The Church Confronts Modernity

MIC LIBRARY
WITHDRAWN FROM STOCK

The Church Confronts Modernity

Catholicism since 1950 in the United States,
Ireland, and Quebec

edited by LESLIE WOODCOCK TENTLER

MIC LIBRARY
WITHDRAWN FROM STOCK

The Catholic University of America Press
Washington, D.C.

Coláiste
Mhuire Gan Smál
Luimneach

Class	282·09045
Suff	CHU
M	1800 1286

Copyright © 2007
The Catholic University of America Press
All rights reserved

The paper used in this publication meets the minimum
requirements of American National Standards for Information
Science—Permanence of Paper for Printed Library Materials,
ANSI z39.48-1984.

∞

LIBRARY OF CONGRESS CATALOGING-IN-PUBLICATION DATA
Tentler, Leslie Woodcock.
    The Church confronts modernity : Catholicism since 1950
in the United States, Ireland, and Quebec / edited by Leslie
Woodcock Tentler.
        p. cm.
    Includes bibliographical references and index.
    ISBN-13: 978-0-8132-1494-8 (pbk. : alk. paper)
    ISBN-10: 0-8132-1494-7 (pbk. : alk. paper)   1. Modernism
(Christian theology)—Catholic Church.   2. Catholic
Church—History—1965–   3. Catholic Church—History—
20th century.   4. Catholic Church—United States.
5. Catholic Church—Ireland.   6. Catholic Church—Québec
(Province)   I. Title.
    BX1396.T46 2007
    282.09′045—dc22

                                        2006026501

Contents

Comparative Perspectives

Acknowledgments

I would like to thank the Louisville Institute, which provided a grant that partially underwrote the conference for which the essays in this volume were initially written. Thanks as well to the Life Cycle Institute at the Catholic University of America and its then-director, Dean Hoge, and to the university itself for its generous support of the Center for American Catholic Studies.

The Church Confronts Modernity

LESLIE WOODCOCK TENTLER

Introduction

The March 2003 conference at the Catholic University of America that gave rise to the essays in this book coincided almost exactly with the U.S. invasion of Iraq. The city of Washington was awash in rumors of an impending terrorist attack. The eight invited speakers, four of whom were coming from outside the United States, gamely agreed to show up anyway, for which I remain profoundly grateful. But would they address an empty hall? I had already had a stream of cancellations from out-of-towners who thought it prudent to remain at home. I can still remember the anxiety-laced drive to campus on the first morning of the conference, with war news and Orange Alerts blaring from the radio. To my near astonishment, I found a hall packed with eager listeners—the first of four well-attended and intellectually lively sessions that added up to one of the best conferences I'd ever been part of.

In the days following the conference, I heard from many of the no-shows—including, most memorably, a Pentagon staffer who'd been kept at his desk for the whole of the conference weekend. Would we be publishing the conference papers, he wanted to know. I marveled at the apparent interest, which was new to me as a veteran of the academic conference circuit. What was it about the subject matter—offbeat, by most calculations—that elicited such a response? I think it had mainly to do with a shared intuition: that the recent history of Catholicism in Quebec and Ireland had something important to tell us about Catholicism in the United States. Most of the conference participants were Catholic and at least middle-aged, which meant that they had lived the history we were gathering to examine. They had witnessed the erosion of the Catholic ghetto and the certainties it embodied, seen the near collapse of vowed religious life and the graying of the priesthood. Some of their own children were among the legions of young Catholics who have drifted away from the Church. And then there was the sex-abuse scandal—on every Catholic mind in the room. These were people who wanted to make sense of it all, but in a context sufficiently broad that all the relevant variables could be identified. Whatever their depths of ignorance with regard to Quebec or even Ireland, most Americans know that these were once intensely Catholic societies. Had the same things happened there as well? And if so, why?

We conference organizers were similarly motivated. Only one of us had expertise on Ireland; none of us—quintessentially American in this regard—knew much about Quebec. But we were all deeply interested in American Catholicism and especially the insights into it that might be gained by a comparative perspective. We knew that comparative studies of Catholicism were few in number, even for the change-filled years since the Second Vatican Council (1962–1965). Theologically minded scholars, for their part, have tended to treat the Church as a unified global entity, downplaying or even ignoring Catholicism's varied expressions in national and regional contexts. Many sociologists have been similarly oriented, impressed by the Church's centralization and its formally uniform beliefs. One does see a different perspective among historians and historically minded sociologists. Perennially drawn to the particular, these scholars have gravitated to studies of ethnic and national Catholicism—of enculturated Catholicism, if you will. But they have had much less to say about the larger reality of a global Church. Genuinely comparative scholarship, after all, is enormously difficult and almost insuperably time consuming.

Hence our eagerness to embark on what I would call the beginnings of a comparative project. We hoped to start a conversation, across not just national boundaries but disciplines as well, and to offer a collaborative model for future comparative research. We knew that our own comparative choices were to some extent arbitrary. We might have substituted the Netherlands for Ireland, or Bavaria for Quebec. Catholicism was in each of these locales in an apparently thriving condition in 1950, as it was in the United States. We were also aware that our three choices posed many difficulties for comparative purposes. Catholicism may have been thriving in the 1950s in Ireland, Quebec, and the United States, but these were otherwise very different places. The United States, including its Catholic population, was far wealthier in 1950 than either Quebec or Ireland. It was far larger, far more industrialized, and far more varied in its racial and ethnic makeup. Ireland and Quebec were Catholic societies both numerically and in terms of self-understanding; Catholics in the United States were a numerical and cultural minority. Quebec and Ireland were both defined by histories of conquest and external domination; the United States, always excepting the die-hard South, has long understood itself as a proudly autonomous nation, even a nascent imperial power. Its Catholic population, fierce patriots historically, have eagerly acceded to this dominant national myth.

Notwithstanding these differences, we believed that much could be learned by comparing the recent trajectories of Catholicism in Quebec, Ireland, and the United States, and not just because the three locales have grown more similar since 1950. (Quebec and Ireland are far wealthier now than they were then, more urbanized, more heterogeneous, more assertive of secular nationhood.) The essays that follow trace the particulars: change over time in Mass attendance and reception of the sacraments, vocations to the priesthood and religious life, the role of the Church in politics and cultural affairs, the religious loyalties of the young. They also probe the reasons for these changes, identifying in the process both interesting parallels among the three cases and equally provocative differences. Catholic practice has declined in all three locales—most spectacularly in Quebec, least so in Ireland—as have vocations; the young are everywhere more alienated than their elders; the Church has lost substantial political leverage even as it has embraced a more generous social gospel. Sexuality and gender are sources of contentious division no matter where one looks, even in hitherto traditional Ireland. The direction of change has thus been constant in all three locales. But the pace and extent of that change have varied. So has the level of what we might call religious energy—the human and spiritual capital on which Catholic renewal depends.

By way of orientation to the essays that follow, let me now offer thumbnail sketches of the three communities under study. We begin with Quebec, more proximate to the United States than Ireland but less familiar to most Americans. The Province of Quebec in 1950 had a population of roughly four million, 82 percent of whom spoke French as their native tongue. Nearly all Francophone Quebecers were Roman Catholic, which meant that—with the addition of small populations of Irish, Italian, and Polish immigrants—the province had a Catholic majority of close to 85 percent. That majority seemed destined to grow, given the Francophone birthrate. The fertility of French-Canadian farm women in 1950 was nearly as high as it had been in the late eighteenth century, when the birthrate in Quebec came close to the maximum possible in human populations. But in Montreal, home to much of Quebec's English-speaking population, Francophone fertility in 1950 was only about half that recorded on farms, which suggests a nascent tension over Catholic teaching on contraception.[1]

It was not only Catholic numbers that made Quebec a quintessentially Catholic society. Catholicism had been integral to Francophone identity since the British conquest of French Canada in 1763, and an organizing principle of the society that subsequently emerged. Although the Catholic Church was not legally established in postconquest Quebec, the Church was primarily responsible for education, health care, and the administration of social services. (Public moneys underwrote overtly confessional schools, colleges, hospitals, and welfare institutions.) No provincial government prior to 1960 would have introduced legislation of any significance without first seeking the approval of the Quebec hierarchy. "The Church and the Provincial State have historically displayed a most intimate spirit of unity and co-operation," as the sociologist Jean-Charles Falardeau rather delicately put it, writing in 1952.[2] In rural and small-town Quebec, as late as the 1950s, the clergy wielded enormous influence, not simply in the spiritual realm but in the political as well. Lay elites, trained in Catholic colleges and often employed by the Church, were a growing force in Quebec's cities, with consequences that both Kevin Christiano and Michael Gauvreau address in the pages that follow.[3]

Even in 1950, Francophone Quebecers imagined themselves an agrarian people—sturdy, simple-hearted, close to the land. But Quebec by 1950 was already substantially urbanized. Less than 17 percent of its labor force was employed in agriculture, according to the 1951 census, while close to half

1. Jacques Henripin, "From Acceptance of Nature to Control: The Demography of the French Canadians Since the Seventeenth Century," *Canadian Journal of Economics and Political Science* 23, no. 1 (Feb. 1957): 14–15, 16–17.

2. Jean-Charles Falardeau, "The Role and Importance of the Church in French Canada," in Marcel Rioux and Yves Martin, eds., *French-Canadian Society*, vol. 1 (Toronto: McClelland and Stewart, 1964), 342–57. Falardeau's article first appeared in 1952.

3. For an extended discussion, see Michael Gauvreau, *The Catholic Origins of Quebec's Quiet Revolution, 1931–1970* (Montreal: McGill-Queens University Press, 2005).

worked in industry.[4] The situation, to be sure, was of recent origin: Quebec's industrialization had proceeded slowly prior to 1940, when wartime demand fueled the rapid development of mining and hydroelectric power, as well as the chemical and aircraft industries. Depression-idled men streamed into these new jobs and, despite Quebec's vigorous anti-conscription movement, into the armed forces. Few of them returned to the land once the war was over. Of potentially greater significance was the wartime employment of women, some sixty thousand of whom left the farm for the factory between 1940 and 1944. They too remained urbanites after the war, often enough the brides of men who were also recent migrants from the countryside.[5] Many such couples eventually settled in booming Montreal, where the population grew by 44 percent between 1951 and 1961,[6] and where hitherto sheltered French-Canadians were exposed to an unprecedented ethnic and religious heterogeneity. Nearly a third of Quebec's population would reside in metropolitan Montreal by 1971, and few Quebecers by then were immune to the city's economic and cultural influence.[7]

The accelerating pace of social and economic change in 1950s Quebec did not initially seem to affect religious practice. Mass attendance remained very high—close to 90 percent in the province, nearly universal in the countryside and small towns—and there were plentiful vocations to the priesthood and religious life. Even in the mid-1960s, the Archdiocese of Montreal had one priest for every 578 Catholics, while Quebec's other dioceses had similar or better numbers.[8] A certain restiveness was evident, however, especially in the cities and among intellectuals. Quebec Catholicism, in these quarters, was frequently criticized as excessively conformist, quasi-superstitious, and militantly anti-intellectual—themes increasingly heard as well among Catholic elites in Ireland and the United States.[9]

4. Nathan Keyfitz, "Population Problems," 238; Albert Faucher and Maurice Lamontagne, "History of Industrial Development," 270; both in Rioux and Martin, *French-Canadian Society*.

5. Jean-Charles Falardeau, "The Changing Social Structure of Contemporary French-Canadian Society," in Rioux and Martin, *French-Canadian Society*, 112–13. Falardeau's article first appeared in 1953.

6. http://www.demographia.com/db-cancma.htm. Accessed 6/21/05.

7. Kenneth McRoberts and Dale Posgate, *Quebec: Social Change and Political Crisis*, rev. ed. (Toronto: McClelland and Stewart, 1980), 51–52.

8. http://www.catholic-hierarchy.org/diocese/dqueb.html. Accessed 5/23/05.

9. Susan Mann Trofimenkoff, *The Dream of Nation: A Social and Intellectual History of Quebec* (Toronto: Gage Publishing, 1983), 286–87, 291, 293–94.

"Our social milieu is quite similar to Dublin society where Stephan Dedalus had to forge the esthetic instrument of a total definition of himself and
. . . to accept the inevitability of exile," as Jean-Charles Falardeau once observed.[10] Most such critics in the 1950s were practicing Catholics, many
the products of Quebec's Catholic Action movements. Their numbers
even included priests. But no matter how ostensibly friendly the critics,
the swelling chorus was still a sign that an urban and increasingly well-
educated Quebec posed unprecedented challenges for what had only recently been a mostly agrarian Church. The critics were also a force for
change, not just in the Church but in the society the Church had done so
much to define. Most were linked to the "Quiet Revolution" of the 1960s,
when the Church lost control of health care and welfare, and even—
though in limited fashion only—of education, as well as what Gregory
Baum has called "the symbols by which Quebec society defined itself."[11]

Given the rapidity of change in Quebec, one might reasonably expect
an eventual surge in Catholic alienation, particularly in the wake of the
Second Vatican Council. Could a faith so dependent on a swiftly eroding
culture be sustained in its accustomed vigor, especially in a context of religious reform? But no one could have predicted how rapid or seemingly
thorough Quebec's secularization would be. By 1970, as Kevin Christiano
documents, weekly Mass attendance was plummeting. (It seems to have
stabilized by the year 2000 at a self-reported figure of 23 percent, which
may well be too optimistic.) Vocations to the priesthood and religious life
had withered by the 1970s almost to the vanishing point. Quebec's fertility,
the highest in Canada in 1960, had dropped by 1970 to below replacement
level. It has not recovered since: the province today has one of the lowest
birthrates in the world and, not incidentally, one of the highest rates of
abortion among the industrialized countries.[12] Marriage went out of fashion too, with births out of wedlock after 1970 moving rapidly toward an
eventual rate of over 50 percent. "It is curious how quickly vast numbers of
Catholics, trained and often fervent in their disciplined religion, shed the
faith of their ancestors," as Gregory Baum has elsewhere remarked.[13] Que-

10. Falardeau, "Changing Social Structure," 122.
11. Gregory Baum, *The Church in Quebec* (Outremont, QC: Novalis, 1991), 23–24;
quote from 24.
12. Quebec's fertility index stood at 1.45 in 2005.
13. Baum, *Church in Quebec,* 24.

bec's public life has never been stridently anticlerical, even in the 1960s, although films and literature since that time have frequently assailed the Church, and its sexual ethic in particular. But in other respects Quebec today looks more like France than like Ireland or the Catholic portion of the United States. An ironic turn of events indeed, given that Quebec had long envisioned itself as the saving remnant of French Catholicism—a latter-day "elder daughter of the Church."[14]

The remarkable pace of Quebec's secularization is especially striking when the province is compared to Ireland. Like Quebec, the Republic of Ireland has a small population—just under 3 million in 1950, over 94 percent of whom were Roman Catholics.[15] Unlike Quebec's, Ireland's small population as of 1950 had not grown for many decades; it was only in 1966 that the country recorded its first population growth since the Great Famine of the 1840s.[16] The stagnation was due to Ireland's poverty, far greater than Quebec's in the 1950s. A largely agrarian society then, Ireland—like Quebec—was land-poor. The "surplus" offspring of Ireland's small farmers either resigned themselves to stoic bachelorhood (Ireland in the 1950s and for many decades prior had the world's lowest marriage rate), became celibate priests or religious, or opted for emigration. Quebec too had seen many of its sons and daughters emigrate, primarily to the New England states, between 1870 and 1930. But Ireland's numbers dwarfed the Quebec experience. Fully 80 percent of Irish children born in the 1930s emigrated in the 1950s, victims of a severely depressed economy.[17] It did not help the nation's morale that nearly all these youthful emigrants were bound for a booming Britain. What meaning had Irish independence, achieved after long struggle in 1921, if Ireland could not provide for her children?

A principal solace for the Irish, afflicted as they were by poverty and a fragile sense of nationhood, was their Catholicism. "According to many outside observers," in the words of historian David Hempton, "Ireland in the first half of the twentieth century was simply the world's most devout-

14. Falardeau, "Role and Importance of the Church," 350–51.

15. Alexander J. Humphreys, *New Dubliners: Urbanization and the Irish Family* (New York: Fordham University Press, 1966), 5, 58.

16. Charles Townshend, *Ireland: The 20th Century* (London: Arnold, 1999), 172; Donald S. Connery, *The Irish* (New York: Simon and Shuster, 1970), 186–87.

17. Connery, *The Irish*, 168; see also Dermot Keogh, *Twentieth-Century Ireland: Nation and State* (New York: St. Martin's Press, 1995), 216.

ly Catholic country."[18] As in Quebec, Irish identity was intimately bound up with religion: Catholicism was the nation's main link to pasts both real and imagined, and the chief means by which it resisted an English-language commercial culture of unsurpassed wealth and vitality. In Ireland, indeed, Catholicism was probably even more important a bearer of identity than in Quebec, given that the twentieth-century Irish had largely lost their ancestral language.[19] Catholic practice in Ireland was nearly universal, as characteristic of the cities as of the countryside and found in every social class.[20] Weekly Mass attendance was the norm, although many attended more frequently, while substantial majorities went regularly to confession and Communion. "Workers and clerks go to confession on leaving their offices or factories on the eve of First Fridays, or else on Saturday, before going to the cinema," the French diplomat Jean Blanchard reported from Dublin in the late 1950s.[21] The very high rates of fertility among those Irish couples who did marry—marital fertility in Ireland in the 1950s was the highest of any Western nation—suggests widespread conformity to Church teaching on contraception, although marital fertility was lower in the 1950s than it had been early in the century.[22] In any event, contraceptives were not legally available in Ireland until 1979, nor indeed was divorce until the mid-1990s.[23]

As these last-mentioned facts indicate, the Church was a political force in Ireland, just as it was in Quebec. Not that the Catholic Church in Ireland was in any formal sense a state church—it was not, despite being recognized in the Republic's 1937 constitution as enjoying a "special position" in Ireland as "the guardian of the Faith professed by the great majority of the citizens."[24] Irish culture was so thoroughly Catholic, however, and the Church so central an institution, that Irish political arrangements in-

---

18. David Hempton, *Religion and Political Culture in Britain and Ireland: From the Glorious Revolution to the Decline of Empire* (Cambridge: Cambridge University Press, 1996), 91.

19. Patrick J. Corish, *The Irish Catholic Experience: A Historical Survey* (Wilmington, DE: Michael Glazier, 1985), 254–55.

20. J. H. Whyte, *Church and State in Modern Ireland, 1923–1970* (Dublin: Gill and Macmillan, 1971), 6.

21. Jean Blanchard, *The Church in Contemporary Ireland* (Dublin: Clonmore and Reynolds, 1963), 31.

22. Humphreys, *New Dubliners,* 70.

23. Keogh, *Twentieth-Century Ireland,* 325–26, 335.

24. Corish, *Irish Catholic Experience,* 247.

evitably reflected Catholic assumptions and values. If the Irish hierarchy had forbidden its priests after 1921 to participate directly in politics, the hierarchy and indeed the clergy continued to be intimately involved in secular affairs. The Church administered the vast majority of the Republic's schools, which were overtly confessional in nature. Religious orders provided most of the Republic's health care and social services, although these sectors were formally controlled by the state. In rural areas, especially, many parish priests were temporal as well as spiritual leaders, as Lawrence Taylor shows us with regard to southwest Donegal. Nor were the bishops above direct intervention in politics, as Dermot Keogh explains with regard to the "Mother and Child scheme" of the early 1950s. Public life in Ireland, moreover, was permeated by Catholic ritual and symbols, which was also the case in Quebec. "Every important public event is the occasion of a religious ceremony," Jean Blanchard pointed out.[25]

As in Quebec, the Church in Ireland had its critics, artists and intellectuals chief among them. Irish Catholicism, they charged, was pathologically hostile to the body and subversive of even responsible critical inquiry. There was much to sustain the indictment: books, periodicals, and films were rigorously censored in Ireland, for example, while Catholics until 1970 were prohibited from attending non-Catholic colleges and universities.[26] Compared to the Church in the Netherlands, Germany, or France, the Church in Ireland in the 1950s was almost unnaturally insulated from contemporary ferment in the arts and the various academic disciplines. (Despite the claims of home-grown Jeremiahs, this was simply less true of the Church in Quebec and the United States.) But if the critics of the 1950s seem in retrospect to have carried the day, they were few in number and often successfully silenced—at least within Ireland itself. The Church continued to command the loyalty of the vast majority of the Irish, whose sons and daughters in the 1950s flocked in truly amazing numbers to the priesthood and religious life. Ireland's seminaries then were filled to bursting, as they had been for decades, producing not only a sufficiency of priests for Ireland itself—the priest-people ratio in most Irish dioceses was comparable to that in Quebec[27]—but a stream of mis-

---

25. Blanchard, *Church in Contemporary Ireland*, 73.
26. Whyte, *Church and State*, 18, 343, 346.
27. http://www.catholic-hierarchy.org/diocese/ddubl.html. Accessed 6/10/2005.

sionaries whose stations encircled the globe.[28] There were American dioceses, especially in the South and far West, which were even in the 1950s
dependent on Ireland for a sufficiency of clergy.[29]

By the early 1960s, Ireland was a far more optimistic place than it had
been just a few years earlier. With foreign investment stimulating both
industry and the service sector, the nation experienced a temporary end
to emigration and heightened living standards, especially among its bur-
geoning urban population.[30] Like their counterparts in Quebec, the Irish
bishops had long been adept at providing for new urbanites, at least in
terms of churches, schools, and clergy. If Ireland were our only test case,
we would have no reason to believe, at least until very recently, that urbanization has a negative impact on religious belief and practice.[31] But the
1960s brought more than a modest prosperity to an urbanizing Ireland.
The decade also witnessed an unprecedented opening up of Irish society by means of television (introduced in 1962), an easing of censorship,
and a new zest for foreign travel.[32] As in Quebec, therefore, the reforms of
the Second Vatican Council were introduced into a society already in the
throes of far-reaching social change. If, as Gregory Baum maintains, Quebec in the 1960s was in a more intense state of cultural upheaval, the situation in Ireland was still quite capable of undermining cherished verities.

Although religious change has surely come to Ireland, it has come more
slowly and partially than in Quebec or indeed the United States. As Dermot Keogh documents, weekly Mass attendance in Ireland in the mid-
1970s stood at 91 percent. Vocations to the priesthood did not show an ap-
preciable decline until the late 1960s, nor did Ireland see large numbers of
men abandoning the priesthood, as happened in the United States and especially Quebec. (Despite a rapidly aging clergy, Ireland is still among the
world's most priest-rich nations.)[33] More significant change has been evident since the 1990s, a decade of unprecedented prosperity in Ireland and
one that saw a wave of scandals centered on clerical sexual misconduct.

28. Corish, *Irish Catholic Experience,* 238.
29. William L. Smith, *Irish Priests in the United States: A Vanishing Subculture* (Lanham, MD: University Press of America, 2004), 73, 115.
30. Townshend, *Ireland,* 172.
31. Hempton, *Religion and Political Culture,* 90.
32. Keogh, *Twentieth-Century Ireland,* 243–44; see also Tom Inglis, *Moral Monopoly:
The Catholic Church in Modern Irish Society* (Dublin: Gill and Macmillan, 1987), 90–92.
33. Smith, *Irish Priests,* 76.

Vocations plummeted—there were no ordinations to the diocesan priesthood in the Archdiocese of Dublin in 2004—and Mass attendance fell to the neighborhood of 60 percent, which is still the highest in the developed world. The contemporary Irish, if poll data are to be credited, overwhelmingly believe in God, personal immortality, and the efficacy of prayer. The young, however, appear to be seriously alienated from the hierarchy and in fundamental disagreement with Church teaching on sexuality.[34] "It is now possible to live a life in Ireland, especially in some parts of Ireland and within some socio-economic groups, untouched by institutional religion," in the view of a school-based catechist. "It's not so much a matter of ideological, as a sort of *cultural* atheism."[35] There is good reason, in other words, for the Irish seminarians profiled in this volume by Lawrence Taylor to regard their present-day vocations as bravely countercultural.

If Ireland today is imperfectly secularized, to employ a fiercely contested term, the same might be said of the United States. One need only recall the religious particulars of the 2004 election. At first glance, however, the two countries could hardly be more different. Against the poverty and homogeneity of 1950s Ireland, we must pose the wealth and heterogeneity of the United States, whose rapidly growing population in 1950 stood at slightly more than 150 million. Catholics accounted for roughly 20 percent of that population—a much smaller percentage than in neighboring Canada, it might be noted, which was about 45 percent Catholic. But as in Canada, with its Protestant "shadow establishment,"[36] Catholics in the United States were a pronounced cultural minority—more urban than their fellow Americans, more discernibly ethnic, and still regarded in influential quarters as lacking commitment to American liberal values.[37] Their socioeconomic status marked them as a minority, too. Ameri-

---

34. Andrew M. Greeley, *Religion in Europe at the End of the Second Millennium* (New Brunswick, NJ: Transaction Publishers, 2003), especially 155–87.

35. Anne Looney, "Disappearing Echoes, New Voices and the Sound of Silence," in Seán MacRèamoinn, ed., *The Church in a New Ireland* (Dublin: Columba Press, 1996), 28–29.

36. David Martin, "Canada in Comparative Perspective," and John H. Simpson, "The Politics of the Body in Canada and the United States," both in David Lyon and Marguerite Van Die, eds., *Rethinking Church, State, and Modernity: Canada between Europe and America* (Toronto: University of Toronto Press, 2000), 23, 276.

37. On the last-mentioned issue, see John T. McGreevy, *Catholicism and American Freedom: A History* (New York: Norton, 2003), especially chs. 6, 8, 9.

can Catholics in 1950 were still largely working- and lower-middle-class, less educated than white Protestants, and less likely to hold prestigious occupations.[38] Seemingly possessed of a vast religious certitude, American Catholics in 1950 were simultaneously a chosen people and, as Garry Wills remembers it, "chosen to be second-rate."[39]

Living as they did in a pluralist society, American Catholics were presumably more vulnerable than their Irish or Quebecois counterparts to the seductions of moral relativism. But they were protected to an important degree by a dense network of Catholic schools, colleges, devotional societies, and professional organizations, the roots of which went back to the mid-nineteenth century. "Every interest, activity, and function of the Catholic faithful is provided with some Catholic institution and furnished with Catholic direction," as Will Herberg asserted in the mid-1950s, exaggerating only mildly.[40] It was possible to keep one's distance from this dense institutional network, and there were Catholics who did. Prestigious non-Catholic colleges were a particular temptation for the upwardly mobile or socially ambitious. But the "Catholic ghetto" was home to enormous numbers of Americans, who sent their children to Catholic schools, bowled on Fridays with the Holy Name Society, and lined up for confession on Saturday evenings in the company of Catholic neighbors. Their movies were vetted by the Legion of Decency, while provocative literature—which probably belonged ipso facto on the Index of Prohibited Books—was kept by organized Catholic vigilance from local stores and the public library. An American Stephan Dedalus could choose internal exile; it would not be necessary for him to leave the country of his birth. But he could hardly remain in the old neighborhood.

For all its seeming solidity, however, the Catholic ghetto by the 1950s was on the verge of collapse. The rising generation of American Catholics was socially mobile to an unprecedented degree, thanks in good measure to the G.I. Bill and vibrant postwar prosperity. It would not be long

38. Andrew M. Greeley, *The American Catholic: A Social Portrait* (New York: Basic Books, 1977), 38–47; Ralph E. Pyle and Jerome R. Koch, "The Religious Affiliation of American Elites, 1930s to 1990s: A Note on the Pace of Disestablishment," *Sociological Focus* 34 (May 2001): 125–37.

39. Garry Wills, *Bare Ruined Choirs: Doubt, Prophecy and Radical Religion* (Garden City, NY: Doubleday, 1972), 18.

40. Will Herberg, *Protestant, Catholic, Jew: An Essay in Religious Sociology* (Garden City, NY: Doubleday, 1955), 154.

before Catholics equaled mainstream Protestants in income and education, and in some cases even outstripped them.[41] Highly educated young Catholics in the postwar years moved in droves to the suburbs, where—initially, at least—they tended a bumper crop of children. Catholic families between 1945 and the mid-1960s were notably larger than those of non-Catholics, and particularly so among the college-educated.[42] Remarkably—if often resentfully—loyal to Church teaching on contraception, at least in the 1950s, these same Catholics were eager supporters of religious schooling and, albeit to a lesser extent, a reworked menu of Catholic social and devotional organizations. It briefly seemed that the Catholic ghetto might be replicated in the suburbs, for reasons that were as much cultural as religious. With the attributes of ethnicity fast fading, religion in the 1950s was more and more regarded as the single most enduring link to Americans' communal pasts. Catholicism was increasingly experienced as a form of ethnicity in its own right, although often enough—at least outside the fastness of Polish-American enclaves—with a residual Irish flavor. Ethnicity still counted for something, as evidenced by the continued overrepresentation of Irish-Americans in the clergy, the hierarchy, and the women's teaching orders.

But the Catholic ghetto in its suburban guise was an incomplete and ultimately evanescent achievement, due to changes that seemed at the time to stem from the Second Vatican Council. As women religious abandoned their convents and hence their vocations as barely paid teachers, the costs of Catholic schooling soared. Certain lay elites and even clergy assailed the very principle of confessional schooling and "separate development" generally. If ecumenism was a post-conciliar priority, they asked, on what grounds could exclusively Catholic institutions be justified? Men and women of this sort were hardly typical Catholics. Like the lay and clerical elites whom Michael Gauvreau largely blames for the collapse of institutional Catholicism in Quebec, these American elites were often contemptuous of "ghetto Catholicism." (The modal ghetto Catholic, at least according to the radicals, was provincial, intolerant, and religiously immature.) The argument was not new, even as a Catholic formulation. But it was articulated in the 1960s more widely and passionately than ever

41. Greeley, *American Catholic*, 50–68.
42. Leslie Woodcock Tentler, *Catholics and Contraception: An American History* (Ithaca, NY: Cornell University Press, 2004), 132–33.

before, and in a context of enormous institutional vulnerability, as Scott Appleby explains. Emboldened if not created by the Council, the critics addressed a Catholic subculture whose raison d'être had been seriously compromised by several decades of social change. Becoming unambiguously American—the Kennedy election gets its requisite nod—left Catholics dangerously exposed to an increasingly secular mainstream. It also deprived them of an essential imagined "Other"—the deracinated and relativistic non-Catholic against whom the ghetto had defined itself.

The results of the "Catholic 1960s" are generally known to American Catholics, at least those of a certain age. As James Davidson meticulously documents, Mass attendance has declined sharply since the later 1960s, with about 35 percent of Catholics today—and these disproportionately older—claiming to attend weekly. Vocations to the priesthood have fallen dramatically, as have those to the vowed religious life. In nearly every American diocese, a shortage of priests and religious has led to the closing of churches and schools, in some cases almost obliterating the physical patrimony of the immigrant past. Catholic schools remain popular with many parents, including non-Catholic parents in the nation's inner cities, but attendance at those schools is half of what it was in 1960, despite vigorous growth in the Catholic population. Religious intermarriage has increased significantly, far more than would be possible in nominally Catholic societies like Ireland and Quebec. Perhaps most important, a substantial majority of Catholics today negotiate their moral lives in a self-reliant mode, seldom consulting the clergy or Church teachings with which they disagree. We would expect this to be particularly true of younger Catholics, as indeed it is. But it comes as something of a surprise to learn that women are more likely than men to regard such "conscience-based" decision making as the truly moral option.[43] One wonders about the long-term consequences for the institutional Church, at least in terms of its present structures.

The picture is not unremittingly negative, however, as even Scott Appleby concedes. The Church in the United States has impressive stores of what an economist would call human capital. Those American Catholics who do regularly attend Mass, for example, are more likely than their Irish

---

43. William V. D'Antonio et al., *American Catholics: Gender, Generation, and Commitment* (Lanham, MD: AltaMira Press, 2001), 82–84.

counterparts to engage in church-related activities.[44] The American Church has far more permanent deacons than any other: some thirteen thousand in 2001, roughly half of all permanent deacons worldwide. The Irish Church, by contrast, had a total of six in 2003.[45] The American Church likewise employs many more lay ministers: about thirty thousand in 2001, the great majority of them women.[46] (Quebec, long short of priests, makes quite generous use of lay parish ministers, although it lags behind the United States in this regard and especially when it comes to permanent deacons. As of 2004, four of the twenty dioceses in Quebec had no permanent deacons, while several others had fewer than five.)[47] Church-related activity, whether paid or voluntary, tends to be the province of older Catholics, and it is certainly possible that the American Church is living off a diminishing cultural inheritance. Today's young Catholics, having never experienced life as a sometimes despised minority, may be less eager than their parents—should I say mothers?—to devote their energies to an institution that privileges maleness and pays less than munificent wages. On the other hand, Americans still live in a society where voluntarism is a valued cultural norm. Religious life in the free-market United States, moreover, is inevitably competitive in ways that it simply cannot be in societies like Ireland and Quebec, notwithstanding their increased diversity. Perhaps a sufficiency of today's young Catholics, like their evangelical counterparts, will respond to long-standing cultural incentives and become the deacons and lay ministers of tomorrow. Will they also opt in sufficient numbers for celibate religious vocations? That seems much less likely, precisely because of the mainstream values that most American Catholics now accept.

44. Greeley, *Religion in Europe*, 172–73.

45. On deacons in the U.S. Church, see "The Permanent Diaconate Today: A Research Report by the Bishops' Committee on the Diaconate of the NCCB and by the Center for Applied Research in the Apostolate," June 2000; on the Irish Church, see http://www.catholic-hierarchy.org/country/spcie1.html, accessed 5/24/05. The various CARA reports and bulletins can be found in libraries that specialize in American Catholicism, as well as at the Center for Applied Research in the Apostolate, 2300 Wisconsin Ave. NW, Washington, DC 20007.

46. A 1999 study put the number of lay parish ministers in the United States at 29,145; some were women religious, who—canonically speaking—are laypersons. More than two-thirds of U.S. parishes then employed at least one lay parish minister. James D. Davidson et al., *Lay Ministers and Their Spiritual Practices* (Huntington, IN: Our Sunday Visitor Publishing Division, 2003), 20–21. For the 2001 estimate, see the Davidson essay in this volume.

47. http://www.cccb.ca/CatholicChurch.htm?CD=95&ID=71. Accessed 5/23/05.

It is not the place of an introduction, or in the competence of this particular "introducer," to embark on a sustained comparison of the three cases under study. Gregory Baum and Michele Dillon, whose provocative essays conclude the volume, have the task well in hand. I would, however, like to comment briefly on the role of the Church in public life—a topic of more than passing interest to many American Catholics, given recent developments on the domestic political front.

In each of the locales under study, the Church since Vatican II has cultivated an ecumenical public presence, cooperating with non-Catholic groups on issues of mutual concern and speaking a language clearly meant to be heard beyond the confessional divide. Even heavily Catholic Ireland moved vigorously in this direction, impelled by sectarian strife in neighboring Ulster. If the new public posture stemmed mainly from the Council and its emphasis on openness to the world, it was also connected to developments in the immediate pre-conciliar years, when many educated Catholics turned toward greater engagement with the world. Symptomatic was the advent of the priest-sociologist, a hybrid common to all three locales, who had necessarily to downplay the arcane categories of papal social teaching in favor of learning about, and from, life in actual human communities. Catholic social movements in these same years were also drawn to the habit of social investigation, which led in short order to a newly positive view of the state and its responsibility for human welfare. The change was most notable in Quebec and Ireland, where the Church had long been militantly antistatist in its public posture, despite possessing enormous leverage in politics. But change was evident in the United States as well, where many bishops had even in the 1930s been chary of federal power. The Church's long-standing suspicion of liberal capitalism was recast in the 1960s, in each of the cases under study, as full-blown advocacy of the welfare state—a commitment that has not appreciably wavered in the face of resurgent free-market ideologies.[48]

There was less agreement, however, when it came to the politics of the body. The Irish bishops, presiding until very recently over a socially conservative population, have been vigorous opponents not just of abortion,

<hr />

48. Whyte, *Church and State*, 331–333; Keogh, *Twentieth-Century Ireland*, 331; David Seljak, "Resisting the 'No Man's Land' of Private Religion: The Catholic Church and Public Politics in Quebec," in Lyon and Van Die, *Rethinking Church, State, and Modernity*, 138.

which remains illegal in Ireland, but in more muted fashion of contraception and divorce. Theirs was a ringing endorsement of *Humanae Vitae,* the 1968 papal encyclical upholding the ban on contraception. The Canadian bishops, by contrast, responded to *Humanae Vitae* with barely concealed dismay, speaking pointedly of the rights of conscience. More remarkably, they have kept their distance from Canada's antiabortion movement, despite its heavily Catholic makeup. (Abortion was initially legalized in Canada in 1969, with the blessing of a Catholic prime minister hailing from Quebec; the limited restrictive provisions of the 1969 law were voided by the Canadian Supreme Court in 1988.)[49] Nor have they attempted, like certain of their American counterparts, to discipline Catholic politicians who support abortion or gay marriage, which was legalized in Canada in 2005—just three years after Quebec extended full parental rights to same-sex couples.[50] The American bishops would seem to occupy a middle ground: gracefully yielding up the field with regard to the politics of contraception but expending considerable political capital in battles against abortion and gay marriage—albeit less capital, in a great many cases, than conservative Catholics have thought necessary. Tellingly, perhaps, their collective response to *Humanae Vitae* was deeply equivocal—more supportive of the papacy than the Canadian bishops but leaving room for conscience too, if in relatively understated language. The behavior of certain bishops in the 2004 election campaign does suggest a new militancy, at least with regard to abortion. Is this in part attributable to unusual Vatican scrutiny of the large and potentially powerful Church in the United States? The Canadian bishops, for their part, do not appear to be under pressure to discipline Canada's many recalcitrant Catholic politicians. It is possible too that zealous evangelicals—their numbers are proportionately much smaller in Canada[51]—push certain American bishops in a militant direction simply by force of competitive example.

49. Michael W. Cuneo, *Catholics against the Church: Anti-Abortion Protest in Toronto, 1969–1985* (Toronto: University of Toronto Press, 1989), 4, 8–9, 13–14, 33, 218. Pierre Elliot Trudeau, prime minister in 1969, had earlier, as minister of justice in Lester Pearson's Liberal government, promoted liberalization of Canada's laws on divorce and abortion.

50. On the Quebec law, see Clifford Krauss, "With a Quebec Law, Equality for Gay Parents," *New York Times,* June 25, 2002.

51. Roger O'Toole, "Canadian Religion: Heritage and Project," in Lyon and Van Die, *Rethinking Church, State, and Modernity,* 45–46.

It is time now to give way to the experts. The essays that follow are paired—two each on Quebec, Ireland, and the United States, followed by two that are explicitly comparative. The "country-specific" essays are arranged so that the first provides a data-filled overview of the locale in question; the second is more frankly interpretive. The authors come from several disciplines—sociology, history, anthropology, religious studies—as their varying methodologies and prose styles attest. They write from different vantage points, too. Some are unabashed partisans of liberal reform in the Church; others evince a wistful affection for aspects of the world we have lost. Still others stand above the battle, at least when it comes to matters ecclesial. Each of the authors, however, is wise enough to challenge a too-literal reading of "decline and fall"—the phrase that originally served as the conference title, albeit with a question mark. One cannot assume, they caution, that a decline in Mass attendance—to pick a standard marker of institutional health—means a decline in religious interest or sensibility. The religious impulse is notoriously protean, as the variegated richness of the Catholic devotional tradition attests. Nor should one discount the impact of prophetic witness on the part of a vibrant religious remnant. And one should certainly not assume that present trends will necessarily define the long-term future. In this regard, we might profitably conclude with an observation from historian David Hempton. "Probably no church in the British Isles started out from a more unpromising position in the first half of the eighteenth century than the Roman Catholic Church in Ireland," Hempton quite rightly notes, "yet no church was in a stronger position, both in terms of popular allegiance and its social and political influence, by the middle of the twentieth century."[52]

LESLIE WOODCOCK TENTLER
Department of History
The Catholic University of America

52. Hempton, *Religion and Political Culture*, 72.

Quebec

KEVIN J. CHRISTIANO

1. The Trajectory of Catholicism in Twentieth-Century Quebec

You know, way back, everybody here was Catholic, just as in Spain or Ireland. And then, at a very specific moment—it was during the year 1966—in only a few months, the churches suddenly emptied out. A very strange phenomenon, one that nobody has ever been able to explain.

—Father Raymond Leclerc (Gilles Pelletier) in *Les invasions barbares* (directed by Denys Arcand; Cinémaginaire, 2003).[1]

In the space of little more than fifty years, between the end of the Second World War and the close of the twentieth century, the Canadian province of Quebec went from being one of the most socially traditional, politically conservative, and religiously devout regions of the developed world to one of the least.

Existing explanations for these sweeping changes, for both their breadth and their abruptness, are many and varied. They indict a panoply of vari-

I thank Leslie Woodcock Tentler for her organizational initiative and editorial guidance; and Gregory Baum, Calum M. Carmichael, Theodore de Bruyn, Michele Dillon, Martin E. Marty, and Alven M. Neiman for their charitable assistance with, and always sound reactions to, previous forms of this essay.

Unless otherwise indicated, translations of sources from the original French are my own.

1. In the original French, the character of the priest says: "Vous savez, ici, autrefois, tout le monde était catholique, comme en Espagne ou en Irlande. Et à un moment très précis, en fait pendant l'année 1966, les églises se sont brusquement vidées, en quelques mois. Un phénomène très étrange, que personne n'a jamais pu expliquer." Denys Arcand, *Les invasions barbares: Scénario* (Montréal: Les Éditions du Boréal, 2003), 154.

ables, some marked with the impersonality of large-scale social differentiation and others with the intimacy of individual crises of commitment. But
almost all of the prevailing accounts refer at least tangentially to the advent
of what Quebecers have labeled *"la Révolution tranquille"* ("the Quiet Revolution"), a period of rapid and profound social transformation that is or-
dinarily dated from the election in June 1960 of Jean Lesage, leader of the
Liberal Party of Québec, to head the provincial government.[2]

The rise of the Liberals put an end to a streak of conservative adminis-
trations that, with only the slightest interruption, had traversed three successive decades. Yet the *Révolution tranquille* meant infinitely more to the
French-speaking citizens of Quebec than an alternation in ruling parties.
The Liberals quickly put the government to work rooting out favoritism
in procurement contracts and corruption in public works. In a few short
years they augmented agencies of the bureaucracy, expanded the scope
of regulation, and applied professional standards to the civil service. Finally, they set into motion a process whereby institutions such as schools,
which previously had been the all-but-exclusive province of the Catholic Church, were placed in the hands of public authorities. This flurry of
frenetic activity left a permanent mark, so that in our day the *Révolution
tranquille* primarily signifies not the growth of the Quebec state or the ra-
tionalization of its services (although these did occur), but the veritable
coming-of-age of a people in its belated encounter with modernity.[3]

For his part, Charles F. Doran, a leading American observer of Can-

---

2. See Thomas Sloan, *Quebec: The Not-So-Quiet Revolution* (Toronto: Ryerson Press,
1965); and Dale C. Thomson, *Jean Lesage and the Quiet Revolution* (Toronto: Macmillan,
1984). For an account of the same period from the perspective of Daniel Johnson [Sr.], one
of Lesage's opponents and leader of the conservative Union nationale, compare Pierre Godin, *La Révolution tranquille*, vol. 1: *La fin de la Grande noirceur*, Collection "Boréal com-
pact," no. 27 (Montréal: Les Éditions du Boréal, 1991).

Numerous sources set the religious context for this transition in Quebec history. A few
of the more general are works of Jean Hamelin: Hamelin, *Le XXe siècle: De 1940 à nos jours*,
vol. 3, tome 2, of *Histoire du catholicisme québécois*, ed. Nive Voisine (Montréal: Les Éditions du Boréal, 1984); Hamelin, "Société en mutation, Église en redéfinition: Le catholicisme québécois contemporain de 1940 à nos jours," in Guy-Marie Oury, ed., *La croix et
le Nouveau monde: Histoire religieuse des francophones d'Amérique du nord* (Chambray-lès-
Tours, France, and Montréal: Les Éditions C.L.D. / C.M.D., 1987), 217–36; and Hamelin
et al., *Les catholiques d'expression française en Amérique du nord*, Collection "Fils d'Abraham"
(Turnhout, Belgium: Les Éditions Brepols, 1995).

3. Réjean Pelletier, "La Révolution tranquille," in Gérard Daigle, with Guy Rocher, eds.,
Le Québec en jeu: Comprendre les grands défis (Montréal: Les Presses de l'Université de Mon-

ada, detects in the accession of Quebec to a fully modern condition the introduction as well of a persistent anxiety over identity. He describes the changes in Quebec during the second half of the twentieth century with predictable terminology:

> In five short decades, francophone Quebecers lifted themselves out of inferior social status, leaving the farm, entering the university, embracing business, celebrating their language and culture. The clergy that had saved Quebec from the neglect of Louis XV and his court, and from the hardships of survival in a rough land, now became a burden. A Catholic faith that had provided the social cement for the colony, as well as the solace from fear and from societal and job exclusion for its members, became an embarrassing reminder of a past that everyone wanted to forget.

> . . . to be modern, . . . Quebecer[s] had to turn against Mother Church, the institution that had succoured and protected them but that now condemned their materialism. The Quebec Church was the institution that stayed with Quebecers when the French elite abandoned them after the Conquest, that helped defend them against the depredations of the 1839 Durham Report (that proposed to assimilate them), that cared for their sick and educated their children, and that provided cultural continuity across three centuries of difficult survival as a people. Yet under the umbrella of the Quiet Revolution this was the institution against which they rebelled.

Why did they rebel? This is the story waiting to be told.[4]

To inaugurate his telling of it, however, Doran musters a list of suspects that has worn ragged from repetition: the Catholic Church "was co-

---

tréal, 1992), 609–24; and Guy Rocher, "La sécularisation des institutions d'enseignement: Conflit des faits et du droit," in Robert Comeau et al., eds., *Jean Lesage et l'éveil d'une nation: Les débuts de la Révolution tranquille,* Collection "Les leaders du Québec contemporain," no. 2 (Sillery: Québec, Les Presses de l'Université du Québec, 1989), 168–75. But bear in mind the warnings about overstatement that François-Pierre Gingras and Neil Nevitte deliver in "La Révolution en plan et le paradigme en cause," *Revue canadienne de science politique* 16 (décembre 1983): 691–716.

For succinct overviews of the competing interpretations of this period, consult Paul-André Linteau, "Un débat historiographique: L'entrée du Québec dans la modernité et la signification de la Révolution tranquille," in Yves Bélanger, Robert Comeau, and Céline Métivier, eds., *La Révolution tranquille 40 ans plus tard: Un bilan,* Collection "Études québécoises," no. 58 (Montréal: VLB éditeur, 2000), 21–41; and Kenneth McRoberts, "La thèse tradition-modernité: L'historique québécois," trans. Florence Piron, in Mikhaël Elbaz, Andrée Fortin, and Guy Laforest, eds., *Les frontières de l'identité: Modernité et postmodernisme au Québec,* Collection "Sociétés et mutations" (Sainte-Foy, Québec: Les Presses de l'Université Laval; and Paris: L'Harmattan, 1996), 29–45.

4. Charles F. Doran, *Why Canadian Unity Matters and Why Americans Care: Democratic Pluralism at Risk* (Toronto: University of Toronto Press, 2001), 78–79.

ercive and controlling," it consistently supported entrenched interests, it resisted sought-after social changes, and—most of all—"it stood for the anti-modern."[5] Much of this is true, to be sure, but Doran himself admits that the litany of charges misses the "subtlety and complexity" of the "existential" shift that is implicated in this change.[6]

My own approach to this question specifies a dynamic that is neither ideological (properly speaking) nor psychological—which is not to say that the decline of the Roman Catholic Church in Quebec did not and does not have these dimensions to it.[7] Instead, I examine in this chapter the structural and sociological precursors of the Church's diminished salience among francophone Quebecers. The "quiet" tumult of the *Révolution tranquille*[8] and, for that matter, the eager reception accorded in Quebec to the sweeping ecclesiastical reforms of Vatican II,[9] I contend, were more effects than causes. They were, to state the thesis directly, the culmination of a long and fairly intense course of preparation that was conceived well before the 1960s and that largely proceeded under the auspices of the Catholic Church itself. Yet, despite the fact that these labors were guided by the Church's clergy and peopled with its laity, they had the ironic effect of ushering into Quebec society the very trends whose results the faithful remnant and their leaders now lament.[10]

---

5. Ibid., 79.　　　　　　　　　　6. Ibid., 80.

7. For a fuller elaboration of intellectual currents in Quebec Catholicism since the 1950s, see the contribution to this collection by Michael Gauvreau, as well as Gauvreau's book *The Catholic Origins of Quebec's Quiet Revolution*.

8. See Louis Balthazar, "La laïcisation tranquille au Québec," in Jacques Lemaire, ed., *La laïcité en Amérique du nord,* Collection "La pensée et les hommes," no. 14 (Bruxelles, Belgium: Les Éditions de l'Université de Bruxelles, 1990), 31–42; Micheline Milot, "Laïcisation au Canada et au Québec: Un processus tranquille," *Studies in Religion / Sciences religieuses* 33 (2004): 27–49; David Seljak, "Modernization Theory and a New Look at the History of the Catholic Church in Quebec," Thème: "Regards nord-américains sur la religion," *Religiologiques* 11 (printemps 1995): 33–50; Seljak, "Why the Quiet Revolution Was 'Quiet': The Catholic Church's Reaction to the Secularization of Nationalism in Quebec after 1960," *CCHA* [Canadian Catholic Historical Association] *Historical Studies* 62 (1996): 109–24; and Seljak, "Trudeau and the Privatization of Religion: The Quebec Context," in John English, Richard Gwyn, and P. Whitney Lackenbauer, eds., *The Hidden Pierre Elliott Trudeau: The Faith Behind the Politics* (Ottawa: Novalis, 2004), 47–56.

9. For an account of Quebec's influence on the Roman deliberations, see Jan Grootaers, "Le catholicisme du Québec et son insertion dans le milieu conciliaire," in Gilles Routhier, ed., *L'Église canadienne et Vatican II,* Collection "Héritage et projet," no. 58 (Montréal: Les Éditions Fides, 1997), 447–75.

10. Compare Peter Beyer, "The Evolution of Roman Catholicism in Quebec: A Luh-

My focus is on the central role of the Catholic Church in the gradual creation of a new elite for Quebec society. Although the lay members of this elite were carriers of novel ideas in theology and religious thought, they were defined most decisively by a new placement in the changing public sphere. In particular, the formative experiences and concrete skills that a rich Catholic associational life[11] imparted to numerous French Canadians from the beginning of the twentieth century through 1960—in concert with other cultural changes—made possible an unprecedented transition: namely, "the transition of a clerical French Canada to a Québec under the control of the state," whose characteristic force, paradoxically, was "a disenchantment of the world by the honest action, all the same, of Christian activists."[12]

The aftermath of this transition is highly visible in the reduced position of the Catholic Church in contemporary Quebec. Over time, the

---

mannian Neo-Functionalist Interpretation," in Roger O'Toole, ed., *Sociological Studies in Roman Catholicism: Historical and Contemporary Perspectives,* Studies in Religion and Society, vol. 24 (Lewiston, N.Y.: Edwin Mellen Press, 1989), 1–26; André Chevalier, *La paroisse post-moderne: Faire Église aujourd'hui. L'exemple du Québec,* Collection "Brèches théologiques" (Montréal: Les Éditions Paulines; and Paris: Médiaspaul, 1992), 65–68; and Gary G. Meyers, "Religiosity and Reform in Québec: The Role of Catholic Elites in the Quiet Revolution," *Québec Studies* 3 (1985): 57–71.

11. Philippe Couton and Jeffrey Cormier, "Voluntary Associations and State Expansion in Quebec: 1955–1970," *Journal of Political and Military Sociology* 29 (Summer 2001): 19–45 (see esp. 33–34).

12. In French, "le passage du Canada français clérical au Québec étatique," as a result of the ironic workings of "le mouvement de désenchantement du monde par l'action pourtant sincère des militants chrétiens." E.-Martin Meunier and Jean-Philippe Warren, *Sortir de la "Grande noirceur": L'horizon "personnaliste" de la Révolution tranquille,* Collection "Les Cahiers du Septentrion," no. 22 (Sillery, Québec: Les Éditions du Septentrion, 2002), 139, 147, 166, and 171. For a fuller preamble, see 139–42.

This work had its initial appearance as a lengthy article in a special edition of the journal *Société* dedicated to an examination of "Le chaînon manquant" in Quebec history: Jean-Philippe Warren and E.-Martin Meunier, "L'horizon 'personnaliste' de la Révolution tranquille," *Société* 20/21 (été 1999): 347–448.

Although Meunier and Warren trace the ironic implications of religious activism for the secularization of Quebec, they bestow causal priority on the operation of what, after the example of Max Weber, they call the "éthique personnaliste." Compare Michael Gauvreau, "From Rechristianization to Contestation: Catholic Values and Quebec Society, 1931–1970," *Church History* 69 (December 2000): 803–33; and M. Gauvreau, "The Emergence of Personalist Feminism: Catholicism and the Marriage-Preparation Movement in Quebec, 1940–1966," in Nancy Christie, ed., *Households of Faith: Family, Gender, and Community in Canada, 1760–1969,* McGill-Queen's Studies in the History of Religion, no. 2.18 (Montréal and Kingston, Ont.: McGill-Queen's University Press, 2002), 319–47.

103580547

Church and its ubiquitous functionaries had consumed so much of the active space in the civil realm that for them, under pressure from an elite of laity who had succeeded in mastering much of the same secular expertise, no measured withdrawal from power was possible. Instead, the retreat, while orderly, verged on the total, and a virtually complete cave-in of traditional structures ensued. The Catholic Church retained a residue of respect and its remaining clergy clung to their relatively dignified social standing, but each lost crucial influence over common behavior.

A pair of sections that immediately follow in this essay depict in quantitative terms, first, evidence of a precipitous drop in Catholic religious practice in Quebec since the 1940s and '50s, and second, indicators of a corresponding erosion of traditional standards of moral behavior that religion undergirds. The narrative then advances to an analysis of elite formation in Quebec, with a special focus on a case history of the Caisses populaires et d'économie Desjardins, a chain of financial institutions founded with the support of the Catholic Church. The argument attributes to this long-building social development of capable secular elites a share of the causal responsibility for the dismal fate of institutional religion in Quebec. A penultimate section examines religion in Quebec at the present, while a final reflection mulls the challenging but, in the end, unknowable future for faith in that place.

The Decline of Devotion

Statistics of Secularity

One might concede at the outset that measurable changes in such empirical indicators of religiosity as estimates of church membership, rates of attendance at worship, statistics on recruitment to ordained ministry and vowed religious life, and data on the frequency of prayer only imperfectly capture ebbs and flows in the spiritual experiences and behaviors of groups. Nevertheless, there are some cases in which the quantitative evidence speaks so plainly that serious misinterpretation is unlikely. The recent history of Quebec is one of those cases.[13]

13. For the past twenty years, the periodic surveys of Reginald W. Bibby have charted the course of religious change across Canada as a whole, including Quebec. See his quartet of works: *Fragmented Gods: The Poverty and Potential of Religion in Canada* (Toronto: Irwin

Writing in the late 1950s, the eminent Canadian scholar Arthur A. M. Lower could assume agreement from readers of his general history of his country when he closed one chapter on French Canada by repeating a humorous yet instructive riddle about Quebec: "What," he quoted clerical friends of his, "are the three things that God alone knows?" The answer, he wrote: "Where the Jesuits get their money, what the Franciscans live upon, and the number of religious orders in the province of Quebec!" Surely, Lower concluded without a shade of doubt, "The fervent piety of French Canada has always been well attested and it remains to-day unabated. . . . Quebec remains to-day, as it has always been, the land of religious orders and of Catholicism."[14]

In a sense, Quebec is still "the land . . . of Catholicism," in that to the present more than 80 percent of its people (in 2001, 83.2 percent) consistently identify themselves to Canadian census-takers as Roman Catholic.[15]

Publishing, 1987); *Unknown Gods: The Ongoing Story of Religion in Canada* (Toronto: Stoddart Publishing, 1993); *Restless Gods: The Renaissance of Religion in Canada* (Toronto: Stoddart Publishing, 2002); and *Restless Churches: How Canada's Churches Can Contribute to the Emerging Religious Renaissance* (Kelowna, B.C.: Wood Lake Books; and Ottawa: Novalis, 2004). The first of these has appeared in a French translation by Louis-Bertrand Raymond as *La religion à la carte: Pauvreté et potentiel de la religion au Canada* (Montréal: Les Éditions Fides, 1988).

A comprehensive compendium of statistics on religious belief and practice in Quebec may be located in the valuable compilations of social indicators by Simon Langlois and his international associates. See, most specifically: Simon Langlois et al., *Recent Social Trends in Québec: 1960–1990,* Comparative Charting of Social Change (Frankfurt am Main: Campus Verlag; and Montréal and Kingston, Ont.: McGill-Queen's University Press, 1992).

14. Arthur A. M. Lower, *Canadians in the Making: A Social History of Canada* (Toronto: Longmans, Green, 1958), 68.

15. Bibby, *Restless Churches,* 78; Gary Caldwell and Madeleine Gauthier, "Religious Institutions," in Langlois et al., *Recent Social Trends in Québec,* 317, 321; Canadian Centre for Justice Statistics, *Religious Groups in Canada,* Profile Series (Ottawa: Statistics Canada, 2001), 4; Census Operations Division, Statistics Canada, *Religions in Canada,* 2001 Census: Analysis Series (Ottawa: Statistics Canada, Minister of Industry, 2003), 7, 12, 23, 29; and Raymond Lemieux, "Croyances et incroyances: Une économie du sens commun," in André Charron, Raymond Lemieux, and Yvon R. Théroux, eds., *Croyances et incroyances au Québec,* Collection "Rencontres d'aujourd'hui," no. 18 (Montréal: Les Éditions Fides, for the Centre d'information sur les nouvelles religions, 1992), 18.

Notwithstanding this statistic of identification, in 2000 a national survey of younger Canadians found that Quebec youth were considerably less likely than their counterparts in other regions of the country to designate their religion as an "important" factor "in the definition of [their] own identity" (29 percent vs. 37 percent). More tellingly, young Quebecers predicted less importance for religion "in the definition of our society in 2025": 27 percent accorded religion this future importance, while 42 percent of Canadian youth out-

But beyond this nominal continuity, Lower's characterization of Quebec society was being invalidated at the very moment that he published it. It is correct to say, with the historian Jean-Marc Paradis, that for the last quarter- (or half-) century, "traditional religious practice among Québec Catholics [has been] in a free fall."[16] The survey researcher Reginald W. Bibby concurs: "On the surface, the Catholic Church has felt the effects of an astonishing pattern of secularization."[17] Even Peter L. Berger, the influential social thinker who lately has criticized sociologists' faith in an inevitable weakening of religion, confesses that, to explain the state of churches in Quebec, the "so-called secularization theory . . . was valid and continues to be valid."[18]

Personnel

Indeed, the religious orders to which Arthur Lower so confidently referred were among the first Catholic bodies in Quebec to exhibit signs of incipient decline.[19] Among religious communities for women, in fact, indications of deterioration were evident before mid-century, when new vo-

---

side Quebec did so. "Belonging in 2025," *Canadian Issues / Thèmes canadiens* (June–July / juin–juillet 2001): 14–15.

16. "La pratique religieuse traditionnelle chez les catholiques québécoises est en chute libre." Jean-Marc Paradis, "Le remodelage des paroisses catholiques: Le cas de la Mauricie," in Roch Côté and Michel Venne, eds., *L'annuaire du Québec 2003: Toute l'année politique, sociale, économique et culturelle* (Montréal: Les Éditions Fides, 2002), 308.

17. "En surface, l'Église catholique a senti les effets d'un étonnant modèle de sécularisation." Reginald W. Bibby, "La religion à la carte au Québec: Une analyse de tendances," Thème: "Catholicisme et société contemporaine," *Sociologie et sociétés* 22 (octobre 1990): 134.

18. Peter L. Berger, "Sociology: A Disinvitation?" *Society* 30 (November/December 1992): 15. See also Berger, "Reflections on the Sociology of Religion Today" (the 2000 Paul Hanly Furfey Lecture to the Association for the Sociology of Religion), *Sociology of Religion* 62 (Winter 2001): 443–54 (esp. 447 and 451–53).

19. For ample historical data concerning this period, see Micheline D'Allaire, *Vingt ans de crise chez les religieuses du Québec: 1960–1980*, 2e édition (Montréal: Les Éditions Bergeron, 1984); Bernard Denault, "Sociographie générale des communautés religieuses au Québec (1837–1970): Éléments de problématique," in Bernard Denault and Benoît Lévesque, *Éléments pour une sociologie des communautés religieuses au Québec* (Sherbrooke, Québec: Université de Sherbrooke; and Montréal: Les Presses de l'Université de Montréal, 1975), 15–117; Danielle Juteau and Nicole Laurin, *Un métier et une vocation: Le travail des religieuses au Québec, de 1901 à 1971*, Collection "Trajectoires sociales" (Montréal: Les Presses de l'Université de Montréal, 1997); and Nicole Laurin et al., *À la recherche d'un monde oublié: Les communautés religieuses de femmes au Québec de 1900 à 1970* (Montréal: Le Jour, Éditeur, 1991).

cations to convents sagged modestly from 1940 to 1945. (The influence of the Second World War, and the necessity, in a nation drawn into battle, for many women to assume functions that until that time had been reserved for men, are probably related to this numerical change.) The trend line for nuns-in-formation was flat throughout the material prosperity of the postwar boom. Then the 1960s arrived, and counts of students entering preparation for lives as sisters in Quebec dipped dramatically, from almost 2,000 in 1960 to 1,400 just four years later.[20]

The priestly ranks as well were decimated, and then some, in the aftermath of the *Révolution tranquille*. The internal records of the Canadian Conference of Catholic Bishops show that, between 1966 and 1988, the number of secular (i.e., diocesan) priests in Quebec decreased by more than one quarter, from approximately 8,800 to 6,400. By 2005, they numbered around 2,700. The fate of religious orders of men was yet more pronounced. Priests or monks in congregations of men numbered nearly 4,900 at the beginning of this term. Their communities, however, were to be left two decades later with only about 3,200 members, a drop in size of more than one-third. In 2005, membership had hit slightly more than 1,700. Moreover, attrition among religious sisters continued: their number similarly fell, from 35,000 to 23,000, another reduction in force of more than a third. After the turn of the new century, their ranks counted fewer than 15,000 members.

Ordinations, which hit their high point in 1963, when 127 new priests were consecrated for Quebec, dwindled to the degree that in 1988, merely seventeen men received holy orders. In 1996, all the dioceses and communities of Quebec together could claim a total of 127 seminarians in any stage of formation for ministry.[21]

20. Jacques Légaré, "Les religieuses du Canada: Leur évolution numérique entre 1965 et 1980," *Recherches sociographiques* 10 (janvier–avril 1969): 7–21. For a longer view, see the statistics cited in Jean Gould, "La genèse catholique d'une modernisation bureaucratique," in Stéphane Kelly, ed., *Les idées mènent le Québec: Essais sur une sensibilité historique*, Collection "Prisme" (Sainte-Foy, Québec: Les Presses de l'Université Laval, 2003), 145–74 (esp. 152–53).

21. Caldwell and Gauthier, "Religious Institutions," 317–18 and 322–23; and Raymond Lemieux and Jean-Paul Montminy, *Le catholicisme québécois*, Collection "Diagnostic," no. 28 (Sainte-Foy, Québec: Les Éditions de l'IQRC [Institut québécois de recherche sur la culture] and Les Presses de l'Université Laval, 2000), 69–71.

Statistics for 2005 are from the Quebec bishops' conference, the Assemblée des évêques

Participation

In the last fifty years, rates of participation in religious services have declined everywhere in Canada. A Gallup Poll conducted in 1946 found that
two-thirds (67 percent) of Canadian adults attended religious worship in a
typical week, but a similar survey taken in 1996 showed that this proportion had dropped to 20 percent, where it stalled through 2001.[22] Over the
decade separating 1988 and 1998, those who attended church at least once
per month fell from 41 to 34 percent of the Canadian adult population.[23]
This dissipation of devotion was especially acute in Quebec, where month-
ly attendance plummeted from 48 percent in 1986 to 29 percent by 1998.[24]

Indeed, this change was merely the continuation of a much longer
trend. Among French-speaking Roman Catholics nationwide, those who
attended services twice per month or more went from 88 percent in 1965
to 56 percent in 1974—a loss of fully 32 percentage points in just nine
years.[25] The rapid alienation of Catholic Quebecers from a habit of regular
church attendance surely accounts for most of this statistical difference.

With respect to attendance at Mass, which for many believers is the
hallmark of Catholic identity, the data from Quebec are unremittingly
negative. The earliest Canadian survey on record that invited self-reports
of church attendance, a Gallup Poll from 1945, suggests that at the end of
the Second World War, nearly nine out of ten Catholics in Quebec went
to Mass on a weekly basis.[26] The United States, often portrayed as excep-

---

du Québec. Omitted are returns for three French-speaking dioceses that overstep or strad-
dle provincial boundaries.

22. "*Canadian Social Trends* Backgrounder: 'No Religion' Continues to Grow," *Canadian Social Trends* (Autumn 1998): 6; and Census Operations Division, Statistics Canada,
Religions in Canada, 6.

23. Warren Clark, "Patterns of Religious Attendance," *Canadian Social Trends* (Winter
2000): 23. See also Statistics Canada, "Attending Religious Services: 1998," *Ottawa Daily,*
December 12, 2000; and the Canadian Broadcasting Corporation [CBC], "Church Attendance Declining in Canada," *cbc.ca News,* December 23, 2000.

24. Canadian Centre for Justice Statistics, *Religious Groups in Canada,* 5; and Clark,
"Patterns of Religious Attendance," 26.

25. Hans Mol, *Faith and Fragility: Religion and Identity in Canada* (Burlington, Ont.:
Trinity Press, 1985), 179–81. Statistics that are consistent with these estimates may be found
in Reginald W. Bibby, "Religion in the Canadian 1990s: The Paradox of Poverty and Potential," in David A. Roozen and C. Kirk Hadaway, eds., *Church and Denominational Growth*
(Nashville: Abingdon Press, 1993), 278–92.

26. Bibby, *Restless Gods,* 11 and 15–20. See also Michael Higgins, "Canada's Buried Trea-
sure," *London* [England] *Tablet,* August 31, 2002.

tional in the fervor of its faithful, could hardly boast a superior rate of religious practice among its Catholics.

This impressively high rate of Mass attendance held fairly steady through the next two decades: in 1957 it stood at 88 percent and in 1965 at 85 percent. But by 1970 the percentage of Quebecers attending weekly had decreased sharply to 65. In fact, rates of religious participation for Catholics were embarked on what would turn out to be an inexorable downward slide. In five more years (1975), their exemplary figure for weekly attendance from the 1950s had been more than halved, to 42 percent. Mass attendance tumbled to 31 percent in 1985; it fell to 28 percent in 1990; and it slipped again by 2000, this time to 23 percent.[27] (All of this declension occurred, however, without markedly changing the almost unanimous rates at which Quebec Catholics, then and now, profess to believe in the existence of God and the divinity of Jesus Christ, and without undermining the overwhelming majorities who confess a personal habit of at least occasional prayer.)[28]

A closer look at some of these changes is possible through the findings from a 1990 survey of French-speaking residents of the urban area of greater Montreal.[29] In the prior year, the study discovered, only 37 percent of respondents had attended Mass on half or more of the fifty-two weekends. In contrast, a clear majority frequented their church's services on Christmas and Easter. Regular churchgoing, in fact, was a pattern that applied more to those over the age of fifty-five and to those respondents

27. Bibby, *Restless Gods,* 20. This is, with slight variations, an oft-repeated series of contrasts.

28. Bibby, "La religion à la carte au Québec," 137–38; Bibby, *Restless Churches,* 24; and Madeleine Gauthier, "Religious Beliefs," in Langlois et al., *Recent Social Trends in Québec,* 393.

29. See the summaries of this research in Paul-André Turcotte, "Parole cléricale et parole laïcale dans la paroisse québécoise," Thème: "La parole dans les églises," *Lumière et vie* 39/199 (décembre 1990): 11–22; P. A. Turcotte, "Sunday Mass and Participation in Its Rituals: The Acceptance of the Innovations of Vatican II," trans. Kenneth C. Russell, *JET: Journal of Empirical Theology* 5 (1992): 5–17; P. A. Turcotte, "Catholicisme romain ou catholicisme culturel? À propos de la messe et d'autres pratiques rituelles chez les francophones du Grand Montréal," in Guy Lapointe, ed., *Société, culture et religion à Montréal: XIXe–XXe siècle,* Collection "Études québécoises" (Montréal: VLB éditeur, 1994), 157–85; P. A. Turcotte, "Catholic Ritual Practices, Culture and Society in Greater Montreal," Special Issue on "Mediations and Features of Belief," *Social Compass* 48 (December 2001): 505–23; and Turcotte, *Intransigeance ou compromis: Sociologie et histoire du catholicisme actuel,* Collection "Héritage et projet," no. 51 (Montréal: Les Éditions Fides, 1994), 71–72 and 83–96. (The methodology of the study is discussed at 80n1 and 81.)

with lower levels of formal education. Yet more than eight in ten Catholics who were interviewed for the research agreed that parents should have their children baptized in the Church, that couples who marry should have Catholic weddings, and that funerals of Catholics should proceed from the church. Roman Catholicism is thus firmly fixed in the minds and hearts of contemporary Montrealers, but the lines of institutional involvement and popular participation in the Church have atrophied badly.

Piety and Parenthood

Changes in church attendance assume an additional importance in that they correlate, in Canada as elsewhere, with differences in structures of marriage and family life.[30] Rates of religious involvement are substantially higher among young married Canadians (of whom 44 percent attend services regularly) than among single peers of the same ages (26 percent of whom are regular churchgoers).[31] Having children also seems to propel people into a pattern of consistent attendance at religious services.

The Crumbling of Tradition

Accompanying the decline in strictly religious behavior in Quebec has been a broader trend toward the waning of tradition in a main area of religion's former scope: the organization of family life and the governance of private conduct with moral import, especially conduct pertaining to sexuality. Again, the descriptive data are more than merely suggestive.[32]

30. Warren Clark, "Religious Observance: Marriage and Family," *Canadian Social Trends* (Autumn 1998): 2–7.

For additional context, see Kevin J. Christiano, "Church as a Family Surrogate: Another Look at Family Ties, Anomie, and Church Involvement," *Journal for the Scientific Study of Religion* 25 (September 1986): 339–54; and Christiano, "Religion and the Family in Modern American Culture," in Sharon K. Houseknecht and Jerry G. Pankhurst, eds., *Family, Religion, and Social Change in Diverse Societies* (New York: Oxford University Press, 2000), 43–78.

31. Clark, "Patterns of Religious Attendance," 24. Simon Langlois: "La désaffection vis-à-vis la pratique religieuse, la désaffection vis-à-vis du mariage et la dénatalité sont en fait trois tendances qui révèlent des changements culturels encore mal connus." ("The disaffection with respect to religious practice, the disaffection from marriage, and the drop in births are surely three trends that reveal cultural changes that are still badly understood.") Langlois, "Les grandes tendances: Familles et modes de vie," in Roch Côté, ed., *Québec 2002* (Montréal: Les Éditions Fides, 2001), 127.

32. Given what had been the comparatively homogeneous composition of its society, and what, for North America, is the unusual availability of population registers and parish

During the latter half of the nineteenth century and well into the twentieth, mothers in Quebec had rates of marital fertility that rivaled the "natural" (or maximum practical) levels of childbearing that are recorded in environments where conception is wholly unregulated. "The extraordinary fecundity of French-Canadian families is universally known," wrote the French visitor André Siegfried in 1906. "It is manifest," he estimated of the birth rate in Quebec, "that the French-Canadian is one of the highest in the world."[33] French-Canadian women of one hundred years ago also experienced high rates of infant mortality. For example, in 1903, more than one-third of all recorded deaths in Quebec were of children under the age of five years. In response, mothers resorted regularly to substitution for children who had not survived infancy, to the point of conferring on the next child of the same sex the first name of the one who had died.[34]

---

records of vital statistics extending back to the seventeenth century, historical demography is in many respects the pride of quantitative social science about Quebec. Consult Jacques Henripin, "From Acceptance of Nature to Control: The Demography of the French Canadians since the Seventeenth Century," *Canadian Journal of Economics and Political Science* 23 (February 1957): 10–19 (see 10); John T. Krause, "Some Implications of Recent Work in Historical Demography," *Comparative Studies in Society and History* 1 (January 1959): 164–88; and Georges Sabagh, "The Fertility of the French-Canadian Women during the Seventeenth Century," *American Journal of Sociology* 47 (March 1942): 680–89.

For outstanding examples of historical demography, see Gérard Bouchard, *Quelques arpents d'Amérique: Population, économie, famille au Saguenay, 1838–1971* (Montréal: Les Éditions du Boréal, 1996); and G. Bouchard and Jeannette Larouche, "Paramètres sociaux de la reproduction familiale au Saguenay (1842–1911)," *Sociologie et sociétés* 19 (avril 1987): 133–44.

The Quebec experience of the last century is treated in Danielle Gauvreau and Peter Gossage, "'Empêcher la famille': Fécondité et contraception au Québec, 1920–60," Special Issue on "Children and Family in the Twentieth Century," *Canadian Historical Review* 78 (September 1997): 478–510; D. Gauvreau and Gossage, "Canadian Fertility Transitions: Quebec and Ontario at the Turn of the Twentieth Century," *Journal of Family History* 26 (April 2001): 162–88; and Diane Gervais and D. Gauvreau, "Women, Priests, and Physicians: Family Limitation in Quebec, 1940–1970," Special Issue titled "Before the Pill: Preventing Fertility in Western Europe and Quebec," *Journal of Interdisciplinary History* 34 (Autumn 2003): 293–314.

For overviews, consult Kevin McQuillan, "When Does Religion Influence Fertility?" *Population and Development Review* 30 (March 2004): 25–56 (esp. 32–38); Victor Piché, "La démographie sociale au Québec: Un premier bilan," *Sociologie et sociétés* 19 (avril 1987): 9–23; and V. Piché and Céline Le Bourdais, eds., *La démographie québécoise: Enjeux du XXe siècle*, Collection "Paramètres" (Montréal: Les Presses de l'Université de Montréal, 2003).

33. André Siegfried, *The Race Question in Canada* [1906], ed. Frank H. Underhill, Carleton Library, no. 29 (Toronto: McClelland and Stewart, 1966), 176.

34. Siegfried, *The Race Question in Canada*, 181–82 and n2; and Henripin, "From Acceptance of Nature to Control," 13–15.

Compare Patricia A. Thornton and Sherry Olson, "Family Contexts of Fertility and

These practices are signs of a culture that emphasized nuptiality, parenthood, and large families. But even by these values, the frequencies of pregnancy and childbirth in Quebec were comparatively high. The twelve-year-long correspondence of Father Charles Bellemare (1846–1911), a *curé* (or parish priest) in late-nineteenth-century Shawinigan, testifies to just how striking was the local rate of childbearing. Of course, one could reasonably assume support for natalism from a Roman Catholic clergyman. Yet Bellemare reported with no small astonishment to a clerical colleague, a friend in France who shared his surname, "Here, when there are not eight or ten children, people are surprised. The mayor of my parish, for his part, has had sixteen of his baptized. Your French mayors," our writer innocently inquired of his counterpart on the opposite side of the Atlantic, "are they as productive?"[35]

Births, Children, and Families

But much has changed in the hundred years since then. Although high levels of fertility persisted in Quebec through the first half of the twentieth century,[36] reflecting the preference of the Roman Catholic culture, an accelerating change was underway by the late 1950s. The typical *Québécoise* averaged four children in 1957; by 1963, this index had dropped to 3.55 children. A precipitous fall then followed: from 3.41 offspring in 1964 to 2.27 in 1968. By 1970, fertility in Quebec had dipped to 2.09, below the "floor" of 2.1 children per woman which demographers take to define a population that sustains itself through natural "replacement." Without a doubt, the trend was headed down, to a rate of 1.4 children per woman in

Infant Survival in Nineteenth-Century Montreal" [1991], reprinted in Michael D. Behiels, ed., *Quebec since 1800: Selected Readings,* New Canadian Readings (Toronto: Irwin Publishing, 2002), 177–92 (esp. 186); and Thornton and Olson, "A Deadly Discrimination among Montreal Infants, 1860–1900," *Continuity and Change* 16 (May 2001): 95–135.

35. "Ici, quand il n'y a pas huit ou dix enfants, on est surpris. Le maire de ma paroisse, pour sa part, en a fait baptiser seize. Vos maires français, sont-ils aussi prolifiques?" Charles Bellemare to Vital Bellemare, "[Saint-Boniface-de-] Shawenegan *[sic],* 13 septembre 1887," in Nadine-Josette Chaline, René Hardy, and Jean Roy, eds., *La Normandie et le Québec: Vus du presbytère* (Rouen, France: Les Publications de l'Université de Rouen, with L'Institut pluridisciplinaire d'Études canadiennes, 1987), 48.

36. In the 1930s, the *habitant* couples with children in Horace Miner's study of rural St. Denis (Saint-Denis-de-Kamouraska) averaged ten per family. Fully one-quarter of newborns died before their first birthdays, and one-third did not reach the age of five. Miner, "The French-Canadian Family Cycle," *American Sociological Review* 3 (October 1938): 700–708 (see 701 and n6).

1986. (It since has increased slightly, to 1.5, in 2003.) So low has fertility in Quebec become that one in four children there is now being brought up as an only child.[37]

Employing different statistics, the main theme of the post-1950 population story in Quebec is the same: in 1959, Quebec achieved a crude birth rate of 28.3 per 1,000, the highest of any province of Canada. In a scant nine years, Quebec fell to the lowest rank among the provinces, and in 1972 it posted a crude birth rate of 13.8 per 1,000, or less than half its fertility at the conclusion of the 1950s.[38] In 2002, this rate stood even lower, at 9.7 live births per 1,000 population.[39]

As births have decreased in number, abortions have risen. Quebec saw over 7,000 abortions take place in 1976; this amounted to 7.3 procedures for every 100 live births. However, in the ensuing decades this rate practically skyrocketed. Recent statistics confirm that Quebec's abortion rate is one of the highest of any Western society. In 1998, 29,000 abortions were performed in Quebec, a rate of 38 abortions per 100 births.[40] In surveys, eight out of ten Quebecers profess that abortion is "a personal choice," while 70 percent believe "strongly" that "no one has the right to impose morality on others." (A bare majority, 52 percent, in the rest of Canada supports this view.)[41]

---

37. Statistics Canada, "Births: 2003," *Ottawa Daily*, July 12, 2005; André Désiront, "Dénatalité: Le spectre de la décroissance démographique," *FORCES: La voix internationale du Québec* 137 (février 2003): 20; Langlois, "Familles et modes de vie," 136; and Michel Paillé, "Communication: Le contexte démographique québécois dans les années 60," in Robert Coméau, Michel Lévesque, and Yves Bélanger, eds., *Daniel Johnson: Rêve d'égalité et projet d'indépendance,* Collection "Les leaders du Québec contemporain," no. 4 (Sillery, Québec: Les Presses de l'Université du Québec, 1991), 330.

38. Samuel H. Preston, "Changing Values and Falling Birth Rates," Issue Supplement on "Below-Replacement Fertility in Industrial Societies: Causes, Consequences, Policies," *Population and Development Review* 12 (1986): 182. Compare Simon Langlois, "Tendances de la société québécoise, 1999," in Roch Côté, ed., *Québec 1999*, (Montréal: Les Éditions Fides, 1998), 10–11; and Michael S. Pollard and Zheng Wu, "Data and Perspectives: Divergence of Marriage Patterns in Quebec and Elsewhere in Canada," *Population and Development Review* 24 (June 1998): 350.

39. Statistics Canada, Canadian Vital Statistics, Birth Database, and Demography Division (Population Estimates), Table 102–4505: "Live Births, Crude Birth Rate, Age-Specific and Total Fertility Rates: Canada, Provinces and Territories, Annual, 2002."

40. CBC, "Abortions in Quebec Highest Number in Western World," *cbc.ca News,* March 10, 2000; and Langlois, "Tendances de la société québécoise, 1999," 14–15.

41. P. A. Dutil, "Quebec: A Distinct but Unhinged Society. The Loss, and Maybe the Rebirth, of Hope," *Literary Review of Canada* 10 (October 2002): 6.

Marriage (or Not)

In English, demographers have spoken of a "rapid retreat from marriage in Quebec."[42] A French-speaking scholar of population likewise has written that in Quebec, "One is able, indeed, to speak of a genuine turning away from marriage, which appears less and less as a normative institution in the eyes of new couples."[43] Between 1971 and 1991, marriage rates declined across Canada, but they veritably plunged in Quebec. For example, Ontario underwent an 18 percent drop, to 7.4 marriages per 1,000 persons, while Quebec's rate decreased an astonishing 49 percent, to 4.2 per 1,000.

Despite certain protections that provincial law provides exclusively to married partners, couples in Quebec today divorce at the highest rate in Canada,[44] and live in nonmarital relationships at around twice the rate of other Canadians. Common-law arrangements characterized 19 percent of all cohabiting couples in Quebec in 1991, as opposed to just 11 percent in other parts of the country. Five years later, the ratio had inflated: 24 percent of couples in Quebec who lived together were unmarried, whereas the overall percentage for Canada stopped at 12.[45] By 2000, the statistic had risen again: now 30 percent of Quebec's couples lived as common-law spouses (vs. a static 12 percent for Canadians nationwide and 8 percent in the neighboring United States). Quebec's present rate of common-law relationships is comparable to that of Sweden.[46]

In addition, data from the 1990s show that throughout the metropolitan region of Montreal, more than one-third of couples were living in nonmarital consensual unions; far to the east, on the economically de-

42. Pollard and Wu, "Divergence of Marriage Patterns in Quebec and Elsewhere in Canada," 329, 340.

43. "On peut en fait parler d'une véritable désaffection envers le mariage, qui apparaît de moins en moins comme une institution normative aux yeux des nouveaux couples." Langlois, "Familles et modes de vie," 126.

44. CBC, "Fewer Canadian Marriages End in Divorce," *cbc.ca News,* May 4, 2004. For background, see Renée B. Dandurand, "Les dissolutions matrimoniales: Un phénomène latent dans le Québec des années 60," *Anthropologie et sociétés* 9 (1985): 87–114.

45. Langlois, "Familles et modes de vie," 126 and 128; and Pollard and Wu, "Divergence of Marriage Patterns in Quebec and Elsewhere in Canada," 330.

46. Statistics Canada, *Profile of Canadian Families and Households: Diversification Continues,* 2001 Census: Analysis Series (Ottawa: Statistics Canada, Minister of Industry, 2002), 5, 25.

pressed Gaspé peninsula, the proportion was more than one-half of the total.[47] With a crude marriage rate of 3.4 per 1,000 persons in 2000, the people of Quebec are by far the least wedded of any provincial population in Canada, and are surpassed in their singlehood only by residents of Nunavut (3.2 per 1,000), the newest territory of Canada in the remote reaches of the eastern Arctic.[48] In Quebec, "common-law relationships . . . effectively function not just as a 'trial marriage' but as a socially acceptable marriage substitute."[49]

A natural result of the aversion to marriage in contemporary Quebec is an unusually high rate of childbearing that occurs out of wedlock. In 2002, more than half (55.3 percent) of all births in Quebec were to never-married mothers (another 2.7 percent were to mothers who were widowed, divorced, or separated). This fact has been described as "a major and thoroughgoing transformation, parallel to the loss of interest with respect to marriage."[50] Indeed, so widespread is the practice of rearing children in households where the parents are not married that a conservative publication of news and opinion in western Canada labeled Quebec "A Province of Bastards"![51] Census data from 2001 indicate that 47.9 percent of children in Quebec are being raised by a single parent or by an unmarried pair, up from 35.8 percent in 1996. At the same time (1996), merely 31.4 percent of Quebec adults lived in a traditional household—that is, as married parents of at least one child.[52] The causes of these trends and tendencies, to be sure, are complicated, yet one element whose influence they

---

47. CBC, "Common-Law Unions More Popular: Survey," *cbc.ca News,* July 11, 2002; and Nancy Wood, "Unmarried . . . with Children: Quebecers Pass Up Marriage for Common-Law Relationships," *Maclean's: Canada's Weekly Newsmagazine* 106 (August 23, 1993): 40–41.

48. Statistics Canada, "Marriages: 2000," *Ottawa Daily,* June 2, 2003; and Allison Lawlor, "More Canadian Couples Heading Down the Aisle," *Toronto Globe and Mail,* June 2, 2003.

49. Susan Crompton, "Always the Bridesmaid: People Who Don't Expect to Marry," *Canadian Social Trends* (Summer 2005): 5.

50. Statistics Canada, Canadian Vital Statistics, Birth Database, Table 102–4506: "Live Births, by Marital Status of Mother: Canada, Provinces and Territories, Annual, 2002." The quotation, in French, reads "une mutation majeure et radicale, parallèle à la désaffection vis-à-vis mariage." Langlois, "Familles et modes de vie," 128.

51. Michael Jenkinson, "A Province of Bastards: Statscan Catalogues Quebec's Distinct Society—Such as Its 41% Illegitimacy Rate," *Alberta Report* 23 (February 19, 1996): 11–12.

52. Langlois, "Familles et modes de vie," 132–33; and Statistics Canada, *Profile of Canadian Families and Households,* 26.

do not suggest (and have not for some time suggested) is conventional Roman Catholicism.[53]

The Rise of New Lay Elites

The arrival of the *Révolution tranquille* also heralded the final elevation to power of new elites that had been forming in Quebec for most of the half-century before the provincial election of 1960. One of the first scholars of Quebec to point out this change was the sociologist Jean-Charles Falardeau.

According to Falardeau, these elites composed two broad categories: one, flowing out of the universities, was poised to enter the expanding state bureaucracy; and another was rising swiftly through the previously English-speaking ranks of business executives. While members of the latter group undertook to "French-ify" what was St. James Street in Montreal, Quebec's Wall Street *("Ils ont commencé à franciser la rue Saint-Jacques"),*[54] the reform-minded government of Quebec welcomed many in the former group:

> The government is giving our society some new economic and cultural structures. It is becoming a planner. The majority of planning technicians will come from the ranks of the university. These are the successors to the protesters of fifteen years ago. In several cases it is the former protesters themselves who will compose the first teams of governmental technocrats. This is the new élite: an intellectual, rational, technically-oriented, and effective élite. It is superimposing itself on the onetime professionals of politics, the elected representatives, whom it is displacing in taking for itself functions that consist of both making and executing laws.[55]

53. Benoît Laplante, "The Rise of Cohabitation in Quebec: Power of Religion and Power over Religion," *Canadian Journal of Sociology* 31 (Winter 2006): 1–24.

54. Jean-Charles Falardeau, "Des élites traditionnelles aux élites nouvelles," in Fernand Dumont and Jean-Paul Montminy, eds., *Le pouvoir dans la société canadienne-française,* Troisième colloque de la revue *Recherches sociographiques* du Département de sociologie et d'anthropologie de l'Université Laval (Québec: Les Presses de l'Université Laval, 1966), 141.

55. "Le gouvernement donne à notre société des structures nouvelles, économiques et culturelles. Il devient planificateur. La plupart des techniciens de la planification viendront des rangs de l'université. Ce sont les successeurs des contestants d'il y a quinze ans. Dans plusieurs cas, ce sont les ex-contestants eux-mêmes qui constitueront les premières équipes de technocrates gouvernementaux. C'est l'élite nouvelle: une élite intellectuelle, rationnelle, technicienne, efficace. Elle se superpose aux ex-professionnels de la politique, les députés, qu'elle déplace en assumant des fonctions qui comportent à la fois la légis-

A salient fact to which Falardeau alludes only in passing is that many of those who ascended into the new elites were persons who had gained their formative organizational experience as leaders of various movements of Catholic Action ("anciens dirigeants de l'action catholique").[56]

The original movements of Catholic Action arose almost one hundred years ago out of the direction of Catholic energies to the task of "social reconstruction."[57] The call to the service of God on earth (and thereby the transformation of the world) was not to be limited to the clergy or religious, the Catholic Church taught, but was to involve all Catholics, no matter what their status or station. This work, in turn, was to be pursued through group action that was "specialized" to the social milieu of the believer. In every walk of life, wrote the Most Rev. Joseph Charbonneau (1892–1959), the activist archbishop of Montreal, "it is necessary to discover apostles ready to group themselves around the Hierarchy, in order to help it to extend the reign of Christ." Such helpers would "thus be the apostolic leaven which will raise towards God the masses of young people."[58]

Members of the Catholic clergy were not only willing participants but

lation et l'exécution." Falardeau, "Des élites traditionnelles aux élites nouvelles," 140–41. See also Jean-Charles Falardeau, "The Changing Social Structures," in Falardeau, ed., *Essais sur le Québec contemporain: Essays on Contemporary Quebec*, Symposium du centenaire de l'Université Laval (Québec: Les Presses universitaires Laval, 1953), 101–22.

Compare Hubert Guindon, "Social Unrest, Social Class and Quebec's Bureaucratic Revolution" [1964], reprinted in Samuel D. Clark, J. Paul Grayson, and Linda M. Grayson, eds., *Prophecy and Protest: Social Movements in Twentieth-Century Canada* (Toronto: Gage Educational Publishing, 1975), 337–46; and Lemieux and Montminy, *Le catholicisme québécois*, 56–57.

Michel Sarra-Bournet places these changes in the broader context of historical writing about postwar Quebec, up to and including the 1990s, in his essay, "L'ascension de nouvelles élites et l'histoire du Québec," Thème: "L'histoire du Québec revue et corrigée," *Bulletin d'histoire politique* 3 (hiver 1995): 43–73.

56. Falardeau, "Des élites traditionnelles aux élites nouvelles," 139. See also Jean-Marie Fecteau, "Between Scientific Enquiry and the Search for a Nation: Quebec Historiography as Seen by Ronald Rudin" [1999], reprinted in Behiels, *Quebec since 1800*, 43n27.

57. Gabriel Clément, *Histoire de l'Action catholique au Canada français*, Rapport de la Commission d'étude sur les laïcs et l'Église, no. 2 (Montréal: Les Éditions Fides, 1972); and Clément, "L'Action catholique: Les mouvements spécialisés à Montréal de 1930 à 1966," in Rolland Litalien, ed., *L'église de Montréal: Aperçus d'hier et d'aujourd'hui, 1836–1986* (Montréal: Les Éditions Fides, 1986), 295–315.

58. Joseph Charbonneau, *Catholic Action: Pastoral Letter of His Excellency the Most Reverend Joseph Charbonneau, Archbishop of Montreal* [1941], Apostolate Library, no. 1 (South Bend, Ind.: Apostolate Press; and Montréal: Les Éditions Fides, 1943), 31 and 32.

key instigators of lay action, for the sanctification of the world for Christ required as allies a laity that had been awakened and mobilized. For example, Father Joseph-Papin Archambault (1880–1966), Jesuit promoter of "closed retreats" *(les retraites fermées)* and one of the more conservative Quebec clerics of his day, nevertheless preached the necessity of a lay elite to meet the challenge of a society that was becoming increasingly hostile to religious truth:

> More and more, modern society is dividing itself into two quite distinct camps: on one side the followers of Christ, and on the other His opponents. . . .
>
> Now, to which of the two camps, in this vital struggle that surpasses all the others because it involves souls, will go the victory? Will it be to the larger one? Psychology, which incidentally confirms history, teaches us the opposite. It is not the masses of people who, everywhere in the moral realm, carry off decisive battles. It is the élites, that is to say, the groups of men with convictions so profound that they place at the service of these convictions a limitless devotion and fervor.
>
> As custodian of the truth, the Church ought to have these élites in every country.[59]

59. De plus en plus, la société moderne se divise en deux camps bien tranchés: d'un côté les disciples du Christ, de l'autre ses adversaires. . . .

Or, auquel des deux camps, dans cette lutte vitale qui dépasse toutes les autres puisqu'il s'agit des âmes, ira la victoire? Est-ce au plus nombreux? La psychologie, que confirme d'ailleurs l'histoire, nous enseigne le contraire. Ce ne sont pas les foules qui, dans le domaine moral surtout, remportent les batailles décisives. Ce sont les élites, c'est-à-dire les groupes d'hommes aux convictions tellement profondes qu'ils mettent à leur service un dévouement et une ardeur sans bornes.

Détentrice de la verité, l'Église devrait avoir en tous pays de ces élites.

Joseph-Papin Archambault, S.J., "La formation d'une élite," reprinted in Archambault, *Pour un catholicisme conquérant: Allocutions et discours* (Montréal: L'École sociale populaire, 1933), 34–35.

For background on Father Archambault, consult Richard Arès, S.J., *Le Père Joseph-Papin Archambault, S.J. (1880–1966): Sa vie, ses œuvres,* Collection "Les Cahiers d'histoire des Jésuites," no. 5 (Montréal: Les Éditions Bellarmin, 1983); and Frédéric Boily, "Une figure du catholicisme social canadien-français de l'entre-deux-guerres: Le Père Joseph-Papin Archambault, S.J.," *Mens: Revue d'histoire intellectuelle de l'Amérique française* 1 (printemps 2001): 141–61.

The history, some of it quite controversial, associated with Archambault's organization, the École sociale populaire, is recounted in Samuel H. Barnes, "Quebec Catholicism and Social Change," *Review of Politics* 23 (January 1961): 52–76; P.-M. Gaudrault, O.P., *Neutralité, non-confessionnalité et l'École sociale populaire* (Ottawa and Montréal: Les Éditions du Lévrier, 1946); Marie Agnes of Rome Gaudreau, P. de M., *The Social Thought of French*

The creation of this kind of elite was the aim of Catholic Action's many organizations tailored for the situations of youth,[60] students, younger workers,[61] adult workers,[62] farmers, and professionals. (Though not officially affiliated with the movement, there even developed in Quebec a powerful federation of Catholic trade unions.) Leaders in Catholic Action were explicitly barred from using the organization for partisan political ends. Nevertheless, among the secular benefits of a vital Catholic Action movement, predicted Archbishop Charbonneau, would be that it "furnishes to the country a phalanx of exemplary citizens who will favour and defend, not only the interests and rights of the Church, but also those of the State and of domestic society."[63]

Canada as Reflected in the Semaine Sociale, Catholic University of America Studies, vol. 18 (Washington, D.C.: The Catholic University of America Press, 1946); and Gilles Routhier, "La doctrine sociale et le mouvement catholique: L'École sociale populaire (1930–1936)" (M.A. thesis, Faculté de théologie, Université Laval, 1980).

60. Michael D. Behiels, "L'Association catholique de la jeunesse canadienne-française and the Quest for a Moral Regeneration, 1903–1914," *Journal of Canadian Studies* 13 (Summer 1978): 27–41; and Laurier Renaud, *La fondation de l'A.C.J.C.: L'histoire d'une jeunesse nationaliste* (Jonquière, Québec: Les Presses collégiales de Jonquière, 1972). See also Jean-Philippe Warren, "La découverte de la 'question sociale': Sociologie et mouvements d'action jeunesse canadiens-français," *Revue d'histoire de l'Amérique française* 55 (printemps 2002): 539–72.

The Association catholique de la jeunesse canadienne (ACJC) was founded somewhat earlier than the groups that composed Catholic Action, but it was later incorporated as part of that religious movement before adopting a more exclusively nationalist emphasis. See Jacques Cousineau, S.J., *L'Église d'ici et le social: 1940–1960,* vol. 1: *La Commission sacerdotale d'Études sociales* (Montréal: Les Éditions Bellarmin, 1982), 163, 201–2.

61. Louise Bienvenue, *Quand la jeunesse entre en scène: L'Action catholique avant la Révolution tranquille* (Montréal: Les Éditions du Boréal, 2003); Oscar Cole-Arnal, "Shaping Young Proletarians into Militant Christians: The Pioneer Phase of the JOC in France and Quebec," *Journal of Contemporary History* 32 (October 1997): 509–26; Lucie Piché, "La Jeunesse ouvrière catholique féminine: Un lieu de formation sociale et d'action communautaire, 1931–1966," *Revue d'histoire de l'Amérique française* 52 (printemps 1999): 481–506; L. Piché, "Une jeunesse unique? Mouvements de jeunesse et contestation sociale," *SCHÉC* [Société canadienne d'histoire de l'Église catholique] *Études d'histoire religieuse* 67 (2001): 215–26; and L. Piché, *Femmes et changement social au Québec: L'apport de la Jeunesse ouvrière catholique féminine, 1931–1966,* Collection "Religions, cultures et sociétés" (Sainte-Foy, Québec: Les Presses de l'Université Laval, 2003).

62. Jean-Pierre Collin, "La Ligue ouvrière catholique et l'organisation communautaire dans le Québec urbain des années 1940," *Revue d'histoire de l'Amérique française* 47 (automne 1993): 163–91; Collin, *La Ligue ouvrière catholique canadienne, 1938–1954* (Montréal: Les Éditions du Boréal, 1996); and Fernand Dumont, "Recherches sur les groupements religieux," *Social Compass* 10 (1963): 171–91.

63. Charbonneau, *Catholic Action,* 68. For a later perspective, after the demise of much Catholic Action, consult Claude Ryan, "Les laïcs et l'évolution de l'Église au Québec: Ré-

To say the least, this element of Catholic Action's promise as a vehicle for the training of dedicated citizens was amply fulfilled. Members of Catholic Action met regularly in intimate settings, in the absence of the clergy, to read Scripture and to divine its meanings for modern times. They thus learned not merely how to organize themselves, but also how to plan in groups; how to reflect, discern, debate, and decide in a manner free and autonomous; and how ultimately to orchestrate outreach activities.[64] Imbued with Catholic Action's decision-making method of "See—Judge—Act," veterans of the movement, including such luminaries as Pierre Juneau (b. 1922), Marc Lalonde (b. 1929),[65] Jean Le Moyne (1913–1996),[66] Gérard Pelletier (1919–1997),[67] Claude Ryan (1925–2004),[68] and

flexions à partir de l'expérience de l'Action catholique," Thème: "L'Église au Québec," *Relations* 26/302 (février 1966): 54–57.

64. Robert Choquette, *Canada's Religions: An Historical Introduction,* Religions and Beliefs Series, no. 12 (Ottawa: University of Ottawa Press, 2004), 345–50; Roberto Perin, "French-Speaking Canada from 1840," in Terence Murphy and Roberto Perin, eds., *A Concise History of Christianity in Canada* (Don Mills, Ont.: Oxford University Press, 1996), 253–54; and Gilles Routhier, "La rencontre de la théologie et des sciences sociales au Québec," Thème: "Religions et sciences sociales: Un chassé-croisé interprétatif entre histoire, théologie et sociologie," *Revue d'histoire de l'Amérique française* 57 (hiver 2004): 389–405 (esp. 394–95).

65. For autobiographical reminiscences from Marc Lalonde, former federal Cabinet minister, see Lalonde, "What *Cité libre* Means to Me," trans. My-Trang Nguyen, *Cité libre* [English ed.] 28 (Fall 2000): 31–33.

66. See the reflections of Jean Le Moyne, author and political speechwriter, in Le Moyne, *Convergences: Essais* (Montréal: Les Éditions HMH Ltée, 1964).

67. On the life and work of Gérard Pelletier, see Gérard Pelletier, *The October Crisis,* trans. Joyce Marshall (Toronto: McClelland and Stewart, 1971); G. Pelletier, *Les années d'impatience* (Montréal: Les Éditions internationales Alain Stanké, 1983), trans. Alan Brown as *Years of Impatience: 1950–1960* (New York: Facts On File, 1984); G. Pelletier, *Years of Choice: 1960–1968,* trans. Alan Brown (Toronto: Methuen Publications, 1987); G. Pelletier, *L'aventure du pouvoir: 1968–1975* (Montréal: Les Éditions internationales Alain Stanké, 1992); G. Pelletier, "Témoignage de Gérard Pelletier," in Alain-G. Gagnon and Michel Sarra-Bournet, eds., *Duplessis: Entre la Grande noirceur et la société libérale,* Collection "Débats," no. 1 (Montréal: Les Éditions Québec/Amérique, 1997), 21–25; Jean-Philippe Warren, "Gérard Pelletier et *Cité libre*: La mystique personnaliste de la Révolution tranquille," *Société* 20/21 (été 1999): 313–46; and Anthony Wilson-Smith, "Quiet Excellence: Gérard Pelletier Won Respect as a Statesman, Mentor and Friend," *Maclean's* 110 (July 7, 1997): 33.

68. On Claude Ryan, the journalist, editor, and Quebec political leader who died in early 2004, see Tommy Chouinard, "Ses jeunes années à l'Action catholique canadienne," *Le Devoir* [Montréal], 10 février 2004; Jean Dion, "Claude Ryan, 1925–2004: L'homme de tous les débats," *Le Devoir,* 10 février 2004; Aurelien Leclerc, *Claude Ryan: A Biography,* trans. Colleen Kurtz (Toronto: NC Press, 1980); Olivier Marcil, *La raison et l'équilibre: Libéralisme, nationalisme et catholicisme dans la pensée de Claude Ryan au Devoir (1962–*

Jeanne Sauvé (1922–1993),[69] went on to careers of consequence in the media, government, and civil society of Quebec.[70]

Pelletier—in his youth an international officer *(secrétaire-général)* of a major organization in Catholic Action (the Jeunesse étudiante catholique [JÉC]), and later a member of Parliament, a federal cabinet minister, and a Canadian ambassador—can be taken as a suitable representative of the postwar Catholic elite in Quebec. Within Catholic Action for students, he advanced the JÉC mission: "to embody socially our faith" *(incarner socialement notre foi)*.[71] As an adult, committed simultaneously to religious action in the world, to his profession as a journalist and television broadcaster, and to principled public service, Pelletier saw no conflict between the removal of the Church and its ministers from social institutions and the promotion of an authentic faith. In fact, to him the two processes were complementary. To unbelieving friends, Pelletier was inclined to say, as he confided in 1961, "You are persuaded that the withdrawal of the clergy from temporal responsibilities that are not theirs will lead fatally to the practical undoing of all religious life. We judge, to the contrary, that the Church in Québec needs to abandon a rôle that is not its own in order to rediscover its true direction and that it will emerge greater from this transformation."[72]

1978), Collection "Histoire et société" (Montréal: Les Éditions Varia, 2002); Denis Monière, "Le nationalisme de Claude Ryan: Un lien entre le fédéralisme et le catholicisme?" *Le Devoir*, 7 mars 2005, A7; Pierre S. Pettigrew, "Témoignage: Mon ami, Monsieur Ryan," *Le Devoir*, 10 février 2004; Antoine Robitaille, "Claude Ryan, 1925–2004: Fidèle au catholicisme social. Les catholiques engagés se faisaient de plus en plus rare au moment de la Révolution tranquille," *Le Devoir*, 11 février 2004; and Ryan's own posthumously published essays, *Mon testament spirituel* (Ottawa: Novalis, 2004).

69. On Jeanne Sauvé, who would be appointed Canada's first female governor-general, see Barbara Greenwood, *Jeanne Sauvé*, Canadian Lives (Markham, Ont.: Fitzhenry and Whiteside, 1989); and Shirley E. Woods, *Her Excellency, Jeanne Sauvé* (Toronto: Macmillan, 1986).

70. Marc Nadeau, "Pierre Elliott Trudeau and the *JÉC*," in English, Gwyn, and Lackenbauer, eds., *The Hidden Pierre Elliott Trudeau*, 75–79.

71. Quoted in Clément, *Histoire de l'Action catholique au Canada français*, 236; and in Clément, "L'Action catholique," 309.

72. "Vous êtes persuadés que le repli du clergé hors des responsabilités temporelles qui ne sont pas les siennes entraînera fatalement l'annulation pratique de toute vie religieuse. Nous estimons au contraire que l'Église québécoise a besoin d'abandonner un rôle qui n'est pas le sien pour retrouver son vrai sens et qu'elle sortira plus grande de cette transformation." Quoted in Meunier and Warren, *Sortir de la "Grande noirceur,"* 158.

As Catholic Action reached its historical zenith in Canada, however, the seeds were sown for a very different type of society in francophone Quebec, one that would be revealed more fully by the 1960s, at the first opportunity for liberalization of political leadership, of basic schooling, and of the values of the workplace. Religious men and women, many with advanced training, were streaming from the monasteries and convents of Quebec and moving unimpeded into positions within the mushrooming public bureaucracies of education and social service, as well as into increasingly broad-based private corporations. They joined there laypersons whose own fidelity to Catholicism encouraged a devotion to constructing the Kingdom of God in the world of mundane affairs. With the onset of the *Révolution tranquille*, then,

> The social doctrine of the Church henceforth not only admitted the necessity of an expanded intervention by the State, it even went so far as to encourage lay people to work fervently for it. And so that the laity could make of the State a genuine setting for the embodiment and blossoming of spiritual values, the Church gave up its drive to influence temporal structures directly. . . .
>
> For Catholic intellectuals of the post-war period, the lay person thus takes it upon himself to be the mediator between the spiritual and temporal dimensions: the State is his city, the Church his watchman. . . . At the beginning of the 1960s, to join the civil service is not only to unearth a good, steady job; it is for some people also to enter into a new form of apostolate: the *apostolate of competence* at the service of individuals and of the common good. Many were the young holders of university degrees who would opt to serve the interests of the people rather than those of private companies.[73]

73. Dorénavant, la doctrine sociale de l'Église non seulement admettait la necessité d'une intervention accrue de l'État, elle allait jusqu'à inciter les laïcs à y œuvrer ardemment. Et pour que le laïcat fasse de l'État un véritable lieu d'incarnation et d'épanouissement des valeurs spirituelles, l'Église renonçait à sa volonté d'influencer directement les structures temporelles. . . .

    Pour les intellectuels catholiques d'après-guerre, le laïc s'impose ainsi comme le médiateur des dimensions spirituelles et temporelles: l'État est sa cité, l'Église sa vigile. . . . Au début des années 1960, entrer dans la fonction publique, c'est plus que dénicher un bon emploi stable, c'est aussi pour plusieurs entrer dans une nouvelle forme d'apostolat: l'*apostolat de la compétence* au service des personnes et du bien commun. Nombreux furent les jeunes diplômés de l'université qui préféreront servir les intérêts du peuple plutôt que ceux des compagnies privées.

Meunier and Warren, *Sortir de la "Grande noirceur,"* 159–61. (The emphasis appears in the original.)

The sociological irony of Quebec's secularization thus came to a proper fruition: it was not at the hands of modern doubters and scoffers at religion that the core of Quebec society was evacuated of the Catholic Church's once-dominant presence, but rather through the faith-filled intentions of religiously motivated and socially committed Catholic laypersons and of onetime professional operatives of the Church itself. As the historian Éric Bédard has summarized this effect of the *Révolution tranquille:*

> During this time, many members of religious orders decide to leave consecrated life. All of a sudden, it was no longer necessary to be a priest to engage in social action. The product of favor for the lay person and of an activist approach that does not dismiss the sciences of the social, the Quiet Revolution would constitute—and there is its paradox—a "religious departure from religion." . . . Far from being a victory of Reason over religious obscurantism, the Quiet Revolution would appear here in part, in its ideological aspect, as the conclusion of a long process of internal transformations within the Church. The creation of the Québec State would have been welcomed with relief by the thousands of participants in Catholic Action who dreamed of power to resort to such effective tools of social justice to affect society.[74]

The knowledge of coordination; the facility with organizational personnel, funding, and communications; and the skill at administration that time spent in Catholic associations (and, to a different degree, in Catholic communities of men and women) had bestowed on the faithful were all transferable assets. They constituted a kind of human capital that, when eventually cashed, dislodged the Catholic Church—previously the predominant institution—from its paramount position in Quebec society.

The result, perhaps clouded in its causes, is clear enough in its demonstration. Jean Pellerin, an author and newspaper essayist, remarks on these

---

74. Pendant ce temps, plusieurs membres de congrégations décident de défroquer. Tout à coup, il n'était plus nécessaire d'être prêtre pour faire de l'action sociale. Résultat d'un parti pris en faveur du laïc et d'une approche militante qui ne repousse pas les sciences du social, la Révolution tranquille constituerait—et c'est là son paradoxe— une "sortie religieuse de la religion." . . . Loin d'être une victoire de la Raison contre un obscurantisme religieux, la Révolution tranquille apparaît ici en parte, dans son versant idéologique, comme l'aboutissement d'un long processus de transformations internes à l'Église. La création de l'État québécois aurait été accueillie avec soulagement par des milliers de militants de l'action catholique qui rêvaient de pouvoir recourir à de si efficaces outils de justice sociale pour agir sur la société.
Éric Bédard, "Préface," in Meunier and Warren, *Sortir de la "Grande Noirceur,"* 16–17.

changes in his collected editorials. In those pages, he looks back in 1971 on the transmission of authority over *truth* in Quebec society from bishops who were genuine ecclesiastical figures to "bishops" who were their secular equivalents in academia, politics, and the law:

> Québec is lucky. It has always had bishops to speak in its name. Previously, these were real bishops. They wore the miter and carried the crozier, and each time that they opened their mouths, they imagined that they spoke *ex cathedra* and in the name of all of French Canada. This was the *Belle Époche* of unanimity. Canadians, Catholic and French, were in peaceful possession of the truth.

> Today, the bishops of Lower Canada are a little bit closer to all the lay people. They neither wear a miter nor carry a crozier. They dress like everybody else, and it is only just that, on occasion, they allow themselves to wear a cap and gown. Yet they all have titles as long as your arm, and, like their predecessors, they speak *ex cathedra* and in the name of all Quebeckers, without forgetting a single one of them.

> Even so, the era of unanimity is over. Quebeckers have lost some of their certitudes.

> The real bishops of yesteryear derived from the people and were born into the lower middle class *(la petite bourgeoisie)*. The lay bishops of today above all come from the universities of Montréal and of Laval. Certain ones are "political scientists," and predict the past and the future. Others are "specialists in constitutional law," and pronounce sentences without appeal.[75]

---

75. Le Québec a de la chance. Il a toujours eu des évêques pour parler en son nom. Anciennement, c'étaient de vrais évêques. Ils portaient la mitre et la crosse, et chaque fois qu'ils ouvraient la bouche, ils estimaient parler ex cathedra et au nom de tout le Canada français. C'était la belle époque de l'unanimité. Les Canadiens catholiques et français étaient en possession tranquille de la vérité.

> Aujourd'hui, les évêques du Bas-Canada sont a peu près tous les laïcs. Ils ne portent ni mitre ni crosse. Ils s'habillent comme tout le monde et c'est à peine si, à l'occasion, ils se permettent de porter la toque et la toge. Mais il[s] vous ont tous des titres long comme le bras, et, comme leur prédécesseurs, ils parlent ex cathedra et au nom de tous les Québécois, sans en oublier un seul.

> Pourtant, l'ère de l'unanimité est révolue. Les Québécois ont perdu plusieurs de leurs certitudes.

> Les vrais évêques d'antan étaient issus du peuple et de la petite bourgeoisie. Les évêques laïques d'aujourd'hui sortent surtout des universités de Montréal et de Laval. Certains sont "politicologues" et prédisent le passé et l'avenir. D'autres sont "spécialistes en droit constitutionnel" et prononcent des sentences sans appel.

Jean Pellerin, "10 mai 1971," in *La fronde québécoise: Une crise en rappel* (Westmount, Québec: Les Éditions Multimédia Robert Davies Inc., 2000), 79.

An entire set of social institutions experienced similar transformations in this period. No longer, then, was the power to define and to alter Quebec's culture lodged exclusively in the Catholic Church. In the eyes of countless observers and commentators, the power to interpret Quebec's provincial patrimony and to address its national destiny belonged to the new experts of a government and a private sector that spread in tandem throughout the middle part of the twentieth century. "The great majority of the architects and implementers of Québec's entrance into the modern world and prosperity . . . are also the principal people responsible for the considerable weakening of the very institution that put them into the world," namely, the Roman Catholic Church.[76] Something of this process can be glimpsed in a single case from the economic history of Quebec since 1900: the establishment and growth of the Caisses Desjardins.

The Case of the Mouvement Desjardins

The largest banking institution in Quebec—and the sixth-largest in all of Canada—is actually not a bank, but a highly developed international network of credit unions (and providers of other financial services, such as investments, insurance, trusts, mortgage loans, private pension management, and equities trading). The largest private employer in Quebec, it is known throughout the world as the Mouvement des Caisses populaires et d'économie Desjardins.[77]

76. Alain Chanlat and Renée Bédard, "Managing in the Québec Style: Originality and Vulnerability," *International Studies of Management and Organization* 21 (September 1991): 29.

77. Presentations by M. Claude Têtu, Le Mouvement des Caisses populaires et d'économie Desjardins, at the Complexe Desjardins, Montréal, Québec (June 17, 1994); and M. Claude Béland, Président, Le Mouvement des Caisses Desjardins, at the Madison Hotel, Seattle, Wash. (November 18, 1995).
See also John T. Croteau, "The Caisses Populaires Desjardins of Quebec: A Modern System of People's Banks," *Agricultural History* 24 (October 1950): 227–38; Pierre Poulin, *Histoire du Mouvement Desjardins*, tome 1: *Desjardins et la naissance des Caisses populaires, 1900–1920*, Collection "Desjardins" (Montréal: Les Éditions Québec/Amérique, for the Société historique Alphonse-Desjardins, 1990); and Ronald Rudin, *In Whose Interest? Quebec's Caisses populaires, 1900–1945* (Montréal and Kingston, Ont.: McGill-Queen's University Press, 1990).
On some of the most recent changes in the movement, see Claude Turcotte, "Le Mouvement Desjardins: Desjardins a dû repenser son leadership," in R. Côté, *Québec 1999*, 227–31; and, from a critical vantage, René Croteau, *Un patrimoine coopératif défiguré et*

From an opening day of business in 1901 that brought in twelve customers with total deposits of $26.40 (Can.),[78] Desjardins has grown to involve more than one thousand branches, nearly forty thousand employees, eight thousand democratically elected officers, and between five and six million *sociétaires* (member-owners). As of 2004, it controlled an estimated $106.2 billion (Can.) in assets.[79] At one time or another, Desjardins has purchased substantial holdings in a surprising number of Quebec-based enterprises, from health-care companies to computer-assisted animators to a Major League Baseball franchise (the former Montreal Expos).[80] So commonplace are its offices in Quebec (and elsewhere in the francophone communities of Canada and the United States), and so assumed is membership among the public, that Desjardins has been dubbed *une institution plus québécoise que le sirop d'érable* ("an institution [that is] more Québec-like than maple syrup").[81] Another commentator argues that its very development may be "used as a kind of metaphor for the history of Quebec in the 20th century."[82]

---

dénaturé: Le Mouvement Desjardins, 1997–2003 (Sainte-Foy, Québec: Les Éditions Multi-Mondes, 2004).

78. "De la caisse au conglomérat. 1900–1920: Démarrage," in *Mouvement Desjardins: Histoire* (Montréal: La Fédération des Caisses Desjardins du Québec, 2003); and Pierre Poulin, with Pierre Goulet and Andrée Rivard, *Desjardins: 100 ans d'histoire* (Sainte-Foy, Québec: Les Éditions MultiMondes; and Lévis, Québec: Les Éditions Dorimène and the Confédération des Caisses populaires et d'économie Desjardins du Québec, 2000), 16–17.

79. "Mouvement des Caisses Desjardins: No. 56216," *Hoover's Company Capsule Database—World Companies* (Austin, Tex.: Hoover's, 2003); Presse canadienne, "Plus riche, Desjardins paie moins de ristournes," *Le Droit* [Ottawa, Ont.—Gatineau, Québec], 2 mars 2005, 31; Benoît Lévesque, Marie-Claire Malo, and Ralph Rouzier, "The 'Caisse de dépôt et placement du Québec' and the 'Mouvement des caisses populaires et d'économie Desjardins': Two Financial Institutions, the Same Convergence towards the General Interest?" *Annals of Public and Cooperative Economics* 68 (September 1997): 494; and Ghislain Paradis, "The Development of the Desjardins Movement in Quebec, Canada" (Montréal: Développement international Desjardins, 1999), 1.

80. "Diversification des activités: Investissement," in *Mouvement Desjardins: Histoire* (2003).

81. Quoted in Jean-Pierre Girard, "Le Québec et le Mouvement Desjardins," in Alain-G. Gagnon and Jean-Pierre Girard, with Stéphan Gervais, eds., *Le mouvement coopératif au cœur du XXIe siècle* (Sainte-Foy, Québec: Les Presses de l'Université du Québec, 2001), 67.

On the relationship between Desjardins and the heritage of Quebec, see the contributions to Benoît Lévesque et al., eds., *Desjardins: Une enterprise et un mouvement?* Collection "Les leaders du Québec contemporain," no. 9 (Sainte-Foy, Québec: Les Presses de l'Université du Québec, 1997).

82. Historian Ronald Rudin, quoted in Lynn Moore, "Desjardins Turns 150: With Preparations Under Way to Mark the Birth of the Man behind the Caisse Pop, the Spot-

After early careers as a journalist and a publisher, Alphonse Desjardins (1854–1920), founder of the movement that took his name, won employment in Ottawa as a stenographer recording French-language portions of legislative debates in the Canadian House of Commons. One day in 1897, while performing his duties in the Parliament, Desjardins learned of complaints among representatives about the usurious rates of interest that irregular lenders charged to persons of modest means—not to mention families, farmers, and small businessmen—who could not apply or qualify for credit through chartered commercial banks. In his search for solutions to this problem, he discovered a movement in the countries of Western Europe to promote cooperative "people's banks" *(caisses populaires)*. Reading about this movement and corresponding with its architects, Desjardins began to formulate plans for just this kind of bank in Quebec to meet the financial needs of French Canadians, whom the major institutions mostly ignored.[83]

The first *caisse populaire* opened in the small town of Lévis, across the St. Lawrence River from the city of Quebec.[84] A "no-frills" undertaking, its original home office was precisely that: Desjardins used the ground floor of his own house. Over the years, the founder and guiding spirit of the movement was to prove tireless in lobbying Canada's politicians (for advantageous treatment for the *caisses* under the banking laws) and the priests and prelates of the Catholic Church (for their endorsements and assistance on the local level).[85]

---

light Again Turns on How His Vision Has Been Used—or Abused," *Gazette* [Montréal], October 30, 2004, B1.

83. Ian MacPherson, *Each for All: A History of the Co-operative Movement in English Canada, 1900–1945,* Carleton Library, no. 116 (Toronto: Macmillan, 1979), 29–30.

84. For the history of this one branch, see Guy Bélanger, with Claude Genest, *La Caisse populaire de Lévis, 1900–2000: Là où tout a commencé* (Sainte-Foy, Québec: Les Éditions MultiMondes; and Lévis, Québec: Les Éditions Dorimène and Caisse populaire de Lévis, 2000).

85. Jean Hulliger, *L'enseignement social des évêques canadiens de 1891 à 1950,* Collection "La Bibliothéque economique et sociale" (Montréal: Les Éditions Fides, 1958), 294–300; Jacques Lamarche, *Alphonse Desjardins, un homme au service des autres* (Montréal: Les Éditions du Jour, 1977); Lamarche, *La saga des Caisses populaires* (Montréal: Les Éditions La Presse, Ltée, 1985); MacPherson, *Each for All,* 29–33; Yves Roby, *Alphonse Desjardins et les Caisses populaires: 1854–1920,* Collection "La Bibliothèque économique et sociale" (Montréal: Les Éditions Fides, 1964); and Cyrille Vaillancourt and Albert Faucher, *Alphonse Desjardins: Pionnier de la coopération d'épargne et de crédit en Amérique,* Volume-souvenir du cinquantième anniversaire de la Caisse populaire de Lévis (Lévis, Québec: Les Éditions Le Quotidien, Ltée, 1950).

The customary oil paintings of presidents past and directors deceased line the long corridors in the downtown Montreal headquarters of Desjardins, perched high atop an office tower over a modern indoor shopping mall. Unexpectedly, these portraits include several of serious, dour-faced men in black cassocks and Roman collars. The reason for this oddity is that the Caisses Desjardins, fathered by an ardent Catholic layman, were midwived around Quebec initially, and nursed through the first four decades or so of their existence, by parish priests.[86] Nearly every local branch recruited the *curé* or *vicaire* (priests of the parish) as a director. In one sample of sixty *caisses,* almost 29 percent of the elected leaders in 1920 were members of the clergy; by 1955, merely 3 percent were.[87] Long before the institution of offices on main streets or the availability of *guichets* (automatic tellers) on urban corners, the *caisses* often operated out of the rectory or the church basement. (To this day, many *caisses* maintain the name of the patron saint of their founding parish.) "Who would have imagined," wonder two scholars of business organizations about Desjardins, "that the Catholic Church, by giving it access to the basements of its churches, would one day become the origin of a powerful financial empire[?]"[88]

In turn, lay notables of the parish, local men with reputations for industry and probity, were enlisted to govern the *caisse,* to serve on its committees and to execute its shared decisions; in most cases they eventually

86. In 1932, as the economic darkness of the Great Depression settled over North America, the Mouvement Desjardins was saved from insolvency when the archbishop of Quebec guaranteed its debts.

Generally, on the role of the Catholic clergy, see G. Bélanger, with Genest, *La Caisse populaire de Lévis, 1900–2000,* 62–64; François Jacques, "Le clergé québécois et son appui aux Caisses populaires de 1900 à 1920" (M.A. thesis, Faculté de théologie, Université Laval, 1975); Jean-Pierre Girard, "Le Québec et le Mouvement Desjardins" and "Un point de vue québécois," in Gagnon and Girard, with Gervais, *Le mouvement coopératif au cœur du XXIe siècle,* 59–71 and 175–89; Roland Parenteau, "Le Mouvement Desjardins dans le système financier québécois: Une institution différente?" and J. Yvon Thériault, "Les figures changeantes de la communauté des sociétaires Desjardins," in B. Lévesque et al., *Desjardins,* 15–24 and 87–98; Rudin, *In Whose Interest?,* 16–19, 65; and Majella St-Pierre, *Alphonse Desjardins: Entrepreneur,* Collection "Entreprendre" (Montréal: Les Éditions Transcontinental; and Charlesbourg, Québec: Les Éditions de la Fondation de l'entrepreneurship, 2001), 67, 112–16, 128–29, 148–49.

87. Roger Levasseur and Yvan Rousseau, "Social Movements and Development in Quebec: The Experience of the Desjardins Movement," *Annals of Public and Cooperative Economics* 72 (December 2001): 549–79. See, for these findings, 555–57 and Table 1.

88. Chanlat and Bédard, "Managing in the Québec Style," 17.

dominated. At the start, the composition of boards was weighted heavily toward the old elite of Quebec: doctors, *avocats* and *notaires* (types of lawyers), so-called liberal or independent professionals, and of course priests. By the time of the Second World War, however, surging growth in the movement meant that Desjardins "might almost be described as big business."[89] Soon changing economic conditions forced managements of *caisses* to draw on the skills of those who were newly trained in the latest techniques of business and commerce.[90]

From a sociological standpoint, collaboration with parochial clergy was indispensable ("a central factor in the development of caisses," in the words of one student, a *"sine qua non* condition for the founding of a caisse")[91] because any Caisse Desjardins invariably took as its local service area the Roman Catholic parish. The reason for this was simple: the Catholic parish was "conceived . . . as a form of localized spatial organization centered on the supervision of the individual."[92] Indeed, the special genius of the *caisses* was to exploit the areal organization of existing Catholic churches, which historically not only acted as units of civil and religious administration, but also formed tightly bounded communities of mind and spirit.[93] Communities of this sort enabled a shared identity of members to grow and a habit of mutual recognition to flourish. Individuals knew each other—or, at minimum, knew *about* each other—and they used this knowledge reliably to arrange practical relationships and to map safely the extent of their overlapping social worlds.[94] The structure of the *caisse* has its economic advantages, to be sure, but

89. J. T. Croteau, "The Caisses Populaires Desjardins of Quebec," 231.

90. Levasseur and Y. Rousseau trace this transformation in "Social Movements and Development in Quebec," 563–69.

91. In French, "un facteur central du développement des caisses," a "condition *sine qua non* à la fondation d'une caisse." Girard, "Le Québec et le Mouvement Desjardins," 63. (Italics appear in the original.)

92. In French, "conçue . . . comme forme d'organisation spatiale de proximité centrée sur l'encadrement des individus." Gilles Routhier, "La paroisse québécoise: Évolutions récentes et révisions actuelles," in Serge Courville and Normand Séguin, eds., *La paroisse,* Atlas historique du Québec (Sainte-Foy, Québec: Les Presses de l'Université Laval, 2001), 46.

93. Hulliger, *L'enseignement social des évêques canadiens de 1891 à 1950,* 295–96; and Normand Séguin, "La paroisse dans l'expérience historique québécoise," in Jacques Mathieu, ed., *La mémoire dans la culture,* Collection "Culture française d'Amérique" (Sainte-Foy, Québec: Les Presses de l'Université Laval, 1995), 195–202.

94. Two initial sociological attempts to approach the Roman Catholic parish as a social unit were Jean-Charles Falardeau, "The Parish as an Institutional Type," *Canadian Jour-*

a more important factor is the intimacy of a homogeneous parish group in cultivating attitudes that make for successful management; people are willing to contribute time and effort to committee work in a parish organization. They identify the success of the *caisse* with that of the parish. An official of the *caisse populaire* is a parish leader and admired by his fellows. Most important, the parish priest—a powerful person in Quebec—can watch over the progress of the *caisse* and in many ways can assist in its development. The usual parish is large enough to provide an adequate number of members and small enough to dispense with the need for a costly investigation of loan applicants. Pressure by parish neighbors is usually effective in the collection of delinquent loans.[95]

The *caisse,* then, as one historian put it, "draws all its distinctiveness from an application of parochial sociability to ways of economic organization."[96] In such a context, the evaluation of character, the scrutiny of motives, and germination of the trust upon which a holder and lender of money must depend came to the directors readymade. When, a decade after its founding, the movement promulgated its own "catechism" to explain its origins and purposes in layman's (literally) terms, it included a terse justification for the immutable borders of its activities. Of the local *caisse,* the book instructed:

---

nal of Economics and Political Science 15 (August 1949): 353–67; and Joseph H. Fichter, S.J., "Conceptualizations of the Urban Parish," *Social Forces* 31 (October 1952): 43–47.

In the American social-science literature, the most famous ethnographic studies of Quebec Catholic parishes and their surrounding communities are, first, that of Everett Cherrington Hughes, *French Canada in Transition* [Drummondville] (Chicago: University of Chicago Press, 1943), esp. 92–114 and 143–59; and second, those of Horace Miner, "The French-Canadian Family Cycle"; "Changes in Rural French-Canadian Culture," *American Journal of Sociology* 44 (November 1938): 365–78; and *St. Denis: A French-Canadian Parish* [Saint-Denis-de-Kamouraska], Ethnological Series, The University of Chicago Publications in Anthropology (Chicago: University of Chicago Press, 1939), esp. 91–116. Also see Miner's subsequent study in "A New Epoch in Rural Quebec," *American Journal of Sociology* 56 (July 1950): 1–10; then compare Hubert Guindon, "The Social Evolution of Quebec Reconsidered," *Canadian Journal of Economics and Political Science* 26 (November 1960): 533–51.

An admirable historical study of recent vintage is Lucia Ferretti's *Entre voisins: La société paroissiale en milieu urbain, Saint-Pierre-Apôtre de Montréal, 1848–1930* (Montréal: Les Éditions du Boréal, 1992). Observations of more up-to-date Catholic parish life in Quebec are available in a pair of works by Colette Moreux: *Fin d'une religion? Monographie d'une paroisse canadienne-française* (Montréal: Les Presses de l'Université de Montréal, 1969), and *Douceville en Québec: La modernisation d'une tradition* (Montréal: Les Presses de l'Université de Montréal, 1982), esp. 43–52 and 234–53.

95. J. T. Croteau, "The Caisses Populaires Desjardins of Quebec," 233. (The italics appear in the original.)

96. In French, the *caisse* "tire toute sa singularité d'une transposition sur la sociabilité paroissiale de formules d'organisation économique." Yvan Rousseau, "Essor et déclin d'une formule d'organisation économique: La coopération et la mutualité paroissiales," in Courville and Séguin, *La paroisse,* 210.

What is its field of activity?

The parish alone. It would be dangerous to go outside it.

Why not go beyond the parish?

Because, in a parish, the people should know best; they therefore should know best the mentality, the morality, the honesty, the solvency, and the true needs of each member.[97]

Conceived in 1900, the *caisse populaire* obviously predates by several decades most of the manifestations of Catholic Action that the Church, and especially the clergy, propagated in Quebec. (In reality, like a host of tendencies in Catholic life, the *caisse* owes its primary impetus to the papal encyclical *Rerum novarum* [1891] by Leo XIII, whereas Catholic Action relied centrally on Pius XI's *Ubi arcano Dei* [1922].)[98] But many of its most important aspects were similar. Among these was its impact, whether deliberate or not, on upwardly mobile laymen and their families. The persistent exclusion of French-speaking Catholics from the accumulation and exercise of economic power throughout Canada, the broad-based membership of the Desjardins movement, and the participatory character of its internal structure combined to cultivate by mid-century a rising class of Quebecers with several generations of practical experience in agricultural credit, independent business, and small-scale finance.

The Desjardins movement "gave priority to the initiative of the individual, to his capacity to undertake projects and to form associations with others."[99] This experience in the marketplace, moreover, enabled these members of a new francophone middle class to embrace a less defensive and more forward-looking vision of the future for themselves and

---

97. *Quel est son champ d'action?*
La paroisse seule. Il serait dangereux d'en sortir.
Pourquoi pas en dehors de la paroisse?
Parce que, dans une paroisse, les gens connaissent mieux; ils connaissent donc mieux la mentalité, la moralité, l'honnêteté, la solvabilité, les besoins réels de chaque sociétaire.
Philibert Grondin, *Catéchisme des Caisses populaires Desjardins: Sociétés coopératives d'épargne et de crédit* [1909–10], quoted from the tenth [1950] edition in Y. Rousseau, "Essor et déclin d'une formule d'organisation économique," 201.

98. Nive Voisine, with André Beaulieu and Jean Hamelin, *Histoire de l'Église catholique au Québec, 1608–1970*, Rapport de la Commission d'étude sur les laïcs et l'Église, no. 1 (Montréal: Les Éditions Fides, 1971), 59–68.

99. Levasseur and Y. Rousseau, "Social Movements and Development in Quebec," 559.

their institutions. Correspondingly, their open stance toward the world produced as a stable byproduct a religious attitude that was decidedly cool toward the more cramped nationalist tradition of language and faith that the Catholic Church, most of its clergy, and their favored elites had supported.[100] The Quebec social scientist Hubert Guindon saw this clearly when he declared that "What have not been provided for by the cultural traditions are the role models for the new middle-class occupations. For this reason," he continued, "the traditional culture is something far from sacred and useful, very often the object of contempt and ridicule within new middle class circles."[101]

At street level, and through their sidewalk-to-ceiling plate-glass windows, the Caisses Desjardins now resemble closely, in their publicity and products, the small number of mammoth commercial banks in Canada, whose branches span the northern swath of the continent. More and more, the spirit of the Desjardins institutions, designed according to the model of economic mutuality, moved "from partnership toward business, from the parish toward the marketplace, from the member toward the customer, from production toward consumption, from training in saving toward the promotion of credit services, from the dedication of élites to the skills of experts."[102] Yet the historical path that they trod to reach that end still distinguishes them. The presence of the *caisses* in secularized form endures as a potent symbol of what concerted efforts, motivated by religious concern, can accomplish for a people. The *caisses* survive, in addition, as an illustration of what, much later, came to be viewed as a distinctive "Quebec model" of economic cooperation, mutual assistance, and social solidarity.[103]

100. Rudin, *In Whose Interest?*, 104–19; compare Couton and Cormier, "Voluntary Associations and State Expansion in Quebec," 27 and 38–40.

101. Guindon, "Social Unrest, Social Class and Quebec's Bureaucratic Revolution," 345–46.

102. ". . . de l'association vers l'enterprise, de la paroisse ver le marché, du sociétaire vers le client, de la production vers la consommation, de l'éducation à l'épargne vers la promotion des services de crédit, du dévouement des élites aux compétences des experts." Y. Rousseau, "Essor et déclin d'une formule d'organisation économique," 215.

103. Chanlat and Bédard, "Managing in the Québec Style," esp. 24–28 and 34–36; Jean-Pierre Dupuis, "La place et le rôle du Mouvement Desjardins dans le modèle québécois de développement économique," in B. Lévesque et al., *Desjardins*, 201–217; B. Lévesque, Malo, and Rouzier, "The 'Caisse de dépôt et placement du Québec' and the 'Mouvement des caisses populaires et d'économie Desjardins,'" 485–89 and 494–99; and Michel Venne, ed.,

Discussion

Concomitant with improved technical and professional education, access to training for a greater variety of careers, and the open-ended potential for continuing contact with the values of the world at large, the lay Catholics of Quebec came, by the 1960s, to expect a degree of self-direction in their lives, temporal and spiritual, that the omnipresence of their church had not historically permitted. For Quebecers who matured during the *Révolution tranquille, Maintenant ou jamais . . . Maîtres chez nous!* ("Now or never . . . Masters in our own house!") symbolized much more than a political imperative to nationalize the province's vast hydroelectric resources. Once a campaign slogan, the phrase became, ineluctably, an orientation to the entirety of life.

In spite of the fact that religious involvement had played a central role in preparing the laity for this moment, Quebecers ceased to rely faithfully on the Catholic Church to mediate for them with the rest of society. Having done just this for most of the lifetime of any 1960s-era adult in Quebec, however, the Church as an institution stood ill-equipped at this watershed to tend only to purely religious matters. Accordingly, it set out to plot a new course.

Resolved to adapt to the radically new arrangement between the institution and the people it served, the Catholic bishops of Quebec in 1968 established a select commission on the laity and the future of the Church, led by Fernand Dumont.[104] Dumont, a sociologist by profession, was a convinced believer, a humane man of letters, a "public intellectual," and as lofty a cultural hero as a small society can elevate. The work of the Dumont Commission, as elaborated in a series of six careful volumes,[105]

Justice, démocratie et prospérité: L'avenir du modèle québécois, Collection "Débats," no. 10 (Montréal: Les Éditions Québec/Amérique, 2003).

104. See, among his many books, two of his last: Fernand Dumont, *Raisons communes,* Collection "Papiers collés" (Montréal: Les Éditions du Boréal, 1995), and *Une foi partagée,* Collection "L'Essentiel" (Montréal: Les Éditions Bellarmin, 1996), esp. "Du catholicisme québécois," 271–97.

For more from the man, see Michel Vastel, "Entretien: Le bilan de Fernand Dumont," *L'actualité* (15 septembre 1996): 86–88 and 92. For an extension of his thinking on Catholicism, consult Anne Fortin, "Penser à partir de Dumont: La religion catholique dans la société québécoise," Thème: "Mémoire de Fernand Dumont," *Recherches sociographiques* 42 (mai–août 2001): 239–52.

105. See the summary published as *L'Église du Québec: Un héritage, un projet,* Rap-

sought to put the Catholic Church in Quebec on a flexible footing that would sustain it in an increasingly uncertain spiritual and social environment.[106]

The Dumont Report summoned Catholics in Quebec to a *projet* (or plan) at the same time less anchored to the certainties of tradition and more daring in its potential for animating religious practice. But a departure from the safe structures of the past also entertained considerable risk. In preference to hauling into the future the dead weight of a sprawling network of bricks-and-mortar institutions, the Church, the report recommended, should travel alongside Catholics on an uncharted journey toward individual awakening, and with all of the society of Quebec toward a Christian ideal of social justice. However, when a critical eye is cast on the sum of the outcome, Dumont and his colleagues may simply have been making of necessity a virtue, the best of a bad situation.

This is not to assert, however, that in subsequent years there has appeared no evidence of spiritual impulses engaged in Quebec. To the contrary, many of the same sorts of religious innovations that elsewhere confronted the tired practices of the institutional churches blossomed there as well: the Catholic charismatic renewal,[107] Christian base communities along the Latin American model, lay-led prayer groups and divine healing ministries, new avenues for participation in quasi-clerical functions,[108]

---

port de la Commission d'étude sur les laïcs et l'Église, no. o (Montréal: Les Éditions Fides, 1971). Of special interest to historians would be the synthetic volume by Voisine, with Beaulieu and Hamelin, *Histoire de l'Église catholique au Québec, 1608–1970,* Rapport de la Commission d'étude sur les laïcs et l'Église, no. 1.

106. Gregory Baum has written extensively on the significance of the Dumont Commission, and of a subsequent report, *Risquer l'avenir* (1992), for the Catholic Church in Quebec. For examples, see Gregory Baum, "Le Rapport Dumont: Démocratiser l'Église catholique," trans. S. Mineau, Thème: "Catholicisme et société contemporaine," *Sociologie et sociétés* 22 (octobre 1990): 115–25, reprinted in English as chapter 2 in Baum, *The Church in Quebec* (Outremont, Québec, and Ottawa: Novalis, 1991), 49–65; Baum, "Sécularisation et catholicisme au Québec: Analyse d'un débat contemporain," Thème: "Regards nord-américains sur la religion," *Religiologiques* 11 (printemps 1995): 19–32; and Baum, "Catholicism and Secularization in Quebec," in David Lyon and Marguerite Van Die, eds., *Rethinking Church, State, and Modernity: Canada between Europe and America* (Toronto: University of Toronto Press, 2000), 149–65.

107. See, e.g., Jacques Zylberberg and Jean-Paul Montminy, "Reproduction sociopolitique et production symbolique: Engagement et désengagement des charismatiques catholiques québécois," *Annual Review of the Social Sciences of Religion* 4 (1980): 121–48.

108. See Rouleau, "Le catholicisme, vingt-cinq ans après Vatican II," 44nn25, 26.

new styles of meditation and destinations for retreats,[109] and so on. But none of these innovations has been or is sufficient to replace the cultural mass that the Roman Catholic Church had incorporated in the lives of average Quebecers .

If the constituency for Catholic religion had shrunk, diminished also were the aspirations of its leaders. Bereft of the daily commitments of a compliant flock, the bishops and clergy of Quebec—with or without study commissions—were largely at a loss to devise a new and more secure status for themselves in the lives of the people to whom they were vowed to minister. Their future, they feared, entailed a regimen of cultural mourning, institutional retrenchment, and personal soul-searching. A new dispensation had begun, the sole certainty of which was that things would never again be exactly the same—certainly not for individual Catholics, and therefore not for the Church.

Others, too, suspend their analyses of the Catholic Church in Quebec on this tentative note: "Cut adrift in a secularized Quebec partly and unintentionally of its own making," writes Peter Beyer, a Canadian sociologist, "the Roman Catholic church is faced with new and unaccustomed choices that are reshaping it for an indeterminate future."[110]

Conclusion: *"C'est l'histoire, madame"*

On a warm summer morning several years ago, a small contingent of English-speaking guests visited the impressive white Parlement building that stands gracefully on a hillside in the upper part of Quebec, looking down over the old city below. The guide who was assigned to lead the group, a francophone woman of middle age, moved to one side as the hushed visitors filed slowly into the gallery of the bright but stately chamber of the Assemblée nationale, the Quebec legislature.

Immediately one of the guests, a tourist from California, spotted something amiss, and her arm shot up. "What," she inquired of the guide, "is

---

109. As merely a single example, see Sharon Doyle Driedger, with Susan McClelland and Rima Kar, "Soul Searchers: In a Quest for Spiritual Renewal, Faith-Seekers Turn to Retreats," *Maclean's* 114 (April 16, 2001): 42–47. The article describes a thriving business in retreats at a Benedictine monastery, the Abbaye de Saint-Benoît-du-Lac (1941) in Lac-Brome, near Magog, amid the lakes of Quebec's Eastern Townships.

110. Beyer, "The Evolution of Roman Catholicism in Quebec," 24.

that doing there?" The "that" to which the questioner was pointing is an oversized and even somewhat gaudy crucifix that hangs directly above the speaker's chair at the far end of the floor.[111] Initially the guide was flustered and could only think to respond in her native language: *"C'est l'histoire, madame."* ("This is history, madam.") Switching to English, calmer now, she elaborated by stating with pride that Quebec is a modern and democratic state, and as such has established no official church. But this fact did not mean, she insisted, that the people of Quebec could afford to forget the past and to neglect their heritage. Like the *fleurs-de-lis,* the shamrocks, and the many other cultural symbols that decorate the halls and rooms of the Parlement, the cross of Christ was a key to the memory of who Quebecers were and what they had undergone through four centuries of time.

As the parliamentary guide doubtlessly knew, the Catholic Church in Quebec functioned for much of its history as a near-total presence. Through its institutions it controlled the provision of lifelong education, health care, and welfare. Through its moral teachings it shaped family forms and disciplined personal habits. And through the often indefatigable activism of its clergy it regulated local economies and orchestrated social action. Once this structure of control collapsed and the reach of the Church's influence consequently receded, however, Quebecers naturally felt liberated from a thoroughgoing and intrusive code of old restrictions that their religion had imposed. But this realization swept through their lives and culture without leaving behind a residual desire for maintaining allegiance to the more purely spiritual promises of religious conformity. Presciently, Hubert Guindon warned in 1960:

> After having achieved complete control over the social organization, the clergy may discover, perhaps too late, that its population no longer knows what religion and its cherished symbols mean. The symbols may become hollow and meaningless for the population, and even for parts of the clergy. And not because of alien and foreign culture, but as a direct result of the clergy's own successful control of the whole society.[112]

In Quebec today, one finds relatively little openly anticlerical animus, and little of the organized religious skepticism that was once so common

---

111. See Jean-Guy Pelletier, "Le crucifix à l'Assemblée nationale," *Le Bulletin de la Bibliothèque de l'Assemblée nationale* [Québec] 17 (novembre 1988): 7–8.

112. Guindon, "The Social Evolution of Quebec Reconsidered," 551.

in France and that was a cultural bequest to its post-Revolutionary colonial offspring around the world. Rather, the mentality of many average Quebecers toward the Roman Catholic Church—to the extent that it occupies their conscious thoughts at all—is one of polite indifference. As a body, the hierarchy and clergy of the Church in Quebec now receive a mostly passive form of respect: the respect of their people's good-natured inattention. The priests, because they no longer can command anything, together ask very little.[113]

Yes, modern Quebecers are broadly familiar with the Catholic faith through family ties and early education; yes, they appreciate the institutional role of the Church in their own society and its development; but no, they feel little need to lead the lives of active Catholic parishioners, nor do they orient their lives around the Church's rituals, except at intermittent passages in the personal life cycle (e.g., for baptisms, weddings, and funerals) or on infrequent special occasions (e.g., at Christmas and Easter). As Gilles Routhier has observed:

> Indeed, the erection of the Québec State and expansion in the tertiary sector of the economy figure heavily in the development of a perception of the parish whose function is ever more reduced, by law, to rituals of worship and to pastoral life. From this time forward, the parish is situated among that set of institutions that provide public utilities for citizens. Citizens approach it to obtain specialized services of a religious nature: baptism, first communion, confirmation, marriage, funerals, etc. It becomes, in a manner of speaking, a place for the production and distribution of symbolic goods of a certain kind. The relationship that it establishes with a majority of parishioners within its jurisdiction eventually succeeds in resembling very much that which a utility fosters with its users.[114]

113. For example, the Canadian magazine *Maclean's* quotes one seventy-two-year-old priest from Quebec as follows: "We cannot deny what is happening. That would be like looking out the window at a rainy sky and saying, 'What a lovely day!' But we do not condemn, either. We are rather like parents who can no longer control their grown children." (Wood, "Unmarried . . . with Children," 40.) What may be most important in this realization is not that control has collapsed, but that those who in the past were treated as children have definitely grown.

This reticence, whether it be a strategic tactic or a concession to necessity, is criticized from a conservative perspective by Richard John Neuhaus in *Appointment in Rome: The Church in America Awakening* (New York: Crossroad, 1999), 60–61; by Preston Jones in "Quebec after Catholicism," *First Things* 94 (June/July 1999): 12–14; and by Jones more obliquely in "Quebec *Indépendantisme* and the Life of Faith," *Journal of Church and State* 43 (Spring 2001): 251–65.

114. En effet, la construction de l'État québécois et la tertiarisation de l'économie

But the number of ecclesiastical service stations is constantly shrinking. In the last decade or so, the Catholic hierarchy in Quebec has closed or "fused" more than one hundred parishes.[115]

The landscape of Quebec, with its bustling cities and its peaceful villages, is dotted by more than 4,000 religious edifices. Among these are some 2,800 houses of worship, more than two-thirds of which are Roman Catholic. Montreal alone has 468 churches, and more than 300 of them are Catholic.[116] Yet so many of these and other religious buildings in Quebec have fallen into disuse that some have been deconsecrated and rededicated to nonreligious purposes: custom-renovated urban condominiums, group residences for the aging and infirm, public libraries, and even a vocational school for circus performers.[117]

With more than $135 million (Can.) in financial assistance from the Quebec government, other structures that shelter irreplaceable works of sacred art, that possess special historical or cultural significance, or that are themselves architecturally singular have been preserved as "heritage

---

pèsent lourdement sur l'évolution de la perception de la paroisse dont la fonction est de plus en plus réduite, par la loi, au culte et à la pastorale. Désormais, la paroisse est située parmi l'ensemble des institutions qui assurent le service public des citoyens. Les citoyens s'adressent à elle pour obtenir des services spécialisés en matière religieuse: baptême, première communion, confirmation, mariage, funérailles, etc. Elle devient, en quelque sorte, un lieu de production et de dispensations de biens symboliques d'un type particulier. La relation qu'elle engage avec la majorité des paroissiens d'un territoire finit par ressembler beaucoup à celle qu'entretient un service public avec ses usagers.

Routhier, "La paroisse québécoise," 56. Also see Bibby, "La religion à la carte au Québec," 140; Caldwell and Gauthier, "Religious Institutions," 317; André Carbonneau, "La liberté religieuse dans une société sécularisée: L'expérience québécoise," in Pauline Côté, ed., *Chercheurs de dieux dans l'espace public—Frontier Religions in Public Space* (Ottawa: Actexpress, Les Presses de l'Université d'Ottawa, 2001), 183–91; Gauthier, "Religious Beliefs," 393; Raymond Lemieux, "Le catholicisme québécois: Une question de culture," Theme: "Catholicisme et société contemporaine," *Sociologie et sociétés* 22 (octobre 1990): 147–49; and Lemieux, "Croyances et incroyances," 18.

115. Commission de la culture de l'Assemblée nationale du Québec, *Patrimoine religieux du Québec: Document de consultation (juin 2005)* (Québec: Secrétariat des commissions de l'Assemblée nationale du Québec, 2005), 17 and n14.

116. Commission de la culture, *Patrimoine religieux du Québec*, 13 and n1, 19, 35, and 36.

117. Miro Cernetig, "Quebec Churches under Siege: Many Sold for Development, Others Pillaged by Gang of Thieves," *Toronto Star*, November 1, 2003; Katherine Macklem, "Old Habits, New Times: Pressed into Pragmatism, a Once-Cloistered Order of Nuns Now Lives with Lay Folks," *Maclean's* 118 (June 6, 2005): 43 and 45; and Commission de la culture, *Patrimoine religieux du Québec*, 22.

sites," in a process that Quebecers refer to as *la patrimonialisation des ég-lises* (broadly, the "heritagization" or "touristification" of churches).[118] Yet the conservation project does not stop at the built environment. Funding is allocated in addition for the preservation of "nonmaterial" or "intangible" elements of memory: vanishing religious knowledge and expertise. "It accomplishes nothing to protect the religious heritage," states the legislature's Commission de la culture, "if tomorrow nobody knows the meaning of it."[119]

The stylish Lysiane Gagnon, an astute social commentator in Quebec and a popular political columnist for the Montreal daily *La Presse*, described the situation for Catholicism in Quebec well when she concluded an elegiac Christmas meditation by noting that

> The church still has a social function. Young couples who want a romantic wedding marry in a church ceremony. (For many, it is the first time they have set foot in a church.) Most French Canadians, including the non-believers, are carried to their neighbourhood church for the final homage. There still is an emotional, albeit much looser, link between the people and the priests. The clergy has gracefully adapted to its reduced role. The anger against the church, which was virulent in the sixties and the seventies, is gone.[120]

For Quebecers, Paul-André Turcotte has reflected, laxity in conforming to an institutional standard of religious practice in the Catholic Church can nevertheless be combined with "acknowledging the contribution its institutional character makes to the historical continuity of their belief and culture."[121] Whether future generations of Quebecers , more than ever imbued with the secular attitudes of their most accomplished artistic, intellectual, and economic elites (if not the critical foundations of those attitudes), will find such loose attachments to religious tradition either useful or ultimately satisfying is still an open question.

118. Financial figures are from the private, not-for-profit Fondation du patrimoine religieux du Québec, "Quebec's Religious Heritage Restoration Program."

119. In French, "Il ne sert à rien de protéger le patrimoine religieux si demain personne n'en connaît les significations." Commission de la culture, *Patrimoine religieux du Québec*, 19.

120. Lysiane Gagnon, "Inside Quebec: A Meditation on Empty Pews, Families and Christmastime," *Toronto Globe and Mail*, January 2, 1999, D3. Also see Gagnon, "Inside Quebec: Void Left by the Collapse of Catholicism Remains Unfilled," *Toronto Globe and Mail*, May 4, 1996, D3.

121. P. A. Turcotte, "Catholic Ritual Practices, Culture and Society in Greater Montreal," 505; and P. A. Turcotte, *Intransigeance ou compromis*, 69–70.

MICHAEL GAUVREAU

2. "They Are Not of Our Generation"

Youth, Gender, Catholicism, and
Quebec's Dechristianization, 1950–1970

They have organized many frequent communions,
Many stations of the cross.
They have turned the Temple of God into a collection
Of clowns, of eloquent puppets,
What a bunch of fussy little panty-waists!

One of the most compelling problems of postwar Canadian history was the devastating evisceration of Quebec's Catholic identity in the space of one short decade between 1961 and 1971. In 1961 fewer than 6,500 Quebecers (less than 1 percent) declared themselves to be unbelievers, and Sunday observance, even in the highly urbanized region of Montreal, stood at 61 percent. However, by 1971, Sunday attendance in Montreal had fallen catastrophically to only 30 percent, and more troubling still was the fact that it stood at 12–15 percent for young adults aged twenty to thirty-four, raising the prospect that the Church would not be able to replenish either its faithful or its clergy. Equally disturbing was the apparent defection from Catholic teaching governing personal values. Before a series of

The chapter title, "Ceux-là ne sont pas de notre génération," is from Roger Varin, "Quand on se parle 'En Plein Front,'" *Jeunesse,* déc. 1937; and "Ils ont organisé beaucoup de communions fréquentes, Beaucoup de chemins de croix. Ils ont fait du Temple un ramassis de polichinelles, de fantoches à grands discours. Tas de femelettes artificielles." (Ibid.) [end of unnumbered note on chap. Opener]

amendments to the federal divorce laws in 1968, there were only 500 divorce proceedings per year in Montreal, but between 1968 and 1972, there were 11,300, settling down after that date to about 500 per month.[1] And it must be underscored that these religious changes occurred in a society that displayed, at the end of the Second World War, what was in North America perhaps the most seamless fusion between Catholic values, social practices, and the political order. The weakening of a public culture that synthesized Catholic religion, expansion and promotion of the French language, and nationalism that had served to define Quebec's place within the wider Canadian federation created a crisis of authority within Quebec, and in so doing, ushered in a long period of instability for Canada as a whole, as illustrated by the series of ongoing referenda, in 1980 and 1995, on the question of Quebec independence.

How, then, to interpret this rapid, and extremely devastating, dechristianization? From one perspective, the events of the 1960s were but the brutal backwash of reality as Quebec experienced in extreme and exaggerated form what other Western societies had been undergoing since the late eighteenth century. This approach, however, tends to deny the cultural and historical specificity of Quebec; worse still, it tends to obscure the significance of those social, cultural, and political factors specific to the post–Second World War era by lumping them all together under the rubric of "secularization." The rapidity of Quebec's dechristianization can be traced to the way in which the Church sought to appropriate and direct currents of modernity, in particular, the social and cultural category of "youth" in the early 1930s. In response to the papal encyclical *Quadragesimo anno,* a number of Quebec bishops imported the method of specialized Catholic Action, which had originated among Belgian and French youth. The novelty of this approach was that an influential type of social Catholicism legitimated the idea that "youth" constituted a separate cultural and moral category in modern society.[2] According to a number of influential Cath-

---

1. For these statistics, see Jean Hamelin and Nicole Gagnon, *Histoire du catholicisme québécois: le XXe siecle, tome 2, de 1940 à nos jours* (Montréal: Boréal Express, 1984), 277–78. Rates of religious practice in Quebec's metropolis of Montreal appear much higher than those of a number of large European cities. See, for example, Hugh McLeod, *Piety and Poverty: Working-Class Religion in Berlin, London, and New York, 1870–1914* (New York: Holmes and Meier, 1996).

2. Sian Reynolds, *France between the Wars* (London: Routledge and Kegan Paul, 1996), 51. The cultural notion of a generational divide had developed among young European in-

olics, the nature of the relationship between adolescents and their parents was now adversarial in character. Discussions of the spiritual method of Catholic Action that took place in Quebec during the 1930s and early 1940s always proceeded from a negative reference point: the values of previous generations could offer no guidance or salvation for young Catholics confronted with the pressures and challenges of modern society.

However, two central tensions emerged from the 1930s Catholic youth movements that were to indelibly mark the decades between 1950 and 1970. The current of inclusive activism, oriented to the demands of working-class people and women, sought in particular to reform what they saw as deficiencies in family relationships through a more egalitarian emphasis upon the satisfaction of youth and women, which in Quebec took the form of a greater stress on the sexual, psychological, and emotional factors that underpinned personal identity, marriage, and family life. However, during the early 1950s, this activist current was challenged, marginalized, and eventually fragmented by a particularly conflictual reassertion of Catholic Action's generational thinking. This current, grounded in contemporary social and psychological theories that seemed to lament the loss of male authority in family and society, articulated an elitist cult of spiritual authoritarianism rooted in theological, rather than social, priorities. Sponsored especially by a small but influential circle of Catholic intellectuals, this reassertion of masculine leadership through the parallel dichotomies of tradition/modernity, female/male was frequently stated in terms of a virulent critique of working-class religious identities and devotional practices, which were always conflated with the "feminine" elements of conformity, excessive individualism, and sentimentalism. These were viewed with fear and abhorrence, as promoting both religious conformity and a cultural leveling that was rapidly Americanizing Quebec.

This elitist Catholicism had two serious implications for the dechristianization of Quebec: first, the positing of religious dichotomy between tradition and modernity in the language of conflictual masculine and feminine values produced, in the ensuing decade, an increasing confusion in the Catholic postwar public ideologies that organized sexuality, marriage, and family life. This served to convince many ordinary Catholics that the Church either lacked a firm message, or worse still, was engaged in a systematic campaign to subvert parental authority. Second, increasingly after the mid-1950s, an influential group of senior clergy and those lay activists

who subscribed to Catholic Action's spiritual authoritarianism redefined
the criteria of Christian belief and practice so as to systematically disconnect large segments of Quebec's population from any identity as Catholics. In this way, the rapid and catastrophic dechristianization of the 1960s
was accomplished less as the result of the workings of the anonymous processes of urbanization and industrialization than by a series of conscious
cultural choices made by groups of Quebec Catholics themselves.

Between 1940 and 1960, the surface of Quebec Catholicism appeared
to be very little disturbed, as prewar political arrangements between the
institutional church and the liberal state survived practically intact, with
the exception of the introduction in 1944 of compulsory education to
age fourteen.[3] During this period, the most visible barometer of religious
change in Quebec was in fact provided by transformations in Catholic
thinking about the family and sexuality. Quebec Catholicism's revaloriza-
tion of the family was largely spearheaded by initiatives of the laity, whose
movements were united by a common purpose, which was to reaffirm a
family solidarity imperiled by the Depression while compensating for parental deficiencies as authority figures, and they all sought to marry modern educational techniques to a traditional language that claimed to "restore" the family to a type of original, pristine solidarity of age and gender
relations. Significantly, these groups exerted a particular appeal to women,
so much so that by the mid-1950s, between two-thirds and three-quarters
of the membership of specialized Catholic Action was female. Indeed, this
marked something of an abrupt reversal of the "masculinizing" tendency of
the early phase of Catholic Action, with its privileging of spiritual violence
and confrontation, so much so that one anguished priest privately wondered: "'the feminized nature of our J.O.C. [*Jeunesse ouvrière catholique*]
has always troubled me. Are we to be spiritual directors for a worker's
movement of young women rather than of young men?"[4] However, these

tellectuals during the first decade of the early twentieth century, and had become a "tradition" by the 1920s. See Robert Wohl, *The Generation of 1914* (Cambridge, Mass.: Harvard
University Press, 1979), 205, 229.

3. Dominique Marshall has observed that despite much previous clerical opposition
to compulsory schooling, by the early 1940s, Quebec's bishops, senior clergy, and reform-
minded Catholic laity in both government and educational bureaucracies had reached
a consensus on the necessity of this reform. See *Aux Origines sociales de l'État-providence*
(Montréal: Les Presses de l'Université de Montréal, 1998), 26–38.

4. ANQM, Fonds Jeunesse Ouvrière Catholique [hereafter JOC], P104 art. 4, "Rap-

attempts to elevate the family as something immutable and eternal in an age of economic crisis and social turmoil cannot be viewed as a simple re-imposition of conservatism. In the first place, they entailed a radical shift in Catholic thinking about the nature, purpose, and composition of the family. The effect of this revision was to abruptly shift the function of the family from older economic, political, or institutional considerations to the terrain of psychological satisfaction and emotional fulfillment. Second, they embodied what was in fact *the* mainstream feminist current in Quebec prior to the mid-1960s, one that sought to articulate an equilibrium between Catholic doctrines on male and female identities, which emphasized the notion that women found social and spiritual fulfillment in the context of maternity and familial roles, and a more "personalist" current, which legitimated the spread of more egalitarian views of female intellectual and social potential.[5] These movements powerfully appealed to ordinary Catholics because they employed the same cultural metaphor of rupture between present and past, and at times posited a fundamental conflict of spiritual values between a married laity and a celibate clergy.

---

port de la 17e session JOC canadienne," 27 juin–1 juillet 1962; ANQM, Fonds Service de Préparation au Mariage [hereafter Fonds SPM], P116 art. 2, "Historique du S.P.M." Contemporary observers were well aware of the 2:1 female/male ratio in Catholic Action movements. Subsequent historical research revealed that these estimates were too conservative, and that the figure was at times closer to 75 percent female. See on this point, Hamelin and Gagnon, *Histoire du catholicisme québécois, tome 2,* 127.

   5. There is some debate among historians as to where to place this trajectory of Catholic thinking and action. Recently, Karine Hébert's analysis of the Fédération Nationale de Saint-Jean-Baptiste has used the term "maternalism" because this pre-1940 women's organization that advocated female suffrage lacked an egalitarian argument. See Hébert, "Une organisation maternaliste au Quebec: la Fédération Nationale Sain-Jean-Baptiste et la bataille pour le vote des femmes," *Revue d'histoire de l'Amérique française* 52, no. 3 (hiver 1999): 315–44. However, under the impetus of Catholic Action's brand of personalism after the mid-1930s, discussions of women's nature, roles, and responsibilities took on a considerably greater egalitarian complexion, despite the persistence of powerful cultural and institutional strands of conservatism in Quebec society. For the use of the term "personalist feminism," see Michael Gauvreau, "The Emergence of Personalist Feminism: Catholicism and the Marriage Preparation Movement in Quebec, 1940–1966," in Nancy Christie, ed., *Households of Faith: Family, Gender and Community in Canada, 1760–1969* (Montreal and Kingston: McGill-Queen's University Press, 2002), 319–47. Karen Offen has coined the term "relational feminism" to describe the ideology of a number of European social Catholic women's organizations. See Offen, "Body Politics: Women, Work and the Politics of Motherhood in France, 1920–1950," in Gisela Bock and Pat Thane, eds., *Women and the Rise of the European Welfare States, 1880s–1950s* (London: Routledge, 1991), 144.

What was fundamental to all these spin-offs of Catholic Action was the elaboration of a mystique of marriage, which effectively raised the stature of laypeople. Quebec Catholic activists eagerly seized upon the 1930 papal encyclical on Christian marriage, *Casti connubii,* which, despite ultraconservative surface appearances, defined a new order of priority between marriage and family, shifting kin relations, economic functions, and even children to a lower order of priority. Implicit in the encyclical was the idea that humans were sanctified not by participation in the legal, customary, economic, and political functions of the family, but only by virtue of the sacrament of marriage itself, what Pius XI termed a "sacred partnership" between husband and wife and at another level between God and humans, which stood prior to any previous family bonds or commitments.[6] The implication of *Casti connubii* was that the value of marriage lay in the mutual spiritual satisfaction that husband and wife conferred upon each other. Thus, although the encyclical overtly insisted on procreation, it actually had the effect of subtly downplaying the purely reproductive, or social, nature of the family and of sanctioning a far more individualist current, privileging the psychological and emotional realm of the affections, namely, the mutual enjoyment and physical and spiritual fulfillment of the married couple.[7]

Postwar Quebec, by contrast with a number of European Catholic societies, had not experienced drastic wartime population losses, and as a consequence, the natalist imperatives of Catholic marriage doctrines were often downplayed.[8] Through movements such as the Service de Prépara-

---

6. Pope Pius XI, *Encyclical: On Christian Marriage—Casti Connubii* [1930] (New York: Paulist Press, 1941), 5; Fr. Ferdinand, "Le Mariage: 1. Doctrine catholique sur le mariage," *La Famille* 1:5 (jan. 1938): 75; R. P. Joseph-Papin Archambault, S.J., "Dédication d'ouverture," *Le Chrétien dans la famille et dans la nation,* 17e Semaine Sociale, Nicolet, 1940 (Montreal: École Sociale Populaire, 1940), 1940; Adélard Provencher, "Le chrétien dans la famille," in *Le Chretien dans la famille et dans la nation,* 48.

7. *Casti connubii,* 11–12.

8. Unlike their counterparts in postwar France and Germany, countries that had experienced severe population losses, Quebec Catholicism's support for official natalist state initiatives was rather muted. While Quebec's climate should not be described as "antinatalist," the rather more cumbersome but more neutral "non-pro-natalist" will serve. For these policies and their impact on women in postwar France and Germany, see Elizabeth J. Heinemann, *What Difference Does a Husband Make?: Women and Marital Status in Postwar Germany* (Berkeley: University of California Press, 1999); Robert Moeller, "Reconstructing the Family in Reconstruction Germany: Women and Social Policy in the Republic, 1949–

tion au Mariage (SPM), whose fourteen-week marriage preparation course was first formed in a number of working-class parishes in Montreal after 1942, and which by the mid-1950s had become the most widespread and popularized of all Catholic Action services, reaching roughly 50 percent of all engaged couples in the Montreal diocese,[9] many young Catholics imbibed the message that the primary spiritual value of marriage was the partnership between husband and wife primarily on an emotional, sexual, and psychological level. As a corollary, they maintained that the success of any marriage depended upon the level of intimacy that the couple was able to achieve in their daily lives. While conservative clergy expatiated upon the new papal teaching on marriage as a political bulwark against Communism and the inroads of materialist ideologies,[10] lay promoters of these movements were far more intent on using the new mystique of marriage, with its promise of happiness and mutual fulfillment, as a way of reintroducing young men and women to the responsibility of family formation by combining this imperative with a new scale of individual satisfactions. In exalting a "communitarian" vision of marriage founded upon spiritual and physical intimacy and partnership, Catholic Action brusquely dismissed as obsolete notions of institution or contract that still remained attached to ideas of marriage.[11] This meant, in turn, the popularization of a far more dynamic view of marriage that empha-

1955," in Robert Moeller, ed., *West Germany under Construction: Politics, Society and Culture in the Adenauer Era* (Ann Arbor: University of Michigan Press, 1997); and for France, Claire Duchen, *Women's Rights and Women's Lives in France, 1944–1968* (London: Routledge, 1994), 126. The Canadian federal family allowance policy, the only postwar social legislation that appeared to have natalist implications, was in fact intended to encourage consumption, and was deliberately designed to reduce benefits to large families. See Nancy Christie, *Engendering the State: Family, Work, and Welfare in Canada* (Toronto: University of Toronto Press, 2000), final chapter. A Quebec provincial policy of family allowances had to wait until the late 1960s, when the connection between Catholicism and the state had become much more tenuous.

9. For a more complete treatment of the structure of the fourteen-week marriage preparation course, see Gauvreau, "The Rise of Personalist Feminism." The Quebec Catholic Action initiative provided the inspiration for similar initiatives by other national Catholic churches in the United States and Latin America.

10. Mgr. L.-A. Paquet, "La doctrine de l'Eglise," *Ordre Nouveau*, 1936.

11. AUM, Fonds Action Catholique Canadienne [hereafter ACC] , P16/R.61, "Prêtre et Famille," *Le Prêtre et la Famille: Revue de pastorale familiale*, nov.–déc. 1947: *"communautaire,"* "Il ne s'agit pas pour les jeunes gens qui se marient de *faire* quelque chose ensemble, mais d'*être* désormais ensemble."

sized ongoing mutual emotional and psychological adjustment, encapsulated in the words "understanding" and "mutual pleasure." Certainly by the early 1950s, for Catholic laity the reworking of marriage as a spiritual partnership entailed an explicit divinization of the sexual act itself within the bonds of marriage, thus assigning almost exclusive weight to sex as the one element that provided an ongoing sanctification for marriage. And because the quality of spiritual intimacy and thus stability depended upon the degree to which husband and wife were capable of a satisfying sexual relationship, this strand of Catholicism maintained that young people had to be overtly prepared for the psychological and emotional demands of marriage.[12]

While it must be remembered that these late-Depression and wartime Catholic Action initiatives were inspired by socially conservative motives, the injection of the notion of generational conflict subtly altered the implications of these movements. Particularly during the late 1940s, the ideal of marriage preparation was advanced in reference to a strident metaphor of sharply conflicting generational sexual awareness and values. Gérard Pelletier, for example, defended the new personalist vision of marriage based on love, free choice, emotional compatibility, and sexual intimacy, openly mocking the values and experience of the pre-Depression generation and lambasting as hypocrisy the silence that surrounded the sexual facts of marriage.[13] For Catholic laity, the radical novelty of postwar Catholicism's sacralization of marriage depended entirely upon the revalu-

12. "Le courrier de José," *Le Front ouvrier* (Montreal) [hereafter *FO*], 30 nov. 1946; Jacques B., "Vers l'avenir . . . Face à l'éternel féminin," *FO*, 9 déc. 1944; Lionel Pelland, "Mariage et bombe . . . atomique," *Relations* [hereafter *Rel*], mai 1948, 135–37; Mme. Claudine Vallerand, "Madame Vallerand de l'École des Parents nous invite a soigner notre ÉDUCATION SENTIMENTALE," *Vie étudiante* 18, no. 4 (avril 1952). Quebec Catholics were not alone in proclaiming the sacredness of human sexuality. For the existence of a similar, although later, current within the United Church of Canada, see the analysis by Nancy Christie, "Sacred Sex: The United Church and the Privatization of the Family in Post-War Canada," in Christie, ed., *Households of Faith*, 348–76.

13. ANQM, Fonds SPM, P116 art. 2, "Semaine des fiancés, 1949," Gérard Pelletier, "Réflexions sur un mot malheureux," *Le Devoir*, 8 jan. 1949. For similar views, see ibid., art. 1, "Semaine des fiancés, 1955," Marie Bourbonnais, "Les fiancés d'aujourd'hui sont les parents de demain," *La Presse*, 8 jan. 1955; ibid., art. 1, Chanoine Clavel, "La semaine de la famille et la préparation au mariage," *Le Canada*, avril 1950; ibid., art. 24, "Conférences donnees au Service, 1947–1954," "Substance de la conférence de M. Marcel Clément, nov. 1954"; Thomas-A. Audet, O.P., "Sainteté des époux," *Revue Dominicaine* [hereafter *RD*] 51 (juillet–août 1945): 4.

ation of the place of sexual relations within marriage and the equation of satisfying sex with the highest form of spiritual perfection.[14]

In the religious atmosphere of postwar Quebec, which was strongly permeated by a tension between Catholic Action and the more institutional side of Catholicism, the positive revaluation of sex within marriage served, for many Catholic activists, to demarcate a cultural and moral fissure between clergy and laity, a division that had repercussions for the wider social authority of Catholicism in Quebec. As a way of overcoming their own sense of insecurity in the face of what they believed was the fact that they had been relegated to adolescent status under clerical tutelage, lay Catholic militants drew upon new psychological theories that equated a healthy sexuality with emotional maturity, and thus human freedom. By implication, those, such as the celibate clergy, who failed through lack of sex to move to a higher plateau of humanity remained repressed and thus stunted as persons, with a question mark over their fitness to wield social authority. It was no surprise, then, that some Catholic laity posited an absolute moral dualism between the new values of youth, directed to fulfillment, community, and spiritual authenticity—in which mutual sexual satisfaction sanctified marriage itself—and those of an older generation, whose puritanism—linked to immature, "medieval," and clerically inspired definitions of human personality—tolerated marital sex as an evil necessary to ensure reproduction, but certainly not something to be openly discussed, much less enjoyed.[15] Indeed, it is difficult to escape the conclusion that a number of articulate Quebec Catholics used the promotion of the new sexualized marriage spirituality to foster anticlerical attitudes, and in particular, to dispute the control and expertise that an un-

14. See Jean LeMoyne, "Du sens et de la fin du mariage," *La Relève* [hereafter *LR*] 4, no. 8 (1938): 237–43; and ibid., 4, no. 9 (1938): 276–82. Le Moyne's articles were based on the work of the German theologian Herbert Doms, whose teachings were later condemned by Rome. See also Simone and Roland Germain, "Le mariage, route de sainteté," *La Famille* [hereafter *LF*] 14, no. 8 (oct. 1950): 478–89. For clerical commentary, see Robert-E. Llewellyn, "Problèmes," *LF* 10, no. 2 (fev. 1946); Marie-Joseph d'Anjou, S.J., "Respect du mariage chrétien," *Rel*, jan. 1952, 8, 10.

15. Alex and Gerard Pelletier, "L'amour humain chez les jeunes," *Cahiers d'Action Catholique* [hereafter *CAC*] 113 (jan. 1942): 148: "a revenir aux vieilles erreurs origenistes et jansénistes, et à considérer les tendances sexuelles et passionnelles comme mauvaises en soi, alors qu'en soi elles sont belles et bonnes"; AUM, P16/G2, 1.38, "Spiritualité étudiante—numéro spécial," *CAC* (dec. 1944); Chartrand, *Ma vie comme rivière, tome 2* (Montréal: Les éditions du Remue-ménage, 1982), 87.

married clergy had always exercised over the realm of marriage and family. A number of these Catholic militants came close to proclaiming a sacerdotal conception of marriage and sexuality that raised these above virginity and the religious vocation.[16]

Two important consequences followed from the new Catholic marriage ideal. The first entailed a restructuring and redefinition of what the boundaries of the family were and, as a corollary, subtly recast lines of hierarchy and function within the family itself. Under this rubric, the family, as stated by Camille Laurin, a psychologist and Catholic Action militant in 1950, "has become a strictly functional entity, limited to its immediate members,"[17] and what is striking about postwar Quebec Catholicism is its firm commitment to the affectional-nuclear family as a cultural ideal, as opposed to the existence of a number of different models of family in Quebec prior to 1940.[18] While some worried about the temporary social "disequilibrium" attendant upon the cultural clash between two models of family, they maintained that only in the modern nuclear family could parents and

16. Gérard Pelletier, "Le laique marié, image de l'union du Christ et de son Eglise," *Le role des laics dans l'Eglise*, Carrefour 1951, organisé par le Centre Catholique des intellectuels canadiens, Université de Montréal (Montréal: Fides, 1952), III: "mystère," "sacré," "routine."

17. ANQM, JOC, P104, art. 104, "Rapport Camille Laurin": "autarcique"; Pierre Laplante, directeur des sections d'études du Conseil central des oeuvres de Québec, "En attendant les 'unions de familles," *Rel*, sept. 1951, 246–48. Camille Laurin, a Catholic Action militant, was president of the Université de Montreal student body in the late 1940s. During the 1950s and 1960s, he was a prominent Montreal psychoanalyst and commentator on family issues. In 1967, he played a key role in founding the sovereignist *Mouvement souveraineté-association,* the direct precursor of the present *Parti québécois*. A leading figure in the first government of René Lévesque, elected in 1976, he was the principal architect of Quebec's current language legislation.

18. For the existence of economic-interdependent, extended kin ideologies and practices of family in Quebec and Canada prior to 1940, see in particular Christie, *Engendering the State,* which demonstrates that during the 1930s, the federal state undertook a concerted effort to decisively marginalize these types of families. See also Nancy Christie, "Introduction: Interrogating the Nuclear Family" in Nancy Christie and Michael Gauvreau, eds., *Mapping the Margins: The Family and Social Discipline in Canada, 1700–1975* (Montreal and Kingston: McGill-Queen's University Press, 2004). For the persistence of the model in working-class Montreal, see Bettina Bradbury, *Working Families: Age, Gender and Daily Survival in Working-Class Montreal* (Toronto: McClelland and Stewart, 1993). See also Marshall, *Aux origines sociales de l'État-providence,* which explores the extent to which in the period after 1940, Quebec rural and working-class families continued to adhere to the older model of the economically interdependent family, contesting attempts by reformist Catholics and provincial and federal governments to promote the idea of the nuclear family with a single breadwinner.

children effectively cultivate "personal relationships," the type of spiritual, psychological, and emotional intimacy that alone could balance individual satisfaction and maturity with social responsibility.[19] Younger social scientists such as Guy Rocher and Fernand Dumont, who as students had taken a prominent role in Catholic Action, were the most intent on identifying the connection between family nuclearity, the achievement of "modern" cultural values, and spiritual efficacy.[20] The critical elements in the elaboration of a new family ideology in the period 1940–1955 among Quebec Catholics was a synthesis between Catholic Action personalism and American social science, both of which posited the closed nuclear family, radically eviscerated of economic functions and extended kin, as an absolutely essential benchmark of modern cultural values and forms of social organization.[21] At a more popular level, elements of the Catholic marriage preparation course aimed directly at equipping young couples to establish exclusive nuclear families, teaching them especially to budget so as to be able to establish a household physically separate from parents or relatives. Young couples were repeatedly advised by the SPM that living with parents or in-

19. AUM, Fonds ACC, P16/O4.88, "École des Parents—Journées d'Etude," 16–17 fev. 1957, Dr. Claude Mailhiot, "L'Évolution de l'École des Parents": "déséquilibrés," "rapports personnels." Mailhiot drew directly upon the early work of the historian Philippe Ariès, a French social Catholic whose work was available in the mid-1950s. See Ariès, "Le XIXe siècle et la revolution des moeurs familiales," in R. Prigent, ed., *Renouveau des idées sur la famille* (Paris: Les Presses Universitaires de France, 1954), 111–18. See also "Après la guerre," *Jeunesse Ouvrière* [hereafter *JO*], fév. 1943; Guy Rocher, "La Famille dans la Ville Moderne," *Le Service Social* [hereafter *SS*] 4, no. 1 (printemps 1954): 81; Marc A. Lessard, "Individualisme dans la Famille," *LF* 18, no. 10 (oct. 1954): 483–85.

20. For the involvement of Guy Rocher and Fernand Dumont in the Jeunesse Étudiante Catholique in the 1940s and its influence on their social thinking, see Guy Rocher, *Entre les rêves et l'histoire: Entretiens avec Georges Khal* (Montreal: VLB Éditeur, 1989), 12–25; Fernand Dumont, *Récit d'une emigration* (Montréal: Boreál, 1997), 69–71.

21. For the influence of Talcott Parsons, the leading American theorist of the nuclear family's psychological and emotional functions, especially upon young Catholic sociologists trained at Laval University, see Fernand Dumont, "Les causes de la désintegration familiale: les facteurs socio-culturels," in *La prévention de la désintegration familiale* (Montréal: Caritas-Canada, 1956), 31; and Rocher, *Entre les rêves et l'histoire*, 32–33. During the 1970s, Rocher authored a treatise on Parsons's thought. For the influential role of University of Chicago sociology and Parsons's appropriation of Freudian psychology in postwar definitions of the family, see the critical account by Christopher Lasch, *Haven in a Heartless World: The Family Besieged* (New York: Basic Books, 1977), 29–33, 35–7, 39, 112–13. For a discussion examining the wider impact of these strands of sociology on shaping postwar views of the Canadian family, see Michael Gauvreau, "The Family as Pathology: Psychology, Social Science and History Construct the Nuclear Family, 1945–1980," in Christie and Gauvreau, *Mapping the Margins*.

laws was a prime cause of marital dispute and would stunt the emotional maturity of their own children.[22]

In the postwar cultural climate shaped by Quebec Catholicism, such thinking had enormous resonance precisely because the discussions of family functions took as their point of departure the new Catholic doctrines that had recast the nature of marriage in terms of an emotional, intimate partnership in which the quality of the sexual relationship between husband and wife assumed overwhelming importance. Married love, the SPM courses in premarital counseling never tired of repeating, was a "gift of the self,"[23] and such a total communion at the sexual and emotional levels was possible only if husband and wife were psychologically secure in their identities of male and female. Catholic family activists in Quebec fully accepted the prevailing psychological wisdom that such identities were shaped very early in childhood, and that naturally the most important element of family formation, after marriage itself, was to "apprentice children to conjugal life."[24] The guiding principle of the modern marriage ideal, aside from procreation and the cultivation of intimacy between husband and wife, was to enable children to in turn replicate this spiritual partnership in their own marriages by assuming the primary parental responsibility, "in a simple truthful manner to undertake by gradual stages the sexual education of their children."[25]

22. Renée Geoffroy, "Dans une société qui ne va pas, l'amour est le premier atteint," *Le Travail,* 11 juin 1954, 6: "Les époux ne se reconnaissent plus, ne se regardent plus avec les memes yeux. L'indifférence, l'habitude s'installe. . . . L'amour n'est peut-être pas mort, mais il vit à peine." See also ANQM, Fonds SPM, P116, art. 2, "Semaine des fiancés, 1949," "Quelques conseils pratiques"; "Le courrier de José," *FO,* 21 sept. 1946; ibid., 18 oct. 1947; ibid., 17 jan. 1948; "C'est ma belle-mère qui mène dans mon ménage!," *FO,* 11 juillet 1953. It should be noted in this context that as late as 1961, over 67 percent of the population of Montreal rented, rather than owned their dwellings, and that much of even the new construction consisted of multifamily dwellings. See Paul-Andre Linteau et al., *Histoire du Québec contemporain, tome 2, de 1930 à nos jours* (Montreal: Boreal, 1993), 279–80. On the Catholic Action crusade for working-class housing, see Jean-Pierre Collin, "La Ligue Ouvriere Catholique et l'organisation communautaire dans le Québec urbain des annees 1940," *Revue d'histoire de l'Amérique française* 47, no. 3 (automne 1993): 163–91.

23. ANQM, Fonds JOC, P104 art. 4, "17e Session Intensive," Jacques Champagne, "S.P.M. 1952": "don de soi."

24. Louise-M. Lamonde, "Préparation au mariage," *Rel,* juin 1953, 162: "faire l'apprentissage de la vie conjugale"; ANQM, Fonds Jeunesse Étudiante Catholique [hereafter JEC], art. 42, "Vie sentimentale des jeunes."

25. Marcel Côté (ancien president, JIC), "La préparation au mariage," *Le Foyer: Base de la Societe,* 27e Semaine Sociale, Nicolet, 1950 (Montreal: Institut Social Populaire, 1950),

However, it was at this point that the new Catholic family ideal exhibited a profound ambivalence, which flowed from the attempt to reconcile the imperative toward generational solidarity through family formation and to continue to assert a link between the newer youth sociability and an unbridgeable cultural rupture between the values of the present and the past. On the one hand, postwar Catholics of both conservative and reformist tendencies were agreed that education in sex roles and responsibilities was of primary importance and that it was best given by parents within the intimate setting of the family itself, rather than in schools or in large group settings.[26] However, contacts between Catholic activists and Quebec adolescents during the postwar period, particularly in the context of the SPM's premarital advice courses, seemed to reveal an appallingly low level of sexual knowledge and self-awareness exhibited by young men and women.[27] Even as late as 1962, 55 percent of women and 57 percent of men attending the courses stated that they had not been well informed by either parents or teachers about sexuality.[28] Of those who felt that their knowledge of these matters was adequate, what was more telling was that only 61 percent of women and 34 percent of men credited their parents with providing them with such information. A shockingly high percentage of young men and women had *never* been informed about marriage, sex, and reproduction before attending the SPM courses.[29]

68: "simplement, franchement et par étapes [faire] l'éducation sexuelle de l'enfant." See also Louise-M. Lamonde, "Préparation au mariage," *Rel*, juin 1953, 162–63; Joseph D'Anjou, S.J., "Parents, c'est vous que ça regarde," *Rel*, mars 1959, 68–69.

26. Mgr. A. Camirand, "L'éducation sexuelle," *LF* 2, no. 7 (mars 1939): 145–46; "L'amour humain chez les jeunes," *CAC* 113 (jan. 1950): 147. On the discourse surrounding the sexual instruction of Catholic youth in Quebec, see Gaston Desjardins, *L'Amour en patience: la sexualité adolescente au Québec, 1940–1960* (Sainte-Foy: Les Presses de l'Université du Québec, 1995), 78, 118. Desjardins observes that a number of Catholic circles in the 1930s recognized the need for sex education for youth, but that Catholic commentators resolutely sought to avoid a collective sexual instruction given in educational institutions.

27. ANQM, Fonds JOC, P104, art. 171, "Rencontre nationale des responsables et aumôniers du S.P.M.," 3–4 déc. 1955; ibid., art. 4, "Suggestions de programme d'action, 1961," "Amour entre garçons et filles"; ibid., art. 175, "Enquête auprès de 329 fiancés qui ont suivi le S.P.M. sur la préparation économique des jeunes au mariage," 1954.

28. AUM, Fonds ACC, P16/D5, 1.14, "Compilation du sondage auprès des fiancés sur l'amour," 1962. This was a study based upon the responses of 133 couples in five Quebec dioceses and eight cities. See also ANQM, Fonds SPM, P116 art. 1, "Situation des fiancés, 1955–56," which pointed to the very late sexual awareness of Quebec youth. Fully 60 percent of young people questioned stated that they had acquired their sexual knowledge after age 14.

29. AUM, Fonds ACC, P16/D5, 1.14, "Compilation du sondage," 1962; ibid., P16/H18.84, "Conclusion du Comité Exécutif du S.P.M., jan.–mai 1956."

The central point was not that these surveys were an accurate measure of the state of sexual knowledge among postwar Quebec youth, but that they marked an ongoing attempt to define the family—and sexual identity itself—as the central terrain of cultural difference between the religious values of "youth" and those of the previous generation. Although on the one hand "intimacy," with all its connotations of sexual partnership, and the cultivation of the emotions represented aspirations for family solidarity and community in an ideologically troubled, impersonal world of mass institutions, its pervasive use by an influential segment of Quebec Catholicism also indicated that it was a slogan in an ongoing effort to elaborate a cultural polarization between present and past in Quebec society. Youth's lack of sexual awareness and therefore the firm psychological identity essential to form stable marriages and families was unanimously interpreted as the inadequacy and abdication of the previous generation of parents in fulfilling the primary function of the modern family: the psychological integration of all its members through constant education in sex roles.[30] Such failure would mean social disequilibrium because inability to impose the new model of family structure and function spelled the persistence of older economic and extended-kin family ideals and practices. This, Catholic reformers believed, would prolong and intensify a state of cultural adolescence, a perpetual identity crisis that would affect not only the individual, but because of the public character of the family, the wider Quebec society.

A second key consequence of the Quebec Catholic promotion of the affectional-nuclear family was that between 1940 and 1960, Catholic social movements and publications became the principal channels for the spread of contraceptive information and practices. Within the framework of the extremely popular marriage preparation movement, there was considerable emphasis placed upon women's equal access to sexual pleasure as one of the key determinants of a successful, stable marriage. So well attended were the sessions on male and female anatomy and techniques of mutual pleasure that one organizer ruefully complained that young peo-

---

30. See ANQM, Fonds SPM, P116, art. 24, "Substance de la conférence de M. Marcel Clément," ca. 1954; ibid., art. 2, "Semaine des fiancés, 1950," Chanoine Clavel, "Les ennemis de la famille et la préparation au mariage"; AUM, Fonds ACC, P16/G3, 9.2, R. P. Jules Godin, S.J., "Le service de préparation a la vie," ca. 1951; ibid., P16/G5, 8.1, "Le problème des jeunes qui ne fréquentent plus l'école," 6 dec. 1942; "Famille-École," CAC 134 (oct. 1951): 75–76; "Le courrier de José," FO, 4 dec. 1946.

ple were "flocking to the courses for sexual information and not to explore the spirituality of marriage."[31] A key element of the post-1930s reorientation of Catholic teaching on marriage was a partial, if never complete, disentangling of sexuality from strictly reproductive imperatives. Could parents, and especially mothers, who were more directly implicated in education and child-rearing, best cultivate these roles in families with large numbers of children or in families where the conjugal couple had exercised some prudent planning and foresight, and made an effort to adjust their available physical and emotional resources to the numbers of children that they could effectively raise? And could husband and wife effectively cultivate their own intimate relationship under the pressures of raising large numbers of children, or indeed have a satisfying sexual relationship under the psychological stress of the wife always becoming pregnant? Of equal significance, if women's sexuality—read as the foundation of postwar family stability itself—was not just synonymous with reproduction, could the sexual needs of wives be satisfied without some form of family limitation?

In answering these questions, an important current of Quebec Catholicism did far more than simply oppose or haltingly accommodate itself to the supposedly "secular" practice of birth control. Through various forms of lay activism, Catholic Action promoted an ideal of family planning, one that emphasized women's control because it was based upon using recent scientific knowledge of the female menstrual cycle, and relied upon the "mutuality" and intimacy that the marriage preparation movement sought to instill in the very relationship between husband and wife to allow couples to adjust the frequency, nature, and timing of their sexual expression. In Quebec between the mid-1930s and the widespread use of the Pill during the later 1960s, one type of birth control—the much-maligned Ogino-Knaus, or rhythm, method—was in fact central to the type of marriage spirituality that Catholic Action aspired to promote.[32] Because Catholic laity, and especially women, dominated the postwar Catholic Action movements, there began to emerge within this strand of Catholicism a palpable gap between the official doctrines that stressed the

31. ANQM, Fonds SPM, P116, art. 1, Session d'étude 1955, "Commission des couples."
32. In fact, the Service de Préparation au Mariage deployed a large number of medical professionals to directly instruct couples on the practice of the rhythm method. See AUM, Fonds ACC, P16/H18.83, "Commission médecins-infirmières," 2 octobre 1955.

imperative of procreation and the way the issue was dealt with and softened in practice by chaplains and spiritual directors. Clergy such as Father Jules Paquin, a popular lecturer who attempted to popularize a type of sexual technique that maximized female pleasure, explained that Catholic doctrine permitted the use of the rhythm method—what he termed "periodic continence"—to allow the spacing of children so as to ensure their proper care and education. Paquin nuanced official teachings by emphasizing that the key factor was not external authority, but the consent of both spouses and their own personal assessment of their needs and resources.[33]

In this way, reformist Catholics allied the new morality and techniques of contraception to the new psychological and affective ideal of modern marriage and parenting to launch a full-scale assault on pre-Depression Quebec popular values that had lauded a high rate of fertility. They effectively severed these older notions from any connection with Christianity, and assimilated the older cultural ideal of the unremitting cycles of birth with the instinctual, "irrational" social and cultural forms of a rural society that had subordinated human values to the play of blind natural forces. "The procreation of children," stated the proceedings of one postwar conference on family spirituality, "is not necessarily the expression of chastity: it is perhaps more closely linked to a purely bestial sexual instinct, or to ignorance, what some would call 'bad luck.'"[34] It would not be an exaggeration to state that this type of Catholic teaching on family planning, what one commentator termed a "baptized Malthusianism,"[35] was responsible for a contraceptive revolution that occurred among the cohorts of Quebec

33. ANQM, Fonds SPM, P116 art. 24, "Compte-rendu de la rencontre des conférenciers du S.P.M. avec le Reverend Père Jules Paquin, s.j.," 16 mars 1960: "L'église n'a jamais été pour le plus d'enfants possible dans le moins de temps possible," "continence périodique." Official teaching as expressed in *Casti connubii* had permitted the use of the rhythm method, but envisioned it as something exceptional and temporary, certainly not to be practiced by couples on a regular basis with the overt intention of spacing births. Paquin's sexual technique was a type of "reserved intercourse," similar to aspects of the Kama Sutra, in which the male partner held off ejaculation for the longest possible time, thus allowing maximum female pleasure.

34. AUM, Fonds ACC, P16/R.62, "Spiritualité familiale, problèmes pratiques et expériences," s.d.: "La procréation d'enfants n'est pas nécessairement l'expression de la chasteté: elle tient peut-être a un pur instinct sexuel bestial, ou a l'ignorance, a la 'malchance,' dit-on."

35. Hervé Blais, O.F.M., *L'Éducateur: Revue des parents et des maîtres* 1, no. 4 (mai 1942): 53: "malthusiansime baptisé."

women born between 1921 and 1935. It should be noted that this "revolution" in social practices was not at first manifest in an actual decline in the birthrate; indeed, women born within this age group seem to have had the same average number of children as those born between 1906 and 1910. However, within the later age cohorts, women increasingly chose to space and limit births over the course of their childbearing years, and more particularly, made the decision to have all their children while younger, employing a combination of contraceptive practices to ensure that the cycle of births was closed. Of women born between 1921 and 1925, 47 percent used some form of contraception; those born between 1926 and 1930, 59 percent; and those born 1931 to 1936, 64 percent. Significantly, the latter two groups were those most likely to have been influenced by the personalist teachings of Catholic Action, and in particular to have had some contact with the marriage preparation movement. Women of these age groups relied upon the supposedly "traditional" combination of rhythm method and periodic abstinence, the only forms sanctioned by Roman Catholicism, to introduce into Quebec the "modern" practice of limiting births.[36] Quebec's introduction to contraception between 1931 and the early 1960s signaled not the mass rejection of Catholic values, but the engrafting of a particular strand of Catholicism onto wider social practices. However, one of the consequences of this successful infusion of Catholic values into the lives of ordinary people was the seamless equation between religion itself and a moral calculus, implicit in the new Catholic spirituality of marriage, in which the individual was allowed to oscillate between sexual pleasure and self-denial, both of which were assigned spiritual value. But what would happen if large numbers of Catholic faithful came to see sexual abstinence as having no positive personal or spiritual value?

36. For these figures, see Danielle Gauvreau and Peter Gossage, "Empêcher la famille: fécondité et contraception au Quebec, 1920–1960," *Canadian Historical Review* 78, no. 3 (Sept. 1997): 478–510. These historians do not examine the wider cultural influence of Catholic Action, but they do note that 80 percent of Catholic women relied exclusively upon the rhythm method and abstinence to regulate births. Contemporary social surveys also revealed the heavy prevalence of the rhythm method among Catholic families. See Philippe Garigue, *La vie familiale des canadiens-français* (Montréal: Les Presses de l'Université de Montreal, 1962), 89. As early as 1957, the demographer Jacques Henripin observed that "Parents control their fertility more effectively *after* they have had a few children." See "From Acceptance of Nature to Control: The Demography of the French Canadians since the Seventeenth Century," in Marcel Rioux and Yves Martin, eds., *French-Canadian Society*, vol. 1 (Toronto: McClelland and Stewart, 1964), 213.

After 1955, however, Catholicism's attempt to use the family to hold a delicate balance between competing currents of democracy and authority was fundamentally destabilized by two cultural currents that had, by 1970, largely uncoupled Catholicism both from Quebec's public culture and from the realm of personal belief and practice. The first was the reassertion, during the early 1950s, of some of the conventions of the elitist spirituality of the 1930s by a number of articulate middle-class and university-educated men. Associated with the critical magazine *Cité libre,* the Faculty of Social Sciences at Laval University, and the upper echelons of Catholic Action, these intellectuals have been generally identified with a reformist political liberalism because of their unbending opposition to the conservative regime of Maurice Duplessis.[37] However, what is less well known about them is their unbending cultural conservatism, which between 1950 and 1960 elaborated an exceedingly corrosive synthesis that combined an intellectualized Catholicism that looked with disdain on manifestations of popular religion, anxieties over the spiritual vacuity of middle-class professionals, contemporary fears for masculine leadership in both family and society that identified feminization with clericalized religion, and a critique of the type of humanistic education offered in Catholic educational institutions. The overall effect was to posit a belief that Catholicism was in "crisis" and was somehow incompatible with the realities of a rapidly urbanizing and industrializing society. This was a notion that not only was embedded in subsequent historical treatments of the Quiet Revolution and thus powerfully informed the larger context of the relations between Catholicism and Quebec society, but also dictated a number of Catholic initiatives that drastically narrowed and polarized the criteria of religious belonging during the 1960s.

The "spiritual athletes" who clustered around *Cité libre* and who styled themselves a "Christian Left" in close imitation of their French mentor, Emmanuel Mounier, were all former male veterans of Catholic Action whose transition to adulthood during World War II coincided with a realization that the new type of Catholic social activism, heavily biased to-

---

37. The links of this group of intellectuals to political liberalism have been explored by Michael D. Behiels, *Prelude to Quebec's Quiet Revolution: Liberalism versus Neo-Nationalism, 1945–1960* (Montreal and Kingston: McGill-Queen's University Press, 1985); and Leon Dion, *Quebec 1945–2000, tome 2, Les intellectuels et le temps de Duplessis* (Quebec: Les Presses de l'Universite Laval, 1993).

ward youth and women, offered very few leadership possibilities for married men beyond a return to activities in more traditional parish-based associational life, where their initiatives would be guided and shepherded by the clergy.[38] This left modern men with a lack of spiritual substance, their roles narrowed to being biological procreators and economic providers.[39] What these activists most wished to constrain in both family and the wider society was the "hypertrophying of the maternal figure," what American commentators would term "Momism."[40] From these sharp distinctions between male/female, reason/emotion, public/private, an articulate group of Quebec Catholics postulated a struggle between two types of Catholicism: one authentic, heroic, spiritually pure, communitarian, appealing to masculine reason, the other, routine, sentimental, unthinking, overly pious, excessively individualistic, appealing primarily to women and the less educated. What gave a hard, confrontationist edge to this dialectic was this group's belief that "traditional" Catholic religious attitudes and practices were driving men away from the faith. Quebec society, they believed, had entered a vicious circle in which the persistence of old-style ritualism as the primary expression of Catholicism had persuaded many middle-class and professional men that "religion was only good for women,"[41] and that inward-looking, feminized styles of piety simply did not resonate with the needs of modern men for spiritual fellowship based upon activity and engagement. The end result was that this emasculating of Catholicism would simply expose male public elites to the inroads of more aggressive, secularist ideologies, and would, despite Quebec Catholicism's impressive institutional armature, inevitably privatize religion. Clearly, in the estimation of this elite, the entire Quebec society was

38. Pierre Elliott Trudeau, "In Memoriam: Albert Béguin et Jacques Perreault," *Cité libre* 17 (juin 1957): 2: "athlètes de l'esprit."

39. Pelletier, "Le laique marié," 121: "duperie," 115: "un laicat désorienté," "en proie à toutes les passivités comme à toutes les rages intérieures," 120: "notre vocation la plus haute et la plus authentique, notre vocation au mariage."

40. Guy Rocher, "La famille dans la ville moderne," 82: "une hypertrophie de la figure maternelle"; AUM, Fonds ACC, P16/R.62, "Spiritualité familiale," "Spiritualité familiale: problèmes pratiques et expériences," s.d.; Ryan, *Les classes moyennes*. For "Momism" on the postwar social and cultural scene in the United States, and its links to both conservative and liberal discourse, see Ruth Feldstein, *Motherhood in Black and White: Race and Sex in American Liberalism, 1930–1965* (Ithaca: Cornell University Press, 2000), 41–43.

41. François Hertel, *Leur inquiétude* (Montréal: Éditions "Jeunesse" A.C.J.C., 1936), 125: "La religion bonne pour les femmes."

suffering from advanced symptoms of "Momism," which had produced "a hollow aching dichotomy" that according to the sociologist Jean-Charles Falardeau "is tearing apart our Catholic souls and intellects" through endless "inoffensive repetitions of acts of piety."[42]

By the mid-1950s, a vocal section of Catholic opinion in Quebec had adopted the notion of an unbridgeable chasm between two diametrically opposed religious mentalities as the key to the historical development of Quebec society, which had reached the proportions of a cultural and spiritual crisis. As represented by the church institution, religion was, for the most part, purely "sociological," an adjective that was always negatively contrasted with "personalist." "Sociological" religion was an amalgam of long-standing popular folk practices, translated into an unthinking reflex of conformity to a series of devotional acts, and was not anchored in any intellectual commitment or understanding of Catholic doctrine. For this reason, they offered the diagnosis that "the religious life of the average French-Canadian is totally devoid of cultural roots,"[43] and was increasingly governed by "a practical agnosticism."[44] What this particular Catholic elite most feared was an actual convergence between the formalist, sociological "traditional" Christianity, represented by what they saw as the clericalized, institutional Church, and the conformist pressures of standardized North American society. What was striking about their social analysis was that it was simply wrongheaded: from 1940, Quebec's educational and social welfare sectors were in the process of becoming less, rather than more, dominated by clergy.[45] For all their self-identification with reform-

42. Jean-Charles Falardeau, "Comment préparer l'après-guerre," *RD*, juin 1941, 312: "Une sourde et névralgique dichotomie est en voie de déchirer notre pensée et notre coeur catholiques," "une facilité traditionnelle à répéter inoffensivement des actes de piété."

43. AUM, Fonds ACC, P16/B6, 3.18, Claude Ryan, "Rencontre de Deux Mondes," ca. 1955: "La vie religieuse du Canadien-français moyen est sans racines culturelles." See also ibid., P16/E3, 6, 4.3, "Congrès International—Rome 1961," "La femme canadienne-française, instrument d'unité": "sociologique."

44. Jean Francoeur, "Les témoins d'une crise?," *Vie etudiante* 22, no. 4 (mars 1956), "agnosticisme pratique."

45. As noted by Jean Hamelin, in 1942, 23 male religious communities and 51 female communities were involved with teaching, and comprised 48 percent of the total number of teachers employed by the Department of Public Instruction and 59 percent of the teaching personnel of the private secondary institutions. By 1960, however, religious communities represented only 30.5 percent of the public sector teaching personnel, the result of an aggressive campaign by lay teachers' federations, which in 1951 had persuaded the Montreal Catholic School Commission that despite the financial savings involved in the employ-

ist liberalism, their outlook was marked by a profound anti-Americanism, and the primary issue at stake was a profoundly conservative one, the "historical indissolubility of French Canadian culture and Catholic religion" and the primacy of a "theological" culture, which they adamantly maintained must persist as the foundation of collective identity.[46] The use of the term "theology" was in this connection a most revealing one, because in its identification with rationality and the intellect, it served as an emblem by which to distinguish "authentic" virile Christian faith from its formalist, feminized, quasi-pagan counterpart. For them, the institutional Church, the Catholic clergy, and the religion of ordinary people were active agents of cultural Americanization, a process that could be arrested only by the urgent and imperative transfusion of a new kind of spirituality that would eradicate "conformity," "routine," and "individualism." Only a violent religious purification, the evisceration of a whole series of religious practices, could secure Catholicism's role as the religious underpinning of any viable civic order.

What ultimately accelerated and widened the process of dechristianization was the large-scale defection from the Church's doctrines of contraception and prescribed family roles that occurred among adult Quebec Catholics between 1960 and 1968. By the end of the 1950s, the combination of increasingly higher rates of married women working outside the home and the rise of a discourse even within Catholic women's movements that acknowledged that an exclusive focus on women's familial obligations was stunting the female identity, a critique that in some ways presaged that advanced in 1963 by Betty Friedan, established a very difficult terrain for Catholicism to navigate. This was a consequence of the ambiguity inherent in the delicate balance postwar Catholic activists had established within the ideology of family between male authority and female aspiration. Although there was considerably more flexibility within these identities than historians have previously acknowledged, the overall emphasis was on the stability of woman's maternal role.[47] Personalist femi-

---

ment of nuns and teaching brothers, only lay teachers could replace laity who retired from teaching.

46. Jean-Charles Falardeau, "Les recherches religieuses," in Fernand Dumont and Yves Martin, eds., *Situation de la recherche sur le Canada français* (Québec: Les Presses de l'Université Laval, 1962), 208–9: "une indissolubilité de la culture canadienne française et de la religion catholique"; "théologique."

47. For a more complete analysis, see Michael Gauvreau, *The Catholic Origins of Que-*

nism, however, had postulated "spiritual" rather than physical definitions of maternity, and by actively promoting access to forms of contraception, populist strands of Catholicism had overtly encouraged the idea that maternity was an act of female choice.

However, because the new Catholic culture of "regulated births" eschewed artificial means of contraception, it relied almost entirely for its effect upon an exalted sense of personal responsibility and awareness by individual women and upon a delicate, and frequently frustrating, calibration of sexual pleasure and the self-sacrifice demanded by abstinence. The psychological critique of female domesticity and an exaltation of personal sexual expression within the wider ambit of Western society began to unsettle this Catholic synthesis. Increasingly, the post-Depression Catholic morality of contraception was identified as "a received cultural heritage of 'the evils of the flesh,'" a particularly oppressive compound of interdictions, folklore, fears, and taboos that acted as the primary obstacle to women's sexual fulfillment.[48] New medical evidence indicated that the rhythm method could be successfully practiced only by the minority of women who had completely regular menstrual cycles, and because it was not entirely reliable, it was increasingly judged as a technique that favored fertility and natality. Second, the rhythm method was identified as a principal culprit in the sexual and psychological dissatisfaction of women, especially in light of the accepted sexual wisdom (widely propagated by Church-sponsored marriage preparation movements) that both husband and wife needed a complete orgasm to achieve sexual fulfillment. "The long periods of abstinence required to assure the maximum effect of the rhythm method," stated one expert in 1964, "often led to serious difficulties in the home, the husband feeling frustrated, and the wife, fearing that she was already less sexually ardent, risked becoming completely frigid."[49] Although most surveys from the early 1960s revealed a strong

---

bec's *Quiet Revolution* (Montreal and Kingston: McGill-Queen's University Press, 2005), 175–246.

48. AUM, Fonds ACC, "La femme canadienne-française, instrument d'unité": "L'héritage culturel reçu sur la 'perversité de la chair'"; Solange Chalvin, "Un teach-in prend l'allure d'un cours magistral sur la sexualité," *Le Devoir,* 12 mars 1970, citing the address of Jean-Marc Samson, theologian.

49. Marie-Josee Beaudoin, *Pouvez-vous 'empêcher la famille'?* (Montreal: Les Éditions de l'Homme, 1964), 18–19: "Il fut prouvé que les longues periodes de continence exigées pour assurer un maximum de garantie à la methode ont souvent crée de serieuses difficultés dans

commitment among Catholic couples to having four or five children during the course of their marriage, there was also compelling evidence of widespread acceptance, particularly among the expanding middle classes, of the logic of the affectional-conjugal family in which, given the total psychological and emotional commitment involved in modern parenting, this could be accomplished only in situations where they had deliberately chosen to restrict family size.[50]

More alarming still, however, was evidence of an apparent connection between difficulties with Catholic notions of birth regulation and defection from all forms of religious practice. Surveys from a number of Quebec urban centers undertaken in 1963 by Catholic Action indicated a rather striking defection from the Church, most evident among Catholics who were trying to limit family size. While 60 percent of Catholic couples practiced birth control, a shockingly high 65 percent of these had entirely abandoned religious practice.[51] It was in order to avert this disjuncture that a number of Catholic groups such as the marriage preparation movement popularized the notion that the birth control pill, widely available in Quebec by the early 1960s, fell within the rubric of the Church's approval. Although a number of clergy were unhappy about the idea that the Pill might free female sexuality from any restraint, they sought ways to integrate this new technique with Catholic teaching.[52] However, the partially unintended effect on a wide section of Catholic laity was to establish a firm identification between Catholicism and the notion that sexuality and contraception were purely private acts, subject only to the dictates of individual conscience. Thus, the results of a 1966 *Maclean's Magazine* survey found that 65 percent of women questioned on contraception claimed that priests had advised them that the Pill was acceptable, and believed that this technique seemed to resolve all problems of conscience occasioned by other methods. Indeed, 80 percent of couples questioned in

---

le foyer, l'homme se sentant frustré et la femme, pour peur qu'elle ne soit déjà pas tres ardente, risque de devenir frigide."

50. On these surveys, see Colette Carisse, *Planification des naissances en milieu canadien-français* (Montréal: Les Presses de l'Université de Montréal, 1964), 99–100; Alice Parizeau, "Contrôle des naissances," *Châtelaine* 4, no. 6 (juin 1963): 25.

51. Beaudoin, *Pouvez-vous 'empêcher la famille'?*, 72; AUM, Fonds ACC, P16/D1, 4.15b, "Sondage à Chicoutimi." See also ibid., P16/G2, 2.1.3, "Problèmes à la centrale de la J.E.C., 1961–62," "Jean Francoeur."

52. ANQM, Fonds SPM, P116, art. 24, Paquin, "Compte-rendu, 1960."

the Montreal diocese stated that "they found birth control such a normal practice that they did not even speak about it any more in the confessional because the Church had nothing to say in the matter."[53] When in 1968 the pope reiterated Catholic moral teaching and the Church's opposition to what he termed "artificial" types of birth control, it entailed an immediate and massive erosion of adherence among Catholicism's traditional constituency: married couples with families.

If growing tensions and ambiguities within Catholic public ideologies of sexuality, youth, and gender constituted the principal axis of Quebec's trajectory toward a more secular culture in the early 1960s, something else is required to explain the catastrophic fall in rates of religious participation among Quebec Catholics in the years after 1965. In that year, Quebec could still wear the label "Catholic society," given the fact that 88 percent of people attended Mass twice or more each month, indicating a high level of personal and public identification with Catholicism. By 1975, however, this figure had been almost halved, with only 46 percent indicating this close identity.[54] While it would be easy to point the finger at popular resentment against the liturgical changes introduced by Vatican II, there was an element present in Quebec that was more fundamental, which involved the very way in which "authentic" and "sociological" Christianity had been posited as a dichotomy between the religion of an activist, modernizing spiritual elite and an inert, traditionalist mass of ordinary Catholics. In this way, the most cathartic act in the drama of that society's dechristianization was enacted through the appropriation, by senior clergy and the institutional Church itself, of these dichotomies, which were in the 1960s enunciated in such a way as to appear as the official policy of the Quebec Catholic Church. Indeed, it should be reiterated in this context that the erosion of Catholicism's public authority was not a simple case of displacement of the church by the state. The reforms of public education and social welfare that took place in the early 1960s were undertaken by a re-

53. "Sondage—la régulation des naissances—comment se comportent les Québécoises?," *Le Magazine Maclean,* juin 1966, 11–13; Colette Carisse, "Le nombre des enfants," *Châtelaine* 5, no. 6 (juin 1964): 27, 63–65; Beaudoin, *Pouvez-vous,* 57, citing the opinion of "Anne," a university student, who declared that she had consulted a priest, who referred her to a doctor who prescribed the Pill.

54. For these figures, see Reginald Bibby, *Fragmented Gods: The Poverty and Potential of Religion in Canada* (Toronto: Irwin Publishing, 1987), 19–20.

formist laity who desired to preserve and strengthen the equation between religion and national identity; in the words of the minister of education, Paul Gerin-Lajoie, himself a veteran of the Depression-era Catholic student movements, the intent was to accomplish a "grand quiet revolution" in both church and state by bringing to an end "the opposition of clergy and laity, the spiritual and the temporal, religion and politics."[55] The new education structures, while under definite state management and financial control, did not eviscerate religion, but rather, incorporated confessionality (and the teaching of Catholic religious doctrine) directly into the structure of the state. However, this meant that the state in fact gained a certain control over the very *content* of Catholic doctrine, because the Church hierarchy lost its power to dictate where and when to build schools and how much religion could be taught in the overall curriculum; more importantly, Catholic doctrine could no longer be presented implicitly in the teaching of other subject matters, but had to be compartmentalized from the rest of the curriculum.[56]

A unifying central premise underwrote these educational reforms on the part of both political and clerical elites. This was the idea that the entire direction of post-Depression Catholic social action, with its central emphasis upon the family, had failed, particularly in the communication of religious values, and that only a massive institutional intervention, in the form of a restructured school catechesis, and radical reform of the life of the parish community could ensure the integration of Catholicism and the public values of a modern nation. The early 1960s was dominated by the apprehension that the faith of most ordinary Catholics was at best

55. National Archives of Canada, Fonds Paul Gerin-Lajoie, MG 31E106, Vol. 64.12, "Discours 1965," "Allocution à l'occasion du 25e anniversaire du sacerdoce de Mgr. H. Aganier, vicaire-général du diocèse de Valleyfield, 26 juin 1965, au séminaire de Valleyfield": "La grande révolution tranquille," "c'est que l'on cesse d'opposer le clergé et les laics, le spirituel et le temporel, la religion et la politique."

56. For a more complete analysis of the meanings of "confessionality" during the 1960s and the articulation of a political theory combining the liberal state and Catholicism, see Gauvreau, *The Catholic Origins of the Quiet Revolution,* chapter 6. If the pop sociology of the era has any validity, and the "medium was the message," then the very nature of Catholic doctrine was radically changed by an altered presentation in the school system. There are a number of historical parallels for this particularly close relationship, whose axis was the supremacy of the state. One of these was the Constitutional Church created in the early years of the French Revolution. See Nigel Aston, *Religion and Revolution in France, 1780–1804* (Washington, D.C.: The Catholic University of America Press, 2000), 140–64.

"shaky" or at worst nonexistent and that this defective popular religion of the older generation constituted a cultural "crisis" because it was mired in a religion of acquisitive individualism utterly foreign to an ideal of spiritual and social solidarity.

What was most striking about the statements of a number of prominent Quebec clergy after 1964 was the notion that the vast majority of the people of Quebec no longer possessed a viable Christian commitment. As stated by Father Jacques Grand'Maison in 1965, "the Fathers of the Church baptized converts, but we have to convert the baptized."[57] In this way, the gendered dichotomy that pitted the virile "authentic" Christianity of a prophetic minority against the "feminized," passive Catholicism of the Quebec masses was elevated to the status of theological and social-scientific orthodoxy. Among both clerical and lay intellectuals, a certain type of French religious sociology enjoyed a particular vogue. This style of investigation and interpretation of religion presented a bleak prognosis that rested upon three interlocking convictions, given "objective" status through the deployment of statistical discourse. These were the inevitable paganization of the industrial working class, the ineffectiveness of "traditional" Catholic practices and organizations, deemed hopelessly "bourgeois," in competing with secular ideologies, and, as stated by its principal Quebec devotee, the sociologist–lay theologian Fernand Dumont, an absolute religious divide between the authentic Christianity of heroic, missionary, activist minorities, appropriate for a modern "global" society, and the conventional religious life of the parish, a holdover of an obsolete rural culture, a hopeless amalgam of folklore and unthinking naturalistic ritual practiced by pious Catholics who conceived salvation in purely individualistic terms.[58]

Catholicism in Quebec, stated Dumont in 1964, was anchored upon "a dog's breakfast of pseudo-beliefs that are in reality superstitions barely disguised by a thin coat of Christian veneer."[59] The significance of such

57. Jacques Grand'Maison, ptre, "L'Église du Quebec en état de concile—III: Les provocations missionnaires du mouvement de sécularisation," *Le Devoir,* 1 oct. 1965: "Les pères de l'Eglise baptisaient des convertis, nous avons à convertir des baptisés."

58. For a self-appraisal of this intellectual and spiritual itinerary, see Dumont, *Recit d'une emigration;* and for a more critical appraisal of his encounter with radical French personalism, social democracy, and sociology, see Gauvreau, *The Catholic Origins of the Quiet Revolution,* chapter 7.

59. Dumont, "L'authenticité de l'expérience chrétienne dans la société d'aujourd'hui," *Communauté chrétienne* 29 (sept.–oct. 1966): 382: "toute cette quincaillerie de pseudo-

a negative reassessment of the religion of ordinary Catholics was that it was no longer restricted to a small coterie of intellectuals. After 1956, it formed the underlying assumption of the *grandes missions,* systematically undertaken in a number of dioceses, which directly imbibed the French notion that it was only intellectualized religion that really counted. This style of Catholicism no longer considered that faith was a cultural given, or that youth was naturally Christian, in contrast to older forms of periodic missionizing that aimed at revivifying the tepid faith of a population presumed to be Christian in belief and practice. The fundamental assumption, articulated by Father Grand'Maison, was that "in daily life, the mass of Christians are still in fact at the level of pre-evangelization. Faith never intervenes practically in human relations. Many have retained the religious habits of their forefathers without holding on to their faith." The new concern was directed at provoking a "crisis of conscience" at the level of community, so that "the theological dimension of the faith was understood and embodied in the daily life of those baptized."[60] This primacy of theology expressed the intent of a self-conscious group of Catholic modernizers who wished to draw a fundamental distinction between what they meant by "authentic" or "adult" faith, and the religion currently practiced in Quebec, continued adherence to which would only perpetuate a conformist "evasion" into individual, petit-bourgeois self-satisfaction, and ultimately aggravate both individual and social pathologies.

In this respect, the "crisis" model of faith proposed by these modernizing senior clergy and lay social scientists induced them to agonize less over the defections of traditionalist Catholics than about the perceived dechristianization of the educated middle classes of Quebec society. Far better the loss of traditional Catholics, whose faith was at best "infan-

---

croyances qui souvent d'ailleurs sont des superstitions à peine recouvertes d'une mince couche de peinture chrétienne." See also the views advanced by Maurice Bouchard, an economist at the Université de Montréal in "Conformisme religieux," *Maintenant,* nov. 1964, 330.

60. Mgr. Paul-Emile Charbonneau, "Renouveau pastoral," *Rel,* fev. 1966, 42–44: "crise de conscience," "la dimension théologale de la foi n'arrive pas à prendre corps dans la vie quotidienne des baptisés"; Grand'Maison, "L'Église du Québec en état de concile": "Dans la vie quotidienne la masse des chrétiens est de fait au plan de la pre-évangélisation. La foi n'intervient pas dans les relations humaines. . . . Plusieurs ont gardé les habitudes de leurs pères sans retenir leur foi." See also Colette Moreux, "Le Dieu de la québécoise," *Maintenant,* fev. 1967, 67. For the *grandes missions,* see Hamelin and Gagnon, *Histoire du catholicisme québécois, tome 2,* 214–15.

tile," if it existed at all, than a compromise that would offer at best a "ghetto Christianity" of blind adherence to ritual. This would only succeed in marginalizing the Church from the new currents of public life, which required a self-conscious engagement with social reality,[61] what for a certain Catholic elite in 1960s Quebec meant a commitment to a sovereignist neo-nationalism, anchored upon the supremacy of the political state as the central organizing principle of national life, but with a Catholicism radically purged of its kitschier, "folkloric," "individualist" excrescences, offering a type of communitarian solidarity. It was precisely this theological-political understanding of the place of Catholicism that informed the outlook of the Commission d'etude sur l'Eglise et les laics, appointed by the hierarchy in the wake of the collapse of Catholic Action in 1966, to suggest a new interface between Catholicism and Quebec society. Chaired by Fernand Dumont, this body can best be described as a case of "the usual suspects"—former prominent Catholic activists who shared a basic commitment to the "crisis" model of religious development—and included no advocates of more "traditional" religious approaches. Despite its mandate to search for new ways of expressing the public presence of the Church, the Dumont Commission remained dominated by a particular vision of the past, a fundamentally anachronistic reversion to a type of Gallican political Christianity, and by an inflexible cult of personalist elitism. These emphases offered no solace to those troubled about the relativization of the Christian message, and seemed to seriously compromise the independence and universality of the Church. Perhaps the most revealing comment on the exercise was the complete fissure between traditionalists and reformers in the very way in which religion was understood. As one conservative Catholic expressed the perplexity and rage against the new orthodoxy of religious elitism, "Quebec is sprouting mini-sociologists!"[62] But the most compelling symbol of the extent of Quebec's dechristianization, of a great reversal in a society that had accepted Catholicism as the meeting point of private and public values, was the lament of the religious

61. AUM, Fonds Paul-Larocque, P52/F1, Louis O'Neill, "La formation religieuse": "Christianisme du ghetto"; H.-M. Robillard, O.P., "La Religion du péché mortel," *Maintenant,* mai 1965, 175: "âmes grossières et lourdes . . . les âmes delicates, les âmes d'artistes, les âmes . . . profondément religieuses."

62. Archives Nationales du Quebec, Quebec, Fonds Action Sociale Catholique, P428S2, Action Catholique (Journal) "La parole est aux lecteurs," 1958, A. Larouche, Le Mouvement social chrétien, "Quand le Chat sort du sac!": "Le Québec foisonne en mini-sociologues."

experts on the Dumont Commission that abandonment of Catholic practice was an act accomplished in the realm of private values, and indicated a complete lack of interest by ordinary Quebecers in a continued linkage between Catholicism and the "fundamental values of our people."[63] However, after two decades of increasingly shrill hectoring and denigration by a self-appointed spiritual elite, why indeed would the masses even be remotely interested in a project of defining a synthesis between Catholicism and nationalism in which their religious experience was no longer included?

63. Commission d'Etude sur l'Eglise et les laics (Commission Dumont), *L'Église du Quebec, un héritage, un projet* (Montreal: Fides, 1971), 20: "Serait-ce parce que ces débats ne tiennent déjà plus aux valeurs essentielles de notre population?"

Ireland

DERMOT KEOGH

3. The Catholic Church in Ireland since the 1950s

In the fifty years between 1950 and the twenty-first century, Ireland has undergone the most profound and historic changes. From a country of mass emigration in the 1950s, it was in the early 2000s a receiving nation. Those coming to the island were not only returning Irish forced by economic circumstances to leave decades before for the United States, Britain, or other industrial destinations. The migrant workers of the 1990s and early twenty-first century come from the European Union, particularly the Eastern European countries, and from Africa, Asia, India, and Latin America. Thus, the Catholic Church in Ireland today is being reinforced by the active participation in parish life of believers from Poland and the Philippines, from Nigeria and Lithuania. Ireland has a rising Muslim population and a radically declining Jewish community. There is a sharp increase in the number of evangelical Christians and in the growth of various sects.

In the context of the radical economic change that has given Ireland the reputation of having become the "Celtic tiger," little thought has been given to the role of the Catholic Church in the process of modernization. In the eyes of Tom Garvin, it was an inhibiting factor, preaching as it did an anti-materialist message.[1] However, that is merely one aspect of a Catholic legacy that has contributed greatly to the social and economic trans-

---

1. Tom Garvin, *Preventing the Future: Why Was Ireland So Poor for So Long?* (Dublin: Gill and Macmillan, 2004).

formation of the state; it has cross-subsidized that state through its contribution to education, social welfare systems, medical care, and support of
those with special needs. But that is an argument for another forum.

In the early twenty-first century, the Catholic Church in Ireland faces many challenges. Secularization has taken place at an accelerated pace
since the 1980s. The Catholic Church has had to face a succession of scandals over clerical child sexual abuse and the treatment of children in the
care of religious. The full implications of those revelations for the future
life of the Church in Ireland have yet to be calculated and assessed. Suffice it to say that it has caused the greatest crisis of credibility for the Irish
Catholic Church in the last three centuries.

Yet, in the middle of the last century, Irish Catholicism was the odd
one out in Europe. It defied the strong trends toward secularization in
the countries of Western Europe. The economic transformation of many
countries in the 1950s was conducted under the watchful eye of Christian
Democratic governments in Germany, Italy, and France. The movement
toward greater economic integration was a project led by Robert Schuman
(France), Alcide de Gasperi (Italy), and Konrad Adenauer (Germany). Ireland observed the march of progress in Western Europe. Eamon de Valera, a survivor of the 1916 Rising and the single most important politician in Ireland in the twentieth century, shared the political philosophy
regarding the integration of Western Europe. But he did not feel that Ireland should be a part of that project. That policy position was determined
to a great extent by the anti-European policy of neighboring Britain, the
recipient in the 1950s of over 80 percent of Irish exports. (That position
would change in 1961 when both countries tried unsuccessfully to enter
the EEC.)

While Britain boomed outside the EEC, Ireland stagnated. Economic protectionism was an outmoded government policy having its roots in
the very different world of the 1930s. De Valera's Ireland stagnated in the
1950s. The only Irish people to "never have it so good" were those who
emigrated to Britain, where the conservative government of Harold Macmillan led his country to greater and greater prosperity between 1957 and
1963.

Ireland's arrested economic development had a number of interesting
consequences, not least being the artificial conservation of a traditional
society where religious observance was anomalous compared with patterns

of religious observance in Western Europe. Ireland was perceived as being atypical. Religious observance remained very high, and the mass exodus away from the churches, so much a feature of Western Europe, was not replicated in Ireland. Why was Ireland different from other Western European countries in this respect? The usual answer given was circular in character: Ireland was very religious because Ireland was Ireland. It had a distinctive historical experience. The Catholic Church had played a central role in the achievement of Irish independence. But how long would that conjunction between Catholicism and nationalism be sustained? This chapter attempts to provide an answer to those questions.

The 1950s—the Lost Decade: Catholic Church Structures and Devotional Catholicism

The Catholic Church in Ireland is divided into four archdioceses and twenty-six dioceses. It is organized on an all-Ireland basis, making no genuflection to the political divisions on the island between Northern Ireland (six counties) and the Republic of Ireland (twenty-six counties). Northern Ireland was founded in 1920 with a Protestant majority and a Catholic minority. Operating under a local parliament, it provided a Protestant government that tolerated, if not encouraged, discrimination against the minority Catholic population. The Irish Free State, founded in 1922 and called the Irish Republic after 1949, was over 95 percent Catholic. The remaining population were members of the Church of Ireland, Presbyterians, Society of Friends, and the like. Both Northern Ireland and the Irish Free State together had a small Jewish population of over six thousand, with more than four thousand being citizens of the Irish Free State. The Irish Free State established diplomatic relations with the Holy See in 1929. The nuncio is accredited to the Irish church in all Ireland. The National Conference of Bishops, one of the oldest in Europe, provided a decision-making framework capable of corporate decisions in a relatively efficient manner at times of crisis.

Jean Blanchard, a French scholar writing about the Irish Catholic Church in the 1950s and early 1960s, noted that the "exceptional importance and influence of the Bishops, and respect that is paid to them" was a "unique aspect" that usually impressed foreigners. Bishops were typically appointed to their native dioceses and were rarely transferred outside their ecclesiastical province. Blanchard also noted the resemblance to the medieval Church, "whose traditions she has almost completely preserved." He was struck by the large number of dioceses in the country "and their relatively small areas, their irregular boundaries and the manner in which they frequently inter-penetrate. These peculiarities originated in the distant past, and their cause is often forgotten."[2] Blanchard contrasted the stability and intimacy of the Irish diocesan system with France, where "the bishops are liable to be appointed to any of the seventeen metropolitan provinces." He saw as a further strength the "coherent clerical education" that was given by the national seminary at Maynooth.[3]

There were 1,141 parishes in Ireland administered by 1,090 parish priests in the late 1950s. In all, there were 3,798 secular priests for about 3.28 million Catholics in Ireland. That was a ratio of one priest for about 860 laity. The ratio was, of course, much lower if priest members of religious orders were included. There were 2,514 parish churches and chapels. Blanchard noted that "parish priests are permanent," and it was customary to exclude religious orders from parish or diocesan administration. He noted that the parishes were large and had many curates who usually were given a district of their own to work in. He was struck by the practice of the "stations," which brought the parish priest into houses in remote parts of the parish to say Mass and hear confessions: "Ireland rightly preserves and values its many traditions," he wrote. The houses of religious orders or communities in the 1950s and 1960s were plentiful, and there were large numbers of vocations. The number of houses of religious in the 1950s grew from 128 houses of priests, 176 of brothers, and 597 of nuns to 140, 192, and 648 respectively.

These houses of male and female religious played a central role in the delivery of education at primary and secondary levels. Members of male and female religious orders expanded education at the secondary level to a much wider range of students than would otherwise have been the case in a highly stratified and poverty-stricken country. Leaving school at fourteen was the fate of many in the 1950s, however, and the boat to England

2. Jean Blanchard, *The Church in Contemporary Ireland* (Dublin: Clonmore and Reynolds, 1963), trans. from the French *Le Droit Ecclésiastique Contemporain D'Irlande* (Paris: R Pichon and R Durand-Auzias), 86–87.

3. Blanchard, *Church in Contemporary Ireland* (Dublin: Clonmore and Reynolds, 1963), 87.

their only hope of employment. The Irish educational system was denominational in structure. State funding was provided for the running of the schools and the payment of teachers. The state received an indirect subsidy from the salaries of the religious working in the schools. That money was usually put back into the running of the schools. The long hours worked by religious, male and female, in the running of boarding schools were not remunerated by the state.

The universities were state funded. Unlike the case in the secondary schooling system, the staff in the universities was overwhelmingly lay. But the ethos in the 1950s of the National University of Ireland Colleges, in Dublin, Cork, and Galway, was distinctively Catholic. The hierarchy had made a special effort to place clergy in professorial positions in the disciplines of philosophy and sociology. Theology was taught only at the Cork campus, not at Dublin or Galway.

Blanchard, in his study, saw Ireland as being "one of the most ancient and loyal countries of the Catholic World."

> Despite the fact that she is traditionalist, nationalist and conservative, she remains the Church of the ordinary people, not of any privileged class. Once a ferment of revolt, she now appears as the guardian of order. The symbol of liberty among a free people, she is prone to direct public opinion; she has a strong hierarchical structure and her clergy wield an unrivalled authority. While she insists on being the "social conscience" of a Catholic nation, yet she remains democratic in spirit, and her missionaries plant the seeds of liberty in distant continents.[4]

Blanchard correctly identified the local nature of the Irish Catholic Church. The bishop was a local, the clergy were local, and very often the men and women religious in a diocese were also local. There was a closeness between priests and people even if that relationship was unquestionably hierarchical and sometimes authoritarian.

The postwar Ireland in which that church ministered remained in a state of economic depression and stagnation throughout the 1950s when other countries in Western Europe were enjoying the fruits of "economic miracles." The 1950s was, for many people, a decade of enforced departures, economic depression, and despair. The young, in particular, were leaving the country for economic reasons. Emigration had been rising steadily since the end of the war in 1945. The rise of the welfare state in

4. Ibid., 89.

Britain, together with the promise of employment, held attractions for many at home faced with the dole queue and subsistence. With unrestricted entry for the Irish, they left in their tens of thousands for Britain. Brendan Kennelly, in his poem "Westland Row"—the Dublin point of departure for Britain—captured the melancholy scene:

> Brown bag bulging with faded nothings;
> A ticket for three pounds one and six
> To Euston, London via Holyhead.
> Young faces limp, misunderstanding. . . .
> Take your place. And out of all the crowd,
> Watch the girl in the wrinkled coat,
> Her face half-grey,
> Her first time.[5]

In the 1950s, the German novelist Heinrich Boll watched as people left St Andrew's Church, Dublin, after evening benediction: "[S]o I was left with the impression of an overwhelming piety as it flooded Westland Row after the Tantum ergo; in Germany you would not see that many people coming out of church after Easter Mass or at Christmas."[6] Boll had witnessed a moment of Catholic piety. Had he the time, he would have witnessed many more throughout the country. Benediction, Mass, and confessions were well attended in the 1950s throughout the country. There were other forms of devotion: forty hours' adoration, holy hours, first Fridays, novenas. Local Irish saints, such as St. Brigid and St. Finbarr, were strong in their localities, as were a myriad of other Irish saints. There were visits to holy wells, patterns, and the stations.

The cult of the saints was promoted by the different religious orders. There was a strong devotion to St. Jude, patron of hopeless cases and matters despaired of. St. Therese and St. Rita were very much associated with the Carmelite order. St. Clare, St. Ann, St. Philomena, St. Bernadette, and St. Martin de Porres were very popular. There was strong devotion to the Infant of Prague. Scapulars and blessed medals associated with the saints were popular to wear. Members of the Third Order of St. Francis wore a cord around the waist. Devotion to Our Lady was very strong. The Marian Year in 1954 and the centenary of Lourdes in 1959 further deepened

5. Quoted in Dermot Keogh, *Twentieth Century Ireland* (Dublin: Gill and Macmillan, Dublin, 1994), 216–17.

6. Heinrich Boll, *Irish Journal* (London: Secker and Warburg, 1967), 10 (originally published in German under the title *Irisches Tagbuch* in 1957).

that piety. The building of shrines to Our Lady had always been popular, and in the 1950s many more were added. The Marian shrine of Knock was a popular place of devotion in the 1950s. There was a strong local devotion in Ireland to Our Lady of Perpetual Succour, Our Lady of Good Counsel, and Our Lady of Fatima. The strength of that devotion was very much in evidence in May, when flowers were placed on the shrines and processions took place around the country. The time coincided with confirmations and first Communions. The Corpus Christi procession was also held in May.

The annual parish mission brought out large numbers to hear the order priests give forensic sermons about the state of morality in the country. There was a strong emphasis on hellfire, damnation, and sin. Much of Irish Catholic spirituality was associated more with Plato than with the New Testament. Dualism was very much the prevailing orthodoxy. There were dire warnings against company keeping, special friendships, occasions of sin, and impure thoughts, and casuistic analyses of "How far can I go." Catholic Truth Society pamphlets warned about the dangers of Freemasonry, Protestantism, and world conspiracies. Casuistry was a built-in feature of religious practice—How late do I have to be before I miss Mass? In Cork, one bakery devised a means of bending but not breaking the fast. The local bishop, Cornelius (or Connie) Lucey, was strict in his application of the law. He permitted two biscuits per collation. The local bakery concerned made very large biscuits known popularly as "Connie Dodgers." Irish Catholicism was a world surrounded with boundaries, negativity, and a sense of sin. People purged themselves of sin by going on pilgrimage to Croagh Patrick in County Mayo and to Lough Derg in County Donegal.

Religious culture in Ireland in the 1950s did not place a high value on individual freedom and personal choice. The laity had to be protected from evil literature, immoral plays, and the dangers from Hollywood. The novelist Bryan MacMahon wrote in the early 1950s "in Ireland today the conception of sin is everywhere, even from the earliest years. Send a child of four years of age or so to an Irish school, and on his return on the very first day he will begin to cry out, 'that's a sin!'"[7] The emphasis on sexual morality and the dangers of "company keeping" was fulminated from pulpits across the country.

---

7. Bryan MacMahon, "Getting on the High Road Again," in *The Vanishing Irish*, ed. John A. O'Brien, 2nd impression (London: W. H. Allen 1955), 210.

Authoritarianism and the Catholic Hierarchy

The episcopal/clerical/religious anxiety to keep "the flock" out of the way of temptation was emblematic of Irish Catholicism in the 1940s and 1950s. Patriarchal and patronizing, the Catholic Church's endemic authoritarianism was matched by an antipathy to openness. Archbishop of Dublin John Charles McQuaid was the undisputed and unchallengeable leader of the Catholic Church in the mid-twentieth-century era. Appointed in December 1940, McQuaid held the post until Pope Paul VI accepted his resignation in December 1971. Born in 1895, the son of a doctor from County Cavan, he was educated in a diocesan college, then by the Holy Ghost Fathers at Blackrock College, and finally by the Jesuits at James Joyce's old school, Clongowes Wood. He joined the Holy Ghost order, and after ordination he took up teaching duties in the 1920s at Blackrock College, of which he later became president. In the late 1920s and 1930s, McQuaid became very friendly with the family of Eamon de Valera. The latter became president of the Executive Council (title changed to taoiseach after 1937) in 1932. His children went to Blackrock, where he himself had gone at the turn of the century. Both men enjoyed a close friendship. But in their respective roles as taoiseach and archbishop of Dublin, that friendship was not strong enough to prevent tension and conflict in relations between church and state.

In order to set down the basis for McQuaid's understanding of church and state, it is necessary to revert back to the 1930s and the drafting of the Irish Constitution. The future archbishop of Dublin was heavily involved in the process. He was largely responsible for the wording of the first draft article on religion, church, and state.[8] His teacher, friend, and confrere, Father Denis Fahey, C.S.Sp., influenced his thinking in many

8. There is a substantial file of over fifty pages in the de Valera papers, file 1055, which shows the amount of work that McQuaid put into this article on religion. Leo XIII's encyclical *Immortale Dei* is quoted very frequently. If these extracts were sent very early in the process, then they formed the basis of the article on religion, church, and state. There is another possibility: McQuaid drafted the article and later provided the sources on which his work was based. (The file number above refers to the referencing system in the de Valera papers when held in the Franciscan Archives, Killiney, Dublin. Since this research was undertaken, the de Valera papers have been removed to the Archives Department, University College Dublin. They have been reclassified and renumbered. All references in this article are to the Franciscan numbering system.)

areas.[9] Fahey represented a strand of theological thought that owed much to the antirevolutionary, antimodern stance of French Catholicism. Mc-Quaid was not quite as "singular" in his views, but he shared Fahey's ultramontane position on the relationship between church and state. Those ideas found expression in the first draft Article 42, "Religion, Church and State":[10]

1. The State acknowledges the right of Almighty God to public worship in that way which he has shown to be His Will.

2. Accordingly, the State shall hold in honour the Name of God and shall consider it a duty to favour and protect religion and shall not enact any measure that may impair its credit.

3. The State acknowledges that the true religion is that established by our Divine Lord, Jesus Christ Himself, which He committed to His Church to protect and propagate, as the Guardian and interpreter of true morality. It acknowledges, moreover, that the Church of Christ is the Catholic Church.

4. The State recognises the Church of Christ as a perfect society, having within itself full competence and sovereign authority, in respect of the spiritual good of men. [. . .]

There is a striking contrast between the first draft article and what ultimately appeared in the final draft of the constitution. The difference, as can be seen by comparing both texts, was quite radical:

Religion: Article 44:[11]

1. (1) The State acknowledges that the homage of public worship is due to Almighty God. It shall hold His Name in reverence, and shall respect and honour religion. (2) The State recognises the special position of the Holy Catholic Apostolic and Roman Church as the guardian of the Faith professed by the great majority of the citizens. (3) The State also recognises the Church of

9. Fahey taught a few generations of Holy Ghost priests. He also found time to write but had difficulty in later years getting ecclesiastical approval for some of his work. Quite ironically, Fahey could not get permission to publish one of his books in the Dublin archdiocese when John Charles McQuaid was the prelate. The latter had written a preface to one of Fahey's earlier works.

10. See Preliminary Draft, with name of [Joseph] Walshe [no. 6] written on it in the hand of John Hearne, privately circulated by de Valera, S9715A (Franciscan Archives).

11. Bunreacht na hÉireann, Article 44; sub-sections 1.2 and 1.3 were deleted following a referendum in 1972.

Ireland, the Presbyterian Church in Ireland, the Methodist Church in Ireland, the Religious Society of Friends in Ireland, as well as the Jewish Congregations and the other religious denominations existing in Ireland at the date of the coming into operation of this Constitution.

McQuaid did not have success in relation to the wording of the religious article. He did, however, have a profound influence on the drafting of other sections of the constitution.

As archbishop between 1940 and 1972, he continued to act pastorally on the basis that the discarded article on religion in the constitution was operational in the de facto relationship between church and state. The Mother and Child crisis, 1950–1951, exemplifies both the archbishop's relationship with the state and his profound mistrust of the state itself. This was less a church-state crisis than an internal government crisis. But the crisis does reveal the growing integralist impulse of the leadership of the Catholic hierarchy—a desire to secure certain Catholic principles as the underpinning for social legislation. Although a strong Catholic, de Valera and his Fianna Fáil party, in power between 1932 and 1948, did not share a belief in the integralist principles espoused by the archbishop of Dublin. Under the new constitution of 1937, de Valera set his sights on a more distant relationship between the Irish state and the rightwing Catholic ideas prevalent in Franco's Spain and Salazar's Portugal. By the end of World War Two and the early years of the Cold War, Ireland was not a member of the world of Catholic authoritarianism in Europe. Ireland was a democracy in which the Catholic Church enjoyed "a special position" and extensive power and influence.

Nevertheless, the Catholic hierarchy wrote anxiously to the taoiseach (prime minister), Eamon de Valera, in spring 1947 expressing concern about the departure to urban Britain of so many young people, and particularly young women. Concern was expressed about the existence of foreign agents working to recruit women to go abroad "with promises of lucrative employment." The moral welfare of young Irish women was to the fore of the bishops' concerns. Ideally, the bench of bishops would have wished the government to intervene to halt the emigration. De Valera replied on February 16, 1948, a year later, expressing his deep concern at the unnecessary emigration of many young men and women. The development of the economy was the solution, he argued. But he ruled out any embargo:

The denial to individuals of the opportunity to seek a livelihood or a career abroad would, in the Government's view, be the restriction of a fundamental human right which could only be justified in circumstances of great national emergency.[12]

This episode was revealing of a particular episcopal mindset—the expectation that the state could and would use draconian legislation in peacetime to restrict the freedom of movement of citizens in order to protect their moral welfare.

The Inter-Party government that replaced Eamon de Valera and Fianna Fáil in March 1948 sent a telegram after its first cabinet meeting to Pope Pius XII desiring

> to repose at the feet of your Holiness the assurance of our filial loyalty and our devotion to your August Person, as well as our firm resolve to be guided in all our work by the teaching of Christ, and to strive for the attainment of a social order in Ireland based on Christian principles.[13]

The new minister for external affairs, Seán MacBride, was well disposed to the introduction of a travel ban on young women, and a memorandum was drafted for cabinet. But this policy was never implemented. A political confrontation in 1951 brought an end to the Inter-Party government of which he was a member. This became known as the Mother and Child crisis. From the vantage point of the early twenty-first century it is hard to imagine what possible objections there could have been to a scheme that proposed to introduce a free, non-means-tested program to take care of all mothers and children up to the age of sixteen. But the secretary to the National Conference of Bishops, Bishop Staunton, wrote in his official capacity to then Taoiseach John A. Costello on October 10, 1950, stating that the scheme was in direct opposition to the rights of the family and of the individual and was liable to "very great abuse." If adopted, the letter continued, it would "constitute a ready-made instrument for future totalitarian aggression." It was the view of the hierarchy that the right to provide for the health of children belonged to parents and not to the state. The state had the right to intervene only in a subsidiary capacity, to supplement and not to supplant. Staunton continued: [my emphasis] *"It may help indigent or neglectful parents; it may not deprive 90 per cent of parents of their rights*

12. Quoted in Keogh, *Twentieth Century Ireland*, 164–166.

13. Dermot Keogh, *Ireland and the Vatican: The Politics of Church-State Relations 1922–1960* (Cork: University Press, Cork, 1995), 232.

because of 10 per cent necessitous or negligent parents." The bishop, on behalf of the hierarchy, told Costello that it was not sound social policy to impose a state medical service on the whole community on the pretext of relieving the necessitous 10 percent from the so-called indignity of the means test. Staunton also wrote that the right to provide for the physical education of children belonged to the family and not to the state:

> Gynaecological care may be, and in some other countries is, interpreted to include provision for birth limitation and abortion. We have no guarantee that State officials will respect Catholic principles in regard to these matters. Doctors trained in instruction in which we have no confidence may be appointed as medical officers under the proposed service, and may give gynaecological care not in accordance with Catholic principles.

Staunton further claimed, on behalf of the hierarchy, that the proposed scheme destroyed the confidential relationship between patient and doctor. It also meant for the hierarchy the elimination of private medical practitioners by a state-paid service.[14]

The vehemence of the sentiments in the letter might have been better addressed to an anticlerical government. The motivation for such an intransigent stance sprang from a growing mistrust of the independence of the state. Behind the actions of the bishops—and here it might be more appropriate to speak of the leadership of the hierarchy—was the fear that the state might one day be controlled by a secular socialist government. Therefore, it was necessary to make a determined stance in order to defeat the "socialistic" project known as the Mother and Child scheme. Another old fear also manifested itself at that time—mistrust of Trinity-trained doctors. The minister for health in the Inter-Party government, Noel Browne, was a graduate of Trinity College. He had taken over the implementation of the Mother and Child scheme from the previous Fianna Fáil government.

But Costello and his ministerial colleagues were devout Christians— most of whom had made a pilgrimage to Rome in 1950 for the Holy Year. During the course of the crisis, Costello told the Dáil: "I am an Irishman second; I am a Catholic first." MacBride, in notes he put on file, stated that due weight had also to be given to the heads of other religious denominations: "In this case [the Mother and Child issue] we are dealing with the considered views of the leaders of the Catholic Church to which

14. This episode is discussed in my book *Twentieth-Century Ireland,* 201–12.

the vast majority of our people belong; their views cannot be ignored." Noel Browne was also prepared to defer to the ruling of the bishops in moral matters. He felt, however, that there was room for an alternative opinion when dealing with social policy. Without the support of a single member of the cabinet, Browne was forced to resign on April 10, 1951.

The political crisis caused by the resignation brought the government down, and de Valera and Fianna Fáil were returned to power in the election of 1951. The new minister for health, James Ryan, took over the implementation of the scheme. He was again confronted by episcopal intransigence. The hierarchy went so far as to issue a letter in April 1953 to all the national papers, with the exception of the Irish *Times*. De Valera confronted his former school friend, Cardinal John D'Alton, and the letter was withdrawn. A strong denunciation of the Ryan scheme, it was couched in somewhat less robust language than the Staunton missive referred to above.[15] Ambassador Joseph Walshe provided an unsolicited commentary on the text being forwarded to him in Rome:

> The declaration is fearfully ill-digested. In no country, not to speak of a Catholic Country, would the Bishops make so many general assumptions about the possibly unchristian and immoral or amoral attitude of State Servants. [. . .] The declaration is so biased, ill-prepared, badly written that it must have been a last minute decision, perhaps taken under pressure from the Doctors Group—and the Bishops put themselves in the position of being protectors of privilege. As I read the position, they owe a lot to the Taoiseach for having taken their heads out of the noose. Had he allowed the situation to develop as it was surely going to develop, helped by Jack Costello's unparalleled bad judgment, their prestige and power would have received a great blow indeed.[16]

The hierarchy had indeed cause on that occasion to be grateful to de Valera. He had prevented a church-state crisis that the bishops would have lost decisively. It was clear that the leadership of the church in the 1950s, notwithstanding the presence of John Charles McQuaid, was very weak. A number of its leaders had excellent negative minds. But besides showing themselves to be out of touch with contemporary developments in Catholic social teaching, they had made a significant error of judgment

15. For text, see John Whyte, *Church and State in Modern Ireland 1923–1979* (Dublin: Gill and Macmillan, 1980), 449–52.

16. Keogh, *Ireland and the Vatican*, 338–39.

by allowing themselves to be manipulated by the medical profession. The late bishop of Ferns, Donal Herlihy, told me: "We allowed ourselves to be used by the doctors, but it won't happen again."[17] With the growth of special interest groups inside and outside the church in the latter part of the twentieth century, the wisdom of Bishop Herlihy's comment has enduring relevance.

The relationship between church and state remained close, particularly as mediated through McQuaid, but his expectations of state action, particularly in relation to the censorship of films and books, were not realizable. His overtures were treated with great respect, but de Valera and his ministers refused to act.

There was one example of both political and popular resistance to McQuaid during the 1950s. Ireland was due to play Yugoslavia in a soccer match in 1955. McQuaid's intervention in 1952 had prevented the game from taking place. But three years later, twenty-two thousand spectators turned out to see the godless Yugoslavs defeat the god-fearing Irish by four goals to one.[18] The former Fianna Fáil minister for defence, Oscar Traynor, officially welcomed the teams. That was in spite of the fact that the Football Association of Ireland had received many calls and letters urging that the match be postponed. However, McQuaid did have influence, and he also had a network of vigilantes who kept him informed on activities in his archdiocese. There is a strongly held belief that the archbishop was involved in the moves that led to the police, in 1957, closing down a production of Tennessee Williams's play *The Rose Tattoo* at the Pike Theatre.[19]

In summary, the Archbishop McQuaid model of church was highly suspicious of the state. Therefore, it was necessary to maximize church influence through the clergy and male and female religious in primary and secondary schooling and within designated colleges of the National University of Ireland. McQuaid forbade Catholics, without his express permission, from attending Trinity College, Dublin. The archbishop preserved a strong hold over the delivery of health care in the clerically run voluntary hospitals, a number of which also provided courses for the ed-

17. Keogh, *Twentieth-Century Ireland,* 213.
18. Ibid., 228.
19. See Gerard Whelan with Carolyn Swift, *Spiked: Church-State Intrigue and the Rose Tattoo* (Dublin: New Island, 2002).

ucation of the nursing profession. He mistrusted the laity and sought to exercise an influence over what was available to be read, over what films might be shown and what plays were put on in the theatre. He did not have absolute power. But he did have great moral authority and an ability to scrutinize different developments in his archdiocese, rooting out dissent and divergence of opinion. A biographer has exaggeratedly subtitled his work *Ruler of Catholic Ireland.*[20] However, he exercised much greater power than any of his immediate predecessors or successors over his archdiocese and over his fellow bishops.

There were three great moments of Catholic mobilization in the 1950s and early 1960s—Holy Year in 1950, Marian Year in 1954, and Patrician Year in 1962. All provided the opportunity to demonstrate the devoutness of people and their commitment to their religion. But did such outward displays of religious devotion reflect a deep popular and personal faith? Or was attendance at Mass, Benediction, novenas, devotions, holy hours, retreats, and pilgrimages an act of subservience in an authoritarian clerically patrolled society? What would happen with the onset of industrialization, urbanization, modernization, and wider social access to education?

Diagnosing the Defects of Irish Catholicism

Bruce Francis Biever S.J., a U.S. sociologist, wrote on this subject in the early 1960s. He argued that there was a lack of intellectual content in Irish Catholicism. Asserting that fear was a prime motive in securing lay obedience and religious practice, his criticism of Irish Catholicism was very severe:

> There is little value or encouragement placed upon freedom of expression. Those who do take the liberty of speaking out on church-related issues are viewed with great suspicion by their peers and the clergy alike, and of course, ultimately in the Irish system they are silenced. We may recall again the general atmosphere of hostility, defensiveness, and fear with which this interviewer was met on more occasions than he would like to enumerate. Why? Because of the inveterate fear that word of their talking to a foreigner might somehow get back to the parish priest. . . . Defenders of Irish Catholicism would say that this is only "reverence for the clergy," but *fear* describes the case far more

20. John Cooney, *John Charles McQuaid: Ruler of Catholic Ireland* (Dublin: O'Brien Press, 1999).

accurately. A single word from the local parish priest can destroy a man's reputation in his community, take away his livelihood, and make him a pariah in his own family.[21]

Biever argued that that clerical invasiveness had "progressively estranged the intellectual class" and that lack of intellectual orientation was coupled with "an emphatic legalism in the church's presentation of doctrine and in the area of morals an almost Jansenistic rigorism." The religion preached from the pulpit was unremittingly negative, with sex and alcohol being "constantly reiterated themes in clerical instruction." He found that the Irish educational system was flawed and clerical domination of the profession was a source of resentment in schools, particularly since clerics dominated the better-paying and high-prestige administrative positions. School facilities were "poor, especially in the rural districts where they are almost pitiable in their inadequacy." Teachers were "overworked, under-paid, and in many cases faced with an almost impossible pedagogical task of attempting to instruct children from the age of seven through fifteen in a single room with a single instructor."[22]

Whatever the defects of the educational system, Biever recognized its centrality to Ireland's religious homogeneity and what Biever called its "apathetic complacency." Only a handful of believers—and these culturally marginalized—grasped the extent to which Irish Catholicism had turned its back on modernity, enshrining authority rather than "reasoned conviction" as the basis of faith. But with a changing social milieu, would authority continue to hold sway? Biever thought not:

> The utter deficiency of this pattern of educational training in matters of faith has been underscored by the utter liability for the Irish Catholic, once removed from this native hothouse atmosphere, to cope with intellectual challenges to the faith, as the plight of the Catholic Irish emigrants to England bear irrefutable testimony.

Biever did not necessarily see an imminent crisis—the critics with whom he obviously sympathized were still marginalized at the time of his research. He believed, nonetheless, that these critics would eventually triumph, simply because social conditions in Ireland were changing so rapidly.

21. Bruce Francis Biever, *Religion, Culture and Values: A Cross-Cultural Analysis of Motivational Factors in Native Irish and American Irish Catholicism* (New York: Arno Press, 1976), 499.
22. Ibid., 499–501, 511.

We have indicated our own hypothesis that the power struggle (if it can be glorified by such a title) in Irish Catholicism is not found between clergy and laity, but between clergy and the traditionally oriented laity against the intellectual "new breed." In our considered opinion they represent the greatest challenge which traditional Irish Catholicism will have to face in the next decade.[23]

Biever's thesis was submitted to the University of Pennsylvania in 1965 and published in 1976. Did his critique have any impact on episcopal policy in the 1960s? I have found no such evidence. The U.S. sociologist diagnosed what many Irish critics from the 1920s to the 1950s had described in their writings, short stories, novels, and poetry. Clergy and religious had also pointed out the defects of a Catholicism built upon devotionalism, anti-intellectualism, authoritarianism, and fear.

The 1960s, the Second Vatican Council, and the Modernization of Irish Society

Despite the economic gloom and the cultural bleakness of the 1950s, the Irish Catholic Church was not synonymous with Archbishop John Charles McQuaid. There were reformists amongst the clergy and laity. Many members of the clergy were not authoritarian and certainly not anti-intellectual. For example, *The Furrow*, founded in 1950, had an inspired and liberal editor in Canon Cecil McGarry. It had a wide clerical and lay audience. Its name was borrowed from a journal once published in France before it ran into difficulties with authority. It provided a very lively analysis of the nature of religious practice, the deficiencies of Irish society, and the need for change within the Church itself. In contrast, the long-established Irish *Ecclesiastical Record*—also published from St. Patrick's College, Maynooth—retained a more staid and conservative approach. The *Irish Theological Quarterly*, revived in 1951 after an absence of nearly thirty years, evolved in its editorial policy, highlighting new trends in modern theology.

In the mid-1950s, Father Austin Flannery became the editor of the Irish Dominicans' publication *Doctrine and Life*. The order had previously published the *Irish Rosary*, a journal with a strongly intemperate and in-

23. Ibid., 511, 515.

tolerant tone. Father Flannery played a progressive role in Irish Catholic life. He personally translated the documents of the Second Vatican Council and made them available in an accessible format. His review became a debating ground for central themes of the Vatican Council. Father Flannery himself played a prominent role in dialoguing with dissident and disaffected Catholics. He commanded great respect in many sectors of Irish society and was highly regarded amongst those on the political Left who had broken ranks with the Catholic Church.

The Irish Jesuits published a devotional magazine, *Sacred Heart Messenger.* This enjoyed a very wide circulation in the 1950s and 1960s. But a question mark hangs over the extent to which it was read in the homes to which it was delivered. The Jesuits also published *Studies,* a quarterly in existence since 1912. It followed a cautious editorial line but in the 1960s opened its pages to many progressive Catholic writers such as a former Jesuit student and future foreign minister and taoiseach, Dr. Garret FitzGerald.[24]

Those journals listed above reflected a desire for radical change in the Catholic Church and a shift away from devotionalism, anti-intellectualism, and authoritarianism. At the beginning of the 1960s, that desire for change was reinforced by the creative political leadership of Seán Lemass. He took over from Eamon de Valera in 1959 and held the position of taoiseach until 1966. Although both men were veterans of the 1916 Rising, Lemass was considerably younger than his predecessor. He was just over sixty and of a very radical bent of mind. Having implemented since 1932 Fianna Fáil's sacred doctrine of protectionism, Lemass switched to favor a policy of free trade and to advocate Irish membership in the Common Market as soon as possible. In 1963 General Charles de Gaulle's veto of British entry also thwarted Ireland's plans to enter the EEC. Dublin suffered another rebuff in 1967. In preparation for eventual membership, the Irish economy was opened up to external investment and to trade liberalization. The results produced economic growth and newfound pros-

---

24. There was also a range of popular Catholic magazines that focused on the life of the Church and the missions. *The Word,* published by the Divine Word Missionaries, was an example of high-quality journalism. Other magazines in the same category were contemporary with the *Word* or emerged later: *Africa, African Missionary, The Far East, Medical Missionary of Mary, Oblate Missionary Record,* and *Lourdes Messenger.* Each, its own way, prepared the way for more openness in the Catholic Church in Ireland in the 1960s or later.

perity. Many immigrants returned home to take up jobs in the building trade and in the new factories set up by U.S. and continental multinationals. Increased industrialization exacerbated the flight from the land. Many people moved to the cities and, in particular, to Dublin. Educational reform in the 1960s resulted in the introduction of free secondary school education. This decision revolutionized access to education for the poorer socioeconomic groups and meant that many who might have left school for the workplace or the emigrant ship at the age of fourteen were in a position to complete their studies at eighteen. That, in turn, increased the demand for access to university. Educational expectations rose, and by the late 1960s the country was on the road to mass third-level education.

Meanwhile, the content of secondary education also changed as the country sought to produce a diversity of new economic, entrepreneurial, and technical skills necessary to supply the new industries with a well-prepared labor force. That educational revolution took place against a backdrop of a new openness in Irish society and greater sense of personal freedom. The relaxation of book and film censorship placed new responsibilities on the individual citizen. The establishment of a National Television Station (RTÉ) in 1962 reinforced the trend to question authority in church and in state. The migration to the cities weakened the authority of the rural clergy. The church in urban areas was never in a position to exercise the same authority over a laity living in very large parishes in the suburbs or in inner-city flat-land. Young people working in Dublin often lived between two worlds. At weekends, they returned home to the countryside to socialize. However, the increase in the number of motor cars meant that young people could travel to dances outside their parishes— dances now more frequently run by new lay entrepreneurs rather than by the parish priest. In Ireland, the 1960s also witnessed the beginnings of mass travel for leisure to Mediterranean resorts outside the jurisdiction of parental or priestly control.[25]

It is in the context of an improving economy and a greater sense of optimism and hope in the country that the impact of the Second Vatican Council has to be evaluated. Without wishing to romanticize the 1960s,

25. A similar thesis has been put forward by the University College Dublin political scientist Prof. Tom Garvin in *Preventing the Future;* see my review of that work in the *Irish Times,* 11 September 2004.

the Irish Church in that decade was partially characterized by a growing openness and by a willingness to change. This was not uniformly the case, and I do not wish to present a unilinear view of the history of the decade. But the Second Vatican Council had obliged all—conservatives and liberals alike—to confront the issue of change. However, having to shift from a majoritarian mindset to a concept of church in a pluralist society was a quantum leap for those raised and formed within the traditional model of the Irish Church. The ideas of Vatican Two on religious freedom were subversive of clericalism, juridicalism, and triumphalism. This work on religious freedom had been carried forward in Ireland by a new generation of theologians, who had learned their theology in the United States, where Catholics are a minority religious grouping.[26]

The elderly archbishop of Dublin, John Charles McQuaid, clung to old ways, and his concept of church was to prove much more enduring and resilient than his numerous critics in the 1960s anticipated. Returning from the Vatican Council, Archbishop McQuaid reassured his flock gathered in the procathedral in 1965: "One could not but feel that the Holy Spirit had guided our deliberations." To those who might have been worried, he said: "Allow me to reassure you. No change will worry the tranquillity of your Christian lives."[27] Rooted in the majoritarian mentality, Ireland was perceived as being a Catholic country, and this was reflected in her laws—an accommodation reached by the Church with successive Irish governments. The dominant position of the Church in Irish society could be preserved only, according to the above school of thought, if the practice of the politics of informal consensus were continued. Church/state relations were a zero-sum game. There could be no concessions, as the state could not be trusted.

In the first half of the 1960s, the Catholic Church underwent a renaissance in the numbers entering seminaries and religious orders. It was a period of great optimism about the future of the Irish Church, which had again proved itself to be the exception in Western Europe. The 1961 census showed Ireland to be 94.9 percent Catholic. In the early 1960s, Professor John Whyte believed that "a practice rate of 90% is plausible for

26. For a good overview of American Catholicism, see Jay Dolan, *The American Catholic Experience* (New York: Image Books , 1985).
27. Keogh, *Twentieth-Century Ireland,* 262.

Ireland."[28] In Northern Ireland, the 1961 census put the number of Catholics in the state at 34.9 percent. A survey in 1968 found that 95 percent of Catholics claimed to go to church at least once a week. Whyte is inclined to round that figure down to about 90 percent—the same as in the Republic of Ireland.[29] Mass attendance in other "Catholic" countries on the continent was much lower. In Austria, Whyte estimated that, at its highest, about 40 percent attended Mass weekly. In Belgium, he gave the figure of 50 percent; in France, he accepted the figure of about 25–26 percent; in Italy, Whyte put the practice rate at around 45 percent; in West Germany and Australia, about 50 percent; in New Zealand, about 60 percent; and 65 percent in the United States and in English-speaking Canada. The figure for Quebec, Whyte stated, was 85 percent.[30]

The "healthiness" of the Irish situation cautioned men such as Archbishop McQuaid to hold the ship on a steady conservative course. However, confronted by the defensiveness of the previous decade, a large section of the Irish Catholic Church began to lay down a challenge to its conservative wing or wings. While there were forces within the Church that opposed change and fought a strong rearguard action, it appeared that new forces were liberating the institution from the vestiges of the old siege mentality. The Church reformers were greatly supported and buoyed by the teachings of Vatican II.

The government of Seán Lemass was anxious to address a number of the unresolved constitutional problems that affected the principle of parity of esteem between churches in the eyes of the state. His all-party committee on the constitution reported in the mid-1960s and tackled a number of the thorny issues that still confronted Irish society in the mid-1990s. The report recommended a change in Article 3 of the constitution to read: "The Irish nation hereby proclaims its firm will that its territory be re-united in harmony and brotherly affection between all Irishmen." On divorce, the committee felt that it could be argued that Article 41.3, which stated that "no law shall be enacted providing for the grant of a dissolution of marriage," was "coercive" and "unnecessarily harsh and rigid and could, in our view, be regarded as being at variance with the accepted

---

28. John Whyte, *Catholics in Western Democracies* (Dublin: Gill and Macmillan, 1981), 142.

29. Ibid., 143.   30. Ibid., 138ff.

principles of religious liberty as declared at the Vatican Council and else-where." On Article 44, it was felt that the decisions of the Vatican Coun-cil also had a direct impact:

> It is clearly to be inferred from these documents, and the comments made on them by competent persons, that the Catholic church does not seek any special recognition or privilege as compared with other religions and that her primary interest is to see that all citizens enjoy equal freedom in the practice of their religion whatever it may be.

That formula reflected the growing parity of esteem in the 1960s between the different churches.

Cardinal William Conway, who was appointed archbishop of Armagh in September 1963, stated in a speech in 1966 that the state should allow the maximum of freedom that was compatible with the common good. It was a carefully worded speech. But it might be read as an indirect apology for the hierarchy's stance in the Mother and Child crisis. Speaking about the expanded role of the state, he said: "I think it is true to say that peo-ple understand this problem more clearly now than they did 20 years ago, and that some of the fears which were widely held at that time now ap-pear to have been exaggerated." Conway said in September 1969, "I per-sonally would not shed a tear if the relevant sub-section of Article 44 were to disappear." A month later, a meeting of the hierarchy in Maynooth en-dorsed the cardinal's statement as representing the bishops' view.

Article 44 was amended by referendum in 1972, and the "the special position" clause was gone from the constitution. This was done in the context of the growing violence in Northern Ireland and motivated by the need to better relations between the different religious traditions on the island. Thus ended the debate that had first begun in 1937 between de Valera and John Charles McQuaid. The latter, too, was gone by the end of 1971. He had offered his resignation at 75 and Pope Paul VI had ac-cepted it.

Despite the strong conservatism of the Irish bishops, there was a strong willingness to implement many council ideas. Episcopal Commissions were established to involve the laity, including Justice and Peace, Laity, Emigra-tion, and the Liturgy. The Catholic agency CURA was set up to provide help and counseling for women with unplanned pregnancies. Trocaire, meaning "mercy" in Irish, gave expression to much social idealism in the country. Popular goodwill toward the problems of the Third World was expressed in the generous donations to the annual Trocaire Lenten collection. That money was used to support development projects abroad. The bishop of Kerry (1969–1976) and later of Galway (1976–1992), Eamon Casey, played a very important role in the building of Trocaire in the 1970s and 1980s. He had been a curate in two inner-city Limerick parishes between 1951 and 1960 before he went to Slough, England, where he became director of the Catholic Housing Aid Society and head of the British Council of Churches' Housing Trust. Casey was also a founder of Shelter National Campaign for the Homeless. His work in Britain on behalf of the homeless and of poor emigrants was significant. When he returned to Ireland, he brought that reforming zeal with him.

The Irish Church geared up to work in the modern world. The Catholic Communications Institute of Ireland was established together with the Catholic Press and Information Office. Radharc, an initiative endorsed by John Charles McQuaid, was staffed by priests trained in filmmaking. The priest filmmakers were Joe Dunn, Tom Stack, Dermod McCarthy, Peter Lemass, and Billy Fitzgerald. They examined issues of great social sensitivity in films entitled: *The Young Offender, Honesty at the Fair, Smuggling, Down and Out in Dublin,* and *The Boat Train to Euston.* Many of these programs gave insights into the inequalities in Irish society and the urgent need for reform.[31]

In the Catholic print media, *Studies, The Furrow, Doctrine and Life, Herder Correspondence, Reality,* and *The Word* had opened up their pages to debate on church reform, the liturgical renewal, and the changing place of religion in Irish society. Lay Catholic voices in the 1960s were strong in their support for the social change that many of the Radharc films implied was necessary. A young economist, Dr. Garret FitzGerald, also employed his pen to argue in favor of church reform and social change.[32] He wrote in *Studies* in 1964:

> If we can successfully graft these liberal and socialist ideas, themselves largely Christian in their origin and inspiration, on to the particular form in which the Christian tradition displays itself in our country in this generation, we may succeed in developing an internally consistent philosophy of our own,

31. See Joseph Dunn, *No Tigers in Africa: Recollections and Reflections on 25 Years of Radharc* (Dublin: Columba Press, 1986).

32. Keogh, *Twentieth-Century Ireland,* 285; see also Garret FitzGerald, *All in a Life: An Autobiography* (Dublin: Gill and Macmillan, 1991), 63–111.

appropriate to the needs of the time in which we live, and clearly superior to the excessive conservatism sometimes found in Catholic attitudes, as well as to the wishy-washy liberalism common in Britain, and the doctrinaire socialism of other countries.[33]

FitzGerald, who later entered Irish politics and became minister for foreign affairs (1973–1977) and taoiseach (twice in the 1980s), was searching for a way to modernize the Irish Church in concert with the modernization of Irish society. There was a radical, reforming voice—clerical and lay—in the Irish Church.

When voices of protest were raised by church people about the lack of public housing in the capital, they felt the brunt of public criticism from a number of politicians. Father Austin Flannery, then editor of *Doctrine and Life,* was also the producer of a successful television program, *Outlook.* When the Jesuit Michael Sweetman shared a TV studio with the leader of the Irish Communist Party, Michael O'Riordan, to discuss the housing crisis, Flannery was called a "gullible priest" by Charles Haughey. The minister for local government, Kevin Boland, called him a "so-called cleric." In response, Flannery said that his only intention as a Christian and as a priest was to speak on behalf of people who were in need. He was not alone in that task. Members of the Catholic Church—lay and clerical—contributed to the growth of a radical social critique of Irish society in that decade.

The appointment of Professor Dermot Ryan as archbishop of Dublin to succeed John Charles McQuaid reinforced the perception that a "progressive" had been appointed to what is the most important archbishopric on the island. Ryan was a biblical scholar at University College Dublin and a person likely to be sympathetic to those who sought significant change in the structures of the Church and in the relationship between church and state. Ryan was a friend and former colleague of Dr. Garret FitzGerald, who became minister for foreign affairs in a Labour/Fine Gael coalition government that came to power in 1973 and was defeated in 1977.

Ireland had joined the European Economic Community (EEC) in 1972, giving hope of a rapid upturn in the national economy and in agriculture. Membership did not disappoint, and there were major cash trans-

---

33. Keogh, *Twentieth-Century Ireland,* 285; see also FitzGerald, *All in a Life,* 65.

fers to Ireland in the form of infrastructural grants and subsidies to farmers. However, the international oil crisis of the mid-1970s dealt a severe
blow to European, and to Irish, expectations for rapid prosperity.

The conflict in Northern Ireland, having erupted in 1968–1969,
reached levels of unprecedented violence by the early 1970s. The clash of
ideologies in the North, very often fuelled by sectarianism, presented a
great challenge to the leaders of the Catholic Church and other churches. It also set down a challenge for the government in Dublin. The conflict between Catholics and Protestants in Northern Ireland was part of
the motivation behind the holding of a referendum in December 1972,
amending Article 44 of the constitution. For the taoiseach, Jack Lynch,
that move was directed toward building a bridge between the divided religious communities north and south of the border. The violence in the
North challenged southern politicians to work toward a peaceful solution
to the problems on the island. That required, according to FitzGerald, the
need to change Irish laws and the constitution to make southern society
more inclusive. The focus of the coalition government was on the need to
change the laws preventing the sale of contraceptives in the state. Thinking of that kind sought to disconnect the law of the state from Catholic
moral teaching. On November 26, 1973, the Catholic hierarchy issued a
joint statement on church and state. It reaffirmed the teaching that the
use of artificial contraception was morally wrong, adding:

> It does not follow, of course, that the state is bound to prohibit the impor-
> tation and sale of contraceptives. There are many things which the Catholic
> Church holds to be morally wrong and no one has ever suggested, least of all
> the Church herself that they should be prohibited by the State.

Archbishop Ryan was placed at the heart of that potential conflict between church and state. He was the leader of the Catholic Church in the
South. Commenting on the period, Professor John Whyte said:

> By the standards of advanced industrial societies, Ireland in the seventies re-
> mained a conservative country. Abortion and divorce were prohibited; laws
> against contraception, although increasingly a dead letter, remained on the
> statute book. Education remained preponderantly in the control of the
> Churches. Almost the whole active population continued to go to church on
> Sundays. But traditional standards were being increasingly questioned.[34]

---

34. Whyte, *Church and State in Modern Ireland,* 386.

Contraception was an issue of growing importance at the time. Archbishop Ryan strongly asserted the teaching of the Catholic Church on the matter. This view was at variance with that of his Catholic friend and government minister, Dr. Garret FitzGerald. He was a legislator. A private members' bill on contraception had failed in the Senate. However, in 1974, the coalition government published a Contraception Bill as it was obliged to do in response to a court ruling.[35] In 1975, the bishops published the joint pastoral: "Human Life Is Sacred." It reaffirmed Catholic teaching on the question at issue. The pressure on members of the Irish legislature was intense. The taoiseach, Liam Cosgrave, together with six Fine Gael members of Parliament, voted on July 16, 1975, against the bill and stopped its passage through the Dáil.

The minister for foreign affairs, Dr. Garret FitzGerald, and the taoiseach, Liam Cosgrave, represented two very different philosophies regarding morality and the law. FitzGerald was convinced of the need to separate church and state in Ireland. His ideas were colored by his desire to seek reconciliation between the two parts of the island and bring Southern Ireland more into line with a society based on ideas of religious pluralism and respect for all secular and religious minorities. His family background also influenced his stance. His mother was a northern Presbyterian and his father a southern Catholic. FitzGerald took the opportunity to unveil his ideas to the secretary of state, Cardinal Agostino Casaroli, at one particular meeting. His plans to separate church and state in Ireland were not warmly received by the Holy See.[36]

---

35. This was made necessary by the ruling in the case taken by Mrs. Mary McGee. Customs had seized the contraceptives she was importing for her own personal use. The judge ruled in December 1973 that the ban on the importation of contraceptives under the 1935 Criminal Law Amendment Act was unconstitutional.

36. This interpretation is supported by certain passages in Dr. Garret FitzGerald's memoirs. When Dr. FitzGerald was minister for foreign affairs, he met the papal secretary of state, Cardinal Agostino Casaroli, in Helsinki in 1973. He explained in an informal meeting the concern of the Irish government to establish good relations with unionists as well as nationalists in Northern Ireland. He mentioned the areas of mixed marriages and integrated education as being most problematical. Returning home, FitzGerald prepared a memorandum that he had agreed he would send to Casaroli. He sent it first to the taoiseach, Liam Cosgrave, whose views, according to Dr. FitzGerald's memoirs, "on these issues I knew to be much more conservative than mine." There were no negative comments from the taoiseach. Before finalizing and sending the document, Dr. FitzGerald incorporated comments sent to Iveagh House by the Irish ambassador to the Holy See. FitzGerald had also spoken about

On a visit to Strabourg in February 1977, FitzGerald was encouraged by Archbishop Benelli (later cardinal archbishop of Florence)[37] to see Pope Paul VI about Northern Ireland. FitzGerald had an audience with the pope at the end of March, where he hoped to lay out his ideas on the separation of church and state in Ireland. The pope read a text in French, which lasted for about six minutes.

> The theme was uncompromising. Ireland was a Catholic country—perhaps the only one left. It should stay that way. Laws should not be changed in a way that would make it less Catholic. . . . [Dr FitzGerald then spoke about the tragedy in Northern Ireland to which the Irish state was trying to respond in a Christian way.] Before I could go any further he intervened. He knew how tragic the situation was there, he said, but it could not be a reason to change any of the laws that kept us a Catholic state. At that I more or less gave up. I left the audience somewhat shell-shocked.[38]

Rome, through the papal nuncio, probably alerted the Irish hierarchy to the dangers of such a strategy. Monsignor Gaetano Alibrandi was papal nuncio to Ireland between 1969 and 1989. He played a central and assertive role in the appointment of bishops to almost all the dioceses during those twenty years. Many of the choices were not popular with the cler-

the matter to the nuncio, Archbishop Gaetano Alibrandi, who had advised Rome that unity would not come soon.

When FitzGerald met Casaroli in Rome some weeks later (the memorandum had been sent on August 14, 1973), the latter said that certain points relating to doctrinal questions had been sent to the Sacred Congregation for the Doctrine of the Faith for comment. Casaroli inquired that since the proposed changes would not bring about unity, "should we be upsetting people in our state by making such changes now?" FitzGerald agreed that unity would not be achieved "soon." However, he stressed the need for an interim stage of reform, which might help shift unionist opinion in order to bring about a majority in Northern Ireland in favor of unity. The legalization of contraception was raised. FitzGerald also spoke about integrated education and laid great stress on the need for a change in Church law regarding mixed marriages, where the Catholic partner had to promise orally to do his or her best to have the children brought up as Catholics.

Casaroli "kicked for touch at this point," according to FitzGerald, and he added: "Casaroli did, however, go so far as to say that he was now of the opinion, having heard my case, that the Nuncio had given him the wrong slant; his—Casaroli's—comprehension of the complexities of the problem had been changed by our discussion. I wondered—not for the last time—just what the Nuncio had said to him." See FitzGerald, *All in a Life*, 184–85.

37. Benelli, who held the position of prime minister—according to FitzGerald's description—at the Vatican, had served in Ireland in the early 1950s. While he was serving at the Vatican, two Irish Medical Missionaries of Mary from Drogheda had served as his administrative assistants. They both continued to work with him in Florence until his death.

38. FitzGerald, *All in a Life*, 186.

gy of the respective dioceses. There was a general view that the best candidates had not been selected. By the end of the 1980s, the Irish bench of bishops was particularly weak, according to Father Joe Dunn, who wrote a book entitled *No Lions in the Hierarchy.*[39] There was a sense that a number of those appointed were simply not up to the job. There was a concern that most of the appointees shared a very defensive approach to matters of church and state.

There was at least one exception to that view. Cardinal William Conway died in 1977 and was replaced as archbishop of Armagh by a professor of history from St. Patrick's College, Maynooth, Tomás Ó Fiaich. An Irish language enthusiast and a strong nationalist, he offered a different and more populist style of leadership to the Catholic Church in both parts of Ireland. His archdiocese straddled the border and was in the two political jurisdictions. As a northerner, paradoxically, he appeared to be far less fearful than his southern episcopal counterparts of the influence of the state on the pastoral and institutional life of the Catholic Church. His attitude toward church-state relations south of the border was quite relaxed.

Fianna Fáil swept in to power in 1977 with Jack Lynch back as taoiseach. He appointed his strong political opponent Charles Haughey to the portfolio of health. The latter had to confront the question of introducing legislation governing the sale of contraception. Haughey successfully brought in the Health (Family Planning) Act of 1978. He consulted widely with members of the different churches, including the Catholic Church. Barry Desmond, a future minister for health in the Fine Gael/Labour coalition of 1982–1987, had access to the files. In his memoirs, he recounts what happened. The bishop of Kerry, Kevin McNamara (future archbishop of Dublin) led the delegation that also included Cahal Daly (future cardinal archbishop of Armagh, 1990–1996). Daly, according to Desmond, argued the case on social rather than on theological grounds. He is quoted as being totally against making contraceptives available to single people.[40] The Health (Family Planning) Act came into force in 1979. What the act did was to provide for contraception, including condoms, to be made available on prescription for medical reasons or for "bona fide"

39. Joseph Dunn, *No Lions in the Hierarchy: An Anthology of Sorts* (Dublin: Columba Press, 1994).

40. Barry Desmond, *Finally and in Conclusion: A Political Memoir* (Dublin: New Island, 2000), 233–35.

family planning purposes. Such legislation was part of a liberal agenda that would radically change Irish society for the worse, bishops and many clergy argued. But there were others among the clergy, religious, and laity who felt that, to use a popular phrase, it was time that the "the bishops were no longer in the bedrooms of the nation."

In the midst of the debate on contraception and the liberal agenda, Pope John Paul II visited Ireland in autumn 1979. In studying the Irish file, he would have read his predecessor's words to Dr. FitzGerald in 1977 that the tragic situation in Northern Ireland was not a reason to change any of the laws "that kept us a Catholic state." That visit intersects the period under review. On the occasion of the papal visit, more than 1.2 million people attended Mass celebrated by the Holy Father in Phoenix Park, Dublin. The occasion had echoes of the Eucharistic Congress of 1932, when over one million people heard Mass celebrated by the papal legate, Cardinal Lorenzo Lauri, in the same venue. Wherever the Pope traveled in Ireland, he brought out the crowds. At the Marian shrine in Knock, County Mayo, there were almost as many as the 300,000 that had greeted him in Galway. There were 40,000 to greet the Pope at the monastic ruins of Clonmacnoise, and 60,000 at the national seminary of St. Patrick's, Maynooth. Over 300,000 assembled at Limerick race course to hear the pope preach and celebrate Mass before his departure to the United States. Those figures do not include the thousands who thronged the streets of Dublin and other cities to see the papal motorcade. The visit was a major pastoral success. It was also a significant national occasion, and church and state cooperated closely to ensure the visit was accorded all due ecclesiastical and official ceremony.[41]

It had been part of the original papal plan to include a visit to Northern Ireland. The grounds of St. Patrick's, Armagh, had been chosen as the venue for an open-air ecumenical service of reconciliation. The attendance would have included many of the people maimed by bomb blasts and victims of the violence. However, his trip to Northern Ireland had to be canceled due to the volatile security situation that followed the killing on

41. I was working for the visit as a journalist with RTÉ, the national radio and television station. As the religious affairs correspondent was on holidays, it fell to me to do much of the daily reporting for TV and radio on the pope's trip to Ireland. Two weeks before the visit, I was part of a team sent to Rome to provide daily news reports for the main evening news. They ran the week before the pope arrived.

August 27, 1979, of eighteen British soldiers near Warrenpoint, County Down. On the same day, Dowager Lady Brabourne, Lord Mountbatten of Burma, his fourteen-year-old nephew, and a fourteen-old crew member were blown up by an Irish Republican Army (IRA) bomb in their boat off Mullaghmore, County Sligo. On security advice, the Holy See reluctantly agreed to cancel the papal trip north of the border.[42]

However, the pope did visit the Archdiocese of Armagh, which is on both sides of the border. He delivered a forceful speech to a large congregation near Drogheda on the violence in Northern Ireland. Ever conscious of conflicting philosophies in Ireland on issues such as contraception and divorce, he told a congregation in Limerick shortly before his departure to the United States:

> It is true that the stability and the sanctity of marriage are being threatened by new ideas and by the aspirations of some. Divorce, for whatever reason it is introduced, inevitably becomes easier and easier to obtain and it gradually comes to be accepted as a normal part of life. The very possibility of divorce in the sphere of civil law makes stable and permanent marriages more difficult for everyone. [. . .] And so I say to all, have an absolute and holy respect for the sacredness of human life from the first moment of its conception. Abortion, as the Vatican Council stated, is one of the "abominable crimes."[43]

The Catholic hierarchy quoted a passage from that sermon in their statement prior to the coming into force of the Health (Family Planning) Act at the end of 1979:

> Dear fathers and mothers of Ireland, believe in your vocation, that beautiful vocation of marriage and parenthood which God has given to you. Believe that God is with you—for all parenthood in heaven and on earth takes its name from Him.[44]

Reviewing the visit from the perspective of the early twenty-first century, there are those who look nostalgically to those days of fervor and devotion in 1979. The papal visit is viewed as a high watermark of a particular kind of Catholic devotionalism—a world that has been lost. But there is another point of view. The papal visit represented a final phase for

42. This information was given to me by an Irish bishop. I was given further confirmation of the intended visit to Northern Ireland by the pope at the Vatican in August 1979.

43. *The Visit—John Paul II in Ireland—A Historical Record* (Dublin: Veritas, 1979), 87–88.

44. Text of statement from the Irish Catholic Hierarchy on the Health (Family Planning) Act 1979.

a form of Catholicism that had been radically challenged in the previous two decades by the forces of modernization and secularization. Few, however, could foresee in 1979 the succession of crises to be experienced by the Catholic Church in Ireland—crises that were all the more damaging because of the growing levels of lay alienation and frustration with the institutional Church and the repeated failures of its leadership.

The papal visit in autumn 1979 almost coincided with a change of leadership in Fianna Fáil. Lynch retired without warning. Charles Haughey, the pioneer of the family planning legislation, replaced him as party leader and taoiseach. Dr. Garret FitzGerald had become the leader of Fine Gael in 1977. He was also leader of the opposition and the politician most likely to become taoiseach in the event of a change of government. The philosophical differences between FitzGerald and Archbishop Ryan placed a strain on their long-standing friendship. Nevertheless, the opportunity existed for dialogue and for the establishment of new mechanisms for consultation between church and state. FitzGerald was a devout Catholic, and both he and his wife, Joan, were known to be keen lay theologians whose household was often the center of vigorous debate on issues of church and state. However, FitzGerald was mistrusted by many of the bishops. The fact that the coalition government in 1977 was alleged to have objected to the appointment of Tomás Ó Fiaich to Armagh may not have helped relations in that quarter. Haughey, a bon viveur and man about town, had lost credibility in episcopal circles over his stance on contraception. But he was a pragmatist and probably, on balance, was preferred to FitzGerald.

It is difficult to make any link based on archival evidence between the papal visit and the emergence in Ireland in the early 1980s of strongly organized lobbies against abortion. The political uncertainty of those early years in the decade and the swift changes in government did create a climate of unease. It was a fertile environment in which different lobbies might work. Changes in Ireland were influenced by wider developments within the international church. This movement must be set in the context of the growing phenomenon of neoconservatism that was manifest, in particular, in the United States, in Latin America, and in Britain. Professor Enda McDonagh has commented:

> There have been religious fundamentalists in Ireland. . . . Separated from political causes, they have not been so threatening. The present rise of funda-

mentalism in the wider world and the movement toward more closed and conservative views among many church leaders, Protestant, Catholic, and Orthodox, might make our situation more serious.[45]

Ireland was atypical in Europe. The process of modernization had not resulted in rapid secularization if attendance at Mass was a reliable barometer. A survey conducted in 1974 found that Sunday Mass attendance was 91 percent. A 1984 survey reported that the figure had dropped to 87 percent. In the late 1990s, the figure was an estimated 60–62 percent. However, such national statistics may have been misleading as they did not reflect the practice among differing socioeconomic groups.

Between 1980 and 1983, the country experienced unprecedented volatility in national politics. Dr. Garret FitzGerald led a short-lived Fine Gael/Labour coalition in 1980. Charles Haughey returned to head an even more short-lived Fianna Fáil government in 1982. It was a very ugly time in Irish politics and a very difficult period in Anglo-Irish relations. The violence in Northern Ireland spiraled downward. Hunger strikes, the Falklands war, turmoil in Anglo-Irish relations, and the weak state of the economy made 1982 a very difficult year to be in government.

Dr. FitzGerald brought a Labour/Fine Gael coalition back into power in November 1982, and it remained in office until 1987.

The issues of abortion and divorce dominated church-state relations in the first half of the 1980s. It is very difficult to analyze at this point the reasons for the emergence of the Society for the Protection of Unborn Children (SPUC) and the launching of the Pro-Life Amendment Campaign (PLAC).[46] The laity led that organization. It appeared to be quite well funded, and it had strong clerical backing.

The years 1980–1983 revealed a strong level of alienation on the part of a large group within the state. Dr. Garret FitzGerald had announced as taoiseach in September 1981 a "crusade" to change the confessional and nationalist aspects of the Irish constitution.[47] The announcement took

---

45. Enda McDonagh, "New Forces for Positive Change in Ireland," in Dermot Keogh and Michael Haltzel, eds., *Northern Ireland and the Politics of Reconciliation* (Cambridge, UK: Cambridge University Press, 1993), 148.

46. See Tom Hesketh, *The Second Partitioning of Ireland: The Abortion Referendum of 1983* (Dun Laoghaire, Dublin: Brandsma Books, 1990).

47. Richard Sinnott, *Irish Voters Decide: Voting Behaviour in Elections and Referendums since 1918* (Manchester, UK: Manchester University Press, 1995), 226–27.

many people by surprise, even many of those who were sympathetic to his line of argument. The use of the term "crusade" was singularly ill-judged. A crusade for pluralism might be said to be a contradiction in terms. Both SPUC and PLAC found further justification to mistrust the state and therefore intensified their efforts to campaign to amend the constitution to include an explicit prohibition on abortion.[48] As taoiseach in 1983, Dr. FitzGerald accepted the wording of an amendment drafted by the outgoing government. Many well-informed citizens, not seeing the necessity for this constitutional amendment, worried about the looseness and ambiguity of the wording, which read:

> The state acknowledges the right to life of the unborn and, with due regard to the equal right to life of the mother, guarantees in its laws to respect, and as far as practicable, by its laws to defend and vindicate that right.[49]

How was the amendment drafted, and who drafted it? These questions are worthy of scholarly investigation, as is the question of why it was considered necessary during the referendum on the Maastricht Treaty in 1992 to add a protocol on abortion to that document.[50] Despite the best professional advice available to the government of the day from the attorney general, Peter Sutherland, the wording was put to the people following a campaign that reached levels of unedifying acrimony, probably not witnessed in the country since the post-treaty campaigning by rival sides in the run-up to the 1922 general election.[51] The amendment was approved in the referendum by a two-to-one majority in a turnout of 53.7 percent.[52]

The 1980s was the most difficult decade for church-state relations since the foundation of the state itself. When the Catholic Church delegation appeared before an oral hearing of the New Ireland Forum on February 9, 1984, the members had an opportunity to outline the thinking of the Catholic Church in the context of a debate on religious pluralism in the

48. See Emily O'Reilly, *Masterminds of the Right* (Dublin: Attic Press, 1988).

49. Sinnott, *Irish Voters Decide*, 227.

50. I have been informed, on good authority, that a draft of that protocol in 1992 included a reference to the constitutional ban on divorce. This was removed from the final draft after a determined intervention by senior civil servants.

51. According to oral sources, the attorney general, Peter Sutherland, is believed to have written a memorandum to government of over 100 pages outlining his negative observations on the wording.

52. Joe Lee, "Dynamics of Change in the Irish Republic," in Keogh and Haltzel, *Northern Ireland and the Politics of Reconciliation*, 124.

Irish context. A written submission had been received from the hierarchy in January 1984. It consisted of five papers, covering ecumenism; the family; pluralism; alienation of Catholics in Northern Ireland; and the Catholic school system in Northern Ireland. The document had a comprehensive introduction by Cardinal Ó Fiaich. But no attempt had been made to provide a synthesis of the position of the Catholic Church.[53] The hierarchy did not consult members of the laity. The document lacked gravitas, focus, and coherence. The paper on pluralism contained the following interesting passage on "the views of the majority":

> To require in the name of pluralism that public policy tolerate or even facilitate forms of public morality of which the majority of the citizens could not approve may sometimes be reasonable in the interests of the common good of harmony between all the citizens; but where the offence to the moral principles of the majority of the citizens would be disproportionately serious it is not unreasonable to require sacrifice of minorities in the interests of the common good. Britain, for example, does not allow polygamy even though certain of its citizens accept it from their religious convictions.[54]

A Catholic Church delegation, made up of bishops, senior clergy, and laypeople, appeared at a public session of the forum on February 9, 1984. Their performance, although somewhat uneven, was much more convincing than the written submission. To the discerning eye, too, there was a diversity of approach in the group. The bishop of Down and Connor, Cahal Daly, told the forum:

> The Catholic Church in Ireland totally rejects the concept of a confessional state. We have not sought and we do not seek a Catholic State for a Catholic people. We believe that the alliance of Church and State is harmful for the Church and harmful for the State. We rejoiced when that ambiguous formula regarding the special position of the Catholic Church was struck out of the Constitution by the electorate of the Republic. The Catholic Church in Ireland has no power and seeks no power except the power of the gospel it preaches and the consciences and convictions of those who freely accept that teaching. The Catholic Church seeks only the freedom to proclaim the gospel. It proclaims the same doctrinal and moral message under whatever constitutional or political regime operates in this island. The Catholic Church has always carried on its mission on the basis of a Thirty-two County Ireland. . . . So far as the Catholic church and questions of public morality are

53. *Submission to the New Ireland Forum from the Irish Episcopal Conference, January 1984* (Dublin: Veritas, 1984).
54. *Submission to the New Ireland Forum.*

concerned the position of the church over recent decades has been clear and consistent. We have repeatedly declared that we in no way seek to have the moral teaching of the Catholic Church become the criterion of constitutional change or to have the principles of Catholic faith enshrined in civil law. What we have claimed, and what we must claim, is the right to fulfil our pastoral duty and our pastoral duty is to alert the consciences of Catholics to the moral consequences of any proposed piece of legislation.[55]

While the perceptive questioning of the forum members revealed an impasse on a range of issues, the forensic skills of the late Fine Gael TD John Kelly evoked what he termed "an extremely frank and revealing statement" from Bishop Joseph Cassidy of Clonfert on the vexed question of mixed marriages. John Kelly asked whether there would be a case for seeking a special regime tailored to the Irish conditions that would leave Protestant (his word) partners in mixed marriages feeling in a condition of absolute equality with the Catholic partner so far as making decisions about children's upbringing is concerned. Cassidy replied:

> I appreciate the point that you are making. It is something to which the Irish Episcopal Conference gave consideration and we did consider, in view of the attention given to and the sense of injustice that is sometimes felt due to this particular promise, we did consider that we might appeal to Rome for a derogation. I think we should only have appealed to Rome if we felt that there was some chance, even a slight chance that Rome would accede to that particular appeal. We did not feel that.[56]

Dr. FitzGerald wrote the following in his memoirs:

> A decade later I smiled to myself when I heard Bishop Cassidy at the New Ireland Forum kicking that ball back to Rome, saying that the Irish bishops had considered appealing to the Holy See for a derogation from the requirement that the Catholic partner promise orally to do his or her best to have the children brought up as Catholics, but that they had not gone ahead with this, as they felt there was not even a slight chance that Rome would accede to such an appeal. Two Government departments seeking to shift the bureaucratic onus to each other could not have been more skilful.[57]

The same coalition government pressed forward with an amendment to the Haughey Health (Family Planning) Act. The minister for health, Barry Desmond, had initiated a departmental review of the workings of

55. *New Ireland Forum Report*, 2.
56. Irish Episcopal Conference Delegation, report of proceedings, 9 February 1984, 48.
57. FitzGerald, *All in a Life*, 185.

the act soon after coming into office in December 1982. That review was completed by February 1983. It concluded that there were no figures available of the number of chemists who sold contraceptives in accordance with the terms of the 1979 act. But there were figures for the numbers of outlets in towns supplied by those licensed to sell contraceptives. The number was 118. Desmond also suggests in his memoirs that there were large numbers of chemists who refused to stock condoms for sale even on prescription. However, the Well Woman Clinic and Family Planning Services Ltd. did supply the public. A new Health (Family Planning) Bill, liberalizing the sale of contraceptives in Ireland, was introduced and passed in 1985.[58]

Many Irish people's attention was deflected from the developing tensions between church and state by more pressing matters. The Anglo-Irish Agreement was signed, giving hope of a settlement in Northern Ireland. The national economy was in a weak state. Unemployment was high. Emigration had returned, and young people left in tens of thousands to seek employment in the United States, many of them as undocumented workers. There was an air of great despondency in the country. An unusually wet summer added to the feeling of general gloom. The summer of that year was also unusual in another respect. As early as February 1985, a group of children had claimed to have seen a statue of Jesus move. At Ballinspittle, County Cork, a woman and her daughter claimed in July that the statue of Our Lady in the local grotto had moved. Crowds gathered and continued to gather amid claims that others had also seen the statue move. Official church skepticism did not dampen the popular enthusiasm for visiting the roadside grotto.[59] By the end of the summer, there had been over thirty other locations to which people had flocked following claims that a statue had moved or that there were reports of other paranormal activities. The epiphenomena died away later in 1985.

In September 1985, the minister for foreign affairs, Peter Barry, spoke after a lunch in Iveagh House.[60] He may have been the first minister since independence to give a speech on the topic of the principles underlying

58. Desmond, *Finally and in Conclusion,* 237–50.

59. Tim Ryan and Jurek Kirakowski, *Ballinspittle: Moving Statues and Faith* (Cork: Mercier Press, 1985).

60. The taoiseach, Dr. Garret FitzGerald, had not been told in advance that the speech was going to be made.

church-state relations. His guest was the cardinal secretary of state for the Holy See, Agostino Casaroli.[61] A number of bishops were present, including the cardinal. The minister paid tribute to the role of the churches in Irish society and to their fine missionary records through the centuries. But then he continued

> It cannot seriously be denied that during the fifty years which followed the establishment of an independent Irish State, there was a considerable intimacy between the state and the Catholic Church. The extent of this intimacy has been greatly exaggerated in some quarters, and, in many ways the close relationship which marked that period was quite understandable, given the prevailing historical factors and the overwhelming proportion of Catholics in the population. Nevertheless, in retrospect, it has been argued—most notably by the Catholic Bishops at the Public Session of the New Ireland Forum on 9 February 1984—that the alliance of Church and state was harmful for both parties. That is why the Catholic Bishops, to quote one member of the Hierarchy "rejoiced" when the provision concerning the special position of the Catholic Church was removed from the Constitution, following the referendum of 1972.

The minister then spoke about the change in the relationship between the state and the various churches since 1972 that had sometimes led to instances of misunderstanding: "Measured against international standards, the causes of these difficulties have been minor, but in an Irish context they have occasionally been allowed to assume major proportions." That was a source of regret to the government not least because little or no benefit is derived by church or state when they are seen to be at loggerheads: "The government accepts, however, that these episodes are the price that has to be paid for a relationship with the Churches that is based on equality and mutual respect." The bishops had accepted at the forum the two principles on which that proposition was based:

1. Every church and religious denomination had, subject to the provisions of the Constitution, the right to speak out on any issue they wish.

2. The members of the Oireachtas [Parliament] have the right to legislate according to their conscience and in what they consider to be the best interests of the Irish people.[62]

61. Dr. FitzGerald, it will be remembered, had met Cardinal Casaroli in 1973 in Helsinki and had had discussion with him later at the Vatican on the content of a memorandum that he had sent there.

62. See Keogh, *Ireland and the Vatican,* 365–68.

The bishops present on that occasion may have felt a captive audience. Oral sources confirm that at least some of the bishops present, if not the papal party, remained somewhat underwhelmed.[63]

The Status of the Child Act, abolishing the concept of illegitimacy in Ireland, was passed with the approval of the churches. Thus ended discrimination against children born out of wedlock. There was further trouble ahead for church-state relations in 1986. In July 1983, the government had established a Joint Oireachtas Committee on Marriage Breakdown to consider the current state of marital relations in Ireland. Consensus was difficult to achieve. But the committee report, issued on March 27, 1985, recommended that a referendum be held on the issue of divorce. Consultation took place with delegations from most religious bodies in the country, all of whom, except the Catholic Church and the Mormons, recognized the necessity for legislation on divorce.

On April 24, 1986, FitzGerald's government announced that a referendum on divorce would be held on June 26. Unlike the 1983 referendum on abortion, where a new section was added to the constitution, the proposal in 1986 required the removal of the constitutional ban on divorce in Article 41.3.2 and its replacement with a wording that permitted divorce in specific circumstances, including that the marriage had failed for a period of five years with no hope of reconciliation between the spouses and that adequate provision was made for any dependent spouse or children. The Church published a pastoral entitled *Love Is for Life*. It was read at Mass for three consecutive Sundays. The hierarchy opposed the referendum on moral and social grounds. The bishops warned about the proliferation of divorce in Ireland with all the consequent social evils. It highlighted the dangers to women and to children. The episcopal arguments against divorce were rooted in a defense of the common good.[64] While

63. It may be apocryphal, but one of the comments passed after the speech on church and state had been delivered before Casaroli was: "It would not have happened in a banana republic."

64. For a general background to this referendum see the following works: Maurice Reidy, "Civil Divorce: Clarifying the Issues," *Doctrine and Life* 36, no. 8 (August 1986): 483–95; Kieron Wood and Paul O'Shea, *Divorce in Ireland: The Options, the Issues, the Law* (Dublin: O'Brien Press, 1997); William Binchy, *Is Divorce the Answer?* (Blackrock: Irish Academic Press, 1984); Michele Dillon, *Debating Divorce: Moral Conflict in Ireland* (Lexington: University Press of Kentucky, 1993); Louise Fuller, *Irish Catholicism since 1950: The*

the official episcopal position was not to participate in the campaign, a number of prominent bishops broke ranks, including Kevin McNamara, who had been translated from Kerry to the archbishopric of Dublin on November 21, 1984. (He died on April 8, 1987.) McNamara provided vigorous anti-divorce leadership. A highly professional Anti-Divorce Campaign (ADC) was launched at the end of April 1986. It was supported by Family Solidarity, which had been founded in 1984 in order to counter threats to the family. The professor of moral theology at Maynooth, Dr. Patrick Hannon, later wrote that the debate was about "the relationship between a moral belief and the law of the state." As the main issue was a question not of morality but of the morality of law, a Catholic was free to approach the issue from a sociological perspective rather than from a religious one. He concluded that it was not the case that "a Catholic has no choice but to oppose the introduction of divorce."[65]

Charles Haughey and Fianna Fáil opposed the referendum. The government conducted a lamentable campaign, failing to put in place the necessary supporting legislation governing inheritance rights and the protections of the rights of the spouse and children. "What will happen to the family farm," was a theme echoed throughout the campaign. The government realized their error too late and only compounded their weak position by making pledges to introduce legislation concerning the rights of the family. On June 26, 1986, the proposition was rejected by 63.48 percent to 36.3 percent. The turnout was 62.7 percent. Dublin constituencies voted narrowly in favor of divorce while the countryside and urban Cork, Waterford, Limerick, and Galway voted against.[66] It was a major

---

Undoing of a Culture (Dublin: Gill and Macmillan, 2002); Chrystel Hug, *The Politics of Sexual Morality in Ireland* (London: Macmillan Press, 1999); Tom Inglis, *Moral Monopoly: The Catholic Church in Modern Irish Society* (Dublin: Gill and Macmillan, 1987); Vincent MacNamara, "Morality and Law: Experience and Prospects," *Studies* 74, no. 396 (Winter 1985): 373–93; and Patrick Hannon, *Church, State, Morality and Law* (Dublin: Gill and Macmillan, 1992).

65. Patrick Hannon, "Catholics and Divorce," *Furrow* 27, no. 8 (August 1976): 473; quoted in Kerry J. Begley, "The Defeat of the 1986 Divorce Referendum," essay submitted to Prof. Dermot Keogh, December 16, 2003.

66. Analyzing the results, Brian Girvin found that in only six constituencies was there a "yes" vote, and within Dublin (where all these pro-divorce constituencies are located) the difference between "yes" and "no" is only 0.20 percent. Outside of Dublin, the rejection of the proposal was much clearer. The further away from Dublin the constituency, the more likely it was to return a "no" vote, while closeness to Dublin or another urban center increased the relative size of the "yes" vote. In predominantly rural constituencies and in the

reversal for the government. FitzGerald lost power to Charles Haughey and Fianna Fáil in 1987. However, it fell to another coalition government to call a second referendum on divorce on November 24, 1995. The margin in favor, 50.23 percent, was the narrowest in the history of the state. The margin was little more than 9,000 votes out of more than 1.6 million cast. The 1996 Family Law (Divorce) Act states that the court will grant a decree of divorce if the court feels confident that the applicants are aware of the alternatives to divorce and that there is no possibility of reconciliation. The number of divorces granted in Ireland between 1997 and 2003 rose from 93 to 2,710, while the number of judicial separations in the same period declined from 1,431 to 998.[67]

In 1992, abortion was back as a central political issue. Controversy surrounded the X case of a fourteen-year-old statutory rape victim who became pregnant and whom the authorities prevented from traveling to England for an abortion. The Supreme Court found that she could have an abortion on the grounds that she was suicidal and that represented a threat to her life. Pressure was then placed on the government to amend the 1983 antiabortion amendment to the constitution. The fears expressed in 1983 about the wording had been realized. Many who had dogmatically supported the 1983 wording became its strongest critics. In November 1992 another referendum was held, and two of the three propositions were carried. Irish voters supported a constitutional amendment to allow access to abortion information and also supported the right to travel abroad for an abortion. A third clause, the substantive issue as it was called, which would have limited the extent of the X case ruling, was defeated. The Regulation of Information Act was passed in 1995. The government-established Constitutional Review Group recommended in 1996 that legislation should be introduced to implement the X judgment. The government established an Abortion Working Group in 1998 following another case involving a thirteen-year-old rape victim. This became known as the C case. A Green Paper on abortion was published in September 1999 setting out seven possible options.

---

west of Ireland, the "yes" vote rarely exceeded 30 percent. Brian Girvin, "The Divorce Referendum in the Republic: June 1986," *Irish Political Studies* 2 (1987): 96.

67. Sources: *Courts Service Annual Report 2002*, 94; and *Courts Service Annual Report 2003*, 115.

In 2000, an All-Party Oireachtas Committee was set up. To date no legislation has been brought forward. In 1991, 4,154 traveled abroad for an abortion; in 1992, the figure was 4,402, and it was 5,340 in 1997. In 1999, 6,226 Irish women traveled to have an abortion. About 6,391 left in 2000 and 6,673 in 2001. Some 6,490 Irish women traveled abroad in 2002 for an abortion.[68]

Legislation governing contraception and divorce had been strongly opposed by the Catholic hierarchy in Ireland between the 1970s and the 1990s. There was strong support for the bishops' stance among the laity. But the weight of support tilted toward those who viewed such matters as issues for citizens' consciences. The question of the legality of abortion in Ireland provoked the most intense and terribly bitter debate in the 1980s and 1990s. That contentious and divisive matter remains in abeyance awaiting legislation in 2006.

Catholic Church Faces Major Difficulties in the 1990s

From the early 1990s the Catholic Church in Ireland faced a succession of difficulties, including revelations concerning prominent clergy fathering children, scandals concerning sexual abuse by a small number of clerics, and allegations concerning sexual and physical abuse in state institutions run by religious orders. The mismanagement of the initial response to the allegations by the hierarchy and religious orders turned these events into a crisis of credibility for the Catholic Church, leading to public outrage and a series of investigations. The Catholic Church bore the brunt of the backlash, with few critics pondering the role of the state, which had ultimate responsibility for many of the institutions in these matters.

That series of scandals began with the resignation of the bishop of Galway, Eamon Casey, in May 1992 on instructions from Rome, following press reports that he was the father of a child who was then in his early teens. Casey was among the best known of the Irish bishops, noted for his strong stance on issues of human rights, poverty, and development in the Third World. He was very high profile, receiving wide TV and radio exposure in March 1980 for his presence in San Salvador at the funeral

68. Source: Irish Family Planning Association Website, http://www.ifpa.ie/abortion/iabst.html.

Mass of Archbishop Oscar Romero. He later gained world headlines for his absence from Galway on the occasion of a visit by President Ronald Reagan to receive an honorary doctorate from the local university. The bishop found that his pastoral commitments took him to a rural parish in his diocese on the day in question. Bishop Casey, who was very popular, went into exile, working first in Ecuador and later in a parish outside London. He returned to lead a quiet retirement in rural Galway in 2006.

Another clerical celebrity, a priest of the Dublin archdiocese, Father Michael Cleary, had two children by his housekeeper. Cleary had his own radio program and was well known around the country as a performer with a group of singing priests known as "The Holy Show." Ironically, he had been on the podium in Knock in 1979, together with Bishop Casey, to welcome Pope John Paul II to the best-known Marian shrine in Ireland. Both were known as stout defenders of church teaching on priestly celibacy. The contradiction between theological posture and practice, rather than their personal actions in private, was what generally shocked the laity most and caused scandal, adverse comment, and great hurt. Both cases became the subject of best-selling popular accounts, ghosted by two journalists, but based on firsthand accounts by their respective partners.

Although those two cases caused hurt and wounded clerical credibility, the damage they did to lay confidence in the clergy and hierarchy was minimal compared with the succession of revelations throughout the 1990s regarding the involvement of a small number of clergy and religious in child sexual abuse. Between 1983 and 2000, eighteen diocesan priests were convicted of such abuse in Irish courts; a further three Irish diocesan priests were convicted abroad, and two former diocesan priests were also convicted. During the same period, ten religious order priests, nine religious order brothers, and a number of former religious order brothers were also convicted. During this period there was a total of forty convictions for clerical child sexual abuse in the Republic of Ireland and eight in Northern Ireland.[69] Figures for the Archdiocese of Dublin released in March 2003 indicated that allegations of abuse had been made against thirty-five priests who had served in the archdiocese over the previous fifty years; some 107 victims had approached the diocese about this matter; the

69. I am grateful to the religious affairs correspondent of the *Irish Times,* Patsy McGarry, for providing me with these figures.

archdiocese had paid compensation in twenty-nine cases involving allegations against diocesan priests, while thirty more cases were continuing.[70]

One case in particular—that of Father Brendan Smyth—exposed the inadequacy of the church authorities' response to clerical child sexual abuse. It demonstrated the complete absence of protocols and procedures and revealed the extent to which church authorities sought to resolve matters "in house." Smyth, a member of the Norbertine order, abused children from the early 1960s. In 1968 he was sent back to Ireland in disgrace from the Diocese of Providence, Rhode Island, where he had abused young children.[71] He worked in Belfast in the 1980s, where he abused the children of at least one family. Arrested in 1991 in Northern Ireland on charges of pedophilia, he was released on bail and returned to his monastery in the South, where he refused to return to Belfast to stand trial. The Royal Ulster Constabulary (RUC) issued warrants for his extradition in 1993. The Irish government took no action. When this came to light in 1994, it became a matter of high politics. The Labour Party, critical of its Fianna Fáil partners in coalition, resigned from office, and the government fell. In April 1997, Father Smyth was found guilty in a Dublin court on seventy-four charges of indecent and sexual assault; he died in jail later that year. In 1995, the journalist Chris Moore published a study of the Smyth case entitled *Betrayal of Trust*. Father Kevin Hegarty, in his preface to the book, stated: "If the church listens humbly to what the scandals have revealed about its structures, this time of tragedy and pain can also be a time of redemption. . . . The less defensive the church is about its failures, the more open it is about its need to learn, the more able it will be to proclaim the Good News."[72] The Smyth tragedy was a case study for ecclesiastical authorities on how *not* to handle current and future cases of clerical child sexual abuse.

Serious allegations were also made against state-funded and religious-run orphanages and industrial schools. Many of the allegations related to events going back to the 1940s and 1950s. Two television programs set the

70. My thanks to Fr. Damien McNiece for a copy of the press release containing this information, March 14, 2003; see http://www.cps.dublindiocese.ie/article_20.shtml.

71. See Chris Moore, *Betrayal of Trust: The Fr Brendan Smyth Affair and the Catholic Church* (Dublin: Marino Books, 1995), 205.

72. Ibid., 13. This scandal was also the subject of a TV documentary made in Belfast for the UTV *Counterpoint* program.

framework for public discussion in this area. *Dear Daughter,* broadcast on RTÉ on February 28, 1996, was the autobiography of Christine Buckley, who told the story of her time in St Vincent's Industrial School, Goldenbridge, Dublin, run by the Sisters of Mercy. Her account was an indictment of the manner in which the school allegedly operated. The program was part documentary and part drama, reconstructing the painful experiences of the narrator in a most forceful form. Unfortunately, the response to the broadcasting of *Dear Daughter* was almost exclusively popular rather than academic or scholarly. There was, of course, a necessity for both kinds of reaction, and the work of Harry Ferguson in particular sought to provide an academic counterpoise to the popular, not to say populist, tone of much of the commentary at the time.[73] But Ferguson's work, no less than earlier studies by Joseph Robins in 1980 and Jane Barnes in 1989, was overshadowed in the public debate that followed transmission.[74]

The second television program was a three-part documentary entitled *States of Fear,* which was screened by RTÉ in April and May 1999. Made by Mary Raftery, a senior producer and director with RTÉ, the series explored in shocking detail the industrial school system in Ireland. The broadcasting of *States of Fear* produced an unprecedented public response, ranging from shock and disbelief to anger bordering on fury. Kilometers of newspaper columns and many hours of broadcasting time, on both radio and television, were devoted to the issues raised in the screenings. It would not be an exaggeration to say that there was a palpable sense of anger in the air, aimed generally at the Catholic Church and more particu-

73. See Harry Ferguson, "Protecting Irish Children in Time: Child Abuse as a Social Problem and the Development of the Child Protection System in the Republic of Ireland," in Harry Ferguson and Tony McNamara, eds., *Protecting Irish Children: Investigation, Protection and Welfare,* special edition of *Administration* 44, no. 2 (Summer 1996): 5–36; see also Harry Ferguson, "Learning from the Past: Child Abuse and Institutional Care in Historical Perspective," in National Conference of Priests of Ireland, ed., *Child Abuse in Institutional Care: Learning from the Past and Hoping for the Future* (papers from a public conference held in Kilkenny, April 3, 2000), 22–40, and Harry Ferguson, "Child Abuse Inquiries and the Report of the Kilkenny Incest Investigation: A Critical Analysis," *Administration* 41, no. 4 (Winter 1993–94): 385–410.

74. Joseph Robins, *The Lost Children: A Study of Charity Children in Ireland 1700–1900* (Dublin: Institute of Public Administration, 1980); Jane Barnes, *Irish Industrial Schools 1868–1908* (Dublin: Irish Academic Press, 1989). An earlier contribution to the literature on this subject was a pamphlet published in 1966 by the London branch of Tuairim and entitled *Some of Our Children: A Report on the Residential Care of the Deprived Child in Ireland.*

larly at the male and female religious orders under whose care most of the children had been detained in industrial schools.[75]

Mary Raftery followed up the screening of *States of Fear* with the publication, in cooperation with Eoin O'Sullivan of Trinity College Dublin, of a valuable book entitled *Suffer the Little Children: The Inside Story of Ireland's Industrial Schools*.[76] The book is an important contribution to our understanding of the culture, ethos, and history of the Irish industrial school system in the twentieth century. It is all the more important because it was written with full access to many of the relevant records on the subject held in the Department of Education and Science. *Suffer the Little Children* offers one reconstruction of Ireland's "best kept secret."

Having said this, however, the publishers' contention that the book is a "definitive history of industrial schools in Ireland" is somewhat overstated, since there are some inherent weaknesses in it. Firstly, the book emerged from the television series and, perhaps in part due to these origins, the structure of the book is conceptually weak; it might, for instance, have been more appropriate to divide the project into two books—the first based on transcripts of the testimonies of those who suffered abuse in industrial schools and the second consisting of a historical analysis of the industrial school scheme in general. A second weakness, which is particularly surprising since the authors had access to the relevant files in the Department of Education and Science, is the fact that the first three chapters, providing the historical background to industrial schools in Ireland, are academically weak: polemical in tone, they lapse all too easily into generalization.

Another weakness of *Suffer the Little Children* is what may be called "presentism"—judging the past by the standards of the present and projecting contemporary ways of thought backward in time. The past can be fairly judged only on the basis of its own norms and culture. Unfortunately, the authors of this book all too easily succumb to the temptations of presentism. Finally, and perhaps most fatal in the context of a claim to

75. Two books published in 1998 and 1999 respectively provided further personal testimony on life in Irish industrial schools: see Susan McKay, *Sophia's Story* (Dublin: Gill and Macmillan, 1998), and Bernadette Fahy, *The Freedom of Angels: Surviving Goldenbridge Orphanage* (Dublin: O'Brien Press, 1999).

76. Mary Raftery and Eoin O'Sullivan, *Suffer the Little Children: The Inside Story of Ireland's Industrial Schools* (Dublin: New Island, 1999).

be a definitive history, the book is based on an analysis of only a portion of the historical record. Through no fault of their own, the authors were not in a position to examine the records of the religious-run institutions themselves since these records were not made available to them, on legal advice. Therefore, although the book is excellent in terms of unearthing the facts and of disabusing us of many of the myths associated with the industrial school system, its analysis of how and why this system developed as it did is inadequate, leaving some important questions and avenues largely unexplored.

However, the TV journalists involved had performed a great public service. The most shocking revelations to emerge related to the sexual abuse of children. It was contended that this abuse was widespread, was constant, and spanned a number of decades. There is no need here to give a verbatim account of the personal testimonies of the abused: suffice it to say that the term "sexual abuse" fails to convey the physical and emotional pain suffered, and the feelings of degradation and worthlessness and the lasting psychological damage endured as a result. The past must be unmasked. The injustices suffered by children in the care of the state must be addressed. There is no escaping the burdens of the recent past. The television documentaries need to be supplemented by informed debate rooted in scholarship.

These observations also apply to understanding another facet of the Irish state's "child care" system. At different stages, the Sisters of Mercy and the Good Shepherd Sisters ran ten Magdalene asylums. As the name suggests, those homes were for unmarried mothers and/or "fallen women." The taboo associated with sex outside of marriage, and the stigma of illegitimacy, meant that young single pregnant girls were often taken away to religious-run institutions in order to have their babies. When they had given birth, the girls remained with their babies for a few months. They were then transferred to the Magdalene home, which was often situated a few hundred yards from the orphanage where their children lived. Usually the children were given up for adoption or put into foster care. These institutions are the subject of a rather incomplete study by Frances Finnegan entitled *Do Penance or Perish*.[77]

77. Frances Finnegan, *Do Penance or Perish: A Study of Magdalene Asylums in Ireland* (Piltdown, Kilkenny: Congrave Press, 2001). Peter Mullan has made a feature film on the

The general debate on these areas at the beginning of the twenty-first century is characterized by outrage and incomprehension. How could it have happened? The answer will require a very painful examination of the public's complicity in the running of such institutions. There were many innocent victims of the harshness of such institutions. But there were also willing collaborators in all levels of official life. There were the bystanders. It may be very painful to accept the fact that industrial schools and Magdalene laundries were convenient institutions in which to lock away many of the darker secrets of a not-so-perfect Christian Ireland. Girls made pregnant through rape and incest may have found their way to such homes while the perpetrators of these crimes went free.

What insight is there into the religious personnel who ran these institutions on the state's behalf? Teresita Durkan, a former member of the Sisters of Mercy, was sent to the twenty-three-strong Goldenbridge community in 1959, but she was not assigned to the industrial school that was the focus of the TV program *Dear Daughter*. Nevertheless, her pen-portrait of the manager of Goldenbridge industrial school and the central authority figure in *Dear Daughter*, Sister Xavieria (like herself a Mayo woman), is revealing.[78] Durkan reflects on the lack of resources available in those times: Xavieria "didn't have to do it all by herself, of course. But funding and staffing were so meagre, personnel so poorly paid, training for childcare work in Ireland unknown or just acquired on the job, psychological and other support services and structures as yet hardly on the horizon."[79] Durkan portrays a person working under extreme professional stress in a world close in years to 2005 but a universe away in terms of what has happened in the intervening years regarding the development of the profession of child care and the provision of support and training for those working in the profession. Here were children with special needs—emotional and educational—and the state did nothing to provide for those special needs.

---

topic entitled *The Magdalene Sisters*. It is claimed that some 30,000 Irish women worked in the Magdalene laundries.

78. Teresita Durkan, *Goldenbridge: A View from Valparaíso* (Dublin: Veritas, 1997), 76–78.

79. Ibid., 77–78; Durkan spells the name as "Xaveria."

Responses and Responsibilities

The hierarchy set up an advisory committee on child sexual abuse issues on April 27, 1994, under Bishop Laurence Forristal of Ossory. It had a broad charge, including advising on an appropriate response by the church to allegations of child sexual abuse and identifying guidelines and procedures. A wide process of consultation with various parties took place, including "listening days" in January and February 1995 with organizations in the statutory and voluntary sectors involved in child protection and welfare. The advisory committee heard the views of religious superiors, and the Irish Bishops' Conference was briefed on a regular basis. The guidelines were published in 1996 in *Child Sexual Abuse: Framework for a Church Response,* which came to be known as the Green Book. In 2006, it was reported that each of the twenty-six dioceses had complied with a key recommendation—the setting up of a support resource.[80]

On April 1, 2002, the archbishop of Armagh, Seán Brady, and the archbishop of Dublin, Desmond Connell, issued a press statement stating that "the sexual abuse of children by priests is an especially grave and repugnant evil. To all victims of such abuse, to their families and to their parish communities, we again offer our profound apologies."[81] This statement followed the resignation of Bishop Brendan Comiskey of Ferns earlier the same day as a consequence of his handling of the case of Father Seán Fortune, a priest who committed suicide while facing child sexual abuse charges. The bishop said that he had found Fortune "impossible to deal with"; he had confronted him regularly, removed him from his ministry, sought professional advice in several quarters, tried compassion and firmness, but never succeeded in managing a satisfactory outcome. Comiskey admitted that he "should have adopted a more informed and more concerted approach to any dealings with him and for this I ask forgiveness."[82] A judicial inquiry into the handling of child sexual abuse matters in the Diocese of Ferns was later set up; this inquiry is ongoing at the time of writing.

On June 27, 2002, it was announced that Judge Gillian Hussey would

80. Information provided by Child Protection Office, Maynooth, June 2005.

81. Press release, April 1, 2002, Catholic Communications Office [cited 20-09-2004], http://www.catholiccommunications.ie/Pressrel/1-april-2002.html.

82. Press release, Diocese of Ferns, April 1, 2002.

chair a new and fully independent church commission on child sexual abuse. Established jointly by the Irish Bishops' Conference, the Conference of Religious of Ireland (CORI), and the Irish Missionary Union (IMU), its charge was to establish "the truth about the extent of child sexual abuse within the Catholic Church in Ireland, and the response of Church authorities to complaints of such abuse."[83]

Cardinal Desmond Connell came under pressure and issued two statements outlining his responses, since becoming archbishop of Dublin in 1988, to allegations of child sexual abuse against members of his clergy. He explained how he had provided resources for priests who had offended in the form of professional advice and residential care in treatment centers. He had removed priests from pastoral ministry and introduced disciplinary measures, including dismissal from the clerical state. He had ordered an examination of the diocesan archives for the past fifty years. The names of seventeen priests against whom allegations had been made had been handed over to the police. His archdiocese had followed the 1996 guidelines.[84]

However, an RTÉ *Prime Time* investigation into Connell's handling of allegations of clerical child sexual abuse raised further questions. Amid demands for his resignation, on October 23, 2002, Cardinal Connell issued another statement outlining the record of his archdiocese. There was growing criticism of the Hussey commission. Cardinal Connell felt obliged to defend it. But the commission was stood down in December 2002.

This followed an announcement by the minister for justice, equality and law reform, Michael McDowell, that the government, at its meeting on December 2, had approved a proposal from him for the preparation of a scheme for a new statutory-based mechanism for investigating matters of significant and urgent public importance. The proposed legislation was informed in the first instance, he said, by the public concern expressed following the RTÉ *Prime Time* program as well as by the minister's consultations with victims' organizations, representatives of the Catholic hierarchy, and other interested parties.[85]

83. Press release, June 27, 2002, Catholic Communications Office [cited 20-09-2004], http://www.catholiccommunications.ie/Pressrel/27-june-2002.html.

84. Press release, Archdiocese of Dublin, Cardinal Connell's letter on child sexual abuse, October 5, 2002, http://www.cps.dublindiocese.ie/article_13.shtml, accessed 30 April 2005; Cardinal Connell's statement on October 12 following *Prime Time* program.

85. Department of Justice press release of statement by minister, December 3, 2002,

On December 30, 2002, two abuse victims, Marie Collins and Ken Reilly, met Cardinal Connell to discuss a number of issues connected with clerical child sexual abuse. As a follow-up to that meeting, Collins and Reilly met with a number of church representatives and other groups and expressed serious concerns about what they saw as the archdiocese's inadequate pastoral support for victims. These concerns, they pointed out, applied particularly in the case of those who had recently reported for the first time that they had been abused. Collins and Reilly stressed that, irrespective of when the abuse may have taken place, victims felt particularly vulnerable at the time when they first reported it. Seeking to address this criticism, Cardinal Connell committed resources to provide a support network.[86] A follow-up meeting in July 2004 with Connell's successor, Archbishop Diarmuid Martin, reported progress.[87]

In June 2003, the Irish Bishops' Conference, CORI and the IMU established a Working Group on Child Protection to develop a comprehensive and integrated child protection policy. It was chaired by Maureen Lynott and had representatives from a number of bodies as well as two survivors of clerical sexual abuse. The group concluded its work in September 2004, and in January 2005 it produced its final document, *Our Children, Our Church,* which sets out a comprehensive and integrated child protection policy for the Irish Catholic Church.

The Fianna Fáil–Progressive Democrat government first discussed the need for a formal response to the needs of victims of childhood abuse in March 1998. A subcommittee of the cabinet was established in December 1998. The minister for education and science, Micheál Martin, was named as chair. It included the tánaiste (deputy prime minister), Mary Harney, and had eight members in total. The subcommittee made a number of important recommendations that were accepted by cabinet. These included commitments to amend the provisions in the Child Care Act relating to residential centers for children with physical and mental disabilities; to

---

http://www.justice.ie/80256E01003A02CF/vWeb/PCJUSQ5ZYJH7-en; accessed April 30, 2005.

86. Joint statement from Marie Collins, Ken Reilly, Cardinal Connell, and Bishop Eamonn Walsh, December 30, 2002, Archdiocese of Dublin press release, http://www.cps.dublindiocese.ie/article_19.shtml; accessed April 30, 2005.

87. Press release, Archdiocese of Dublin, July 14, 2004, http://www.cps.dublindiocese.ie;article_108.shtml; accessed April 30, 2005.

introduce legislation to cover the compiling of a register of sex offenders; to make fully operational the Social Services Inspectorate in the Department of Health and Children; and to modernize facilities and services for young offenders.

On May 11, 1999, the taoiseach, Bertie Ahern, made an unprecedented public statement: "On behalf of the State and of all citizens of the State, the Government wishes to make a sincere and long overdue apology to the victims of childhood abuse for our collective failure to intervene, to detect their pain, to come to their rescue." Ahern quoted from the short preface to the 1970 Kennedy Report on industrial schools, which states "All children need love, care and security." He continued: "Too many of our children were denied this love, care and security. Abuse ruined their childhoods and has been an ever present part of their adult lives, reminding them of a time when they were helpless. I want to say to them that we believe that they were gravely wronged, and that we must do all we can now to overcome the lasting effects of their ordeals."[88] Ahern also indicated that the cabinet that same day had endorsed the setting up of an inquiry, later provided for under the Commission to Inquire into Childhood Abuse Act, passed by the Oireachtas in 2000. A High Court judge, Mary Laffoy, was appointed to chair the commission. Religious orders that had once been responsible for the running of reformatories and industrial schools could be called to give testimony before this commission. There was also provision for religious orders to provide a written report on the history of the institutions for which they had responsibility.

The government and eighteen religious orders signed an indemnity on June 5, 2002. The religious orders agreed to pay €128 million (€78.5 million of this in land) to the Statutory Redress Scheme, which was set up under the Residential Institutions Redress Act 2002 "to assist the recovery of persons who as children were resident in certain institutions and who suffered or who have suffered injuries that are consistent with abuse while so resident."[89] The deed was not to be construed as an admission of liability

88. Speech by an taoiseach, Bertie Ahern, TD, announcing government measures relating to childhood abuse on May 11, 1999, copy supplied by press office, An Taoiseach's Department.

89. Quoting from the Indemnity, paragraph A; copy supplied to me by the Department of Education and Science. Figures are quoted from Mark Hennessy, "Dáil Committee Investigates Abuse Claim Ceal," *Irish Times,* February 1, 2003.

by either party with regard to any alleged injury suffered by any applicant. "Any payment made under the scheme would be without admission of liability or responsibility for any alleged acts of abuse and no liability or responsibility was or would be apportioned between the said parties or any other person arising out of any sums paid from the special account under the scheme."[90] The indemnity limiting the eighteen religious orders' liability to €128 million was quickly seen as having been far too generous on the part of the state, whose ultimate liability remained uncertain and could potentially run into billions of euro in compensation for survivors of abuse.

A Stewardship Trust was set up in 1996 by the Catholic bishops to take responsibility for paying compensation to victims of clerical child sex abuse. The four archbishops act as trustees. Each of the twenty-six dioceses was required to make a contribution to the fund.[91] Since the establishment of the Stewardship Trust in 1996, 143 claims against thirty-six priests who had worked in dioceses in Ireland have been settled at a cost to the Stewardship Trust of €8.78m. The claim costs in 2003 amounted to €1.9m and in 2004 were €2.9m. Most of these cases occurred prior to 1996 and thus are not covered by any existing insurance policy. Since the total sums agreed in 1996 and 1999 are nearing depletion, new resources need to be provided. Accordingly, the bishops decided that the operation of the Stewardship Trust requires review, and this process is being undertaken by the trustees.[92]

No matter how generous the diocesan contributions may prove to be, the total sum may not be nearly enough to meet the large number of compensation demands now registered. There may be little alternative but to sell some of the assets of the dioceses. That concern is borne out by the publication in October 2005 of the Diocese of Ferns, the result of an investigation by the minister for health and children to inquire into complaints or allegations made against the clergy of that diocese and to consider whether the church response was adequate or appropriate, judged in the context of the time when the complaint or allegation was made.[93] The

90. Quoting from the Indemnity, paragraph F.

91. Patsy McGarry, "Nine Dioceses Yet to Indicate Sex Abuse Trust Contributions," *Irish Times,* March 29, 2005.

92. Excerpts from press release, Catholic hierarchy, March 16, 2005: see http://www.catholiccommunications.ie/Pressrel/16-march-2005.html.

93. As mentioned in the text earlier, the minister for health and children asked George

Ferns diocese, it should be noted, is among Ireland's smallest, with 125 diocesan priests and just 10 priests in religious orders.

The Ferns report identified over one hundred allegations of child sexual abuse between 1962 and 2002 against twenty-one priests operating under the aegis of the diocese. It found that there had been a varied response over the forty years, reflecting in part "the growing understanding by the medical professions and society generally of the nature and consequences of child sexual abuse and in part the different personalities and management styles of successive Bishops." Bishop Donal Herlihy, between 1960 and 1980, had treated child sexual abuse by priests in his diocese exclusively as a moral problem. Priests against whom allegations had been made were transferred to another post or to another diocese and later returned to the former position. By 1980, however, Bishop Herlihy recognized that there was a psychological or medical dimension to the issue of child sexual abuse. He had referred priests to a psychologist, and that was broadly in accordance with the understanding then evolving regarding child sexual abuse. But, the report concluded, "what was wholly inappropriate and totally inexplicable was the decision of Bishop Herlihy to appoint to curacies priests against whom allegations had been made and in respect of whom a respected clerical psychologist had expressed his concerns in unambiguous terms as to their suitability to interact with young children." Equally inappropriate, the report found, was Bishop Herlihy's decision "to ordain clearly unsuitable men into the priesthood when he knew or ought to have known that they had a propensity to abuse children."[94]

In April 2002, Bishop Walsh was appointed apostolic administrator of the Diocese of Ferns. All outstanding allegations of child sexual abuse were reviewed by the administrator and a newly appointed advisory panel. Bishop Walsh made a public appeal for anyone with information relating to clerical child sexual abuse to come forward to the authorities of the diocese, the Gardai (police), and/or the Health Boards. The inquiry found that the current practice of the Diocese of Ferns operated "to a very high level of child protection." But "the regret is that this satisfactory position was not achieved at an earlier stage." It continued:

Birmingham, SC, to prepare a preliminary report on the allegations of child sexual abuse in the Diocese of Ferns, with a view to recommending an appropriate form and terms of reference for an inquiry to inquire into the issues raised. He reported in August 2002.

94. Executive Summary, *The Ferns Report,* October 2005.

With the benefit of hindsight it is possible to see that the Church authorities, the medical profession and society generally failed to appreciate the horrendous damage which the sexual abuse of children can and does cause. The Inquiry was struck by the hurt still borne by mature and fair minded victims who gave evidence before it. The Oireachtas has fixed a maximum penalty of life imprisonment for the more serious offences involving child sexual abuse. The inquiry is of the view that the severity of that penalty is fully justified.[95]

At the time of writing, there is a similar inquiry into the allegations of child sexual abuse against certain clergy of the Archdiocese of Dublin. Its publication in the first decade of the twenty-first century will help the Catholic Church continue to confront the past with honesty and with a determination that this situation will never be allowed to happen again. It was a dark chapter in the history of an institution that showed itself all too reluctant to allow its various sectors to be subjected to more democratic control based on the gospel principles of openness, transparency, and accountability.

Taking Stock: The Catholic Church in the New Century

While public attention was focused on scandal and controversy, the Catholic Church in Ireland faced the critical challenge and the growing strain of fulfilling its basic pastoral and institutional needs in a rapidly changing environment. Vocations to both the religious and the diocesan clergy have declined sharply since the 1990s. The age profile was also very high, most diocesan clergy being over fifty-five. That meant the virtual abandonment of the idea of retirement in the larger dioceses as bishops struggled to keep churches open. There was an inevitable cut in the number of weekday and Sunday masses. In the cities, churches were closed at certain times during the day as there was a danger of vandalism and theft. That would have been unthinkable in the Ireland of earlier decades. In rural dioceses, a shortage of priests meant that it was no longer possible to keep clergy resident in certain parishes. The amalgamation of parishes was unavoidable, and even the merging of smaller dioceses is now a possibility.

The declining number of religious meant a radical reduction in their traditional and central role in secondary education. The era of religious personnel having their salaries reinvested in the running of their schools is

95. Ibid.

virtually over. Lay teachers are now obliged to take over many of the duties traditionally undertaken by religious, such as supervision outside of class hours. The major male teaching orders, such as the Holy Ghost Fathers, the Jesuits, the Vincentians, the Marists, and the Christian Brothers, together with their female counterparts, have already put in place systems for the continuation of the Catholic educational tradition within new legal frameworks. While the religious orders themselves may no longer be present, their schools will continue to operate and will continue to uphold the traditions and spiritual ideas of their founding religious orders. This will mean entrusting laypeople, whether under deeds of trust or as a company, with the running of these schools. The same challenge confronts the voluntary hospitals traditionally run by religious orders such as the Sisters of Charity, Sisters of Mercy, and Bon Secours Sisters. The implications of this trend for the Catholic Church and Irish society are enormous. The hidden subsidies and economic transfers provided by the social capital of church personnel, particularly in the education and health fields, are fast coming to an end. The state will have to face the consequences of this radical change in the coming years.

The Catholic Church experienced a falling-off in attendance at weekly Mass and participation in the sacraments during the 1990s. During the second half of the twentieth century Ireland maintained very high Mass attendance figures relative to other "Catholic" countries such as Italy, Spain, Portugal, and Belgium. By the late 1990s, those figures had collapsed and religious observance in Ireland looked very much like that in other European countries. What was most notable in Ireland was the speed of the collapse. There was strong evidence of a great disillusionment, despondency, and lack of trust in the leadership of the Catholic Church. Priests, once invested with great trust by the laity, were struggling to regain credibility. Many laypeople were discerning; they recognized the idealism and the unselfishness of large numbers of clergy and religious. But mistrust of the institution itself was palpable.

The place of religion in the lives of Irish people ought not to be measured exclusively by the health of the institutional Church. In the summer of 2001, the relics of St. Thérèse of Lisieux were taken in solemn procession around Ireland, North and South. The popular response was overwhelming. Tens of thousands of people—young and old—came out to participate in all-night vigils and to line the streets respectfully as the procession passed through scores of towns. The phenomenon of the warm response to the relics of Saint Thérèse is replicated in the high turnout at the annual pilgrimage to Croagh Patrick, regular pilgrimages to Lough Derg, and the packed cathedral during the annual Galway Novena of Prayers. Other novenas are also well attended in Dublin, Cork, Dundalk, Drogheda, and other towns around the country.

How does an observer read the significance of such phenomena at a time of unprecedented crisis in the institutional Church? Perhaps they symbolize the strong attachment to religious values in a country where the clerical church has lost prestige and esteem. They may also point to a general desire to seek reassurance from great figures and symbols at a time of uncertainty and turmoil. This kind of devotion does not signal a revival of the traditional church or a reversal of the most profound secularization of Irish society. But what it may show is that there is a base on which new Catholic structures can be built in the new century.

The twentieth century in Ireland was the Catholic Century. No institution was more powerful in shaping the lives of most of the people living on the island. That is now in the past. The 1990s brought to public attention the negative legacy of an institution that had helped mold and shape the consciousness of generations of Irish people. There is, however, a need for balance. In striking that balance future historians will look not only to the negative legacy but also to the tremendous contribution of priests, brothers, and nuns to the development of Ireland's education, health, and social services. Irish men and women in missionary orders also did extraordinary work in providing education, health care, and pastoral ministry for people in many countries in Africa, Asia, Latin America, the Caribbean, the United States, Canada, Australia, and New Zealand. This work did not go unappreciated. When Pope John Paul II came to Ireland in September 1979, he expressed his gratitude for the work of the Irish Church at home and abroad. He remained a strong supporter of Irish Catholicism, and intended to make a return visit in 2005, which would include a visit to Northern Ireland. His death on April 2, 2005, ended the hopes of the Irish hierarchy and many Irish Catholics in this regard.

But welcome as his return would have been, the historical reality must be faced: even Pope John Paul's charisma would not have been able to reverse the modernization of a once-traditional society and the manifestation of a secularism with a strong anticlerical bent in contemporary Ireland. Ireland had changed radically between the time of the only papal visit to Ireland to date, in 1979, and the early twenty-first century. It was no longer the exception to the rule in Western Europe. Ireland was no longer a society that could combine economic modernity with the conservation of traditional patterns of Mass attendance and participation in the sacraments. But if Ireland in 2006 was no longer the exception that proved the rule, it was distinctive from many other countries in Western Europe. Irish Catholicism faced the challenge of having to rise in a creative way to a changed society demanding a new approach to mission and to a pastoral presence in the anonymous cities and giant, sprawling suburbs of the Ireland of the new century. In the nineteenth and for much of the twentieth centuries, Catholicism in Ireland had responded to diverse challenges to provide mass education, institutional care, running of hospitals and homes, and a strong presence in a complex parish structure in both urban and rural areas. The post–"Celtic tiger" Ireland presents new challenges. The Catholic presence in the twenty-first century will be different and distinctive. It will neither die nor be extinguished, but its structures will be far less clerical and will depend more and more on the priesthood of the laity, with an increasingly more prominent role being played by women in the decades to come.

LAWRENCE   TAYLOR

4. Crisis of Faith or Collapse of Empire?

I remember very well what it was like back then, when I first came here in 1970. Here in Pugin Hall there would be 600 for dinner. They would file in all in black—they used have to wear those always. And there would be no talking. Only the fellow who'd be up at the lectern reading some religious lesson through the whole of the meal. For the rest of them, not a word. Ten to a table and one of them would be in charge. And the food wasn't very good at all in those days. Fatty meat and maybe you wouldn't like the potatoes there, they mightn't be any good at all. But you'd no choice; that's for sure! Sure, I used feel sorry for them, and I would smuggle out something for the ones I knew or the ones didn't like the dinner. Maybe I'd take bread out to them or something. Under my skirt. I wasn't allowed do that of course. Indeed we weren't allowed to speak or anything to them, nor them to us. But I was headstrong myself and felt sorry for them. Good God, it was awful for many of them. Pushed in here by their families and many of them with no real reason for being here. Naturally they didn't do well. Many of them. And quite a few as took their own lives here. Of course you heard nothing about it. Everything was a secret. It's no different today. That sort of thing is still going on and you will hear nothing of it.

The bleak institution remembered by cafeteria worker Dolores sounds like the now infamous industrial schools, where Irish children suffered abuse and many other forms of cruelty at the hands of religious orders. But she is describing the Irish National Seminary at St. Patrick's Pontifical University at Maynooth, a kind of officers training school for a militantly Catholic Ireland. And not so very many years ago, in the early '70s. The

This chapter would not have been possible without the cooperation and assistance of the staff and students of St. Patrick's College, Maynooth, as well as the clergy and people of Southwest Donegal, here gratefully acknowledged.

black costume she mentions was a soutane—the seminarians' garb from dawn to dusk, as they listened, queued, studied, and walked the well-groomed and ordered neo-Gothic corridors and yards. Up to the locked gates and then back.

Clearly, things have changed since then, and not only at the seminary. The position of the Catholic Church in Irish society—in terms of its social power and cultural authority—has altered dramatically over the last several decades. As Dermot Keogh's detailed recounting and analysis in this volume reminds us, the declining authority and power of the Catholic Church in Ireland is, in one sense, the product of a series of shifts in the social, cultural, economic, and political scene that were in some ways specifically Irish, and in others common to Western Europe and North America. Of undoubted significance in this context were the particular decisions, revelations, and reactions (also treated at length by Keogh) that rocked the Church and nation through these last several decades. Anthropology needs of course to take note of these facts and contexts, but here the focus is on another sort of detail, the kind garnered through an ethnographic interaction that sheds light on the "meaning" that such shifts take on for the people living them, ideally both clergy and laymen.

To return to our remembered seminary, what is being described were clearly crucial elements in a drawn-out rite of passage; this discipline of the body and the material aspects of the place dramatically enclosed, reduced, and constrained the new seminarians—creating a vivid sense of the ritual death of their "civilian" status and of their ensuing liminality. At the same time the stage set portrayed the severe grandeur of the institution not only to which they were subject, but also into which they would, after ordination, be incorporated. For just outside that oppressive hall the diners emerged into a long cloister where they would pass under a series of portraits—a striking visual representation of the place of Ireland and Maynooth in what can be called the "World Irish Catholic Empire." Surely one of the great ironies and unintended consequences of British Protestant domination was the promotion of Ireland to the key position of English-speaking Catholic nation at the center of the world's greatest empire. As Corish remarks, "In the early nineteenth century English-speaking power was expanding all over the world. That power, British or American, was culturally Protestant but ruled over many Catholics. The Catholic Church in all these territories was under the jurisdiction of the Roman

Congregation of Propaganda. In a search for English-speaking priests the Congregation turned naturally to Ireland."[1] Hence the portraits, including not only the bishops of every Irish diocese, but also the complacent, voluptuously robed figures of Ireland's version of the British viceroys—the vicars apostolic of Madras and Kenya, the archbishop of Denver, the bishop of Chicago. They too had paced this corridor and then voyaged abroad to oversee Catholicism in these far-flung dominions. Most Irish missionaries were to come from All Hallows and the regional seminaries. Maynooth, however, initiated the very important missionary order of Saint Columba. (I can remember meeting a group of Korean Catholics in the U.S. all of whom had been convinced by the Columban Fathers entrusted with their education that there was on the other side of the world a place very like their own green land. A beautiful spiritual realm called the Kingdom of Kerry.)

While these reminders of empire were no doubt important to the seminarians' sense of their place in the larger world, the vast majority of ordinates were heading back to their own dioceses as curates, hopeful of promotion to parish priest, if not higher office. And, in those same years Dolores remembers, a different sort of Irish Catholicism might be practiced back home, as it certainly was out in the mountain fastness of Southwest Donegal, on whose rocky shores I first washed up in 1973. There, under the highest sea cliffs in Europe, I chatted, drank, and fished my way through what anthropologists call "fieldwork." By virtue of the patience of many a helpful neighbor, I wrote a dissertation mainly concerned with the socioeconomic aspects of local fishing and so, as one old man liked to put it, *"chuirmuid an ainm doctuir ort"*—we put the title doctor on you. Now ethnography, as most real social scientists will tell you, is a very sloppy and inexact affair, very much at the mercy of the skills of the ethnographer, the whims of the people, and the luck of the match. But it has one great virtue—you might learn something. By which I mean you might discover something you weren't looking for, and for me that something was Catholicism.

Of course I knew the local Irish were Catholics, although earlier anthropological accounts had relatively little to say on that score. What I found, of course, was every manner of belief and practice—popular and

1. Patrick Corish, *Maynooth College: 1795–1995* (Dublin: Gill and Macmillan, 1995), 95.

official—from holy well *turus* to novenas, to missions and Mass cards, to pilgrimages approved and disapproved. All these popular practices were very much embedded in everyday social life and relations, and in many instances strongly linked to the landscape, itself at the foundation of local social worlds. Religion, in this sense, is embodied in what Bourdieu called *habitus,* maintained not only by church ritual but by a thousand minor and major observances, habits of body and mind, moral, conceptual, and emotional inclinations. And of course by stories—a world narrated and performed.

All this did not vitiate the local importance of that living embodiment of "official" Irish Catholicism: the Maynooth-trained priest. Very much the contrary, for he enjoyed an incredible presence, power, and penetration into every aspect of life. During my first years of fieldwork, the parish priest was the famous Father James McDyer. His efforts in organizing cooperatives, bringing water and electric, and generally saving his parish from the devastating effects of emigration and oblivion had been hailed nationally and even internationally.[2] He was not average, but the structural base and cultural authority on which he built his extraordinary career were in fact the basic features of the status, role, and identity of any rural Irish priest. Father McDyer was just particularly adept at developing them. In the words of a local critic, "as a priest, he was a fine businessman, and as a businessman, he was a fine priest." Which was to say that he was a broker in all things—standing between the mass of the then still poor and little educated parishioners and the larger world beyond. And this operated in every realm. For any outsider wishing to accomplish something in the parish, or any parishioner hoping to do the same beyond, he was the necessary connection, the man in the middle. And of course, like all parish priests, he was president of the local school board. As with its role in the health system, the Catholic Church remained, and remains, central to the Irish public school system, a fact that the Irish simply took for granted but that certainly struck me, as an American, as strange. Indeed,

2. See Canon James McDyer, *Autobiography of Father James McDyer* (Kerry: Brandon Press, 1984); Vincent Tucker, "Images of Development and Under-development in Glencolumbkille, Co. Donegal, 1830–1970," in John Davis, ed., *Rural Change in Ireland* (Belfast: Institute of Irish Studies, 1999); Eileen Moore Quinn, "Portrait of a Mythographer: Discourses of Identity in the Work of Father James McDyer," *Eire-Ireland* 38, no. 1/2– (2003): 123–40.

I was able to witness the priest's particular use of that position to reward one local family—whom he counted among his supporters—and literally drive another (a perceived enemy) out of the parish. Even in my little dissertation-world of fishing, the priest was active, trying to organize the local river salmon-netters—poachers to a man—into a cooperative to police the river and one another.[3]

At the same time, I watched other clerics, far less politically involved or adept, exercising another sort of power. These were alcoholic priests, in the extreme removed from their parish pulpits, who by local popular religious theory were thus out from under the *smacht*—the control—of the bishop, and whose power to cure was thus released. And sought. Although I first became acquainted with this kind of priest in stories, there were at least three operating during the time of my fieldwork: one from a hospital, one from home, and one from a pub near Killybegs. Privy to all this priestly potency, I turned my attention to exploring the ways in which Irish Catholicism—at least in its local guise—had come into formation and continued to operate in people's lives. So I did more field research, in the 1980s and early '90s. During that time I accompanied the many people I had come to know by then, as they attended and participated in a long list of what I called *Occasions of Faith*—the title of the book I eventually published.[4]

Now the contrast between the priest as he emerged from Maynooth and his multifaceted identity out in the rural west reminds us that different things may be indicated by the term "Irish Catholicism." On the one hand, there is popular religious practice—itself taking various and changing forms that have combined elements of official Catholic doctrine and practice with other features often described, depending on the fad and the perspective, as superstition or the expression of an earth-oriented Celtic spirituality. The other is the particular brand of institutional Church practice all those men in black were learning at Maynooth. Not that the two were or are wholly different of course. A focus on the position of the priest serves to remind us of the personal continuity between one world

3. Lawrence Taylor, "'The River Would Run Red with Blood': Community and Common Property in an Irish Settlement," in Bonnie J. McCay and James M. Acheson, eds., *The Question of the Commons* (Tuscon: University of Arizona Press).
4. Lawrence Taylor, *Occasions of Faith: An Anthropology of Irish Catholics* (Dublin: Lilliput, 1995).

and another. Father McDyer—like so many others down the years—became a priest in the seminary (in 1937) but in a sense continued to become a priest in the parish. Whether official or popular, the role of the priest, like other aspects of religion, is both created and lived in the world, in and through not only texts, but buildings, objects, and above all social relations. These are not just the "set" or "stage" on which a fully scripted religion is performed. They are, on the contrary, intrinsic features of the Faith. The social dimension of religion is not something after the fact, but rather absolutely central to its experience and hence meaning. After all, religion is about relationships—relations to powers that may heal, harm, transform—and is thus necessarily conceived in the context of other relationships, perhaps especially to those also embodying power in one form or another.

Given this experiential and situated view of religion, one expects anthropologists to attempt ethnography of local, popular religious practice. The halls of Maynooth, however, are a less obvious, but equally important, site for fieldwork. The lack of attention in that direction is in part probably due to difficulty of access, but is also linked, I think, to a fundamental shortcoming in our understanding of religious practice. While we are prepared to think about local and popular religious forms as constructed in the context of an experienced, material, and social world, we think of official practice as simply formal doctrines mediated only by the politics and personality of the leading figures. That kind of mediation is of course very important. It was certainly a series of political moves by both the British and the bishops from the late eighteenth century on that resulted in the formation of a singularly monolithic "religious regime" in Catholic Ireland (see the work of Emmet Larkin, for example). Perhaps nowhere else in the Catholic world did an episcopal hierarchy enjoy such unrivalled domination. Perhaps nowhere else in the Catholic world did one seminary enjoy such a prominence in the formation not only of priests, but of the particular brand of Catholicism they were charged with bringing to the people. However, Dolores's evocative description of the dining hall, as well as such material artifacts as the portrait gallery and awesome neo-Gothic chapel, reminds us that it was not just the texts and lectures that "formed" the priests. All instruction was as embedded in the material, experiential, and social aspects of everyday life there as popular religion was out in the parishes, as Corish's historical survey of Maynooth shows.

Of course it is too late for the ethnography of the Maynooth that produced Father James McDyer in the 1930s, though focused, anthropologically informed historical studies of various periods would certainly prove very useful. However, even a preliminary look within the national seminary at the current time of crisis and change should prove as suggestively fruitful as a return to the parish in West Donegal.

Certainly, there is no doubt that things have changed dramatically, at both the center and the edge of Irish Catholicism, but those changes have taken and are taking place in precisely the contexts of the historical trajectory of Irish Catholicism. Can it be a coincidence, for example, that Irish Catholicism here in Ireland and in its colonial form in North America have been the most rocked by scandals of clerical abuse? If there are two characteristics whose centrality most distinguishs Irish from other forms of Catholicism, it is clerical authority and antisexuality. Clearly, neither is unique to Irish Catholicism, but perhaps nowhere else have these two features been so developed, so prone to taking center stage in both narrative and practice. Whether or not these features—both of which are definitive of the position of the priest—are a contributing cause of the high incidence of clerical sexual abuse I cannot say, but I have no doubt that they very much contributed to the reaction to and effects of the scandals. Ironically, it was the clergy themselves who gave sex its particular weight here in Ireland. That weight must at once heighten the awful power of the experience of abuse for the victims even as it more directly undermines the power and authority of the Church here than it might elsewhere. In order then to begin to understand the present circumstances, I offer a preliminary foray, a temperature taking of the current state of Irish Catholicism at the center—Maynooth—and one particular edge—Southwest Donegal.

We begin at Maynooth, taking another turn through the cloister in the very shaken and much diminished institution that is the seminary in 2003. The portrait gallery is still there: the latest in the series was hung only a few months ago, the long torso and meditative hawkish face of Cardinal Connell, his brilliant red robes scintillating against an electric blue background. Unlike earlier portraits, the Cardinal faces sideways, thus avoiding the spectacle confronting the other grave figures, all of whom stare unblinkingly forward across the hallway at a series of photographic class portraits: the ever-diminishing ordination classes.[5] Thirty years ago, there were about six hundred students in all seven years; now there are sixty-four. Thirty years ago, about half the entering students made the whole journey. Now the attrition rate is better than two-thirds. At that rate, we are looking at very small graduating classes indeed. To some extent this decline is of course a function of the calamitous events of the past decade—specifically the pedophilia cases and the attendant prevarication, obfuscation, and obdurate refusal on the part of the hierarchy to come to adequate terms with the situation. It certainly can be argued, however, that such a sea change was in the works and would have greatly accelerated in the circumstances of the all too brief but heady economic boom that began in the late '90s. To judge from the figures, the 1960s was a crucial decade here as it was in so many other places around the world. The entry numbers were higher than ever, following the continuing momentum of the '50s and perhaps the slow economic improvements of that decade. But a larger percentage of these entrants than ever before left before ordination.

One might suggest a number of contributing factors here, which could be the useful subject of direct enquiry. Since in those days their families propelled most seminarians into Maynooth, the choice to enter the seminary was not wholly the student's own. On the other hand, once in, the decision to leave was undoubtedly far more under his control. So we can read the figures as at once expressing a continuing allegiance to the central social value of vocations among the middle-aged and older, and a younger generation's growing doubts and sense of independence. Nothing surprising in that, of course. The national scene in Ireland in this period was certainly one of great change on all fronts. The decade is typically seen as one of modernization, in which the beginnings of economic improvement, an easing off of the twentieth century's worst period of emigration, and the beginnings of alternative cultural voices with the inauguration of RTE television all combined to undermine older structures and patterns of life. Those priests who did remain in formation were often quite taken with the Church's own version of modernization in the form of Vatican II. But whether enthused or not, there is no doubt that their numbers continued to decline through the 1970s and 80s. Not only did fewer enter the semi-

---

5. The following figures were generously provided by the seminary.

nary each year, but also an increasing percentage of those that did enter left before ordination.

It was in this context that the scandals began, beginning with the revelations concerning Bishop Casey in 1992. An astounded nation learned that this very popular and highly visible figure had fathered a son by an American cousin and that he had been supporting the boy in the United States for nearly eighteen years with diocesan funds. Far darker stories about other clerics emerged after that, featuring horrific cases of child abuse and the consistent efforts of the hierarchy to protect their priests and their institution rather than their congregants. Naturally, this emerging new narrative of the Irish Church enraged many of its formerly loyal followers, and there followed a precipitous decline in vocations. The 2003 ordination class numbers just twelve and is composed not only of Maynooth seminarians but others from the few remaining seminaries elsewhere in Ireland—all of them now closed.

What can it be like to be a seminarian in these circumstances, and what can they tell us about the future of Irish Catholicism? I met with several of this year's modest ordination class in the very same dining hall described so vividly by Dolores, now a subdued and relaxed place with no clerical garb in sight. Given the national situation, the six smiling men gathered around the table were remarkably comfortable. Four did most of the talking. The youngest was Francis, a pale young man in his midtwenties from the rural West.[6] Michael and James were both Dubliners, by accent of middle- and working-class backgrounds respectively. Both were men around forty, James a bit more watchful and restrained, Michael charming, self-confident, and voluble. Donal, from the North, was around the same age, though with balding, monkish head and deep brown eyes, he seemed older. I asked, first of all, if they could say something about what brought them to Maynooth. Only Francis had entered directly from secondary school, a last remnant of what would have probably been a typical trajectory a few decades earlier.

> I am from the West. I suppose I always wanted to be a priest from as far back as I can remember. My parish priest was a big inspiration to me. Like, I wanted to be like him. He was a real leader in the community and he really rejuvenated our whole parish as far as emigration from it, single-handedly. He was a

6. These names are pseudonyms to protect the men's privacy.

great man, so I suppose he would have inspired me in many ways and I came to Maynooth in 1996.

When he arrived, Francis found a place with vestiges of the old regime, but clearly in precipitous decline and/or change, depending on one's perspective.

> It was a strange environment coming here. First of all, it was my first time actually away from home. I remember particularly our first month in September. We were sort of locked into the college. You couldn't make any contact with home, you could write letters but you couldn't ring home, you couldn't talk to anybody, you couldn't leave the college grounds. We were the lowest class ever to enter the college. Eighteen of us started off. Of those, two were already ordained priests. There are three of us still in formation, so all the rest of them left over time. So, when people were leaving that was always very hard, it sort of shook you up a little. When I came to Maynooth, there was 160 students here and now there is 64 so that is a huge big drop. And there was a great atmosphere when I came here as well. At the start, you know, I mean even queuing up here, there would be a queue out to the door you know. So that has changed. The place has become a lot quieter as the years have gone by, and also students that are coming in are much older now and that also changes the atmosphere and the environment. At the start when I came here, I think the youngest students actually influenced the older ones, because the older ones would become more young, you know you'd find like men in their fifties going on with water fights and stuff like that. You would really regress. Now, with the younger ones, it is the other way around.

Michael, the handsome and self-assured Dubliner, leaned across the table to tell a different story—of a more tortuous route to the priesthood.

> This is actually my second time around. I originally started in the mid-'80s and left after four years. The reasons I left were several. One was celibacy, I wasn't sure I wanted to be celibate or that I could be. The other one was I had a particular vision of what the Church should be . . . and I suppose the Church I felt I was being trained for seemed not to live up to that. I felt a lot had gone wrong there and I couldn't reconcile it. So I left. And I suppose what ultimately started bringing me back was relationships with other people—I was working with homeless people for a number of years. During that time I was basically doing social work and while I think that was very important, social work wasn't ultimately the answer, you know. So if there was an answer, what was it? At the same time, I slowly started to develop a sense of God loving me. At the time I didn't try to live according to Catholic values, I lived what I considered a good life, in the best sense of that word and in the worst. But I just came to have this sense of God loving me very genuinely, despite everything. Like there was nothing I could do "that would stop God loving me" and that had a huge effect on my life in general. Basically I started

looking around and asking myself, "well, what am I going to do with this?" I wanted to share it with other people. And the best way I felt I could share that with the most people was by being a priest.

In the meantime, I have learned to be easier on myself and that made it easier to live with the mess, the complexity, the things that are wrong in the Church. Then there's the whole celibacy thing. I still struggle, but I see a lot of advantages to it. I do think for me personally it is something that I feel at this stage I can live relatively comfortably with. It helps me to be available to people, to be available to God. It is a commitment, no more than marriage is, and this is my commitment.

I found the differences between Francis and Michael both striking and interesting. Young though he was, Francis seemed in a way rooted in an "older" world—the rural West, while Michael was more typically urban. They told different stories of self and Church. While Francis seemed uncertain of his place in a faltering, if not unraveling, narrative that began with his heroic role-model priest, Michael was already well ensconced in the more labile tale of personal and institutional development, of quest and self-realization. Not surprisingly, on most issues young Francis was to prove the most conservative in the group. Yet they all agreed about the root problem they felt the Church faced, and Francis did not hesitate to express his disappointment and unease with the way things were going.

All that sort of stuff happening in the Church would have affected me a bit as well. I suppose I would have felt very angry. First of all when the scandals broke, when the bishops drew up their guidelines in 1996 and then each year the same stuff seemed to come up again and again and again. It was sort of like [the film] *Groundhog Day*. There seemed to be no end to it. I suppose I would have felt disappointed in our leaders. . . . I had a strong sense that people out there are very forgiving of the Church, and very forgiving of the priests. There is still a huge amount of good will there. But that good will can't last forever. It is not being harnessed in any way and I'd feel very saddened by that.

I see the crisis in the Church, not so much as a crisis of faith, I think it is a crisis in the clergy. The clergy really do need to be reformed. And part of the problem, I suppose, on child abuse is that most priests have not been involved and they are feeling very dejected and very down. But still there are other problems in the clergy like motivation, manpower and resources. But because the clergy are feeling so dejected, those issues aren't being dealt with. And you know, in the long run that is going to have serious implications. The whole energy of the Church in Ireland has been totally focused on solving these problems, but there is a huge number of other problems out there and they are not being addressed at all.

Francis's reference to the recurring scandals, and especially to the hierarchy's failure to deal adequately with them, was a view clearly shared by those around the table, all of whom shook or nodded their heads in sad recognition. Donal, the northerner, pushed back from the table and spoke softly of the bishops.

I suppose I always feel, as seminarians, we see things from two perspectives. Like we can be very disappointed with the bishops and very angry and annoyed with them, but yet we encounter them on an individual basis and we know that individually as human beings they are generally very good men and very well meaning men. And on a personal level you feel a huge deal of sympathy for them, you're sort of pulled apart because you feel angry with them, but you feel sorry for them at the same time.

I suppose you put yourself into the position, "well, if I was a Bishop, how would I handle it?"

As I looked around the table, it seemed they all thought they would, in fact, have done—and will do—better. Donal continued:

Yes, I believe that it should have been handled it a lot better. I would be quite angry with most of them, thinking that they could have done a better job, you know, in that situation, instead of covering it up, particularly when the guidelines were implemented. My own bishop, he came on the local radio after the program on UTV saying that there was four new cases that came into the diocese and we still don't know who they are, you know. You know and he hasn't even talked to us.

Weary recognition from around the table. Donal now spoke with some emotion:

Until the bishops start being confronted personally by people who have been abused . . . Unless you are sitting there, you can only talk in the abstract about these things. We all know it is awful, but if you are sitting there looking at someone who is talking about what this has done to his life. What it is to be raped by somebody over a period of time or whatever. And see what has actually been the effect on his life in terms of his emotional life, his physical life, his sexual life or spiritual life, his faith life. You know it has just impinged on so many aspects of their lives. I really don't think it has started sinking in. You know, the reality of it. And I suppose the image that comes across is still the protection of the institution. "God forbid, if we give any sign of weakness, it will begin the crumble and collapse."

My mind's eye returned to the cloister just beyond the room in which we sat, to the phalanx of bishops and cardinals adorned with the regalia of high office. I agreed with Donal about the "image" of the bishops, especially in the early days of the scandals, when they felt powerful enough to try stonewalling the media. But weren't they, in some sense, right about the threat to the "institution," at least as it had come to be in Ireland? Not surprisingly, Donal—and the others—entertained a different view.

> I think maybe the bishops see themselves as guardians of the faith. But they are only one part of the institution. Do the bishops actually trust the people? Do they really trust the people to have a legitimate say in Church affairs? I think that is the real issue coming up now.

Francis agreed and added:

> And do the bishops actually trust the priests? Because the impression that comes across, and the feeling among priests, is that they don't. The bishops, if you hear them at Mass, will talk about this huge unity there is between the bishops and the priests. But in reality, there is a huge union between the priests and the people and there is a gulf between that group and the bishop then. And again, it is all about that trust thing. I think the way the papers will present certain stories, they try to create a rift between the priests and the people. Obviously there are some cases, but the people are very, very united with the priests who serve them in the parish, and I think the priests are very united to the people. The rift is between that grouping and the bishops.

Thinking further about that rift, James, the quiet Dubliner, remarked:

> The question that comes up here for me is why will the people accept human sinfulness and ordinariness in their priests but it doesn't transfer to those who are commonly referred to as the Church—the hierarchy? We do have a fundamental problem with language here and the understanding of Church at a parish level would be limited in that sense. "Church" still refers to hierarchy. It is only those who are somehow involved at a parish level who would see it differently. Whereas in the American Church, it would be very widely understood that "Church" means all people together. We have a huge amount of catechetical work to do at a fundamental level.

While I took his point on the effects of involvement on the parish level, I could not help wondering whether there were other aspects to this general understanding of bishop/hierarchy as Church. For one thing, in an anthropological sense, it is precisely that equation that is performed at every level, from parish to nation. In all cases, bishops appear with and in the "charisma of office," as Weber put it, and never as simple priests, much less people. Their dress, comportment, ritual offices, pronouncements—all of it is meant to convince people that they are, in fact, the embodiment of the Church. James's comparison of Ireland with the United States points to the crucial importance of the current and potential flow of influence in that direction. However, any observer of the work of the Massachusetts-based lay organization Voice of the Faithful cannot but note that the predominantly Irish-American group, if Irish in the "faith," speak with an American "voice" in relation to notions of authority, independence, and so on.

In any event, this line of conversation about the relation of bishops to both priest and people naturally led the seminarians to the topic most on their minds: their own role vis-à-vis potential congregations. Their remarks reveal the difficulty of their perceived position. James led off.

> I think the whole thing is about finding your role. We talk amongst ourselves about the role of priests. It is up to the priests to hand over and say "this is your parish, take responsibility." Although the priest would stay as the figure of Christ leading the people, ultimately it is up to the parish to lead itself, you know. At the center of everything we do is Christ . . . some priests are prepared to go out nearly thinking that they are the Christ. "I am your God in the parish, worship me," you know, and people will try to hold on to that. You have to be willing to let go and give people the freedom. You are there as a shepherd but not as . . .

As his voice trailed off, I was struck by the ambivalence and ambiguity—if not outright contradiction—in James's imagined priest. He "would stay as the figure of Christ" and yet should not slip into thinking he was Christ. What, I wondered, would this new kind of priest actually look like? I had the distinct impression that such was the question on all their minds. Michael, as usual, had something to say on the topic.

> The priests used to have to write the letter for somebody going to America or whatever, but that day is gone and we have to find our own place among them again. What exactly is our role in the parish? I think it goes back to being a particularly spiritual element and enabling the people to make sense of life and all its mechanisms and intricacies, [to help them see] that God is still there amidst it all. But this thing of being the social worker who does everything in the parish, that day is definitely gone.

But some of the others—maybe particularly those from rural areas—were reluctant to abandon precisely the vision of priest-leader that drew them to the position in the first place. The inherent difficulties of this role and the real ambivalence it presents for the seminarian were explored by Donal.

I might disagree with that slightly. I think there is a danger that the priest would withdraw too much and that we can marginalize ourselves further. I think the priest in the past wanted to be in some sense a social worker. Now, like dealing with family breakdown and things like that, it is very easy to refer all those matters to professionals. But you need to be also in there yourself in some way, because if you aren't, then you are alienating yourself more and more from the people. And also, you know, I think you would also damage vocations further. Because the model now is that the priest is there to empower the people, he is there to draw people's gifts and talents out and let the people do, he is an overall manager, helping people to do things for themselves. But if you take the priest forty years ago, like say my parish priest, his job was to build schools, build churches, go out and save souls. If you have a choice between being a savior of souls and power to the people, savior of souls is sort of a more attractive option if you are eighteen or nineteen you know.

The nature of their role, I reminded them, would also be a function of numbers. That is, decreasing numbers of clerics would mean higher and higher priest/people ratios. How did they think that would affect their experience? Donal continued:

I think there is a difficulty there, because in the end that is how the people get to know the priests, from one-to-one contact. From the priest going to the house because somebody has died, or to fill in prenuptial forms or things like that. Really, when people get an opportunity to talk to a priest, it is the same as being a human being and not somebody who just stands up on the altar. I suppose if there is less and less priests, there is going to be less opportunity for that to happen.

Michael added:

How do you catechize a whole generation of people who haven't been catechized effectively? I mean most of my friends have very little sense of any of this. They believe, but it doesn't impinge on their lives in any way, and that is diluted. And what they are passing onto their kids is diluted. So I think part of the challenge is how do you work with them and with those who are still very faithful? And how do you help them to spread the word in their every day lives?

This possible dependence on laypersons reminded them of the fact that Maynooth, along with a few other institutions, was in fact producing far more degrees in lay theology than in divinity. If there were only sixty-four seminarians in all seven years, St. Patrick's College was at the same time teaching over two hundred lay theology students. Michael noted:

You have the same in Milltown; you have the same in Mater Dei. So there is still a level of interest and a level of expertise and professionalism. But to what extent are we as Church prepared to put them into parishes, to give them a decent wage? And to what extent are the people ready to pay for that? The Church in the States does it very well. I don't know if our culture would take to it in the same way.

In fact the signs were not good. At this point the vast majority of such lay theology students—of whom about two-thirds are usually female—go into teaching. The impact of their formation in theology may of course contribute to the shaping of an evolving Catholic perspective, but the Church shows no sign to date of recruiting them to take up any of the pastoral burdens from the clergy.

The conversation then turned back to the seminary as an institution, whose curriculum and style of delivery had in fact changed dramatically over the last few years. The dwindling number of seminarians had in fact led to a structural innovation that might have important repercussions, for beginning the next year lay theology students and seminarians were to be brought together in the same classes. The seminarians thought this would be good for all concerned, and they were all very happy with the increasingly "hands on" approach of pastoral education, which had them all serving internships in everything from prisons to homeless shelters. The more egalitarian atmosphere of classes combined with this "real world" experience was conducive to a growth in feelings of competence and confidence—further fostered by "an emphasis on the whole thing of human growth, human development in ourselves and other people."

After so glowing an account, I could not resist asking why, if it was so good at the seminary, did so many leave? Francis, to everyone's immediate agreement, ticked off the two issues.

I think celibacy has a big part to play in it. It is a huge issue, yeah. And I think obedience can be a bigger problem than the celibacy. You know, the obedience thing. I suppose you can't choose to do what you want to do. You have to hand yourself over to either your bishop or the authorities here but even with the future, what you would like to do, you don't always get your own way, and I suppose it is hard to give that up.

Michael suggested a rather different reading of "obedience," and one with interesting ramifications for that central feature of Irish Catholicism—clerical authority.

I love going back to the root of the word: *obidere*. I think to be obedient to someone is to listen to them and to take on board what they are saying. And

> I think that obedience derives from the bishops in many ways. They are our guides and guardians in many ways. I mean you can listen to them, but we also need to listen to ourselves. There are things we feel comfortable with and feel confident about. But there are certainly things that I do not feel confident about, and I would be much more at ease being obedient to myself. Saying "no, you don't have to deal with that." You can't deal with it all. You deal with where your particular strengths are and be prepared to leave the rest. So the obedience thing is more than just doing what you are told, it is much more a pervasive listening. And I think listening, if it is done well, has to be a two-way process, you know. So if you are talking about obedience in terms of the bishops, you know, you have to listen very closely to hear what they are saying. He has a duty to listen as well, because it is communication.

Probably not the definition of obedience most bishops would have in mind, I could not help thinking. We all rose to part company, but before I left, Michael wanted to put the Church into the larger context.

> I think we need to broaden the whole thing a little bit. We are talking about the issues facing the Church internally. But the things that are affecting the Church are external as well. You know, the secularization of society in general. The whole thing of the authority of the Church being undermined for better or for worse—a bit of both maybe—is going on elsewhere in society. You know, the political system has been undermined through corruption and the justice system has been undermined. So every system that has traditionally had some kind of authority is being challenged, being undermined at some kind of level. I would say that some of that is for the good, but I think that some of it is not. If you carry through on that you end up with utter chaos. You end up where nothing means anything.

Michael's words about the general changes in Irish society echoed in my head as I stood, a few weeks later, high on the bare flanks of the mountain Slieve League in Southwest Donegal, looking out over the several townlands of Teelin and across the river and tidy bay to the parish of Kilcar. Certainly he was right about the general challenge to authority and, more broadly, about the effects of social change on religious practice. Even out in this edge of western Ireland, where, like in Maynooth, there were significant changes afoot long before the priestly scandals hit. In some ways, the particular forcefulness of Father McDyer obscured the degree to which he was the last of a breed. Or rather, the local worlds in which priests like him began their work in the 1950s and '60s were radically reshaped over the ensuing decades.

From the windy heights of the upper Agharagh townland, the most visible changes were in the local relationship to the land and the water. How different the scene had looked when I first arrived there on a fine June day, nearly thirty years before. Then, men in caps with spraying canisters strapped to their backs had moved up and down between the hand-dug, neat summer rows of potato plants, white flowers bobbing over deep green. And arable land that did not grow potatoes grew hay, for nearly every family had a cow or two. There were many sheep above on the mountain, and small boats down on the bay, each with a crew waiting for the leap of the salmon. Now, not a single thatched roof gleamed on this bright winter's day, and spring, I knew, would bring no plowing or digging beyond a few modest kitchen gardens. Nor would there be more than a boat or two with crews patient enough to catch the few salmon still making their way home to the Glen River. In fact, this virtual extinction of what had been the underlying basis of local life was already achieved when I had returned to do fieldwork in the mid-1980s. By then most potatoes locally consumed came from Cyprus or Italy, few families bothered with hay or cows, and a greatly reduced number of sheep roamed the mountain and bog—where by then turf was cut almost entirely by machine. Through those and the ensuing decades the prosperity of the region rose and fell with the nation. Emptied again by emigration in the '80s, the district was the scene of holiday and returned-migrant homes in the prosperous late '90s. But these economic fluctuations did not interrupt the inexorable change in the relation to the land and water. Beginning in the '70s, when the old folks retired, the younger generation—those now in their forties and fifties—had no intention of continuing what had come to be seen as economically irrational practice. These men and women had jobs in factories, trades, shops, and so on. They no longer saw the point in spending long hours and hard labor on poor land and water.

But did such economic changes have any impact on religion? Yes, in at least two important respects. First, the relation to land and landscape was fundamental to popular religious conceptions of power, chance, and reciprocity—a set of ideas and feelings perhaps best and most clearly expressed in devotion to local holy wells. Second, relations with the land strongly impacted on relations with neighbors, interdependence with whom was largely a function of both agricultural and maritime pursuits. Common property in land and water, mutual assistance, inheritance, even conflict and feud were all a function of these economic pursuits and stood at the heart of everything summed up in the words "household" and "community." The weakening of these bonds—particularly those associated with the support, performance, and re-creation of these social units—was bound to affect religious practice. Moreover, the degree to which local worlds were horizontally integrated and lacked vertical access to resources beyond in Dublin (though not to resources in the United States and Britain, which had long been reached through emigrant networks) was crucial in creating the mediatory, broker role for the parish priest. That role was further accentuated by the typical educational distance between the priest and the locals, for up to the late 1960s, there were only very few people with secondary school and university degrees in the parish—the small and important middle class. Others who had managed to obtain higher degrees were typically gone, having gone where the jobs were. But that too had changed, first with the opening of a public secondary school in the parish in the late '60s, and then with increasing participation in third-level education over the ensuing decades. So that by the time the Church scandals hit, the position and role of the local priest, even in places like this, had already slowly but inexorably changed. Family and community were still important, but the degree to which both exercised a strong, and religiously sanctioned, social control had been greatly reduced. And the priest stood before a congregation considerably "leveled up": not at all as distant from him as their parents had been, and with their own connections to the world beyond. This was as true culturally as socially, for the great growth of the media and the increasingly alternative and sometimes highly critical vision they offered certainly undermined the cultural and moral authority of the national/religious master narrative. Institutionally, however, the last but still critical base of priestly power remained—control of the local schools.

For all that, the Sunday scene in Carrick in the winter of 2003 was certainly not unfamiliar. Cars lined the streets, and the church was nearly full with dutiful parishioners who sat through the priest's characteristically slow lilt in Irish and English. The word was that a certain number were going to the young curate's Mass in Glen, because it was typically shorter. If so, there were still many in the Carrick pews, and Father Gallagher reckoned attendance at something like 75 percent. Down from the over 90 percent that had regularly attended ten or fifteen years earlier, but enough to give the general impression of a still regularly practicing parish.

Confession, however, was another story. Numbers at that sacrament, by the priest's reckoning, had dropped precipitously in recent years, so that only a minority of the parish regularly attended.

After Mass, I visited a local family I knew well. Margaret is a bright and reflective fifty-year-old schoolteacher from a middle-class family in the parish. Were she in Boston instead of Donegal, she would likely be a stalwart member of the Voice of the Faithful. Margaret would be classed as a devout or strong Catholic, and certainly a regularly practicing one. She was hopeful, like her New England counterparts, that the Church would emerge from its current troubles stronger and more authentic than before—interpreting these turbulent times as a necessary purge. She even remarked, as did a number of others I spoke with, that those avoiding Mass "were the ones that never wanted to be there in the first place." But she is also angry and frustrated with the hierarchy. If the scandals and cover-ups have not kept her from going to church, she was neither surprised by, nor did she obviously disagree with, those who were no longer going to confession. And she was openly and strongly critical of the bishops. When her elderly mother meekly suggested that perhaps the bishops had learned their lesson, Margaret replied, "Nothing has changed, look at your man in Carrick and with no word of explanation." She was referring to a priest, native to the parish, who had suddenly appeared at home about a year earlier, apparently discharged from duty in a parish to the north. The locals were given to understand that the diocese was obligated to find any priest a home, but there was no explanation of his presence there. Given the endemic problem of clerical abuse, naturally many suspected the worst, but apparently were unable to get any further word on the subject. As I made my rounds of friends over the next several days, this matter was nearly always alluded to. "Well, now we are openly talking about it, and that's a good thing. But the bishops are still secretive—look at your man up in the village! And the people here talk, but they don't do anything about it. Not like in America."

Once again, the reference to America is instructive. Clearly another unintended consequence of "empire" is that the dominions are leading the way, and perhaps eventually influencing what is and will be happening in Ireland. But I could not help wondering whether in setting themselves up once again as the distant authorities, the bishops weren't in some ways presenting a familiar target and thereby creating the possibility that the locals would see their own parish and priest in a contrasting and hence good light. That, I remembered, was precisely the wishful thinking of the seminarians back in Maynooth. In fact, out here most people did seem to like their own priests, though perhaps in different ways.

The new curate, just merged from Maynooth, was carefully finding his role as young, activist priest. After very few months on the job, he had a following, especially among the younger parishioners, a number of whom told me they were going to Mass because of him. On the other hand, he had already run afoul of other locals by getting into a serious dispute with a veteran teacher in the National School. A latter-day Father McDyer? At the least a man who, like Francis back in Maynooth, had grown up with the West of Ireland "local hero" model of the office. He seemed to still interpret the role of priest as community leader and was perhaps destined accordingly to have his avid supporters and entrenched resisters. But the school was in fact the last institutional setting where such secular authority could be exercised, and the degree to which he will prevail is still unknown. Looking at such local contexts, one can have little doubt of the repercussions of the Church's final retreat from the schools. Now, the parish priest is still the president of the local board and hires and fires teachers. Removing him from this position would forever change not only the role of the priest, but also perhaps at least one important aspect of local community structure.

However, another sense of community is perhaps embodied in the figure of the parish priest across the bogs in Carrick. In Father Eddy locals seem to recognize, I think, almost a nostalgic image of their own lost innocence. And of the Church's lost innocence as well. That sometimes comical, even blundering, very local and human fellow "with nothing Oxford about him" could not be imagined in the role of child abuser. In fact, two very young "altar girls" were unproblematically entrusted to his service. Father Eddy seemed genuinely stunned and confused by the very existence of practices he had heard nothing of in earlier, happier times. And all the locals I spoke with believed him, noting without my raising the question, that "poor Father Eddy can't imagine such things!" There seemed to be a sense in which they are saying that they too can't imagine such things and are taking the priest as emblematic of a collective innocence of place and people that firmly places corrupting evil beyond parish bounds. On the other hand, of course, their worries about the possible crimes of the mysteriously returned priest reveal that such a view is tenuous. Meanwhile, however, Eddy is a comforting presence. "Whatever the books and all he had in Maynooth," a local man commented, "they couldn't knock the corner of Glenn Finn off of him!" But it was not just his "innocence" that was valued. Significantly, when any locals—though particularly older ones—were talking about him, they would say something like "he's very good about visiting, about sickness and death." I was reminded of the folktales relating priestly prowess in penal days. A favorite theme was the priest—however he might be thwarted by evil Protestants and natural calamity—who would arrive in time to perform the last rites. All the changes in local society and in even in the position of the Church had not unseated death as the definitive personal and communal moment.[7] It was perhaps no coincidence that the comic stories told about Father Eddy, like the praise, centered on such visits and wakes.

> Old Conny was up in the room—he had been slowly dying for weeks—and Father Eddy came to visit. Well, there was another bed in the room and the priest would take a lie down in it when he came to visit, do you see? So, one time he was there, and the old fellow on his way out, and Old Conny shouts down to his son below in the kitchen. So the young one goes up thinking Conny was about to go—but he was sitting up in his bed. "Would you ever go and get the camera, he said, and take a picture of Father Eddy?" He was fast asleep in the other bed.

There were other similar tales, none told without affection. And, of course, there are the main events themselves, as when the priest leads the rosary at the wake. There were two in one night during my visit, and Father Eddy lumbered into the modest home on the mountain road, and kneeling, transformed all within into the ancient congregation, kneeling on the hard floor, reciting the Hail Marys in Irish and English. If the priest is most identified with the institutional Church in the confessional—and hence to be avoided—at these moments he is most at one with the community's imagination of its self, and hence to be embraced.

Right up to the present crisis, the tortuous tale of Irish Catholicism attests to several aspects of religion as practiced. It is a story of resilience in the face of adversity, of the recurring local creativity of what we might

---

7. See Lawrence Taylor, "Bas-in Eirinn: Cultural Constructions of Death in Ireland," *Anthropological Quarterly* 62, no. 4 (1989): 175–87.

call a religious imagination, but above and beyond all that, of the crucially formative social and political dimension of religion. Moreover, this dimension has always operated at all levels, from the very local to the international. Locally, religious practice certainly continued to include a wide variety of nonorthodox belief and practice, but the collective expression of religion, from family rosary to local pilgrimage to the regular and life-cycle sacraments, came to be dominated, orchestrated, and led by official Church doctrine and personnel. Nationally, the colonial equation of Catholicism with a certain form of nationalism won out over more radical versions, and attained a tremendously central position in the Irish state, controlling not only general moral discourse and practice, but the main institutional settings in which the person and society were formed. Finally, internationally, Irish Catholicism became the standard form in, and its personnel in command of, the English-speaking Catholic world, and that fact has to be one of the great unintended consequences of British conquest and empire.

The present crisis in the Church can in fact be seen to operate at all these levels. Locally, the sort of social world in which the priest and his Church controlled so many crucial settings and acted as brokers between locals and the outside world has been radically altered. A leveling up, a decrease in the importance of local social groupings, and the introduction of alternative and competing discourses through the media have all had the effect of diminishing the position and authority of the priest. These same kinds of changes have of course occurred nationally as well. The media have increasingly represented not only alternative but often absolutely antagonistic voices and narratives to those of the Church, and alternative identities—different ways of being Irish and/or European—that do not require Catholicism are on offer. Internationally, there is a further ironic unintended consequence of Ireland's historical centrality in the English-speaking world Catholic empire. That is the awareness of and influence of events and processes underway in the "colonies." Riding the train back to Dublin from Maynooth one evening I found myself sitting across from a middle-aged lady who was poring over the front-page story on the resignation of Cardinal Law in Boston. She was a traditional Catholic from Bundoran, County Donegal, where—as she explained to me—although she continued attend Mass regularly, she had ceased contributing money these past four years. "I still believe in God, in the Mass, and so on. I just couldn't give money to those people!" Naturally, she was very interested in the fate of Cardinal Law at the hands of the "faithful" in Boston. "I wonder," she said, looking up, "could we ever manage to do that here. To get rid of Cardinal Connell?" In the end they did, but not as yet with the concomitant creation of a strong, organized lay group, as was the case in Boston.

All these vignettes and voices from the center and the edge catch something of the current sense of continuity and rapid change that indeed characterizes not only the Catholic Church here, but Irish society and culture. In a larger, structural sense, the current crisis amounts to a kind of "dis-establishment" of the Catholic Church. With the *smacht* of the bishops removed—to paraphrase the people of Southwest Donegal—a political, social, and cultural space has been opened. Certainly, Catholic religious forms and practice continue to support local social worlds where they persist—as is the case to an extent in places such as Southwest Donegal. They also continue to play a central role in such lay-originating events and processes as the Prayer House in Achill (where the relative weakness of hierarchical control these days may actually afford more latitude). For increasing numbers of Irish people, however, life is taking on either the standard Western European form of secularity punctuated only by life-crisis rites-of-passage or the American search for personal meaning and identity. In the latter instance, Catholic forms have been and are available, including pilgrimages. Croagh Patrick and Lough Derg continue to draw large numbers, perhaps because they allow not only "traditional" readings, but also those of interpretive communities who speak of them in therapeutic and/or new age idioms.[8] These Catholic practices thus combine and/or compete with Reiki and an ever-increasing range of alternative "Spiritualities."[9] Whether all this amounts to the chaos that seminarian Michael feared, it is certain that the failed master narrative has left space for competing stories—stories that were already being told but not heard, and new stories.

8. Arnaud Tagnachie and Keith Egan (Ph.D. program, NUI Maynooth) are currently conducting field research on Irish and European pilgrimages that bear out this interpretation.

9. Peter Mulholland's "Reiki and the Roman Catholic Tradition: An Anthropological Study of Changing Religious Forms in Modern Ireland" (Ph.D. thesis, NUI Maynooth) reveals a fascinating mixture of personal religious/therapeutic practice among contemporary Irish Reiki devotees.

United States

JAMES D. DAVIDSON

5. The Catholic Church in the United States

1950 to the Present

Introduction

According to the brochure for the conference for which this paper was originally written, "The United States, the Republic of Ireland, and the Canadian province of Quebec were in many respects quite dissimilar places in 1950. But the Catholic Church in all three places enjoyed an apparently high degree of institutional vigor, particularly when compared to the Church in Western Europe." A lot has changed since then. The Church in all three locales has experienced very broad and very deep changes. The purpose of this conference was to assess these changes in two respects. In the words of the organizers, the first goal was purely descriptive: "to explore the 'Catholic trajectory' in each of these locales from 1950 to the present—to chart trends in Mass attendance and devotions; reception of the sacraments (especially the Sacrament of Penance); vocations to the priesthood and religious life; attendance at Catholic schools and colleges: support for Church teaching on social, political and sexual issues; and financial support of the Church." The second goal was more analytic: to discern the underlying forces that have propelled these trends. As the conference organizers saw it, "A comparison of these 'trajectories' should help us understand the forces leading to recent changes in Catholicism in Western nations."

With these two goals in mind, I offered conference participants a summary and an assessment of the trends that have taken place in the United

States. Subsequently I have updated my analysis for this book. My under-standing of the trends and the forces that lie behind them is unchanged, but some parts of my analysis have been extended and some new research has been added.

My Approach

I bring two attributes to this task. For one thing, I am a practicing Catholic who was born in 1942. As a result, I have personal experience with many of the changes that have taken place in the Church since 1950. I was an altar boy in the 1950s and still have fond memories of responding in Latin to my pastor, who faced the altar, not the people, as he said Mass. I also recall the day in 1958 when the principal of the public high school that I attended pulled me aside to say that we had a new pope (John XXIII). My days in undergraduate school at Fairfield University (1960–1964) and graduate school at the University of Notre Dame (1964–1968) were enhanced by the parallel occurrence of Vatican II (1962–1965). My years since then have taken me down two tracks: a personal history of marriage and helping my wife, Anna, raise two post–Vatican II children (our son, Jay, and our daughter, Theresa), and a professional life of study-ing the sociology of religion in general and Catholicism in particular.

All of these personal and professional experiences have contributed to the approach I take in this chapter. I begin with my approach to the Church, then turn to the way I will interpret the changes that have taken place in the Church.

Documenting Changes in the Church

Theologically, the institutional life of the Church cannot be separated from the beliefs and the practices of the people who comprise its mem-bership. However, from a sociological point of view, these two entities can be treated separately. The institutional Church contains policies and practices that may or may not be reflected in the thoughts and actions of the laity. The two can be closely related or only loosely connected. There-fore, I treat their relationship as an empirical question, not a given. The evidence shows that the two were more closely aligned in the 1950s than they are now.

My analysis pays attention to four dimensions of church life.[1] One is the structural or bureaucratic nature of the Church. Like any other complex organization, the Church consists of many "bureaus" or units that are linked by a vertical distribution of authority, which flows from the Vatican to the laity. I contend that there have been important structural changes in the American Church since the 1950s.

The second dimension has to do with human resources—that is, the attributes and actions of people in the Church. This includes members of the hierarchy but also the laity. I show that the theological and ecclesiastical orientations of the hierarchy have changed over the years, as have the laity's demographic characteristics, beliefs and practices, and leadership roles in parishes and dioceses.

The political dimension concerns power relations in the Church. Sometimes, cooperative and harmonious relationships prevail in an organization, as members strive to achieve common goals and objectives. But at other times, especially times of uncertainty and change, relationships become more frayed, as various factions or "parties" try to shape the organization according to their own values and interests. In the case of the Church, I call special attention to the changing relationships between liberal clergy and laity, on the one hand, and conservative clergy and laity, on the other.

The fourth dimension highlights the symbolic or cultural nature of organizational life. If we are to understand the Church in the United States, we must understand the values, beliefs, rituals, and traditions that comprise its culture. Here, I pay special attention to fluctuations between what Eugene Kennedy has called Culture I and Culture II Catholicism.[2] I will develop these concepts in more detail later but, for now, let me say that the two are not mutually exclusive types. Instead, they represent opposing ends of a continuum that ranges from pure Culture I to pure Culture II. The Culture I orientation emphasizes the institutional nature of the Church and the authority of the Magisterium. The Culture II orientation stresses the personal nature of faith and locates authority in the conscience of the believer.

1. Lee G. Bolman and Terrence E. Deal, *Reframing Organizations* (San Francisco: Jossey-Bass, 1997).

2. Eugene Kennedy, *Tomorrow's Catholics, Yesterday's Church* (San Francisco: Harper and Row, 1988).

FIGURE 1. My Approach

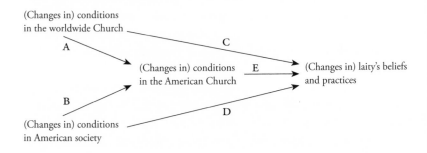

Interpreting the Changes

In addition to documenting changes in the Church, my other task is to interpret the changes. My interpretation starts with what sociologists call an "open system" approach.[3] That approach emphasizes the constant interaction between the Church and its environment. From this point of view, the boundaries between the Church and its environment are very porous, with the environment always influencing the Church and the Church always trying to impact its environment.

I concentrate on two contextual influences: the worldwide Church and the religious context of American society (see Figure 1). By focusing on the worldwide Church, I take into account influences that enter the American Church from the top. I am especially interested in the extent to which authority is centralized in the Vatican or shared more widely with bishops throughout the world. I also examine the extent to which authority is in the hands of theological conservatives, who promote a Culture I orientation to faith and morals, or theological liberals, who promote a Culture II orientation. The religious context of American society includes influences that enter the Church from the side. Here I focus on

---

3. James D. Davidson and Andrea S. Williams, "Megatrends in Twentieth Century American Catholicism," *Social Compass* 44 (December 1997): 507–27; James D. Davidson, *Mobilizing Social Movement Organizations* (Storrs, Conn.: Society for the Scientific Study of Religion, 1985), 15.

the nature of the relationship between American Protestants and Catholics. That relationship has ranged from quite hostile to quite harmonious over the years. I argue that changes in American Catholicism are responses to changes in the relationship between liberals and conservatives in the worldwide Church and the relationship between Protestants and Catholics in the United States.

Arrows A and B in Figure 1 indicate that changes in the worldwide Church (especially the Vatican) and American society (especially Protestant-Catholic relations) have produced changes in the institutional life of the Church in the United States (or, as it is usually called, the American Church). Arrows C, D, and E indicate that changes in the worldwide Church, American society, and the American Church also have affected the thoughts and actions of the laity.

I apply this model to three time periods. The first is the pre–Vatican II years of the 1950s—essentially, the years during which Pius XII was pope (1938–1958). The second period (1960–1977) encompasses the two years of anticipation leading up to Vatican II and the thirteen years of transition that followed. It starts with the papacy of John XXIII (1958–1963) and encompasses Pope Paul VI's reign (1963–1978). The last period is the post–Vatican II years of 1978 to the present. It stretches from the beginning of Pope John Paul II's reign to his death and the naming of Pope Benedict XVI as his successor.

I begin with the 1950s because that was the starting point selected by the planners of this conference. While the 1950s serve as a temporal benchmark for my analysis, I do not assume they are a normative benchmark. I do not treat the Church of the 1950s as a model that should transcend time and place. Instead, I assume it was simply a function of conditions in the worldwide Church and American society at the time. If similar circumstances were to occur at another time, a similar pattern of church life might reappear. Under other circumstances, the pattern is likely to be quite different.

For data, I have consulted historical and theological analyses of the worldwide Church and the institutional Church in America. I also have reviewed research on Protestant-Catholic relations in the United States and Catholics' religious beliefs and practices.

The 1950s

Let me begin with the pre–Vatican II world of the 1950s. I start with conditions in the worldwide Church, then move to conditions in American society, before examining the policies of the American Church and the orientations of American Catholics.

The Worldwide Church

In the 1940s and '50s, authority was highly centralized in the worldwide Church.[4] Popes, cardinals, and bishops claimed to have final authority on issues of faith and morals, and—as I will show—for the most part, the laity granted them such authority. Positions throughout the hierarchy were occupied by leaders, such as Pope Pius XII, who belonged to the pre–Vatican II generation and were formed by the pre–Vatican II Church.[5] These leaders stressed what Kennedy has called Culture I Catholicism. Its emphasis was on the importance of Catholic identity, sacraments, the Nicene Creed, concern for poor, and participation in local parishes. It also stressed the concept of the Church being an end in itself, the hierarchical nature of the Church, and the legitimacy of episcopal authority. Other elements of Culture I Catholicism included the importance of knowing church teachings, an emphasis on obedience (with the Magisterium seen as the locus of authority), belief that the Catholic Church is the One True Church, and a negative view of modern society.[6]

Culture I Catholicism was on full display in John Walsh's book *This Is Catholicism*. Two passages illustrate Culture I's approach to the teaching authority of the Church. In the first one, Walsh wrote:

> The Church teaches truths which are beyond the scope of the unaided human intellect—truths which the mind could never discover by itself, since they concern the invisible God and the life of the world to come. These supernatural truths are most precious and practical, because they tell man where he came from, where he is going, and what he is to do while he is here. God, in His goodness, has disclosed these facts to men through His incarnate Son, Jesus Christ. And Christ's Church unerringly transmits them down through

4. John Seidler and Katherine Meyer, *Conflict and Change in the Catholic Church* (New Brunswick, N.J.: Rutgers University Press, 1989), 16–18.

5. Gene Burns, *The Frontiers of Catholicism* (Berkeley: University of California Press, 1992).

6. Kennedy, *Tomorrow's Catholics, Yesterday's Church*, 10–33.

the ages, to all men, to all parts of the world. It is the duty of man to accept in humble gratitude the message that the infinite God has been pleased to send him.[7]

Walsh had this to say about the laity's duty to obey church teachings:

Catholics accept the fact that Christ endowed the Church with full authority to rule, in matters religious and moral, their entire lives. On a religious or moral question, the voice of the Church is for a Catholic the voice of God, and he no more resents her maternal solicitude than he resents the watchful providence of God; in fact he regards the former as simply an aspect of the latter.[8]

American Society

In the Cold War period of the 1950s, Protestants and Catholics had a mutual interest in defending American social institutions. Both groups emphasized the importance of conforming to the American way of life.[9] For their part, Catholics were fiercely nationalistic and vigorously opposed to fascism and communism.[10] Senator Joseph McCarthy—whose fiery brand of anticommunism captured national attention in the early 1950s—was Catholic, and Catholics played a major role in having the phrase "under God" inserted into the Pledge of Allegiance in 1954.[11]

But Protestants and Catholics were different in other ways. The vast majority of Americans were Protestant. In 1950, the country's 29 million Catholics comprised only about 20 percent of the total population.[12] Protestants also had a disproportionate share of the nation's power, privilege, and prestige, while Catholics ranked well below the national average in education, occupational prestige, and income.[13]

7. John Walsh, S.J., *This Is Catholicism* (Garden City, N.Y.: Image Books, 1959), 172.
8. Ibid., 347.
9. William F. Whyte, *The Organization Man* (New York: Simon and Schuster, 1956); David Reisman, *The Lonely Crowd* (New Haven, Conn.: Yale University Press, 1950).
10. Mark Massa, S.J., *Anti-Catholicism in America* (New York: Crossroad, 2003), 57–80.
11. James D. Davidson, *Catholicism in Motion: The Church in American Society* (Liguori, Mo.: Liguori Publications, 2005), 43–44; Christopher J. Kauffman, *Patriotism and Fraternalism in the Knights of Columbus* (New York: Herder and Herder, 2001), 123–24.
12. William V. D'Antonio et al., *American Catholics: Gender, Generation, and Commitment* (Walnut Creek, Calif.: Alta Mira Books, 2001), 4.
13. Ralph E. Pyle and Jerome R. Koch, "The Religious Affiliations of American Elites, 1930s to 1990s: A Note on the Pace of Disestablishment," *Sociological Focus* 34 (May 2001): 125–37.

Protestants also considered themselves the nation's religious in-group and viewed Catholics as an out-group.[14] Elite Protestants distanced themselves from Catholics through a network of exclusive neighborhoods, private schools, and elite social organizations.[15] They also disapproved of Catholics' view that the Catholic Church is the One True Church, Catholics' beliefs about Mary and saints, Catholic theology regarding sacraments such as baptism, and Catholics' attempts to convert Protestants.[16] Some Protestants supported groups, such as Protestants and Other Americans United for the Separation of Church and State, that spread hatred toward and fear of Catholics.[17] Some also published best-selling books that were virulently anti-Catholic. For example, in *Communism, Democracy, and the Catholic Church,* readers were told that Catholicism's understanding of its own origins was false:

> [I]t is quite clear from the fragmentary evidence that no authentic documents corroborate the Catholic version of the Church's origin. There is no evidence that Peter ever was a pope or a bishop or that the Founder of Christianity sanctioned the system of ecclesiastical power which Rome has developed in his name. Peter may have preached and died in Rome, but beyond this relatively inconsequential and uncertain fact little is known that could associate him in any way with the Vatican claims of Roman primacy. Yet these historical deficiencies in papal pretensions are never admitted by Catholic scholars.[18]

In the same volume, readers were warned about the Catholic Church's supposedly undemocratic worldview and subversive political intentions:

> [W]hile the Catholic bishops in the United States appeal to the alleged principle of the equal rights of religious groups to receive government support under our Constitution, the Church itself never recognizes the right of any other church to receive government support in any Catholic country. If the United States became a Catholic country, there is no doubt that the American bishops would soon abandon their alleged scruples on the subject and would demand government money for the Catholic Church alone.[19]

14. Catherine L. Albanese, *America: Religions and Religion* (Belmont, Calif.: Wadsworth, 1999), 504–10.

15. E. Digby Balltzell, *The Protestant Establishment* (New York: Random House, 1964), 109–42.

16. David O. Moberg, *The Church as a Social Institution* (Englewood Cliffs, N.J.: Prentice-Hall, 1962), 308–309.

17. Ralph Lord Roy, *Apostles of Discord* (Boston: Beacon Press, 1953), 5–6.

18. Paul Blanshard, *Communism, Democracy, and Catholic Power* (Boston: Beacon Press, 1951), 239.

19. Ibid., 22.

Although Catholics had some favorable images of Protestants—as being fair in their business practices, for example—they also were highly defensive about their status as a religious minority and prejudiced against Protestants. They viewed Protestants as misguided enemies of the Church. Catholic culture in the 1950s

> was more often than not consciously anti-Protestant in content, determinedly defensive and apologetic in tone, and based on Ready Answers to questions which no one outside the walls was really asking. Protestants could be patently sincere, young Catholics learned, but they were also the "invincibly ignorant" victims of an erroneous system of theological thought. The conscientious Catholic for his part was solemnly obliged not to condone such errors by acting as if the were really of no serious consequences for either this life or the next. . . . [I]n their efforts to reach their Protestant neighbors, Catholics were not to make unworthy doctrinal compromises or give scandal by seeming to put their approval on the contemporary Protestant's unfortunate weakness for theological flabbiness. For example, except for funerals and weddings, the good Catholic would stay out of Protestant churches and under no circumstances would he participate in worship services conducted in them. Only Catholics duly certified as thoroughly qualified were permitted to read theological works written by Protestant authors; such books, being an exposition of heretical doctrines, were automatically proscribed by the Index of Forbidden Books. And some rigorists even went so far as to suggest that it would even be wrong to contribute to Protestant charities, since at least indirectly they promoted and strengthen the forces of heresy.[20]

Thus, in spite of Protestants' and Catholics' similarities as Americans and Christians, the social and cultural emphasis was on their differences.[21]

The American Church

As a result, the American Church was highly centralized and tightly controlled by pre–Vatican II leaders such as Cardinal Francis Joseph Spellman of New York, Cardinal Richard Cushing of Boston, Cardinal Dennis Dougherty of Philadelphia, and Bishop Fulton J. Sheen.[22] Culture I

20. John Cogley and Rodger Van Allen, *Catholic America* (Kansas City: Sheed and Ward, 1986), 144–45.

21. John J. Kane, *Catholic-Protestant Conflicts in America* (Chicago: University of Chicago Press, 1955); John J. Kane, "Protestant-Catholic Tensions," *American Sociological Review* 16 (October 1951), 663–72.

22. Charles R. Morris, *American Catholic* (New York: Random House, 1997), 165–227; Massa, *Anti-Catholicism in America*, 82–101.

Catholicism prevailed. As in the worldwide Church, the emphasis was on the importance of Catholic identity, sacraments, the Nicene Creed, concern for the poor, and participation in local parishes. The Church was viewed as the One True Church—as an end in itself. The legitimacy of episcopal authority was stressed, with its emphasis on obedience. Primacy was put on knowledge of church teachings, which included a negative view of modern society.

This approach, with its emphasis on authority and obedience, was communicated to the millions of Catholics who studied the *Baltimore Catechism*. In addition to its treatment of the Ten Commandments, the *Catechism* reviewed "the six *chief* commandments (laws) of the Church" (italics appear as they did in the original text):

- To *assist* at Mass on all *Sundays* and *holydays* of obligation.
- To *fast* (take only one full meal) and to *abstain* (use no meat) on the days appointed.
- To *confess* our sins at least once a year.
- To receive *Holy Communion* during the Easter time.
- To *contribute* (pay our share) to the *support* of the Church.
- To *observe* the laws of the Church concerning marriage.[23]

Priests, sisters, and brothers transmitted Culture I Catholicism to the laity through an array of Catholic institutions that were so segregated from the rest of society and so densely populated with Catholic people that they became known as the Catholic ghetto. That ghetto "began with the maternity ward and ended in the choice of gravesite."[24] Here is how sociologist Will Herberg described it:

> The Catholic Church in America operates a vast network of institutions of almost every type and variety. The social and recreational activities in the Catholic parish—from baseball teams to sewing circles, from bowling leagues to religious study groups—are only a beginning. Every interest, activity, and function of the Catholic faithful is provided with some Catholic institution and furnished with Catholic direction. There are Catholic hospitals, homes, and orphanages; Catholics schools and colleges; Catholic charities and welfare agencies; Catholic Boy Scouts and War Veterans; Catholic associations of doc-

23. Rt. Rev. Msgr. Michael A. McGuire, *Baltimore Catechism No. 1* (New York: Benziger Brothers, 1961), 75–82.
24. Cogley and Van Allen, *Catholic America,* 135.

tors, lawyers, teachers, students, and philosophers; Catholic leagues of police-men, firemen, and sanitary workers; Catholic luncheon clubs and recreation fellowships; there is the Catholic Youth Organization, with some six million members; there is even a Catholic Audio-Visual Educators Association.[25]

In short, the Catholic Church was something of a fortress that was de-signed to protect Catholics from a hostile society and socialize them into a Culture I approach to faith and morals. In this regard, it was very suc-cessful. Conditions in the worldwide Church, American society, and the American Church combined to produce high levels of religious participa-tion and Culture I Catholicism among the laity, all of whom were born and raised in the pre–Vatican II Church.

While Protestant parents taught their children to think for themselves, Catholic parents were more likely to stress the importance of obedience.[26] Vatican officials and American bishops were perceived as legitimate au-thorities whose pronouncements were to be obeyed by laypeople. As a re-sult, laypeople expressed high levels of identification with Catholic faith, attachment to the Catholic Church, and agreement with church teach-ings.[27] For example, comparing Protestants and Catholics on a six-item measure of agreement with Christian doctrine, Lenski concluded: "doctri-nal orthodoxy proved more frequent among Catholics than among Prot-estants."[28] Ninety-eight percent of Catholics believed in God, 95 percent said God is like a loving Heavenly Father, 93 percent agreed that Jesus was God's only Son, 90 percent said God responds to our prayers, 82 percent believed that God expects us to worship him every week, and 72 percent said that some people will be punished in the life after death.[29] This high level of orthodoxy cut across class lines, with high-status and low-status Catholics expressing similar levels of agreement with these beliefs.

Catholics also were highly involved in the Catholic community. They

25. Will Herberg, *Protestant, Catholic, Jew* (Garden City, N.Y.: Doubleday, 1960), 153–54.

26. Duane Alwin, "Religion and Parental Child-Rearing Orientations: Evidence of a Catholic-Protestant Convergence," *American Journal of Sociology* 92 (September 1986): 412–40; Duane F. Alwin, "Trends in Parental Socialization Values: Detroit, 1958–1983," *American Journal of Sociology* 90 (September 1984): 359–82; Lenski, *The Religious Factor.*

27. James D. Davidson et al., *The Search for Common Ground* (Huntington, Ind.: Our Sunday Visitor Books, 1997), 16–20.

28. Lenski, *The Religious Factor,* 57–59.

29. Ibid., 398.

had thick Catholic social networks. In Detroit, for example, 44 percent said that "all or nearly all" of their closest friends were Catholic.[30] Numerous studies also reported high levels of participation in the sacraments. About 75 percent of Catholics attended Mass every week, although only half felt worthy enough to receive Holy Communion.[31] Eight in ten went to confession at least once a year.[32] Most married other Catholics, were married in the Church, and said that most of their relatives were Catholic.[33] There also were high levels of involvement in traditional devotional activities, such as the rosary, forty hours, Benediction, and novenas.[34] Laypeople gave generously to the Church in terms of both their incomes and their Culture I offspring, 53,796 of whom were priests, 168,527 of whom were sisters, and 10,473 of whom were brothers.[35]

1960–1977

In the 1960s and '70s, conditions in the worldwide Church and American society changed rapidly and fostered important changes in the American Church and among its members.

Changes in the Worldwide Church

Shortly after becoming pope in 1958, Pope John XXIII unexpectedly announced plans for a worldwide council of cardinals and bishops.[36]

30. Ibid., 38.

31. Davidson et al., *The Search for Common Ground*, 18.

32. Joseph H. Fichter, *Southern Parish* (Chicago: University of Chicago Press, 1951), 55–56.

33. James D. Davidson and Tracy Widman, "The Effect of Group Size on Interfaith Marriage among Catholics," *Journal for the Scientific Study of Religion* 41 (September 2002): 397–404; Lenski, *The Religious Factor*, 54–55.

34. Chester Gillis, *Roman Catholicism in America* (New York: Columbia University, 1999), 158–76.

35. Andrew M. Greeley and William E. McManus, *Catholic Contributions* (Allen, Tex.: Thomas More, 1987); *Official Catholic Directory* (New Providence, N.J.: P. J. Kenedy and Sons, 1960).

36. Joseph A. Komanchek, "40 Years after Vatican II: The Ongoing Challenge," *Liguorian* (October 2002), 11–14; Joseph A. Komanchek, "Vatican II as Ecumenical Council: Yves Congar's Vision Realized," *Commonweal* 129 (November 22, 2002): 12–14; Dennis Doyle, *The Church Emerging from Vatican II* (Mystic, Conn.: Twenty-Third Publications, 1999); Adrian Hastings, "Catholic History from Vatican II to John Paul II," in Adrian Hastings, ed., *Modern Catholicism* (New York: Oxford, 1991), 1–13.

For the most part, the council participants were traditional, pre–Vatican II leaders. Some, such as cardinals Alfredo Ottaviani and Ernesto Ruffini and Bishop Giuseppe De Carli, were conservative "guardians of the old order."[37] Others, including theologians Yves Congar, Karl Rahner, and John Courtney Murray, were more open to change and thus became known as "progressives."[38]

In the run-up to the council, the conservatives drafted preparatory documents that "reasserted Church doctrine and condemned those who had publicly questioned it."[39] But it did not take long for the progressives to gain the support of the pope, who wanted the council to be more reform-minded. An early struggle took place over the locus of authority in the Church, with conservatives stressing the primacy of the bishop of Rome (the pope) and progressives insisting on "collegiality," by which all bishops would share authority and, when acting as a body, would be just as infallible as the pope.[40] With a more collaborative form of participation in council business, the progressives carried the day on the issue of collegiality. They went on to draft and rewrite many other council documents. They also marshaled enough support to win far more votes than anyone would have predicted at the outset of the council. The result was a series of documents that were enthusiastically supported by progressives, but only grudgingly accepted by conservatives.

In the process, two things happened. There was some decentralization of episcopal authority, and there was "an outburst of religious freedom . . . that few would have imagined."[41] Culture II Catholicism emerged as a theological alternative to Culture I Catholicism. It shared Culture I Catholicism's emphasis on the importance of Catholic identity, sacraments, the Nicene Creed, concern for poor, and participation in local parishes. However, in contrast to Culture I Catholicism, Culture II viewed the Church as the People of God, called for some decentralization of au-

---

37. Hastings, *Modern Catholicism*, 4.

38. Melissa Wilde, "How Culture Mattered at Vatican II: Collegiality Trumps Authority in the Council's Social Movement Organizations," *American Sociological Review* 69 (August 2004): 576–602.

39. Ibid., 578.

40. Ibid., 582.

41. James Tunstead Burtchaell, "Religious Freedom *(Dignitatis Humanae),*" in Adrian Hastings, *Modern Catholicism*, 123.

thority, and emphasized the individual's relationship with God (with the Church seen as a means to this end). It highlighted the importance of faith as a way of life, the integrity of one's own conscience, similarities with other faiths (ecumenism), and a positive view of modern society, which it saw as God's creation.

The documents of Vatican II signify the shift to Culture II Catholicism. "The Declaration on Religious Liberty" *(Dignitatis humanae)* is certainly one of the most important. In light of the strict controls the Church itself had imposed on the laity in the 1950s, the following passage indicates a decided shift toward religious freedom and the primacy of the individual conscience.

> It is through his conscience that man sees and recognizes the demands of the divine law. He is bound to follow this conscience faithfully in all his activity so that he may come to God, who is his last end. Therefore he must not be forced to act contrary to his conscience. Nor must he be prevented from acting according to his conscience, especially in religious matters. The reason is because the practice of religion of its very nature consists primarily of those voluntary and free internal acts by which a man directs himself to God. Acts of this kind cannot be commanded or forbidden by any merely human authority.[42]

Without abandoning Culture I altogether, a passage like this—and many others of a similar nature—indicated a shift in the direction of Culture II. But, as we shall see, reactions to this shift were mixed. Some Catholics were more eager to embrace it than others.

Changes in American Society

In marked contrast to the 1950s, when Protestants and Catholics both emphasized conformity to the norms and values of American social institutions, the 1960s and '70s were marked by a cultural revolution. That revolution called all social institutions into question, including religion. It also championed individual rights and freedom.[43]

---

42. Austin Flannery, ed., *Vatican Council II* (Grand Rapids: William B. Eerdmans, 1992), 801–2.

43. Dean R. Hoge et al., *Young Adult Catholics* (Notre Dame, Ind.: University of Notre Dame Press, 2001); David G. Myers, *The American Paradox* (New Haven, Conn.: Yale University Press, 2000); Wade Clark Roof and William McKinney, *American Mainline Religion* (New Brunswick, N.J.: Rutgers University Press); Robert N. Bellah et al., *Habits of the Heart* (Berkeley: University of California Press, 1985).

At the same time, the relationship between Protestants and Catholics was changing. While Protestants remained a numerical majority, the number of Catholics continued to grow, reaching nearly 50 million—22 or 23 percent of the U.S. population—in 1977.[44] Moreover, Catholics were gaining in power, privilege, and prestige. By the 1960s, studies showed they had moved into the middle class and were roughly comparable to Methodists, who were seen at the time as the quintessential middle-class Protestant denomination.[45] As Charles Morris observed, "In the twenty years from 1950 to 1970, the rate of Catholic socio-economic advancement was faster than that of any other religious subgroup except the Jews."[46]

Protestants and Catholics also bridged some of their religious differences. In the context of Vatican II, Catholics modified some of the beliefs and practices that others considered odd. For example, they started to eat meat on Fridays. Instead of Latin, they began to speak English, Spanish, and other languages at Mass. Catholics also became more ecumenical. They joined interfaith dialogues, exploring the similarities and differences between Christian groups.[47] They also became more actively involved in interfaith ministries, addressing issues of common concern, such as poverty, hunger, and homelessness.[48]

Protestants also were becoming more tolerant of Catholics. Although John F. Kennedy encountered some anti-Catholicism in his run for the presidency in 1960, it was not nearly as intense as the religious opposition Al Smith had experienced thirty-two years earlier. With his victory, Kennedy helped to change the religious climate in America. As Martin Marty has noted, "the worldview of fearful and defensive Protestant, anti-papal America" faded.[49] The net effect of these changes was that historic tensions between the two religious traditions subsided. The similarities between Protestants and Catholics increasingly outweighed the differences.

44. D'Antonio et al., *American Catholics*, 12; *Official Catholic Directory*, 1978.

45. Andrew M. Greeley, *The American Catholic* (New York: Basic Books, 1977), 50–68; Norval Glenn and Ruth Hyland, "Religious Preference and Worldly Success: Some Evidence from National Surveys," *American Sociological Review* 32 (February 1967): 73–85.

46. Morris, *American Catholic,* 256.

47. Robert McAfee Brown and Gustave Weigel, *An American Dialogue* (Garden City, N.Y.: Anchor Books, 1961).

48. Davidson, *Mobilizing Social Movement Organizations.*

49. Marty, *A Short History of American Catholicism,* 181.

Changes in the American Church

The struggle between conservatives and progressives in the worldwide Church contributed to increased conflict between liberals and conservatives in the American Church.[50] Some members of the hierarchy who were formed by and supported Culture I Catholicism—such as cardinals John Cody of Chicago, Patrick O'Boyle of Washington DC, and James McIntyre of Los Angeles and Bishop Vincent Waters of Raleigh moved slowly on the implementation of council documents.[51] Like-minded priests and laypeople also formed groups aimed at defending Culture I Catholicism. For example, Catholics United for the Faith was founded in 1968, and the Catholic League for Religious and Civil Rights was formed in 1973.[52]

But some members of the hierarchy who had been transformed by the council's call for *aggiornamento* (reform)—such as Cardinal John Dearden and Bishop Raymond Lucker—moved ahead more quickly.[53] Their assertiveness culminated in the 1976 Call to Action Conference, which was authorized by the bishops, who listened as laypeople expressed their views on changes in the Church and its role in society.[54] In addition, Archbishop Jean Jadot, the apostolic delegate to the United States between 1973 and 1980, urged Pope Paul VI to appoint a number of progressive bishops, which he did. So-called "Jadot bishops" included Kenneth Unterner (Saginaw), Rembert Weakland (Milwaukee), Roger Mahoney (Los Angeles), Howard Hubbard (Albany), and Theodore McCarrick (then New York, later Washington, D.C.), to mention just a few.

A number of liberal organizations also were formed.[55] These includ-

50. Seidler and Meyer, *Conflict and Change in the Catholic Church;* George Kelly, *The Battle for the American Church* (New York: Doubleday, 1979); James Hitchcock, *The Decline and Fall of Radical Catholicism* (New York: Image Books, 1972).

51. Seidler and Meyer, *Conflict and Change in the Catholic Church,* 75.

52. Mary Jo Weaver and R. Scott Appleby, eds., *Being Right* (Bloomington: Indiana University Press, 1995).

53. Thomas P. Rausch, "Another Generation Gap," *America* 187 (October 14, 2002): 12–15; Anthony J. Pogorelc, "Social Movements within Organizations: The Case of Call to Action and U.S. Catholic Bishops" (Ph.D. dissertation, Department of Sociology and Anthropology, Purdue University, 2002); Seidler and Meyer, *Conflict and Change in the Catholic Church.*

54. Pogorelc, "Social Movements within Organizations"; Seidler and Meyer, *Conflict and Change in the Catholic Church.*

55. Mary Jo Weaver, ed., *What's Left?* (Bloomington: Indiana University Press, 1999); Michele Dillon, *Catholic Identity* (New York: Cambridge University Press, 1999).

FIGURE 2. Cultural Shifts in 1960–77 Period

Declining emphasis on:	Increasing empasis on:
the Church as a bureaucracy	the Church as the People of God
episcopal authority	individual conscience
the distinctiveness of the Church	interfaith similarities
the importance of the Church	one's relationship to God
knowing Church teachings	being a good Christian
obeying Church teachings	thinking for one's self
God as a punitive judge	God as merciful and loving
Mass as a sacrifice	Mass as a celebration
a uniform liturgy in which the	an enculturated liturgy in which
laity plays a passive role	the laity plays an active role
modern society as evil	modern society as God's creation

ed the *National Catholic Reporter* (1964), DignityUSA (1969), Pax Christi (1972), Catholics for a Free Choice (1973), CORPUS (1974), and Women's Ordination Conference (1977).

Thus, there was some erosion of Culture I Catholicism. Put differently, the political and cultural momentum seemed to be in the direction of Culture II Catholicism. Figure 2 summarizes some of the key elements in this shift.

Other changes also were taking place. With Catholics' movement into the middle class and improved relations between Protestants and Catholics, laypeople no longer felt as much need for the protection of the Church. One result was that they did not support the vast array of Catholic institutions as much as they had earlier, and the Catholic ghetto began to crumble. The number of Catholic schools and students, Catholic hospitals, and Catholic colleges and universities all began to decline in the 1960s.[56] Between 1965 and 1970, the number of Catholic professional associations that had once served as safe harbors for Catholics declined by 17 percent.[57] In other words, the institutional base of the "separatist

56. Davidson, *Catholicism in Motion*, 65–67, 75–78.
57. Roger Finke and Rodney Stark, *The Churching of America, 1776–1990* (New Brunswick, N.J.: Rutgers University Press, 1992).

American Catholic subculture" was waning,[58] and Catholics' exposure to the individualism and voluntarism of American culture was increasing.

Changes in the Laity's Beliefs and Practices

Relative to the 1950s, the worldwide Church and the American Church lost some of their control over the thoughts and actions of the laity. Meanwhile, the influence of American society increased. These changes led to declining levels of participation in the Church and an increase in Culture II Catholicism among laypeople.

With their rising levels of education and economic prosperity, laypeople were more convinced than ever of their own talents and more willing to reach their own conclusions on a wide variety of issues, including matters of faith and morals. This self-confidence was reflected in their increasing tendency to teach their children to think for themselves. The child-rearing values of Protestants and Catholics became more and more similar.[59]

While there was no sign that Catholics had abandoned core teachings such as the Trinity, the Incarnation, the Resurrection, or the Real Presence, there was growing evidence of their willingness to disagree with the Church on ecclesiastical issues. As Andrew Greeley observed in the mid 1970s:

> There has been a substantial decline in acceptance of the legitimacy of ecclesiastical authority. In 1963, 70 percent thought that it was "certainly true" that Jesus handed over the leadership of his church to Peter and the popes; ten years later that proportion has fallen to 42 percent. Only 32 percent think that it is "certainly true" that the pope is infallible when he speaks on matters of faith and morals.[60]

They also were more willing to disagree with the Church teachings on sexual and reproductive issues—especially birth control. Their support of the Church's opposition to artificial birth control had been slipping for some time, but plunged sharply in response to the publication of *Humanae vitae* in 1968.[61]

---

58. Morris, *American Catholic*, 319.

59. Alwin, "Religion and Parental Child-Rearing Orientations "; Alwin, "Trends in Parental Socialization Values."

60. Greeley, *The American Catholic*, 128.

61. Andrew M. Greeley, *The Catholic Revolution* (Berkeley: University of California Press, 2004), 55–57; Andrew M. Greeley, *The Catholic Myth* (New York: Charles Scribner's Sons, 1990), 90–105.

Although some laypeople were increasingly involved in "lay aposto-lates" in the 1960s and "lay ministry" in the 1970s,[62] the overall picture was one of declining participation in the Catholic community. Catho-lic social networks increasingly included non-Catholic friends. Interfaith marriages also were increasing.[63] There also were declining levels of partic-ipation in the sacraments. For example, in 1975, only 54 percent of Catho-lics attended Mass weekly.[64] Nearly a third of Catholics said they never or practically never went to confession.[65] There also were declining levels of participation in activities such as visiting the church to pray, reading dioc-esan newspapers, and attending retreats.[66]

Vocations also declined. Although the total number of priests was still higher in 1977 (58,485) than it had been in 1959 (53,796), the number leaving the priesthood rose dramatically between the closing of Vatican II in 1965 and 1977.[67] The number of seminarians also declined from 39,896 in 1959 to just 14,998 in 1977. So did the number of brothers (from 10,473 in 1959 to 8,460 in 1977) and the number of sisters (down from 168,527 to 129,391).[68]

1978–Present

But conditions in the worldwide Church and American society were about to change again, leading to still further changes in the American Church and the beliefs and practices of American Catholics.

Changes in the Worldwide Church

With the selection of Pope John Paul II in 1978, authority became in-creasingly centralized in the Church.[69] Moreover, members of the pre–

62. Donald J. Thorman, *The Emerging Layman* (Garden City, N.Y.: Doubleday, 1962); Zeni Fox, *New Ecclesial Ministry* (Kansas City, Mo.: Sheed and Ward, 1997); Philip J. Mur-nion, *New Parish Ministers* (New York: National Pastoral Life Center, 1992).

63. Alan McCutcheon, "Denominations and Interfaith Marriage: Trends among White Americans in the Twentieth Century," *Review of Religious Research* 29 (March 1988): 213–27.

64. George Gallup and Jim Castelli, *The American Catholic People* (Garden City, N.Y.: Doubleday, 1987), 194–95.

65. Greeley, *The American Catholic,* 127.

66. Ibid., 127.

67. Michael Gaine, "The State of the Priesthood," in Hastings, *Modern Catholicism,* 246.

68. *Official Catholic Directory,* 1978.

69. Rausch, "Another Generation Gap."

Vatican II and Vatican II generations who embrace Culture I Catholicism have reclaimed considerable control of the worldwide Church, mainly through papal appointments.[70] Through the Congregation for the Doctrine of the Faith, the Vatican also has disciplined a number of progressive thinkers, including Hans Kung, Leonardo Boff, Eugen Drewermann, Tissa Balasuriya, Bishop Raymond Hunthausen, Charles Curran, and most recently Thomas Reese. Although the worldwide Church now possesses a greater mixture of the two cultures than in the 1950s, the net effect has been a resurgence of Culture I Catholicism.

This resurgence is reflected in many recent Vatican publications. The encyclical *Veritatis splendor* (1993) reaffirmed the Church's adherence to natural law when the Vatican believed that God's moral law was being challenged by relativists and post-modernists. The new *Catechism of the Catholic Church* (1994) appeared when the Vatican wanted to make clear what are, and what are not, official church teachings. *Dominus Iesus* (2000) reasserted the view that the Catholic Church possesses the fullness of truth when the Vatican felt that fact was being lost in some dialogues with other religious traditions.

Changes in American Society

Protestants and Catholics continued to share a common national identity and, to a considerable extent, a common American culture. Arising from the cultural revolution of the 1960s, two hallmarks of that culture continue to be a celebration of individual freedom and a deep-seated skepticism of social institutions.[71] One symptom has been the growing tendency to distinguish between "spirituality" and "religiosity."[72] These two concepts were inseparable in the 1950s (spiritual people were religious, and religious people were spiritual). Nowadays, many Protestant and Catholic young adults believe it is possible to be spiritual (which they view positively) without being religious (which they view negatively).

70. Helen Rose Ebaugh, "Vatican II and the Revitalization Movement," in Helen Rose Ebaugh, ed., *Vatican II and U.S. Catholicism* (Greenwich, Conn.: JAI Press, 1991), 3–19.

71. David G. Myers, *The American Paradox* (New Haven, Conn.: Yale University Press, 2000); Roof and McKinney, *American Mainline Religion*.

72. Robert C. Fuller, *Spiritual but Not Religious* (New York: Oxford University Press, 2001); Penny Marler and C. Kirk Hadaway, "Being Religious and Being Spiritual in America: A Zero-Sum Proposition?" *Journal for the Scientific Study of Religion* 41 (June 2002): 289–300.

Relations between Protestants and Catholics also continued to change. In 1965, President Lyndon Johnson reopened the doors of immigration. Since then, Hispanic and Asian Catholics have comprised a disproportionately large percentage of the people coming through those doors.[73] Thus, the Catholic population climbed to about 65 million in 2004.[74] Catholics also have grown to at least 25 percent of the total U.S. population. Meanwhile, Protestants—who were nearly two-thirds of the population as recently as the 1980s—are now barely half.[75] Projections are that "the Protestant share of the population will continue to shrink and Protestants will soon lose their majority position in American society."[76]

Moreover, the white European portion of the Catholic population has continued to prosper, comparing favorably with Episcopalians and Presbyterians in terms of power, privilege, and prestige.[77] However, the Hispanic population—which is less educated, more blue-collar, and less well off financially—has continued to grow. The net effect is that Catholics' progress toward the top of America's socioeconomic ladder has slowed in recent years. Overall, today's Catholics can best be described as slightly above the national average in terms of education, occupation, and income.[78]

Some forms of anti-Catholicism persist, and there are numerous flash-

73. Guillermina Jasso et al., "Exploring the Religious Preference of Recent Immigrants to the United States: Evidence from the New Immigrant Survey Pilot," in Yvonne Yazbeck Haddad, Jane I. Smith, and John L. Esposito, eds., *Religion and Immigration: Christian, Jewish, and Muslim Experiences in the United States* (Walnut Creek, Calif.: Alta Mira Press, 2003), 217–53; Kevin J. Christiano, "The Church and the New Immigrants," in Ebaugh, *Vatican II and US Catholicism*, 217–53.

74. *Official Catholic Directory*, 2005.

75. Tom W. Smith and Seokho Kim, "The Vanishing Protestant Majority," *Journal for the Scientific Study of Religion* 44 (June 2005): 211–23.

76. Ibid., 221.

77. D'Antonio et al., *American Catholics*, 3–4; James D. Davidson, "Religion among America's Elite: Persistence and Change in the Protestant Establishment, 1930–92," *Sociology of Religion* 55 (Winter 1994): 419–40; James D. Davidson, Ralph E. Pyle, and David Reyes, "Persistence and Change in the Protestant Establishment, 1930–92," *Social Forces* 74 (September 1995): 157–75.

78. James D. Davidson and Ralph E. Pyle, "Social Class," in Helen Rose Ebaugh, ed., *Handbook on Religion and Social Institutions* (New York: Plenum Books, 2005); Christian Smith and Robert Faris, "Socioeconomic Inequality in the American Religious System: An Update and Assessment," *Journal for the Scientific Study of Religion* 44 (March 2005): 95–104; Ralph E. Pyle, "Trends in Religious Stratification: Have Religious Group Socioeconomic Distinctions Declined in Recent Decades?" *Sociology of Religion* 67 (Spring 2006): 61–79.

points between Protestants and Catholics on issues such as abortion and the funding of parochial schools.[79] Yet, Protestants no longer exclude Catholics from public life the way they did a half-century ago. Today's young adults, like my son and daughter, do not have to deal with as much anti-Catholicism as my mother and father's generation did. Catholic prejudice toward Protestants also has diminished. The Protestant-Catholic boundaries that were so important to Catholics in my parents' generation are largely irrelevant to today's generation.

Changes in the American Church

Changes in the worldwide Church and American society have had a direct bearing on the American Church. For one thing, the Vatican's attempt to recentralize authority in the Church has extended to the American Church. A recent example had to do with the norms for implementing the Vatican 1990 publication, *Ex corde Ecclesiae.* Those norms insisted that Catholic theologians at Catholic colleges and universities obtain a mandatum from their bishop.[80] American bishops generally acquiesced to this Vatican intervention in domestic church affairs.

Pope John Paul II also appointed bishops who supported the centralization of authority in the Church. Examples include Cardinal Edward Egan (New York), archbishops Charles Chaput (Denver), Raymond Burke (St. Louis), Timothy Dolan (Milwaukee), Justin Rigali (Philadelphia), and Donald Wuerl (Washington, DC), and bishops Michael Sheridan (Colorado Springs), John Meyers (Newark), Fabian Bruskewitz (Lincoln), and William Lori (Bridgeport).

The bishops also have reasserted their episcopal authority on the home front. In 2001, they merged two separate but related organizations: the United States Catholic Conference (which had lay members and focused on the Church's role in society) and the National Conference of Catholic Bishops (which dealt with issues in the Church and was comprised of bishops only). The new organization, called the United States Conference of Catholic Bishops, represents the values and interests of the bishops. It addresses both public policy and internal Church issues, but its member-

79. James Martin, "The Last Acceptable Prejudice?" *America* 182 (March 25, 2000): 8–16.
80. Peter Steinfels, *A People Adrift* (New York: Simon and Schuster, 2003), 131–51.

ship and committee chairmanships are limited to bishops, with laypeople serving only as committee members and staff people.[81]

But the recentralization of episcopal authority has been constrained by several forces. One factor has been the declining numbers of priests and sisters, along with the increased presence of laypeople at virtually all levels of church life. As James Burtchaell has observed, laypeople are:

> university presidents, hospital administrators, diocesan chancellors, tribunal judges, financial officers, publishers, editors, press secretaries, theological and canonical experts, marriage counselors and adoption agents, and pastoral associates in parishes. This laicization has interrupted the ability of episcopal or papal authority to direct Church life as before.[82]

Another limitation is the fact that laypeople are not as likely as they used to be to grant bishops final say on matters of church life.[83] This trend began long before the recent sexual abuse scandal, but that scandal has only bolstered the laity's view that it should be involved in virtually all aspects of church life.[84]

The appointment of conservative bishops also has contributed to a resurgence of Culture I Catholicism at the top of the American Church. In addition, there has been a proliferation of conservative organizations, such as EWTN (Eternal Word Television Network), which was founded in 1981, and Legatus, formed in 1987.[85] Conservative websites championing Culture I Catholicism (e.g., www.conservativecatholics.com, www.strc.org, www.hereticalcatholicorganizations.org) also have sprung up in recent years.[86] Meanwhile, the formation of liberal groups has slowed, and the number of liberal websites promoting Culture II Catholicism lags far behind (e.g., www.natcath.com and www.cath4choice.org).

Meanwhile, with the improved relations between Protestants and Catholics in the United States, the institutional base of the old Catholic ghetto

---

81. David Gibson, *The Coming Catholic Church* (New York: HarperSanFrancisco, 2003), 281.

82. Burtchaell, "Religious Freedom (Dignitatis Humanae)," in Hastings, *Modern Catholicism*, 121.

83. Davidson, *Catholicism in Motion*, 85–89; D'Antonio et al., *American Catholics*, 69–86; Burtchaell, "Religious Freedom *(Dignitatis Humanae)*," 121.

84. James D. Davidson and Dean R. Hoge, "Catholics after the Scandal: A New Study's Major Findings," *Commonweal* 131 (November 19, 2004): 13–19.

85. Weaver and Appleby, *Being Right*.

86. Brother John Raymond, *Catholics on the Internet, 2000–2001* (Roseville, Calif.: Prima Publishing, 2001).

continues to decline. Data on Catholic schools are good indications of this overall trend.[87] By 2001, the number of Catholic grade schools had shrunk to 6,903 (down a third since 1960). The number of Catholic high schools was down even more (from 2,433 in 1960 to only 1,247). Despite the continuing growth of the U.S. Catholic population, enrollments in Catholic schools in 2001 were only about half of what they were in 1960.

Changes in the Laity's Beliefs and Practices

These developments have produced dramatic changes in the beliefs and practices of the American laity, only 20 percent of whom belong to the pre–Vatican II generation, one-third of whom belong to the Vatican II generation, and nearly half of whom belong to the post–Vatican II generation.[88] For one thing, there has been a continuing decline in the perceived legitimacy of Church leaders' actions, with liberals opposing conservatives in higher offices and conservatives opposing liberals in lower offices.[89] The recent sex scandal and the accompanying abuse of episcopal authority have only accelerated this decline.[90] Adult Catholics increasingly think for themselves and teach their children to do the same.[91]

The result is that Church leaders have far less control over the laity's beliefs and practices. Although the hierarchy tends toward Culture I Catholicism, the laity—especially members of the Vatican II and post–Vatican II generations—tend toward Culture II. Evidence includes a 1995 national study that used a four-item measure: frequency of confession, willingness to obey Church teachings even if one does not understand them, belief that one must attend Mass on a regular basis, and agreement with the Church's opposition to premarital sex.[92] The results are shown in

87. Davidson, *Catholicism in Motion,* 75–78.

88. D'Antonio et al., *American Catholics;* William V. D'Antonio et al., *Laity: American and Catholic* (Kansas City, MO: Sheed and Ward, 1996).

89. Pogorelc, "Social Movements within Organizations"; Komanchek, "40 Years after Vatican II "; Joseph A. Varacalli, *Bright Promise, Failed Community* (Lanham, Md.: Lexington Books, 2000); Cardinal Joseph Bernadin and Archbishop Oscar H. Lipscomb, eds., *Catholic Common Ground Initiative: Foundational Documents* (New York: Crossroad/Herder & Herder, 1997).

90. Davidson, *Catholicism in Motion,* 86–89; Davidson and Hoge, "Catholics after the Scandal," 12–15.

91. Davidson, *Catholicism in Motion,* 170–72; D'Antonio et al., *American Catholics,* 9–10.

92. Anthony J. Pogorelc and James D. Davidson, "One Church, Two Cultures?" *Review of Religious Research* 42 (December 2000): 146–58.

TABLE 1. Religious Orientation by Generation

Generation	Definitely Culture I	Tending to Culture I	Tending to Culture II	Definitely Culture II
Pre–Vatican II	30%	23%	36%	21%
Vatican II	7	18	36	39
Post–Vatican II	7	14	38	41

Table 1. Fifty-three percent of laypeople in the pre–Vatican II generation tend toward Culture I, while 47 percent tend toward Culture II. On the other hand, about three-quarters of Vatican II and post–Vatican II Catholics lean in the Culture II direction, and only one-quarter are Culture I–oriented.

Within this context, laypeople are distinguishing between what they consider the core of the faith and what they consider peripheral or optional.[93] At the core are "Belief that God is present in the sacraments," "Charitable efforts toward helping the poor," "Belief that Christ is really present in the Eucharist," "Devotion to Mary the Mother of God," and "Belief that God is present in a special way in the poor." On the periphery are "Belief that priests must be celibate," "Teachings which oppose the death penalty," "Belief that only men can be priests," and "The Church's traditional support of the right of workers to unionize." While the vast majority of laypeople believe in the teachings they consider central to the faith, such the Real Presence,[94] disagreement is much greater on beliefs the laity considers peripheral. Only about a quarter of laypeople agree with the Church's teachings related to priestly ordination and sexual-reproductive issues.[95]

There has been an increase in lay leadership in small faith communities, parishes, and dioceses (especially among laywomen). Bernard Lee and William D'Antonio estimate that there are at least "37,000 small Chris-

93. Davidson, *Catholicism in Motion,* 170–72; Hoge et al., *Young Adult Catholics,* 195–205; D'Antonio et al., *American Catholics,* 31–50.

94. James D. Davidson, "Yes, Jesus Is Really There: Most Catholics Still Agree," *Commonweal* 128 (October 12, 2001): 14–16.

95. D'Antonio et al., *American Catholics,* 69–86; Davidson et al., *The Search for Common Ground,* 41–56.

tian communities in the continental United States, with a membership of over a million (including adults and children)."[96] The number of lay ministers working in parishes and dioceses has climbed to over 30,000.[97] The percentage of Mass attenders receiving Holy Communion also has risen dramatically. In the 1950s, less than half of people at Mass went to Communion; nowadays, well over 80 percent do.[98]

However, on average, Catholics are less involved in the Catholic community than they were in the Vatican II period. The thickness of Catholic social networks continues to decline, with Catholics increasingly having non-Catholic friends. Participation in the sacraments continues to decline. In 1999, only 37 percent of Catholics attended Mass weekly. The Center for Applied Research on the Apostolate reports that Mass attendance rates have not changed since then.[99] Two recent studies show that only about 45 percent of Catholics go to confession at least once a year; 55 percent never go, mainly because they do not think it is essential to their faith.[100] Interfaith marriages continue to increase. About 29 percent of today's Catholics are in interfaith marriages, and 57 percent of these marriages have taken place outside the Church. Perhaps even more startling is the fact that 29 percent of marriages between two post–Vatican II Catholics do not take place in the Church.[101]

Participation in traditional devotional activities also continues to decline. Only 20 to 30 percent of today's Catholics pray the rosary or pray to Mary and the saints. Meanwhile, only about 5 percent participate in newer, Scripture-based devotions such as Bible study or prayer groups.[102] Financial contributions to the Church remain low, at about one percent

96. Bernard J. Lee and William V. D'Antonio, *The Catholic Experience of Small Christian Communities* (New York: Paulist Press, 2000), 10.

97. David DeLambo, *Lay Parish Ministers: A Study of Emerging Leadership* (New York: National Pastoral Life Center, 2005). See also Davidson, *Catholicism in Motion*, 116–17; James D. Davidson et al., *Lay Ministers and Their Spiritual Practices* (Huntington, Ind.: Our Sunday Visitor, 2003); Bryan T. Froehle and Mary L. Gautier, *Catholicism USA* (Maryknoll, N.Y.: Orbis Books, 2000); Philip J. Murnion and David DeLambo, *Parishes and Parish Ministers* (New York: National Pastoral Life Center, 1999).

98. Davidson, *Catholicism in Motion*, 62–63; D'Antonio et al., *American Catholics*, 52–55.

99. CARA (Center for Applied Research on the Apostolate), "Mass Attendance Steady over Last Five Years," *CARA Report* 10 (Spring 2005): 10.

100. Davidson, *Catholicism in Motion*, 154–55.

101. Ibid., 155–161; D'Antonio et al., *American Catholics*, 55–57.

102. D'Antonio et al., *American Catholics*, 59–61.

of income.[103] The number of seminarians, priests, brothers, and women religious continue to fall.[104] The 2005 *Official Catholic Directory* reports a total of only 4,330 seminarians (down from 14,998 in 1977), only 44,729 priests (down from 58,485), only 71,486 sisters (down from 129,391), and only 5,504 brothers (down from 8,460). Seminarians and newly ordained priests are far more Culture I–oriented than priests belonging to the Vatican II generation and laypeople in the post–Vatican II generation.[105]

Summary and Conclusions

This chapter has addressed two questions: what sorts of changes have taken place in the American Catholic experience during the last fifty years, and what underlying conditions have prompted these changes? Let me summarize the trends that have occurred in the Church over the last fifty years and the forces that lie behind these trends. I conclude with some reflections on what these findings imply for the future of the Church in the United States.

Trends

In the 1950s, there was a close connection between the policies and practices of the American Church and the beliefs and practices of its members. The Church was a highly centralized collection of segregated institutions that successfully promoted Culture I Catholicism among a pre–Vatican II generation of laypeople. American Catholics were actively involved in the Church and tended to comply with most church teachings. In the 1960–1977 period, there still was a relationship between the American Church and the laity, but that relationship was a bit more frayed than it had been in the 1950s. There was some decentralization of authority as bishops shared more decision-making responsibilities with laypeople, and there were growing theological differences in the hierarchy between con-

103. Charles Zech, *Why Catholics Don't Give . . . and What Can Be Done about It* (Huntington, Ind.: Our Sunday Visitor, 2000).

104. Davidson, *Catholicism in Motion,* 65–57; Rodney Stark and Roger Finke, "Catholic Religious Vocations: Decline and Revival," *Review of Religious Research* 42 (December 2000): 125–45.

105. Dean R. Hoge, *The First Five Years of the Priesthood* (Collegeville, Minn.: Liturgical Press, 2002); Dean R. Hoge and Jacqueline E. Wenger, *Evolving Visions of the Priesthood* (Collegeville, Minn.: Liturgical Press, 2004).

servatives, who defended Culture I Catholicism, and liberals, who advocated reform. The so-called Catholic ghetto began to crumble, Culture II Catholicism became an option for many laypeople, and previously high levels of participation and compliance with Church teachings declined. Since 1978, the gap between the American Church and the laity has grown. Among American bishops, there was been an attempt to recentralize authority and reassert Culture I Catholicism. These efforts have been only partially successful, as laypeople have taken on new leadership responsibilities (thus limiting the centralization of authority) and expressed a preference for Culture II Catholicism. As the ghetto all but disappeared, Catholics' participation in the Church continued to decline.

The findings also reveal distinct trends regarding each of the four dimensions of church life. With regard to the structural dimension, two patterns have emerged. There is a U-shaped pattern, with the hierarchy trying, with only limited success, to reassert episcopal authority and the Culture I approach that prevailed in the 1950s, after a period of some decentralization and theological diversity in the Vatican II period. There also has been a rather steady decline of the organizations that formed the backbone of the old Catholic ghetto. In terms of human resources, there has been a dramatic decline in the numbers of priests, sisters, and brothers, but laypeople have achieved new heights in socioeconomic status, and there has been a marked increase in the numbers of lay ministers working in parishes and dioceses. In terms of the political dimension, the unity that prevailed in the 1950s has declined sharply, as liberals and conservatives now vie with one another to shape the Church according to their values and interests. In terms of culture, the high levels of participation and compliance with Culture I teachings in the 1950s no longer exist, as Catholics have become less involved in the Church and have developed different understandings of what it means to be Catholic (Culture I and/ or Culture II). There continue to be high levels of agreement on issues laypeople consider to be the core of the faith, but increasing disagreement on issues they consider to be peripheral or optional. These trend lines or trajectories warn against the overly simplistic view that the Church has gone downhill since the 1950s. Certainly, there are many indications of decline. But there also are many signs of stability and growth.

What factors have contributed to these trends? The American Church of the 1950s was clearly a product of two contextual influences: the hierarchy of the worldwide Church, in which Culture I Catholicism was the prevailing approach to the faith, and the hostile relationships between American Protestants and Catholicism, which fostered solidarity among Catholics. The 1960–1977 period reflected the decentralization of authority and the theological differences that were found in the worldwide Church. It also reflected the growing status similarity and harmonious relations between Protestants and Catholics. The present profile reflects the worldwide Church's effort to recentralize authority and reaffirm Culture I Catholicism, but also the effects of Catholics' increased participation in American life and culture.

These period profiles point to five trends having to do with the relationships depicted in Figure 1. First, regarding arrow A, the high concentration of authority in the worldwide Church of the 1950s experienced some decentralization in the Vatican II period and some recentralization in the most recent period. The dominance of Culture I in the 1950s gave way to a mixture of Culture I and Culture II in the middle period, before being restored in the present period.

Regarding arrow B, the hostile relations between Protestants and Catholics reinforced the goals of the worldwide Church in the 1950s by fostering a segregated Catholic community over which church leaders had considerable control. As relations between Protestants and Catholics have improved, the ghetto and Catholic solidarity have declined, and Catholic involvement in American life and culture has increased. These trends have increased Catholics' exposure to individualism and institutional skepticism, both of which have contributed to Culture II and thwarted Church leaders' efforts to promote Culture I.

Regarding arrow C, the worldwide Church's impact on the thoughts and actions of American Catholics was considerable in the 1950s, but has declined since then. Meanwhile, regarding arrow D, the influence of American society has remained strong, though instead of reinforcing Culture I as it did in the 1950s, it now stifles Church leaders' efforts to restore that approach.

Regarding arrow E, we already have shown that the American Church and the laity were closely aligned in the 1950s, but the two have become uncoupled since then. This separation reflects the American Church's growing inability to control the thoughts and actions of an increasingly autonomous and less active laity.

Anticipating the Future

What do these findings imply for the future? The future will be shaped by the same forces that have shaped the recent past. The policies and practices in the worldwide Church and the relationships between Protestants and Catholics in American society will affect developments in the American Church, and all three of these factors will affect the beliefs and practices of the laity, but in varying degrees. Based on recent trends, I assume that American society will have more impact on the laity's religious orientations than the worldwide Church and that there will continue to be a significant gap between the American Church and its laypeople.

Worldwide Church. With Pope John Paul II's record of appointing conservative cardinals and bishops, conservatives will continue to occupy the highest offices in the hierarchy for some time to come. The choice of cardinals by Benedict XVI, as John Paul II's successor, signals a continuation of this pattern. Therefore, Culture I Catholicism will continue to be the prevailing ethos, although it will encounter some opposition, mostly on an issue-by-issue basis. Liberals will have some power, but not nearly as much as they had a generation ago. The worldwide Church will continue to exert a conservative influence on the highest-ranking officers in the American Church, resulting in emphases on episcopal authority and Culture I Catholicism.

American Society. Protestants and Catholics are now similar in social status, and the in-group/out-group divisions that have plagued them in the past are not as salient as they used to be. Despite some lingering differences, both parties seem content with their new, more amicable relationship. As a result, American Catholics will increasingly participate in American society, not limiting their participation to the Church as they did in the pre–Vatican II era. They also will continue to endorse American culture, including its emphasis on individualism and its skeptical attitude toward social institutions. These trends will contribute to a continuing decline in Catholic institutions, reinforce the persistence of Culture II Catholicism among some leaders in the American Church, and foster that orientation among laypeople.

The American Church. Assuming Pope Benedict XVI extends Pope John Paul II's practice of appointing conservative bishops, conservatives' access to the highest offices in the American Church will increase in the years ahead. With the tendency for today's seminarians and newly ordained priests to be a conservative subset of their generation, it is likely that the policies and practices of the American Church will become increasingly conservative in the years ahead.

Meanwhile, with their well-developed organizational bases, liberals and conservatives will continue to compete for control of the American Church and the hearts and souls of the laity. If liberals and conservatives succumb to the temptation of ignoring their common concerns and dwelling on their differences, both will lose their grip on the laity, especially today's young adults, most of whom are not interested in the partisan conflicts that have gripped many members of the pre–Vatican II and Vatican II generations. Both parties already are experiencing difficulty attracting members of the post–Vatican II generation, who have been taught to be skeptical of institutions in general and to think for themselves with regard to matters of faith and morals.

Laity. It is likely that the increasingly conservative norms of the American Church will have diminishing effects on the majority of American laypeople. Conservative church leaders will bolster the spirits of laypeople who have a Culture I orientation and want that orientation to be passed on to their children, but they will have far less impact on the majority of laypeople, who tend toward Culture II Catholicism and see it as being more consistent with their allegiance to American society. With little or no data indicating any reversal in Catholics' religious practices, it also is reasonable to predict that recent levels of participation in the Catholic community will continue into the near future.

R. SCOTT APPLEBY

6. Decline or Relocation?

The Catholic Presence in Church and Society,
1950–2000

Introduction

Comparison across national boundaries is a difficult challenge. Historians, idolaters of the particular, are not natural comparativists. In 1992 the *Journal of American History* announced the internationalization of its board and issued a call to comparative history. Forty-six issues later, there is scant evidence of anything like a movement in the direction of sustained comparisons of social phenomena, political cultures, or material culture, much less the formation of religious identity, across national boundaries. The Harvard intellectual historian James Kloppenberg attributes this failure to, among other things, the increasing impossibility of mastering one's own subfield within American history, given the access to sources now available with the click of a mouse, and the rapid proliferation of excellent monographs, articles and other secondary studies. What follows here, unfortunately, only confirms the veracity of this observation.

When we first wrote these papers for a conference, each of us coordinated his or her work with a colleague. I had the good fortune of being paired with Jim Davidson, who first phoned me to discuss the project and then sent me a draft of his paper, followed by a revised version. This left me with the far easier task of following Jim's lead and crafting my paper as a kind of belated response to his.

Professor Davidson's periodization thus provides my starting point. As

I move through his three postwar generations, I sketch ways in which Catholic practices and piety were influenced, and in some instances transformed, by increasing levels of Catholic assimilation into mainstream U.S. society. In an attempt to lend greater nuance to a segmented generational analysis, I argue that developments in U.S. society and culture, much more so than developments in world Catholicism, constituted the framework within which most American priests and religious, and the vast majority of Catholic laity, interpreted and assimilated the changes in Roman Catholicism that are commonly associated with the Second Vatican Council. For working-, middle-, and, eventually, upper-middle-class Euro-Americans, that is, "the U.S. experience" was definitive and even normative; "society" provided the filter though which ecclesial reform and changes in practice were perceived, advanced, embraced, implemented, or ignored.[1]

Moreover, the relevant "developments in U.S. society" since 1950 were part of one sustained process of secularization—the redefinition and relocation of "holy things"—that began after the world wars and continues to this day, affecting Catholicism no less than other institution-based religions in the United States, but having distinctive consequences for the Church. Accordingly, the transformations of American Catholicism that account for the most significant generational differences mentioned by Professor Davidson should be understood as phases or stages in the deepening of this secularization process. As will become clear, I do not see secularization as necessarily inimical to religious practices, spirituality, or belief; but the process has in fact produced complex and largely negative consequences for U.S. Catholic institutions.

According to the argument I present here, then, the event of Vatican II ("event" = "what happened at the Council" *plus* "how what happened

---

1. I restrict my claims to the Euro-American majority, not because I am unaware of the African-American Catholic and growing Latino-American Catholic and Asian-American Catholic presences in the United States during the decades under consideration, but because I believe that their experiences cannot be conflated with the Euro-American experience and that they deserve parallel but separate treatment. Beyond lacking the competence to pull this off, which would not necessarily deter me, I acknowledge that this paper is too long as is. But it would be necessary, in a truly comprehensive study of "U.S. Catholicism," to make a structured comparison of U.S. Catholics across Euro-, African-, Latino- and Asian-American communities. When I use the terms "American Catholicism" or "U.S. Catholicism" in what follows, I am referring only to the largest part of that multiethnic body.

was understood by various parties" *plus* "how it was implemented") was less a watershed in U.S. Catholic history than a particularly vivid and important moment within, response to, and expression of the secularization process that unfolded during the latter half of the twentieth century.

Partial though this emphasis on the priority of national society and culture may be in its explanatory power, it seems a fruitful way to generate instructive comparisons with Ireland, French Canada, and other Catholic (or post-Catholic) nations.

The Creeping Hegemony of the Secular Culture: The Fifties

By now the literature on the varying levels of appropriation of the Catholic faith by recent American generations, from the New Dealers through the Baby Boomers to Generation X, is widely known within Catholic academic and pastoral circles. Each generation, sociologists report, has been more inclined to behave as if religious beliefs, moral convictions, and fundamental values are achieved rather than ascribed, constructed rather than "given." Catholics who came of age in the 1960s and 1970s, steeped in a culture of radical choice, were hardly more resistant than other Americans to the appeal of "expressive individualism" as a religious mode no less than a lifestyle. For "a generation of seekers" who came of age in the 1980s values and identities fluctuated with the rhythms of the marketplace of ideas and customs. Spirituality thrived; religiosity waned. Like other Americans, many Catholics born between 1963 and 1983 raised to the level of operating principles the suspicion of authority and tradition entertained by their skeptical and metaphysically challenged but still believing Boomer parents.[2]

2. Consider the verdict of Dean R. Hoge et al., *Young Adult Catholics: Religion in a Culture of Choice* (Notre Dame, Ind.: University of Notre Dame Press, 2001), 16: "Recent studies of identity diffusion among American Catholics suggest that the gap continues to grow between what official documents and ecclesiologists say about the nature of the church and Catholic identity, and the practical ecclesiology of voluntary associations espoused by many Catholics today. Young adults have a more selective sense of a 'consumer Catholicism' than a practicing or institutionally valid Catholicism. Their knowledge of the faith and of its traditional symbols and root metaphors is limited, fragmentary, or nonexistent. Many appear to have lost much of the core narrative of the tradition and to have little connectedness with Catholic institutional life. In consequence, young adult Catholics have a difficult time articulating a coherent sense of Catholic identity and expressing Catholicism's distinctiveness. Nor, with the exception of Latinos, are many young adult Catholics able to fall back

In the historical narratives crafted from the data, the pre–Vatican II generation stands apart starkly from the subsequent generations of Boomers and Xers. Davidson repeats the phrase "high level of" when describing the pre-conciliar laity's belief, obedience to Church authorities, participation in the sacramental life of the Church, devotional practices, and so on.

Yet while practice, attendance, and participation were indeed robust, secular values were emerging as a powerful competitor to the cultural cocoon created by "ghetto Catholicism." As traditional ethnic communities disintegrated—not just Catholic and Jewish urban villages, but midwestern Lutheran farm towns and southern Baptist hamlets—the '50s witnessed the gradual secularization of the lower and middle classes. From 1950 to 1970 the rate of Catholic socioeconomic advancement was faster than that of any other religious subgroup except American Jews. "The postwar generation was assimilating into a broader American culture that, if not quite areligious, was at least highly latitudinarian," Charles Morris writes. "For the American Catholic Church, which had chosen to tie religious practice so tightly to a uniquely Catholic cultural machinery, that portended a more truly root-and-branch challenge than communism ever did."[3]

Morris's hindsight is confirmed by the contemporaries of the first wave of Catholic secularization. "Probably the greatest danger in public life in the United States today," observed historian Thomas T. McAvoy in 1956, "is the drive for conformity. If enforced, this conformity, besides destroying liberty and spiritual aspirations, must produce a low common denominator in culture and religion."[4] Father Francis J. Connell, a Redemptorist priest at the Catholic University of America who authored an astounding 641 essays for the *American Ecclesiastical Review* from 1940 to 1967,[5] inveighed against mixed marriages, ecumenical youth organizations

---

on ethnic or tribal identity as a re-enforcement of religious identity. As the boundaries of Catholicism become weaker and more diffuse, preserving and transmitting the tradition's norms become more difficult."

3. Charles R. Morris, *American Catholic: The Saints and Sinners Who Built America's Most Powerful Church* (New York: Vintage Books, 1997), 254.

4. Thomas T. McAvoy, C.S.C., "Catholic, Protestant and Jew and Other Problems of Conformity," *Review of Politics* 18 (January 1956): 102.

5. Over five hundred of Connell's essays were answers to questions sent by the many priests who subscribed to the journal. *The American Catholic Who's Who 1964–65* (Grosse

such as the YMCA ("a grave spiritual danger"), non-Catholic godparents and pallbearers, and especially "the wealthy Catholic who, for the sake of social prestige, sends his sons and daughters to secular schools or colleges when he could just as easily send them to Catholic institutions."[6]

In 1952 Connell reported that his fears were being realized in the growing number of Catholics "who, either by their conduct or by their mental attitude, constitute a source of danger to the faith." Their faith, he suggested, "is based on a natural sense of honor rather than on supernatural motives"; this is evident in their openness to the general American trend toward sensuality in entertainment and in behavior, and "above all the use of contraception in conjugal life."[7] The root cause of these problems lay in the increased association of Catholics with their non-Catholic neighbors, especially Protestants, and the need to "go along to get along" in the professional world. Specifically religious cooperation was even more insidious, Connell warned, given that "public non-Catholic religious rites [are] sinful." Accordingly, "Catholics should realize that, if necessary, they must be willing to sacrifice material and social advantages rather than collaborate unlawfully in any activities contrary to the true faith."[8]

It was not to be. In one quadrant of the previously insular subculture after another, Catholics began to take their cues from the mainstream. Immigrant-era devotional culture, for example, had tended toward Christian asceticism in its most extreme form when Catholic penitents glorified suffering and linked virtue to the endurance of pain. To suffer was among the most desirable and holy things that a person could do, for suffering united the sufferer to Jesus and Mary, the archetypal sacrificial victims.[9]

Pointe, Mich.: Walter Romig, n.d.), 75, 135. Joseph M. White, *The Diocesan Seminary in the United States: A History from the 1780s to the Present* (Notre Dame, Ind.: University of Notre Dame Press, 1989), 333. Also see Joseph J. Farragher, S.J., review of *Father Connell Answers Moral Questions,* in *Theological Studies* 21 (1960): 312.

6. Francis J. Connell, "Preserving the Faith Inviolate," *American Ecclesiastical Review* 114 (January 1946): 44.

7. Francis J. Connell, "Dangers to Faith within the Church," *American Ecclesiastical Review* 126 (June 1952): 404.

8. Francis J. Connell, "Co-operation of Catholics in Non-Catholic Religious Activities, Part I," *American Ecclesiastical Review* 134 (February 1956): 101–2.

9. The Sorrowful Mother was to many devout persons the model they intended to emulate in their lives: she bore the most oppressive suffering patiently and with resignation, and as a result was deserving of great honor. The words of one popular hymn expressed the peculiar sentimentality that devotionalism frequently attached to Mary's pain: "Mix'd with

The penitential system of the immigrant Church bestowed upon suffering an intellectual, ritual, and symbolic depth of meaning that permeated the images and practices of the Catholic community. At its most extreme, as historians James Fisher and Robert Orsi have argued, the devotional culture was marked by a "grammar of suffering," an "aesthetics of pain," "a redistributive economy of distress," and a "language of sorrow." Catholic intellectuals criticized the softness of "bourgeois inexpensive pain suppressants," or analgesics, and the marketing of a variety of new products guaranteed to relieve aches and pains. But that market niche quickly burgeoned, as historian James McCartin demonstrates, creating an "analgesic sensibility" that deepened in subsequent years with the increasing reliance upon psychological therapy and psychiatric drugs to relieve emotional suffering.[10] The accompanying shift in broader cultural attitudes toward pain, suffering, and wholeness penetrated the Catholic subculture, gradually casting devotionalism's depiction of suffering "as outmoded and ever more macabre and peculiar." Such dramatic changes in Catholic sensibilities occurred rapidly in some quarters of the Catholic population, more gradually in others, McCartin notes. The rate of change depended in part on upward social mobility. In the lives of people who could not so read-

---

yours let my tears be, / Mourning Him who mourned for me, / All the days that I may live." The popular hymn, "Stabat Mater"—generally translated as, "At the Cross Her Station Keeping"—from which this verse came was sung especially throughout Lent during the Stations of the Cross. The hymn was also included as a part of the Mass ritual celebrated on the feast day of Our Lady of Sorrows, observed twice annually throughout the world. *Saint Joseph's Daily Missal*, 250–54, 1055–56. Also see Robert Orsi, "'Mildred, Is It Fun to Be a Cripple?': The Culture of Suffering in Mid-Twentieth-Century American Catholicism," in Thomas J. Ferraro, ed., *Catholic Lives, Contemporary America* (Durham, N.C.: Duke University Press, 1997), 19–64.

10. On pain and pain therapies, consult Donald Caton, *What a Blessing She Had Chloroform: The Medical and Social Response to the Pain of Childbirth from 1800 to the Present* (New Haven, Conn.: Yale University Press, 1999), 90–129; David T. Courtwright, *Forces of Habit: Drugs and the Making of the Modern World* (Cambridge, Mass.: Harvard University Press, 2001); Ariel Glucklich, *Sacred Pain: Hurting the Body for the Sake of the Soul* (New York: Oxford University Press, 2001), 179ff.; Gerald P. McKenny, *To Relieve the Human Condition: Bioethics, Technology, and the Body* (Albany: State University of New York Press, 1997); Roselyne Rey, *The History of Pain,* trans. Louise Elliot Wallace et al. (Cambridge, Mass.: Harvard University Press, 1995), 125–31, 184–90; and David Healy, *The Antidepressant Era* (Cambridge, Mass.: Harvard University, 1997), 7–24. On the subsequent therapeutic culture, see Ellen Herman, *The Romance of American Psychology: Political Culture in an Age of Experts* (Berkeley: University of California Press, 1996), 304–25; Philip Reiff, *The Triumph of the Therapeutic: The Uses of Faith after Freud* (New York: Harper and Row, 1967), 232–61.

ily avoid suffering through drugs and therapy, devotionalism continued to render suffering meaningful and comprehensible.[11]

Catholics' growing sense of being "at home" in U.S. political culture also inspired changes in Catholic piety and religious practice in the post-war period. Joseph Chinnici has traced the connections between the ju-ridical and moralistic cast of immigrant devotionalism and the Church's modern political struggles with the secular state. The Catholic need to propitiate a rights- and power-bearing God through sacrifice and penance mirrored Catholic interaction with an aloof rights- and power-bearing state. "Sociologically the public political language of the Church found its expression in a unique combination of Americanism and Catholicism," Chinnici writes, "which accommodated both to the ethos of American business and to a strong Catholic identity focused on patterns of urban sectarianism, devotional subculture, and religious privatization." Within this accommodation Christian suffering was domesticated to encompass such activities as "the practice of the rhythm method of birth control, the acceptance by the woman of the 'monotonous minutiae' which comprised her domestic world, the recitation of the rosary and morning and night prayers, payment of fees for parochial education, the cultivation of self-discipline, and the religious duty to care for the poor."[12]

By the early 1950s, however, "the intellectual, political, and social pat-terns that had engendered and sustained the sectarian accommodation to the secular state and society had begun to collapse." The agents of this col-lapse, Chinnici argues, included suburbanization and changing patterns in the family, which undercut the social foundations of sectarian Cathol-icism; the influence of humanistic psychology; and the efforts of intel-lectuals such as John Courtney Murray and Dorothy Dohen to reframe

---

11. James P. McCartin, "The Love of Things Unseen: Prayer and the Catholic Moral Imagination in the Twentieth Century United States" (Ph.D. dissertation, University of Notre Dame, 2003), chapter 1.

12. Joseph P. Chinnici, "Suffering, Spirituality and Evangelization: The Catholic Expe-rience, 1930–1996," paper presented for the Catholic Commission on Cultural and Intel-lectual Affairs Annual Meeting, Notre Dame, 2002. The overarching categories of Church and State as correlative perfect societies with internal laws and purposes dominated Ameri-can Catholic thinking, Chinnici explains, especially after the publication of *Immortale Dei* (1885) and the condemnation of Americanism (1899). See for example Virgil Michel, *The Theory of the State* (St. Paul, Minn.: Wanderer Publishing, 1936); John A. Ryan and Moor-house F. X. Millar, S.J., *The State and the Church* (New York: Macmillan, 1922).

the interpretation of suffering.[13] Other developments in U.S. Catholicism also prefigured and anticipated the Church's "turn to the world" at Vatican II—its biblically inspired focus on social justice and new openness to modern sciences and secular intellectual projects. Well before the conciliar era, the displacement of traditional devotionalism and supernaturalism by an activist orientation to social transformation was already painfully evident to Father Patrick Peyton, C.S.C., whose Family Rosary Crusade came under criticism from both North and South American priests and laity for its inattention to concrete social problems and justice concerns.[14] Distressingly, the Catholic subculture was also found wanting at the very heart of its strength—education and formation. Father John Tracy Ellis's 1955 article on "American Catholics and the Intellectual Life," lamenting the absence of Catholic Einsteins, Salks, and Oppenheimers, and Thomas O'Dea's 1958 book, *American Catholic Dilemma,* with its attack on the Church's "formalism," "authoritarianism," and "neurotic immaturity," signaled a decisive shift in cultural and intellectual role models for Catholics. By the mid-1950s the absence of Catholic graduate students in elite secular universities "was . . . well on its way to being corrected."[15]

Belief and Practice in "the World," 1960–1977

Jim Davidson's generational schema places the Vatican II generation at the center of the story. Who would deny the impact and overall importance of the council on the religious imagination, practices, and self-understanding of American Catholics? The question is the decisive nature of Vatican II, which is often taken for granted.

Yet there is considerable counterevidence to the argument that Vati-

13. See Robert T. Reilly, "Sacrifice in the 1960's," *America* 104 (October 29, 1960): 147–49; Father John E. Corrigan and Donald J. Lehman, "A New Look at Self-Denial," *U.S. Catholic* 33 (March 1968): 13–16; William J. Reask, S.J., "Mortification: An Entry into the Christ Mystery," *Review for Religious* 24 (1965): 363–82; Timothy Kelly, "Suburbanization and the Decline of Catholic Public Ritual in Pittsburgh," *Journal of Social History* 28 (Winter 1994): 311–30. On new interpretations of suffering, see John Courtney Murray, S.J., "The Construction of Christian Culture: I. Portrait of a Christian; II. Personality and the Community; III. The Humanism of the Cross," three lectures given at Loyola College, February 1940, Murray Papers, Special Collection, Georgetown University—quoted in Chinnici.

14. McCartin, "The Love of Things Unseen," chapter 2.

15. Morris, *American Catholic,* 268.

can II was the major catalyst of an "American Catholic revolution." One might consider, for example, the persistent expressions of frustration on the part of religious educators, dismayed well into the 1970s with the low level of lay (and clerical) understanding and appropriation of the council's basic theological and ecclesiological teachings. Most American Catholics of the conciliar era, reformers and catechists complained, possessed at best a superficial notion of the reasoning behind either the reforms introduced by Vatican II or the changes implemented subsequently, "in the spirit of the Council." In 1986, while interviewing approximately seventy-five priests around the country about, among other things, their experiences of the transmission and reception of the council at the parish level, I was struck by the repeated tales of the almost comical inadequacy of the priests' own comprehension of the conciliar theology.[16] To the extent that the deep background of the changes eluded the priests, one could hardly expect the laity they served to internalize a sophisticated understanding of "Vatican II Catholicism." As one pastor put it: "From what little reading and discussion of 'the new theology' we had time for, it's no surprise that our 'training' of the laity went something like this. One day, out of the blue, we told them 'You were *the church militant.* Now you are *the People of God.*' When they asked why, we said, 'Because *we're telling you so.* Take our word for it.'"[17]

Prior to the council, as we have seen, American Catholics were increasingly taking their cues from their Protestant and Jewish colleagues in business, higher education, and the professions. But they were not uncritical in their appropriation of the practices and values of the new American religious consensus (valorized in Will Herberg's Protestant-Catholic-Jew amalgam) that was gathering under an expanding secular canopy. Indeed, lay Catholics occasionally recoiled at the prospect of imitating too closely the rhythms and patterns of secular life—even when the institutional Church seemed to make that very mistake. James O'Toole's recently completed study of the rapid decline in the practice of confession in the mid-1960s underscores the complexity of Catholic reactions to social change and how those reactions affected Catholic piety and religious practice. On

---

16. R. Scott Appleby, "Present to the People of God: The Transformation of the Roman Catholic Parish Priesthood," in Jay P. Dolan et al., *Transforming Parish Ministry: The Changing Roles of Catholic Clergy, Laity, and Women Religious* (New York: Crossroads, 1990).

17. Ibid., 87.

the one hand, O'Toole documents the growing irritation of Catholic laity with the long lines, weary confessors, mechanical ritual, and impersonal absolutions—the "mass production" and impersonalism of the sacrament as practiced in the '50s and '60s. These features they associated all too readily, O'Toole reports, with everyday life in an increasingly bureaucratized and commercialized American society. On the other hand, a growing openness to the equality of women, a cause that was being promoted with increasing intensity in the larger society, created a willingness among some laity to express dissatisfaction with male confessors, a desire to engage with more sympathetic personalities, and, eventually, a disgruntlement with the exclusion of women from the role of confessor and from the priesthood itself.[18]

The so-called conciliar period was also, of course, a period of intense social ferment and cultural revolution in the United States. Recent historical works such as John McGreevy's *Parish Boundaries* have situated the event of Vatican II within the powerfully determinative context of the U.S. civil rights movement, Vietnam, the "new morality," and other dramatic changes unfolding after the assassination of John F. Kennedy and the Supreme Court decisions outlawing prayer in the public schools— two landmarks now seen as the inaugural events of "the long '60s," a period of rapid secularization and social fragmentation in American society.

Skepticism, Religious Illiteracy, Diffusion, and a Fractious Pluralism, 1978–2000

Professor Davidson notes that the "post–Vatican II period" has been a time of resurgence of what he calls "Culture I Catholicism," led by a vigorous pope who is conservative, not to say reactionary, on matters internal to the Church—the role of women in pastoral ministry, the encouragement of a new clericalism, the subordination of the college of bishops to the pope, and the like. Such an analysis dovetails rather neatly with a view of "Catholic culture wars" that reinforces an intra-ecclesial interpretation of post-conciliar U.S. Catholic history.

18. James M. O'Toole, "In the Court of Conscience: American Catholics and Confession, 1900–1975," in James M. O'Toole, ed., *Habits of Devotion: Catholic Religious Practice in Twentieth-Century America* (Ithaca, N.Y.: Cornell University Press, 2004), 171–73.

Viewed from my somewhat different perspective here, which situates American Catholicism first and foremost within an increasingly secularized U.S. social and cultural context, the post-conciliar generation personified by John Paul II and his followers in the U.S. Church can be seen as an era of almost last-ditch Catholic resistance to an encompassing and stifling "culture of disbelief," "culture of death," "crisis of fidelity." One can find this reading of the past quarter-century plausible without embracing the range of papal, neoconservative, or "orthodox" responses. In any case, the historical record substantiates the notion of secularization as an accumulating and cumulative process. The salient developments of the 1980s and '90s, according to this view, have deep roots in the previous thirty years.

In American society, for example, the most recent period has been marked by *the rise of popular skepticism.* Skepticism—taken from the Greek *skepsis* ("consideration" or "doubt")—has assumed various forms in history; its root meaning is the view that reason can come to no reliable conclusions about the ultimate nature of reality. Religious thinkers such as Erasmus and Pascal employed skeptical arguments to support the priority of faith, but in the thought of early modern Enlightenment figures such as Voltaire and Hume, skepticism was a powerful means of discounting or minimizing religious belief.[19] We earn the right to believe a hypothesis only by first treating it with maximum suspicion and hostility: this was the legacy skepticism bequeathed to twentieth-century philosophies of religion. By 1960 the historian of skepticism Richard Popkin, noting the preoccupation of modern philosophy with the problems of epistemology, was able to claim that virtually all contemporary philosophy is either skeptical or concerned with answering the claims of skepticism.[20]

The corrosive effects of skepticism have been compounded since the 1960s by the ascendancy of nonfoundationalism—the denial, under the

19. In his nineteenth-century treatise on *The Ethics of Belief,* William Clifford elaborated the positivist's assumption there is only one (empirical) road to truth: belief must be withheld unless and until all available "evidence" justifies it. William Kingdon Clifford, *The Ethics of Belief and Other Essays,* rev. ed. (Amherst, N.Y.: Prometheus Books, 1999).

20. Richard Popkin, *The History of Skepticism from Erasmus to Descartes* (Assen: Van Gorcum, 1960); also W. L. Reese, *Dictionary of Philosophy and Religion: Eastern and Western Thought* (Atlantic Highlands, N.J.: Humanities Press, 1980), 531–32.

pressure of modern science, of the existence of universal and discernible foundations for knowledge, which entails, in turn, a denial of the possibility of objective truth or an objective moral order.[21] Accompanied by a tribalized version of multiculturalism that exalts the exotic and dismisses the very notion of universal truths, nonfoundationalism migrated in the 1980s and 1990s from faculty lounges and the pages of esoteric journals into pop music, movies, advertising, and mass media. Its rejection of the possibility of universally binding truth finds expression in radical individualism, fashionable cynicism, and unchecked materialism.

While we are piling up the disheartening "isms" spinning off from this virulent form of skepticism, let us not forget the nihilism that the presumed loss of foundations renders plausible. Ennui, rootlessness, and apathy have a new home in the denial of a telos, a purposeful end, to human striving. In the title of a popular John Cougar Mellencamp album from the '80s: "Nothing Matters, and What if it Did."

Indeed, by the 1980s, the virulent skepticism that had taken root in the academy and intellectual culture in Europe, Latin America, and the United States after the Second World War had penetrated popular culture, government, business, schools, and even the home. Agnosticism about the underlying meaning of human life has been elevated to the level of a working assumption in the everyday lives of a significant and growing minority of Americans.[22]

Pope John Paul II, recognizing the roots of this skepticism in the Enlightenment project, has attacked the moral relativism it underwrites. Modern reason, he warns, "in its one-sided concern to investigate human subjectivity, seems to have forgotten that men and women are always called to direct their steps toward a truth which transcends them. Sundered from that truth, individuals are at the mercy of caprice, and

---

21. The denial of universally privileged epistemic and interpretive standpoints is displayed in Ludwig Wittgenstein's language games, W. V. O. Quine's notion of webs of belief, and Richard Rorty's pragmatism (which he defines as "what is good for *us* to believe"). For a basic introduction to the concept (if not the term) of "nonfoundationalism," see "Solidarity or Objectivity?" in Richard Rorty, *Objectivity, Relativism and Truth: Philosophical Papers,* vol. 1 (New York: Cambridge University Press, 1991), 21–34. On realism, anti-realism and anti-representationalism, consult pp. 2–17. See also John E. Thiel, *Nonfoundationalism* (Minneapolis: Fortress Press, 1994), 1–37.

22. Stephen L. Carter, *The Culture of Disbelief: How American Law and Politics Trivialize Religious Devotion* (New York: Basic Books, 1993).

their state as person ends up being judged by pragmatic criteria based essentially upon experimental data, in the mistaken belief that technology
must dominate all." The pope laments the shift from "the investigation of
being" to epistemology. "Rather than make use of the human capacity to
know the truth, modern philosophy has preferred to accentuate the ways
in which this capacity is limited and conditioned," he writes. "This has
given rise to different forms of agnosticism and relativism which have led
philosophical research to lose its way in the shifting sands of widespread
scepticism."[23]

U.S. Catholic philosophers and theologians, whether of the "right" or
"left," generally welcomed the papal project—the defense and promotion
of the very concept of Truth—as being absolutely central to the evangelization of the current and coming generations. The proclamation of the
good news of Jesus Christ and the celebration and communication of his
saving sacramental presence presupposes hearers of the Word and commu-
nicants who seek to be incorporated into the Word. Yet popular culture,
Catholic resisters argued, has now joined the skeptical elite in disseminat-
ing ideas and advocating lifestyles that have the effect of undermining the
possibility of belief in a truth that might exist beyond and apart from the
subjective experience of the individual.

The challenge that skepticism poses to people of faith—and to people who may otherwise be prepared to take the leap of faith and religious commitment—is hardly unique to our time. But the context within
which radical doubt is experienced and confronted *is* new, and has been
deepening since the 1950s. The philosopher Charles Taylor, in attempting to name what is old and what new in "the varieties of religion today,"
takes as his text William James's *Varieties of Religious Experience,* the central themes of which James first introduced in delivering the Gifford Lectures at the dawn of the twentieth century. Taylor compares and contrasts
our sense of "existing without foundations" to James's description of the
melancholy felt by the "sick soul," distraught by a sense of meaningless
and pervasive evil:

> Melancholy is, of course, a phenomenon long recognized. It goes back well
> into the premodern world. But its meaning has changed. The sudden sense
> of the loss of significance, which is central to melancholy, or accidie or ennui,

23. Pope John Paul II, *Fides et ratio,* I:5.

used to be experienced in a framework in which the meaning of things was beyond doubt. God was there, good and evil were defined, what we are called to cannot be gainsaid; but we can no longer feel it. We are suddenly on the outside, exiled. [Melancholy] is a sin, a kind of self-exclusion, for which there can be no justification.

But in the modern context, melancholy arises in a world where the guarantee of meaning has gone, where all its traditional sources, theological, metaphysical, historical, can be cast in doubt. It therefore has a new shape: not the sense of exile and rejection from an unchallengeable cosmos of significance, but rather the intimation of what may be the definitive emptiness, the final dawning of the end of the last illusion of significance. It hurts, one might say, in a new way.

One might argue which mode of melancholy hurts more: my exile from the general feast of meaning, or the threatened implosion of meaning altogether. But there is no doubt which has the greater significance. The first pain touches me, the second everyone and everything.[24]

The "threatened implosion of meaning," far from being merely another momentarily fashionable preoccupation of anxious intellectuals, resonates with the historical experience of millions of postwar Americans. For the immediate postwar generation, "the silence of God" echoes down the corridors of memory of the Holocaust, the Gulag and mass murders of Stalin, the genocides of Cambodia and Rwanda. For the Boomers, "the death of God" seemed of a piece with the upheavals of the '60s, the moral abyss of Vietnam, the degradation of political idealism along a downhill slope dug by Nixon and paved by Clinton. For the Generation Xers, the betrayals occurred from within the most intimate, inward, personal realms: the disintegration of the nuclear family, the scourge of AIDS, the anxiety over steadily declining economic prospects despite the ostentatious wealth of the upper classes. Melancholy is socially imbedded within the generations.

Corruption and decadence, in short, has lost its power to shock. Perhaps the saddest truth about the priestly sexual abuse crisis engulfing U.S. Catholicism is its footnote-like character: Yes, and add that betrayal, too. In this milieu, the central themes of Catholic theology and anthropology, if they are to gain a hearing, must overcome the formidable obstacle of "melancholy," twenty-first century style.

24. Charles Taylor, *Varieties of Religion Today: William James Revisited* (Cambridge, Mass.: Harvard University Press, 2002), 39–40.

Forgetting the Bible

A second and related trend building during the postwar decades, namely, *the erosion of biblical and theological literacy in the United States,* also reached its zenith during the most recent period.

Our brief discussion of nonfoundationalism suggests the larger world of ideas and attitudes within which U.S. Catholics, like other Americans, have gradually but unmistakably absorbed and internalized the assumptions of utilitarianism and expressive individualism, leading them to embody and embrace what Peter Berger first called "a culture of radical choice," and what Stephen Carter has labeled, more ominously, "a culture of disbelief." Certain elements of postmodernist theory help us understand how a concept as esoteric as nonfoundationalism has struck a chord with the masses—or, perhaps more accurately, how the masses, in their behaviors and lifestyles, have provided the raw material for the development of such a concept.

First, postmodernist theory holds that the media and popular culture govern and shape all other forms of social relationships: society has become subsumed within the mass media. It is no longer even a question of distortion of reality, since the term "distortion" implies that there is a reality outside the surface simulations of the media, which can be distorted. But the very existence of that "independent" reality is at issue. Cultural theory suggested that the media not only plays a decisive role in constructing people's sense of social reality, but also places us in relationship to that reality. It is a relatively short step to the proposition that the media itself is the primary shaper of the popular sense of reality.

In a postmodern world, therefore, surfaces and style become exaggerated in importance: "images dominate narrative." Compounding this sense of reality as shifting and unstable—this impression that the world somehow lacks depth and substance—is the postmodern American's experience of space and time as fluid and manipulable. The speed and scope of modern mass communications enhances this impression, as does the relative ease with which people and information can travel. Rapid international flows of capital, money, information, and culture disrupt the linear unities of time and the established distances of geographical space. In this setting, time and space become less stable and comprehensible, and more confused and incoherent. Our previously unified and ideas about space and time begin to be undermined. "In short," Dominic Strinati writes, "postmodern popular culture is a culture *sans frontières,* outside history."[25]

Postmodernists also point to the loss of a sense of history as a continuous, linear "narrative," a clear sequence of events with meaning and direction. As mentioned above, the experience of history as ambiguous, directionless, and random—if not somehow of malevolent design—is not restricted to intellectual or cultural elites; the holocausts of the bloody twentieth century have fixed this possibility of history-as-chaos firmly in the minds of anyone who has been paying attention.

The postmodern consciousness is therefore characterized by a hermeneutic of suspicion toward authority figures, who have been known to abuse their authority and to attempt to legitimate those abuses—from slavery to colonialism to patriarchy—by constructing mythologies and meta-narratives of "progress" and "civilization" and "redemption." Such morality tales are seen to have little or no correspondence to reality (understood to encompass the experience of the oppressed and suffering peoples, who are often written out of the meta-narratives). Hence, meta-narratives are in decline. Suspicion of religion, science, Marxism, and even "universal truth" and "universal human rights" is warranted to the extent that these would-be cultural authorities make absolute, universal, and all-embracing claims to knowledge and truth, or try to read a pattern of progress into history. Postmodernists are highly skeptical about these meta-narratives, and love to exploit and play off their ironies.[26] At this juncture "postmodernism" converges with "nonfoundationalism" to reject any and all claims to absolute knowledge. No social practice can be said to have universal validity.

How has this destabilization of texts and meta-narratives played out in the lives of ordinary Americans during the post-conciliar period? George A. Lindbeck, professor of historical theology at Yale, has lamented the "dramatic weakening" of the historic cultural role of the Bible in American society. Until recently, he notes, most people in traditionally Christian countries such as the United States lived in the linguistic and imaginative world of the Bible. It was "the text above texts," or, as Martin E.

25. Dominic Strinati, *An Introduction to Theories of Popular Culture* (London: Routledge, 1995), 227.
26. The diverse, iconoclastic, referential, and collage-like character of postmodern popular culture clearly draws inspiration form the decline of meta-narratives. Ibid., 230.

Marty put it, "America's iconic book." Biblical stories, images, conceptual patterns, and turns of phrase permeated the culture from top to bottom; Americans spoke colloquially, for example, of a Judas, or a Solomon, a Martha or a Mary. Reviewing the hold of the imaginative universe of the Bible over nineteenth- and twentieth-century secularists who explicitly repudiated its theological claims, Lindbeck contends that a familiar text can remain imaginatively and conceptually powerful long after its claims to truth are denied:

> [T]exts influence minds and hearts even when they are not [literally] believed. Once they penetrate deeply into the psyche, especially the collective psyche, they cease to be primarily objects of study and rather come to supply the conceptual and imaginative vocabularies, as well as the grammar and syntax, with which we construe and construct reality. . . . [I]t is worth recalling that this cultural Christianity, this linguistic and imaginative influence of the Bible, is not religiously unimportant. It has often been a condition for the communal shaping of convictions and conduct.[27]

Thus the fading of both biblical literacy and biblical imagination is a crisis of considerable proportions. There seems to be a consensus among biblical theologians that the decline of biblical literacy has been "abrupt and pervasive"; that language, culture, and imagination have been debiblicized at a remarkable rate in the United States; and that this entails a de-Christianization of culture, but not necessarily of society. The percentage of Americans who profess Christianity, however inexpertly, remains high even as biblical literacy decreases.

Of course the Bible is not the only victim of contemporary forgetfulness: American history, world history, and the corpus of Western classics are fading from collective memory. Our educational system has failed, argues Sandra Schneiders, to transmit the classical tradition, including its Judeo-Christian component, to the several generation of students who have been the objects of so-called universal education. "It is not only the Bible which these students do not know; they do not know Greek and Roman mythology, Plato or Aristotle, the classical poets, Shakespeare or Dante," she writes. "But, in a political system which is nearly paranoid about the separation of church and state, knowledge of the biblical tradi-

27. George A. Lindbeck, "The Church's Mission to a Postmodern Culture," in Frederic B. Burnham, ed., *Postmodern Theology: Christian Faith in a Pluralist World* (San Francisco: Harper and Row, 1989), 39–40, 42.

tion is doubly a victim; as a classic, the Bible is largely neglected; as a canonical religious document, it is virtually proscribed."[28]

The consequences of the fading of biblical literacy, Lindbeck observes, include the impoverishment of public discourse and the loss of a common language in which to discuss the common good. Scriptural references, which once peppered the speeches of Lincoln, King, the Kennedys, and other prominent advocates of civil rights and social justice, have not been replaced by alternative "discourses of transcendence." The lack of effective alternatives to biblical language, as Robert Bellah and others have demonstrated, is underscored by the inadequacy of the regnant American idioms—utilitarianism and expressive individualism.

For Catholics, the analog to the erosion of the encompassing imaginative world of the Bible has been the disappearance, among "postethnic" Euro-Americans if not among Latino Catholics, of the encompassing imaginative world of the Catholic neighborhood (ghetto, enclave). Just as the authority of the Bible depended on the believer's immersion in its language, metaphors, and worldview, so, too, the authority of the Church depended on the immigrant (or recently assimilated) Catholic's immersion in the richly imagined devotional and ritual life of the parish.

The authority of the Church *continues to* depend on the parish—on the liturgical, communal, and sacramental bonds shared by parishioners. The question is whether the new paradigm for Catholic self-understanding proclaimed in the documents of Vatican II and internalized by American Catholics during the post-conciliar period—a neo-apostolic paradigm commanding lay Catholic witness to "the world" alongside participation in, and leadership of, secular society—was sufficiently dominant within the American Catholic imagination to prevent mere *integration into* the world, on its own terms.

The concern, expressed so routinely over the past twenty-five years that we can hardly hear it anymore, is that the post-conciliar thinning of American Catholicism—the perceived withering of identity and presence marked by the diminished numbers of priests and religious, the closing of schools and parishes, the graying of "core Catholics,"[29] the inadequate

28. Sandra M. Schneiders, "Does the Bible Have a Postmodern Message?" in Burnham, *Postmodern Theology,* 56.

29. "Core Catholics," as defined by the Notre Dame Study of Catholic Parish Life

theological education and religious formation of younger Catholics, and so on—has eroded the Church's ability to operate with a sufficient degree of independence from the secular society. Headlong secularization seems more likely in the absence or weakening of countercultural Catholic presences as a regular feature in the lives of increasing numbers of laity.

During "the golden age of the parish" in the 1920s and 1930s, the parish did not stand alone as the center of Catholic formation and practice; it was embedded in a web of devotional societies, parochial and extra-parochial schools, colleges and educational associations, active religious orders, and unambiguously Catholic social service institutions. Catholic Action emerged subsequently as an extra-parochial means of promoting lay Catholic efforts at transforming, or "re-Christianizing," the mainstream society as well as the "post-ethnic" Catholic workplace, home, and school. Throughout the post-conciliar period, however, there has been a casting about for successors to these pre-conciliar Catholic presences within American society.

One candidate has been Catholic social doctrine, and the postwar ascendancy of what David O'Brien has termed the republican mode of Catholic public presence (associated initially with Father John Ryan and the Social Action department of the NCWC, then with John Courtney Murray, S.J., and most recently with the lobbying, policy advocacy, and educational efforts of the U.S. Conference of Catholic Bishops and state Catholic conferences). Central to the mission of the Social Development office of the USCCB, especially under John Carr's leadership, have been systematic efforts to educate and evangelize Catholics in the basic tenets of Catholic social doctrine and to demonstrate the scriptural and theological foundations of the social teaching. One effective site of this educational and formative campaign has been "lobbying days," during which staff and volunteers working on policy issues for the national or state conferences study and discuss the Church's social teaching.[30]

The turn to the public square not only as an arena for civic engage-

---

(1986), are those active participants in the life of the Church, regular Mass attenders who have taken leadership responsibilities, in parishes and other Catholic institutions, for a variety of ministries and service.

30. William Bole, "What Do State Catholic Conferences Do?" in Margaret O'Brien Steinfels, ed., *American Catholics and Civic Engagement: A Distinctive Voice* (Lanham, MD: Rowman and Littlefield, 2004), 98.

ment but also as a platform for conveying Catholic teaching, to Catholics as well as non-Catholics, epitomizes the shifting relationship between individual and communal, private and public, expressions of Catholicism during the post-conciliar period. The Catholic presence in the U.S. public square has become both more diffuse and more focused. The 1980s saw the high-water mark of focused national Catholic presence in public debates, with the publication, dissemination, and widespread discussion (by non-Catholics and Catholics alike) of pastoral letters by the U.S. Catholic Bishops Conference: *The Challenge of Peace: God's Promise and Our Response* (1983), on the nuclear arms race; and *Economic Justice for All: Pastoral Letter on Catholic Social Teaching and the U.S. Economy* (1986).[31] As historical documents the pastorals were distinguished less, perhaps, by their actual content than by the transparently deliberative and broadly consultative process by which they were written, and by their open acknowledgement of internal pluralism within the Church—*a pluralism of theological and ethical principles as well as well as prudential judgments.*

As the less collegially minded bishops appointed by Pope John Paul II gained influence within the U.S. episcopacy, however, the national conference declined in influence and the action shifted to state Catholic conferences, which grew in numbers in the late 1980s and 1990s. Working with the national conference on many occasions, the state conferences necessarily tailored their lobbying, educational, and advocacy efforts to the particular justice issues affecting the state in question. This more diffuse presence was no less important and generally considered to be more effective, in terms of Catholic influence on specific policy issues, than the highly visible presence of the U.S. Catholic Conference (USCC) in the 1980s.[32] As the USCC seemed to take a lower profile in the 1990s, local and state Catholic leaders, most of them lay, attempted to take up the moral and educational role. John Huebscher, the director of the Wisconsin Catholic Conference, was not atypical among state conference directors in his am-

31. United States Catholic Bishops, "The Challenge of Peace: God's Promise and Our Response," in *Pastoral Letter on War and Peace* (Washington, DC: National Conference of Catholic Bishops, 1983); "Economic Justice for All," in *Pastoral Letter on Catholic Social Teaching and the U. S. Economy* (Washington, DC: National Conference of Catholic Bishops, 1986).

32. Stephen J. Pope, "Catholic Social Thought and the American Experience," in Steinfels, *American Catholics and Civic Engagement,* 39–40.

bition to supplement the lobbying agenda with efforts to foster a public conversation about the social good. Yet even Huebscher argues that "If we did nothing but legislative advocacy, we would still be relatively unique, *because most of our advocacy is for someone else*—the unborn, poor children, and others without a voice."[33]

The "republican discourse" of "the public Church" in the post-conciliar years, despite the serious commitment to preserving and featuring explicitly biblical and theological language (e.g., in the pastoral letters on nuclear arms and on the U.S. economy), may have led to the unintended consequence of eroding the distinctively non-American core of Catholic witness in and to the United States. In a presentation for the Pew Project on U.S. Catholics in the Public Square, Michelle Dillon deftly praises "the culturally engaged way in which the hierarchy has framed its opposition to abortion as a public rather than a private issue." What is "sociologically exciting," she argues, is that the bishops were not content merely to invoke the relatively abstract language of natural law in making the case against abortion. Rather, "they have explicitly reworked that language to fit directly with the symbols and themes that are at the core of American political culture." All of the public statements issued by the bishops, Dillon notes, whether in forums, in testimony to congressional committees, or in briefs filed before the Supreme Court, have framed the Church's opposition to abortion "as being consistent with the values enshrined in the U.S. Constitution and Declaration of Independence." In this way the bishops advanced an anti-abortion discourse that challenged their fellow citizens to enact America's founding ideals and presents abortion as a deviation from the nation's guiding values. "What greater claim to cultural legitimacy could the bishops articulate," Dillon concludes, "than to construct a discourse that is consistent with some of the ethics first articulated by the Puritan settlers in American society?"[34]

Yet "cultural legitimacy" came at a cost, not least because the path to it was a one-way street. The elites of the mainstream secular culture bestowed cultural legitimacy, often on narrow and quite specific conditions, and they seldom, if ever, felt it necessary to negotiate the terms, much less

---

33. Quoted in Bole, "What Do State Conferences Do?" 108.

34. Michele Dillon, "The Abortion Debate: Good for the Church and Good for American Society," in Margaret O'Brien Steinfels, ed., *American Catholics, American Culture: Tradition and Resistance* (Lanham, Md.: Rowman and Littlefield, 2004), 72–73.

receive wisdom from a faith community. To the contrary, Catholic participation in the public square often led to backlash, polarization, and the hardening of political camps. Those who work daily in the political realm appreciate the significance of the "creation of enemies." We are familiar with this dynamic within the Catholic community, where the birth control controversy and gender discrimination eroded the authority of the clergy and bishops, and where neuralgic issues such as women's ordination, the liturgy, and the contested interpretation of papal social encyclicals set professional Catholics against one another.

The triggers, depth, and consequences of polarization and backlash in the pluralist public arena, within the beltway or the statehouse, however, were no less harsh. The mainstream political culture marginalized Catholics whenever the latter failed to conform to the underlying values of secular liberalism. The combined effect of the feminist and gay rights movements, John McGreevy argues, was to weaken, perhaps fatally, Catholic credibility on all matters related to sex. "The impact of the women's movement was obvious: even as women achieved positions of leadership throughout American society, they were prevented from doing so within the Catholic church," he writes. In itself, this gender hierarchy did not destroy the plausibility of the Catholic argument on abortion, as pro-life women attested. And yet, McGreevy writes,

> the effect has been devastating: on one side, in a culture where personal experience seemed crucial to the assessment of moral problems, pro-choice women spoke of the terrors of unwanted pregnancy and the dangers of illegal abortions. On the other side, priests and (male) Catholic lawyers outlined in abstract terminology their opposition to the taking of innocent life. . . . [T]he inability of Catholic leaders to offer a compelling vision of sexual ethics, one that takes women's experience seriously, one that honestly acknowledges the importance of sexual identity for its leadership caste, invites criticism.[35]

In short, it cannot be said that Catholics effectively evangelized the public square in these years; to the contrary, John Coleman argues, even after decades of American Catholic public discourse about "the common good," "solidarity," and other key concepts of Catholic social doctrine, such fundamental principles find little or no resonance with Americans, including American Catholics. "Few Americans, or even American Cath-

---

35. John McGreevy, "Anti-Catholicism in the United States: The View from History," in Steinfels, *American Catholics, American Culture: Tradition and Resistance,* 160–61.

olics (for whom it ought to be a heritage), have much of a clue as to what it ['the common good'] actually means," Coleman claims. "Notions of the common good . . . move deeply against the American individualist grain."[36]

These conceptual foundations of U.S. Catholic civic engagement, no less than their theological and ethical counterparts (e.g., virtue, grace, sin, redemption) are imperiled in the waning or absence of a nurturing cultural context that would rescue them from sterility and irrelevance. The parish is not the world, but neither is it unaffected by the cultural and religious (or irreligious) dynamics of the larger society.

Catholics, like other Americans, and indeed like people everywhere, seek meaning and hunger for coherence. They are uneasy in the absence of some kind of binding truth—even if it is only *my* truth. Alongside the experience of anomie and melancholy in modern America there runs a countervailing trend toward what we might call postmodern tribalism. The intensification of identity around "the tribe" is one form of multiculturalism in a pluralist society. "The tribe" might be a sectarian offshoot of a church; a defiantly countercultural religious order that sets its members against their co-religionists; a racial or ethnic or class-based movement or group that pursues its particular interests without reference to, or a sense of responsibility for, the common good.

We might summarize this third trend by saying that *a fractious pluralism threatens to undermine the possibility of a genuinely diverse but unified moral and religious community.* Like the other trends discussed in this section, "fractious pluralism" has its origins in earlier stages of postwar secularization, but it has come to the fore amidst the drift of the post-conciliar period. While it bedevils the Church, the challenges of achieving a genuine pluralism have been writ large in American society over the past quarter century.

Pluralism is not necessarily a threat to the kind of diversity-in-unity that constitutes a vibrant society or faith community. Indeed, the idea of pluralism and its healthy practice serves as a corrective to the very enclave-building tendencies we see in those who exploit pluralism and render it as a license to separate from "the other." Thanks to the developments in

36. John A. Coleman, S.J., "The Common Good and Catholic Social Thought," in Steinfels, ed., *American Catholics and Civic Engagement*, 3.

the sociology of knowledge, psychoanalysis, and cultural psychology, we appreciate better than before that culture deeply matters to people, that their self-esteem depends on others' recognition and respect, and that our tendency to mistake the cultural for the natural and to unwittingly universalize our beliefs and practices causes much harm and injustice to others. All this has led to a greater acceptance of cultural differences and a redefinition of the relation between politics and culture, making culture a politically relevant category and respect for an individual's culture an integral part of the principle of equal citizenship.[37]

A genuine pluralism contributing to social or religious unity demands dialogue and collaboration across cultural differences. Yet the hope for genuine pluralism in church and society waned as the mainstream culture or faith community dissolved into numerous, competing subcultures or enclaves. In the places where this happened, the seeking after certainty and ascribed identity took on the character of a reaction to an experience of marginalization at the hands of the mainstream culture or religious community. In other cases, the resort of "special-interest culturalism" was a reaction to a perceived or actual instability in the mainstream culture or religious community.

Ironically, however, this quest for authority and certainty, because it attains these goods by drawing the circle of the "we" too narrowly, ends not far from where the "culture of disbelief" deposits its adherents, namely, on the edge of solipsism and self-absorption. The truth is not accessible to all; it is the gift of God to the elect, the remnant, the true believer, or, in secular parlance, the moneyed classes, the cultural elite, and so on. Transcendence of "orthodoxy" or cult or class or ethnos is unlikely if not impossible. Again, Pope John Paul II, perceiving the connection between skepticism and the potentially pernicious form of pluralism, has raised a warning:

> A legitimate plurality of positions has yielded to an undifferentiated pluralism, based upon the assumption that all positions are equally valid, which is one of today's most widespread symptoms of the lack of confidence in truth. Even certain conceptions of life coming from the East betray this lack of confidence, denying truth its exclusive character and assuming that truth reveals

---

37. Bhikhu Parekh, *Rethinking Multiculturalism: Cultural Diversity and Political Theory* (Cambridge, Mass.: Harvard University Press, 2000), 7–8.

itself equally in different doctrines, even if they contradict one another. On this understanding, everything is reduced to opinion; and there is a sense of being adrift. While, on the one hand, philosophical thinking has succeeded in coming closer to the reality of human life and its forms of expression, it has also tended to pursue issues—existential, hermeneutical or linguistic—which ignore the radical question of truth about personal existence, about being and about God. Hence we see among the men and women of our time, and not just in some philosophers, attitudes of widespread distrust of the human being's great capacity for knowledge. With a false modesty, people rest content with partial and provisional truths, no longer seeking to ask radical questions about the meaning and ultimate foundation of human, personal and social existence.[38]

"Fundamentalism" is one popular option within this sphere of subversive multiculturalism. The selective retrieval of scriptures and traditions for political purposes, the hardening of religious boundaries, the energies devoted to naming and demonizing the impure or insufficiently orthodox, the facile reliance on inerrancy and infallibility to protect truth claims from rational scrutiny—all of these familiar moves, designed to shore up religious authority and "truth," serve, ironically, to sap the tradition of its catholicity, of the inclusiveness that is its greatest strength. Intended to strengthen religious presence and orthodox religious community, the fundamentalist manipulation of the complex and multivalent tradition ends up narrowing and withering it.[39]

The fundamentalist option, that is, risks becoming yet another form of the ongoing individuation of religious identity—at base, it is a "make your own way" approach to spirituality and religion, dressed up in traditionalist garb. In popular culture, this form of radical individualism is now being "legitimated" by the expansion and celebration of pluralism.

The post-conciliar practice of American Catholics affiliating only partially and occasionally with the parish and the diocese, and pledging their allegiance and most of their resources to self-constituted subcommunities, is not new. U.S. Catholics have a long and often noble history of extra-parochial, extra-institutional presence and practice. But that kind of networking almost always occurred under Catholic auspices. It was rooted in,

---

38. Pope John Paul II, *Fides et ratio*, I:6.

39. See "The Enclave Culture," chapter 1 in Gabriel Almond, R. Scott Appleby, and Emmanuel Sivan, *Strong Religion: The Rise of Fundamentalisms around the World* (Chicago: University of Chicago Press, 2003).

and expressive of, Church-sanctioned lay participation in labor unions, in schools, in business, in social justice witness and activism. Over the past thirty years, a pattern of alternative and sometimes expressly counter-ecclesial self-organization has become a viable option for Catholics from various cultural, class, and educational backgrounds. No one ideology or theological perspective determines this pattern of affiliation. It can be seen in the women's movement and in Catholic feminism; in extra-ecclesial (not necessarily counter-ecclesial) Latino rituals, practices, and beliefs that exist in tension with official Church teaching; and in the willingness of young Catholics to participate in evangelical Protestant activities (e.g., re-treats, Bible studies, fellowship) alongside, or in preference to, Catholic ministries.[40] It is entirely plausible that this tendency toward extra- and a-ecclesial affiliation for religious purposes may increase and even spiral out of control in the coming years, at least in some parts of the country, as a result of the sexual abuse crisis and in reaction against the diminished authority of the U.S. Catholic bishops.

Conclusion

For U.S. Catholics these three trends in American society have fostered a distinctive religious-spiritual milieu characterized by self-determination in forging religious identity, conditional loyalty to the institutional Church, diminished levels of practice among lay Catholics, a diffuse presence in the U.S. public square, and a rift between what Davidson describes as adherents of Culture I Catholicism and adherents of Culture II Catholicism. (I believe the ideological profiles of the sides are more complex than this, however, in that "liberals" and "conservatives" differ not because they choose different "cultures" in toto, but because what they select from each culture and how they prioritize the elements they have selected differ.) Conservatives and prophets of decline, as we have seen, describe this milieu as a "culture of dissent" sustained by a "crisis of fidelity."

In focusing on the national social context within which generational

---

40. Timothy Matovina and Gary Riebe-Estrella, eds., *Horizons of the Sacred: Mexican Traditions in U.S. Catholicism* (Ithaca, N.Y.: Cornell University Press, 2002); Tom Beaudoin, *Virtual Faith: The Irreverent Spiritual Quest of Generation X* (San Francisco: Jossey-Bass, 1998); Robert A. Ludwig, *Reconstructing Catholicism: For a New Generation* (New York: Crossroad, 1995).

change has unfolded, I have concentrated on the negative aspects of secularization in the United States, in part to underscore the contrast to the typically rosy picture painted by people who celebrate the triumphs of Vatican II. There is an abundance of good news in this picture, of course. Core Catholics, now as ever, continue to demonstrate high levels of energy, commitment, and creativity; vital Catholic parishes persist and are growing in some areas of the country, especially where spirits and energies are renewed by new waves of immigrants from Mexico, Vietnam, the Philippines, and elsewhere. More than 30 percent of Catholics nationwide continue to attend Mass regularly and participate in the rituals and practices of Lent and Advent.

Moreover, some evidence suggests that younger Catholics are simply "late bloomers," more typical than atypical of previous generations in their gradual integration of their faith lives and professional and public identities. Their profile as Catholics is no more or less distinctive than that forged by their parents' generation (who reacted against *their* parents). This is not, essentially, "a lost generation" that has inherited little, if any, of the content or sensibilities of Catholicism as a way of life; rather, the core of the generation is solidly, even admirably, committed to Christian belief as celebrated in liturgy and enacted in the social order. The majority in *every* generation has been casual in their appropriation and public expression of the faith; it is the committed core that carries the tradition and ultimately determines the efficacy of public Catholicism in every generation.

The "glass half full" approach is tempered somewhat by the compartmentalization of efforts and a lack of collaboration across sectors. Catholicism still thinks of itself (however quietly these days) as THE Church in some respects, but it still operates well below full capacity as Church. Catholic leaders are aware of this problem and have begun to address the lack of coordination between levels (or within the same building, or on the same floor of the same building). But the post-'60s thinning of the institutional presence and the bickering among professional Catholics regarding the extent and source of a malaise within the American Church conspire to limit progress toward cooperation across intra-ecclesial divides.

For some interpreters of post-conciliar Catholicism, however, American society's declining receptivity to the exercise of moral authority "from above"—indeed, from any source other than the atomized self—betokens a far more troubling explanation for the apparent failures of "transmission" of the Catholic tradition. In an age of skepticism, Joseph Komonchak has remarked, Americans face "loss of a common belief that a public consensus on anything more substantial than democratic procedures is either possible or desirable." Some fear that an unbridgeable chasm has opened between Christianity and an American society increasingly closed to the possibility of "objective" foundations for knowledge and ethical decision making. Indeed, the main challenge presented to Catholic social thought in the contemporary American context, Komonchak contends, lies in the "widespread belief that no ethical, much less religious, beliefs or values are more than the products of personal choice."[41]

"All that is solid melts into air" was Marshall Berman's haunting description of the fate of order, authority, meaning, and truth under the influence of the dynamics of secular modernity. Yet these are the constitutive elements of a culture of Christian belief. Binding meaning, universal truth, and external religious authority became contested ideas within U.S. society and culture during the last half of the twentieth century. Vatican II and the deliriously refreshing momentum of ecclesial renewal notwithstanding, Catholics living in that ambient culture could not, and did not, resist the centrifugal secular tendencies of the age.

41. Joseph Komonchak, "The Encounter between Catholicism and Liberalism," in R. Bruce Douglass and David Hollenbach, eds., *Catholicism and Liberalism* (Cambridge, UK: Cambridge University Press, 1994), 94.

Comparative Perspectives

MICHELE DILLON

7. Decline and Continuity

Catholicism since 1950 in the United States,
Ireland, and Quebec

The selection of the United States, Quebec, and the Republic of Ireland as the focus for a comparative analysis of Catholicism may strike some readers as an odd choice. What could possibly be learned from comparing the world's only superpower with one of the smallest and until recently one of the poorest countries in Western Europe? What could possibly be adduced by introducing a Canadian province into the mix? The answer of course is that it makes sense to compare these three societies because the Catholic Church has a strong presence in each. The results of the charge presented in writing this chapter show that the comparative examination of the United States, Ireland, and Quebec reveals clear patterns of decline in Church authority in important areas of activity. This decline coexists, however, with the continuing presence of the Church and Catholicism across several domains of public and private life in each society.

The Historical and Cultural Status of the Church in Ireland, Quebec, and the United States

Before considering the fate of the Catholic Church since 1950 in each of the three countries it is important first to give attention to a major difference in the institutional status of the Church in the United States compared to Ireland and Quebec. The Catholic Church is a cultural insider in

Ireland and Quebec, whereas in the U.S. it is a cultural outsider. For both Quebec and Ireland, Catholicism and political/national identity have been inextricably intertwined. The centrality of an intellectual and missionary monasticism in premedieval Ireland and its imprint in the country's collective memory through Ireland's self-representation as the "Island of Saints and Scholars" gave successive Irish generations what they understood to be a special and unique hold on Catholicism. This legacy was further emboldened by the alignment of popular and institutional Catholicism in the Irish struggle against British domination from the mid-seventeenth century onward. The Irish quest for independence articulated by Daniel O'Connell in the early nineteenth century was explicitly called "Catholic Emancipation." Catholic struggle against British rule was given local expression in secluded country fields where families gathered around "Mass rocks" or altar stones to hear the Mass, whose formal celebration was prohibited by the Penal Laws imposed by the British colonizers. Irishness and Catholicism became symbolically intertwined as the economically and politically dispossessed Irish used Catholicism to demarcate their separateness from England and from Anglo-Irish Protestant landowners.

When political independence was eventually achieved (in 1922), it is not surprising that successive Irish governments used the law and public policy to institutionalize the values perceived as critical to the nation's Catholic identity. This identity was most clearly defined in the Irish Constitution (1937). Among other provisions, the constitution affirmed the "special position of the Holy Catholic Apostolic and Roman Church as the guardian of the Faith professed by the great majority of the citizens." It emphasized traditional Catholic teaching on the family, specifically recognizing the family as the "natural primary and fundamental unit" of society; it committed to protect marriage and the family "from attack" by explicitly prohibiting divorce; and it commended women who, by their "life within the home," give to the State "a support without which the common good cannot be achieved."[1] In sum, in post- as in pre-independence Ireland, to be Irish was to be Catholic. These were two seamlessly intermeshed identities.

The pivotal event in Quebec history is the conquest that took place in 1759 when the British captured Quebec, "the heart" of French Cana-

1. See Articles 41 and 44 of the *Constitution of Ireland* (Dublin: Stationery Office, 1937).

da. Largely as a result of the divisions set in place by the conquest, Quebec became highly differentiated between the French-speaking Catholic majority and the minority English-speaking Protestants, who dominated politically and economically. The Catholic Church was the only major institution under the control of the French Canadians, and, paralleling to some extent the Irish Catholic experience, Catholics bonded to, and appropriated, the Church in their creation of a distinct French Canadian Catholic identity. As Roger Finke and Rodney Stark have argued, in this context of ethnic subjugation and conflict, "mass attendance was inseparable from political and cultural resistance." They draw on the historian Elizabeth Armstrong, who, writing in the 1930s, observed that in the "175 years since the conquest [the Roman Catholic Church] has become more and more closely identified with the interests and aspirations of the French Canadian people until it almost seems that the Church is French Canada." In short, as Finke and Stark note, "For French Canadians, the Catholic Church protected their rights, guarded their institutions, and preserved the French culture and language."[2]

Common then to both Quebec and Ireland is the organic connection between church and culture. The historical narrative of the Catholic Church in America is quite different. The Church in the U.S. is a cultural outsider, an immigrant church that had to forge its legitimacy vis-à-vis the dominant Protestant churches and the Protestantism of the culture as a whole. This cultural gap was deepened because Catholics' participation in a transnational church meant that collective affiliation to the Vatican was a source of tension in the American polity rather than a badge of pride as in Ireland and Quebec; the dual loyalties of American Catholic leaders and laity were seen as weakening the primacy of their American commitment. The many documented instances of anti-Catholicism throughout American history testify to the deep suspicions many Americans have felt and expressed toward their Catholic fellow citizens, whom at various historical moments they have regarded as being somewhat un-American.[3]

2. See Roger Finke and Rodney Stark, "The Dynamics of Religious Economies," in Michele Dillon, ed., *Handbook of the Sociology of Religion* (New York: Cambridge University Press, 2003), 96–109. All the quoted material, including that from Armstrong, can be found on p. 107.

3. On anti-Catholicism, see John McGreevy, *Catholicism and American Freedom* (New York: Norton, 2003).

An additional source of the Catholic outsider status in America is the Catholic doctrinal tradition itself. Many of its core tenets are quite at odds with the American cultural ethos, one that is thoroughly Protestant. As argued by the American social theorist Talcott Parsons (following Max Weber), the impact of the Protestant Reformation was to make the individual a "religiously autonomous entity," but one who, free from authoritarian control, must necessarily assume individual responsibility for both religious and secular activities.[4] The Protestant emphasis on individual self-reliance contrasts with Catholicism's emphasis on hierarchy and community. The rupture between the Catholic worldview and its Protestant counterpart means that the Catholic understanding of the relation between self and society still presents as a somewhat foreign or outsider perspective in American politics. As discussed by Andrew Greeley, the Catholic understanding of God's presence in the world and the related view of the inherent goodness of human nature and of social relations and institutions means that Catholics are significantly more likely than Protestants to have a benign view of the world. Catholics tend to see the value of social and community solutions to structural and individual problems, problems that the Protestant worldview sees as having an individual solution. Consequently, there are substantive differences between American Catholics and Protestants in their social values and attitudes. Catholics, for example, are more likely than Protestants to support government welfare programs for the disadvantaged. Yet, it is the Protestant self-reliant ethic that largely informs American policy on welfare and other issues.[5]

In sum, to be American and Catholic is a less organic identity than being Irish and Catholic or Quebecer and Catholic. As I shall discuss later in this chapter, these contextual differences have presented the Church with different legitimation dilemmas in its efforts to carve out a public voice in each society.

4. Talcott Parsons, *Sociological Theory and Modern Society* (New York: Free Press, 1967), 402–3.

5. See especially Andrew Greeley, "Protestant and Catholic," *American Sociological Review* 54 (1989): 485–502; and Andrew Greeley, *The Catholic Imagination* (Berkeley: University of California Press, 2000).

Comparative Trends of Decline in Roman Catholicism since 1950

The comparative trends in Catholicism since 1950 are quite clear. In the United States, Quebec, and the Republic of Ireland, weekly church attendance and the regular practice of confession have decreased considerably, agreement with official Church teaching on various matters of doctrine and sexual morality has declined, and the correspondence between Catholic moral teaching and public policy has diminished.

Church Attendance and Sacramental Practices

Church attendance is a useful indicator of individual and societal religiousness.[6] For Catholics, attendance at Mass and celebration of the Eucharist is "the center of the Church's life."[7] The continuous assessment of church attendance since the 1940s by public opinion poll organizations makes it a helpful barometer of religious and social change. In 1950, almost two-thirds (63 percent) of American Catholics attended weekly Mass, whereas at the end of the century, this was true of close to one in two (43 percent). In Ireland and Quebec in the 1940s and 1950s, Catholic weekly Mass attendance was almost universal. Today, however, only about one-fifth (23 percent) of Quebec Catholics attend weekly Mass. Church attendance is still comparatively more important in Ireland, but there too there has been a decline, with approximately two-thirds attending Mass weekly. Across all three societies, therefore, there has been a pattern of church exit, and this exit extends to the confessional box also.

There is a dearth of systematic data concerning confession habits. But impressionistic evidence points to the virtual disappearance of confession from the lives of most Catholics, and other than at Easter, also for some of the more devout. In one study, approximately 40 percent of young adult Catholics in America reported having gone to private confession within a two-year period, and in a national poll conducted in 1993, 14 percent of American Catholics said they had gone to confession within the last

6. The accuracy of self-report church attendance rates, however, has been contested in recent years. See Mark Chaves and Laura Stephens, "Church Attendance in the United States," in Dillon, *Handbook of the Sociology of Religion*, 85–95.

7. See *Catechism of the Catholic Church* (Dublin: Veritas, 1994), 1341.

month.[8] In sum, though still on the weekly schedule of parish churches, confession no longer holds the ritualized place that it once held in Catholics' sacramental practice.

For much of the twentieth century, Catholics believed that the confession of sins was a necessary precursor to receiving Communion. But this logic no longer holds. One of the unintended consequences of *Humanae vitae* (Pope Paul VI's 1968 encyclical banning artificial contraception) was the liberation of Catholics from confessing as sins that they in good conscience believed were not sinful. At the time of the encyclical, two-thirds of American Catholics attended weekly Mass, but this figure declined precipitously in the ensuing years and was reduced to just over one-half (55 percent) by the early 1970s.[9] One reason suggested for the decline was that many Catholics were already using birth control, and after the encyclical, aware that they were in a state of sin, some felt unworthy to receive Communion and, by extension, believed it was pointless going to Mass.[10] A similar decline occurred in Quebec; 85 percent attended weekly Mass in 1965, but by 1975 this figure had decreased to a low of 42 percent.[11]

But while the decline continued in Quebec (down to 31 percent by 1985), the post–*Humanae vitae* decline in Americans' church habits leveled off in 1975 at around 52 percent. This return to church and to Communion was not accompanied by a concomitant decline in Catholics' use of artificial birth control. As argued by Hout and Greeley, the return to church marked a significant turning point in Catholics' attitudes toward Church authority. It signified ordinary Catholics' understanding that they could use birth control and still be good Catholics. In short, dissent from official Church teaching no longer prohibited Catholics from attending Mass and participating in the Eucharist.[12]

8. On U.S. youth, see Dean Hoge et al., *Young Adult Catholics: Religion in the Culture of Choice* (Notre Dame, Ind.: Notre Dame University Press, 2001), 158. For American Catholics as a whole see George Gallup and D. Michael Lindsay, *Surveying the Religious Landscape: Trends in U.S. Beliefs* (Harrisburg, Penn.: Morehouse, 1999), 55.

9. Andrew Greeley, *American Catholics since the Council* (Chicago: Thomas More Press, 1985), 53–55.

10. See Greeley, *American Catholics since the Council;* and Michael Hout and Andrew Greeley, "The Center Doesn't Hold: Church Attendance in the United States, 1940–1984," *American Sociological Review* 52 (1987): 325–45.

11. See Kevin Christiano's chapter, this volume.

12. See Hout and Greeley, "The Center Doesn't Hold," 325–45; and Greeley, *American Catholics since the Council,* 50.

Sexual Morality and the Family

Catholics' rejection of the idea that birth control was sinful foreshadowed a shift in their attitudes toward Church authority more generally. Across all three societies Catholics are increasingly at odds with official Church teaching on sexual morality. Even the Irish, for whom contraception was not a legal option until 1979, began to express disagreement with Catholic orthodoxy on sexual morality from the mid-1970s.

Artificial contraception was legalized in Ireland following a Supreme Court ruling that its criminalization violated the individual's right to privacy. The legislation was politically controversial (as I will discuss further in the next section) even though it was quite restrictive: it provided that both medical and nonmedical (e.g., condoms) contraceptives could be purchased only for bona fide family planning purposes and only on the basis of a doctor's prescription. Such restrictions remained in place until legislation in 1985 extended the legal availability of nonmedical contraceptives without prescription to individuals ages eighteen and over. In contrast to a time not too long ago when premarital sex was unthinkable in Ireland, today less than one-third of the Irish believe that premarital sex is always wrong.[13]

There has been a similar shift in Irish attitudes toward divorce and abortion. At the beginning of the 1970s, only one-fifth of the Irish expressed support for the removal of the constitutional ban on divorce, but by the mid-1980s, prior to the first national referendum on the issue, 61 percent were in favor. After nine weeks of vigorous public debate, however, the Irish electorate voted squarely against the proposal. Divorce was eventually legalized in Ireland a decade later, in 1995, in a second referendum, in which just over 50 percent voted in favor of change.[14] Before the 1980s, abortion was a rare topic of private conversation among the Irish and received no attention in the media despite the remarkably influential role of Irish broadcasting in airing all sorts of controversial issues. Yet,

13. See Andrew Greeley, *Religion in Europe at the End of the Second Millennium* (New Brunswick, N.J.: Transaction, 2003), 164.

14. For the details of the first divorce referendum see Michele Dillon, *Debating Divorce: Moral Conflict in Ireland* (Lexington: University Press of Kentucky, 1993). In the second referendum, the margin in favor of the provision that allowed divorce for those couples who had lived apart for four years was just 50.28 percent.

abortion too became a topic of intense controversy and, as in the U.S., is a source of ongoing debate. By 1992, the Irish had legalized limited access to abortion, and in 2002 they voted by a very slim majority (50.4 percent to 49.6 percent) against imposing further restrictions on women's access to abortion.

Currently in America, almost all Catholics (93 percent) think that a person who uses artificial contraception is still a "good" Catholic, a moral liberalism that is also found in their attitudes toward nonmarital sexuality, divorce, and abortion. Catholic attitudes on abortion mirror those of Americans in general: 57 percent of Catholics and 59 percent of other Americans agree that abortion should be legal in all circumstances.[15] A similar pattern demonstrating the decoupling of sexual morality from Catholic teaching is evident in Quebec. In the late 1960s, Quebec liberalized its laws on contraception, divorce, and abortion, a liberalization that was accompanied, as Christiano and Gauvreau discuss in this volume, by dramatic changes in Quebecers' behavior in these domains. This dramatic fall away from Catholic moral teaching is crystallized by abortion: Quebec has one of the highest abortion rates in the West, with 38 abortions per 100 births in 1998.[16]

More generally across all three societies, the increased decoupling of Catholics' sociosexual attitudes and practices from Catholic moral teaching extends to their views of Catholic institutional practices and the doctrinal reasons offered to legitimate such practices. In particular, the Vatican's teachings on women's ordination and on celibacy are the most vigorously contested matters of current Church doctrine. In the United States, for example, celibacy is ranked by lay Catholics as one of the least important aspects of being Catholic, and by the same token, a majority believes that women should be ordained.[17]

---

15. On American Catholics, see William D'Antonio et al., *American Catholics: Gender, Generation, and Commitment* (Walnut Creek, Calif.: AltaMira Press, 2001); and on American abortion attitudes in general, see Gallup and Lindsay, *Surveying the Religious Landscape,* 103.

16. See Kevin Christiano's chapter, this volume.

17. See William D'Antonio, "American Catholics from John Paul II to Benedict XVI," *National Catholic Reporter,* September 30, 2005, 3.

Modernization

The trends indicating church exit and an exit from the fold of the Church hierarchy's authority do not exist in isolation from other social and cultural changes. They are entwined, rather, with the modernization forces encountered in the second half of the twentieth century. Modernization refers to the spectrum of interrelated changes associated with economic expansion and the increased rationality associated with it. Modernization is the twin of industrialization and assumes that as societies move away from tradition-based, agricultural production to mechanized, mass industrial production, this necessitates several other social structural as well as cultural changes. Specifically, increased economic rationality is associated with increased urbanization, the expansion of literacy and education, occupational and socioeconomic mobility, increased dominance of mass media, and an overall increase in institutional differentiation and the specialized functions these social institutions perform. In other words, rather than economy, family, religion, and community being intermeshed and performing interrelated functions of economic productivity and social integration, they, and the emergence of more specialized institutions such as law and education, take on clearly defined and separate functions in society. It is within this process of increased institutional differentiation that sociologists, most notably Max Weber, theorized that secularization would also occur; that religion and religious ideas would lose meaningful authority in shaping both public culture and individual lives.

Clearly, of the three societies under review, the United States is the most industrialized and has been at the forefront of economic production since the middle of the nineteenth century. It was not, however, until the post–World War II period that many Americans, including the majority of Catholics, experienced firsthand the social effects of modernization. Between 1959 and 1969, personal income grew substantially for all American households,[18] and fueled the suburbanization and expanding consumerism of American society. The 1960s and 1970s resulted in significant changes in the lifestyles of American Catholics as they experienced substantial upward socioeconomic mobility, indicated by increases in col-

18. See Claude Fischer et al., *Inequality by Design* (Princeton: Princeton University Press, 1996), 5.

lege and graduate school graduation rates, involvement in high-status professional and managerial occupations, and higher incomes. Catholics have maintained these socioeconomic advances and today are represented more in higher than lower income categories.[19]

While the suburban revolution was occurring in the United States, Quebec was undergoing its own Quiet Revolution, a "period of rapid and profound social transformation" associated with the rise of the Liberal Party in 1960.[20] Quebec's modernization progressed in tandem with the socioeconomic changes occurring in the United States and the West more generally. But it too had its own internal logic. In particular, as discussed by Michael Gauvreau, Catholic lay elites within Quebec were influential in drawing a sharp line between the forces of tradition and the demands of modernity. According to standard historical narratives of the Quiet Revolution, Quebec moved away from its rural Catholic culture toward the creation of a secular state. In this new social formation, educational and social welfare institutions were deconfessionalized, and a secular neo-nationalism was embraced that was based on the power of economics, language, and the primacy of the state rather than the church.

Across the Atlantic, these same decades marked the socioeconomic transformation of Ireland. It moved away from defensive, protectionist economic policies focused on agriculture and toward the creation of a postindustrial and service economy whose impact was visibly evident in changing social trends. Between 1959 and 1963, for example, the annual economic growth rate was 4 percent per annum, and this was accompanied by substantial increases in gross domestic product and personal disposable income. These changes were further fueled by Ireland's subsequent membership (in 1973) in the European Economic Community (currently the EU). The lessening role of agriculture and the expansion of the industrial/service sectors resulted in broader societal change, including the increased concentration of the population in Dublin and in other urban centers, increased participation in education; the expansion of a white-collar middle class; greater participation of women in the la-

19. See Andrew Greeley, *Religious Change in America* (Cambridge, Mass.: Harvard University Press, 1989); and Frank Newport, "U.S. Catholics Vary Widely on Moral Issues," *The Gallup Poll Tuesday Briefing*, April 8, 2005.

20. See Kevin Christiano's chapter, this volume.

bor force; expanding consumerism; and after television was introduced in 1962, the extension of the appeal and reach of the mass media.[21]

In the Western world more broadly, the 1960s and 1970s were also characterized by cultural turmoil—the emergence of movements advancing women's rights, gay rights, and civil rights more generally, making the era a time of political protest and personal experimentation. Although these social movements were most vocal and influential in America, Quebec and Ireland were not immune from public challenges to the status quo.[22] Taken as a whole, the cultural upheavals associated with these decades resulted in a shift away from the authority of social institutions and traditions and opened up possibilities for new ways of thinking about the relation of the self to the larger society.

With all of the macro-level economic, social, and cultural changes that were set in motion in the 1960s and 70s, it is not surprising that as part of this ferment, religion and individuals' regard for religious institutions would also be impacted. Catholicism, moreover, had its own momentous revolution: the Second Vatican Council (1962–1965). As observed by Jesuit Church historian John O'Malley, "The very breadth of the issues which the Council chose to review and to reformulate and the all-inclusive audience that the Council finally chose to address would seem to suggest that we are facing a major turning point in the history of Catholicism, at least in intent."[23]

Although many Catholics may not have been familiar with the theological arguments elaborated by Vatican II, they were well aware that change was happening in the Church, and in ways they would never have anticipated. The unprecedented extent of the coverage of Vatican II news stories in national mass media both during and after the council ensured that millions of Catholics were exposed to its deliberations. More locally, what could be more disruptive to a Catholic's world than to be told that

21. For a useful review of the impact of modernization on Irish society in the 1960s and '70s, see Frank Litton, ed., *Unequal Achievement: The Irish Experience, 1957–1982* (Dublin: Institute of Public Administration, 1983).

22. One iconic event in Ireland, for example, was when a number of well-known feminists (including the now conservative commentator Mary Kenny) went by train to Belfast to buy condoms, and upon their much publicized arrival back in Dublin later that day were confronted by the police and the condoms confiscated.

23. John O'Malley, *Tradition and Transition: Historical Perspectives on Vatican II* (Wilmington, Del.: Michael Glazier, 1989), 24.

eating fish on Friday was no longer a core obligation of being Catholic or to find that the language and structure of the Mass, the Mass that Catholics thought to be immutable, would dramatically change?

The Public Church

The broad-ranging changes that have occurred in sociosexual morality in the United States, Ireland, and Quebec in the latter decades of the twentieth century can readily be seen as evidence of the decline of religious authority, and specifically of the Catholic Church's power to constrain individual and collective behavior. Catholic attitudes and public policy in all three societies are clearly at odds with official Church teaching on contraception, abortion, divorce, and sexuality. Yet this is not the whole story. Concomitant with the declining moral authority of the Church in Catholic lives has been the emergence of the Catholic Church as a fully fledged public church—its emergence as a vocal institutional presence in the public culture. Historical differences in the Church's status created different legitimation dilemmas for the Church in each society. Let us consider first Ireland and Quebec, the two societies where the Church is a cultural insider.

Ireland

The socioeconomic changes associated with the modernization of Irish society proceeded smoothly, but the achievement of cultural modernization was more uneven. The process of crafting a society in which civil laws on sex and marriage would be autonomous of Catholic moral teaching presented the Irish with quite complicated hurdles. How can one legitimate change that deviates directly from Catholic teaching in a society where the Church has deep cultural roots and the vast majority of the people are church-attending Catholics? This is the cultural dilemma that Ireland has had to embrace since the late 1970s, and responding to its challenges has been equally difficult for political and church leaders.

To illustrate the challenge involved in loosening the hold of a monopolistic religious and cultural tradition, it is instructive to consider the legalization of contraception in Ireland. Notably, the impetus for contraception legislation was not the initiative of Irish politicians (who had no problem in taking the lead in economic policy changes) but resulted from a Supreme Court decision. The coerced legislative process was then undertaken by the coalition government in power. The ensuing process highlighted a singularly clear example of the hegemonic power of Catholicism: during the parliamentary vote on the proposed legislation, the prime minister and one of his government ministers voted against their own government's proposal on grounds of conscience. Subsequently, the legislation was redrafted, and when it was brought for a parliamentary vote by a successor government (in 1978), the minister responsible defended its provisions as "an Irish solution to an Irish problem." This meant that medical and nonmedical contraceptives would be available on prescription only and only to married couples for bona fide family planning purposes. In other words, the legislation recognized Ireland's Catholic cultural heritage—and had to recognize it—while simultaneously recognizing and advancing its newly emerging modernization.

A similar dilemma reappeared ten years later when Ireland had its first divorce debate. In introducing a relatively restrictive divorce proposal in 1986, the then prime minister, Garret FitzGerald, had to demonstrate the authenticity of his Catholicism and the attendant belief in the sacramentality of marriage while at the same time arguing in favor of divorce legislation that was clearly at odds with Catholic teaching. FitzGerald, an admirer of the ethics advanced by the French theologian Jacques Maritain, provided an eloquent intellectual defense of the value of differentiating civil law and Catholic morality. Nonetheless, his insistence that one can personally value "indissoluble monogamy" and simultaneously value an individual's right to divorce may have been too complicated for an electorate accustomed to thinking of divorce as both a mortal sin and (a sin) banned by the Constitution.[24] Asking the Irish people to vote in favor of

24. It is noteworthy that FitzGerald felt it important in his opening remarks at the outset of the divorce debate to indicate that the government in their preparation of the divorce proposals had had extensive discussions with church leaders (Protestant and Catholic). He stated: "The government is grateful to the churches for the manner in which they offered their views on the issues dealt with in the amendment and on the statement of the government's intentions with regard to marriage, separation, and divorce. The discussions with the churches were extremely constructive and the arrangements now proposed in relation to a number of these matters bear the mark of the views expressed by the churches. The government recognises, however, that some or all of the churches may have different views on some of the matters dealt with, including the proposals for the provision of divorce, and that the churches will wish to put forward these views to their members." See this quote in Dillon, *Debating Divorce,* 34. In a television interview following the government's press

divorce was asking them to overturn a deeply embedded worldview of the sanctity of marriage, a worldview that, notwithstanding the tides of socio-economic modernization, was not so easily shaken. As indicated earlier, this proposal was defeated by a margin of two to one.

But just as political leaders faced the dilemma of legitimating cultural change in a Catholic society, religious leaders faced its twin: how to defend Catholic teaching in an increasingly modernized society. The Church's ability to adapt to changing times was facilitated by changes within the Church itself, most notably, by Vatican II's affirmation of religious freedom and pluralism. In the early 1970s, for the first time in Irish society, the bishops adopted a new form of collective self-presentation and discourse: they publicly acknowledged the distinction between civil law and Catholic morality. The hierarchy argued that whereas it was the duty of the government to govern, a process in which they did not wish to intervene, it was the duty of bishops to preach. Speaking of contraception, the bishops elaborated:

> The question at issue is not whether artificial contraception is morally right or wrong. The clear teaching of the Catholic Church is that it is morally wrong. No change in State law can make the use of contraceptives morally right, since what is wrong in itself remains wrong, regardless of what State law says. . . . It does not follow, of course, that the State is bound to prohibit the importation and sale of contraceptives. There are many things which the Catholic Church holds to be morally wrong and no one has ever suggested, least of all the Church herself, that they should be prohibited by the State."[25]

It was not easy, however, for the bishops to adhere to their avowed noninterventionism. During the pro-life referendum debate in 1983, the hierarchy forcefully deviated from its previously reiterated stance affirming the autonomy of civil law from Catholic morality. Although the bishops stated that they recognized the "right of each person to vote according to conscience," they explicitly called for a "yes" (antiabortion) vote, which they argued would "constitute a witness before Europe and before the

---

conference announcing the divorce proposals, FitzGerald said: "[T]he Catholic Church has a theological position and also a sociological view which it will, I'm sure, want to put forward. We as a government don't have a theological view. We may have it individually, and indeed we have our own attachment to indissoluble monogamy as individuals. But we do have to take a sociological view and that view is perhaps somewhat different to that of the Catholic Church." See ibid., 41.

25. See ibid., 92–93.

whole world to the dignity and sacredness of all human life from conception to death." But pointing to the political complexity of the Church's situation, one year later, at an official public forum convened to discuss the future of Northern Ireland, the bishops' delegation stated: "The Catholic Church in Ireland totally rejects the concept of a confessional state. We have not sought and we do not seek a Catholic State for a Catholic people. We believe that the alliance of Church and State is harmful for the Church and harmful for the State."[26]

The bishops' vacillation highlights the inevitable tensions the Church confronts in wanting to be "modern" and at the same time needing to defend publicly the moral legitimacy of its teaching. It seemed that the hierarchy finally found a way out of this dilemma in the late 1980s. In the first divorce debate (1986), the Church affirmed the separation of church and state and maintained its right and obligation "to teach the social and moral implications of any piece of legislation." It is noteworthy, moreover, that in articulating these implications the Church does not use a discourse of sin and morality but a social scientific discourse emphasizing the negative social and economic effects of the legislation at issue. Thus the Church opposed divorce not because it contravenes Catholic teaching on marriage, but because, as one bishop explained in a television interview:

> Divorce has very serious consequences for society . . . once divorce is introduced it is very difficult to restrict it. . . . Take a look at the evidence in any country in the world. In 1983, for instance, in America there were 2.4 million marriages and 1.2 million divorces. That's one out of two. In Great Britain at the moment the figure is running two out of every five. . . . There are many indicators that divorce favors men rather than women. One California study found in 1982 that men experienced a 42 percent increase in their standard of living following divorce, while women experienced a 73 percent loss.[27]

Quebec

The Quebec modernization/Catholic culture dilemma shows many parallels to the Irish situation. Indeed, Pierre Trudeau, like Garret FitzGerald, was also strongly influenced by Jacques Maritain and his desire to be pluralistic while not rejecting Christian values.[28] Yet, Trudeau too, notwith-

---

26. Ibid., 93–95.   27. Ibid., 96–109.

28. See Michael Gauvreau, "From Rechristianization to Contestation: Catholic Values and Quebec Society, 1931–1970," *Church History* 69 (December 2000): 21. Gauvreau notes that Trudeau rejected the philosophy of absolute liberalism.

standing an earlier espousal (in 1949) that "only Christianity offers true freedom to the human spirit. . . . Lived Christianity is a social religion, the only one that gives an answer to all problems," subsequently affirmed that the government had no place in Quebecers' bedrooms.[29]

In contrast to its articulation in Ireland, however, the tension in Quebec was most sharply delineated by lay Catholic elites—Catholic Action leaders who argued that Quebecers "must . . . definitively break the conjunction of religion and nation that we have learned to venerate as dogma." At the same time, Catholic modernists in the 1960s wanted the Church to have "a public role as the repository of the religious values of the nation, with a key role in building a more humane civilization."[30] For their part, the Catholic bishops in Quebec (and in Canada as a whole) responded to the changing sociocultural environment and proposed legislative changes using pluralistic discourse similar to the Irish bishops'. In 1966, for example, in response to the government's plans to repeal contraception prohibitions, the Canadian bishops spoke about the rightful differentiation of church and state and, invoking the autonomy of civil legislation from Catholic teaching, stated that they would not oppose the legalization of contraception. In language echoed by their Irish counterparts, they stated, "That which the Church teaches to be morally wrong should not necessarily be considered as indictable by the criminal code of a country."[31]

Later, when Trudeau as minister for justice proposed legislation that would liberalize divorce, the bishops reiterated their views on the differentiation of law and morality. Noting that "Canada is a country of many religious beliefs," they explicitly acknowledged the legitimate role that non-Catholic views of divorce could also possibly play in preserving the common good.[32] It was not so surprising then that in the wake of *Humanae vitae,* the Canadian bishops emphasized the primacy of individual conscience in regard to Vatican teaching.[33] Although the Canadian bishops have taken a less conciliatory stance on abortion (which was liber-

---

29. Ibid., 8.

30. These two quotes are from Gauvreau, "From Rechristianization to Contestation," 12, 14.

31. See Michael Cuneo, *Catholics against the Church: Anti-Abortion Protest in Toronto, 1969–1985* (Toronto: University of Toronto Press, 1989), 26–27.

32. Ibid., 28.   33. Ibid., 35.

alized in 1969), they still, nonetheless, have been far less interventionist than either their Irish or their American counterparts. They too have vacillated between condemning abortion and recognizing the multiplicity of views in a pluralistic society, but have assumed a more detached public policy role than their Irish and American peers. Indeed, it is noteworthy that a critical source of intra-Catholic friction in Quebec and in Canada as a whole is between pro-life activists and the Church hierarchy.[34]

United States

The Church's adoption of pluralistic argumentation is also found in the United States, where the Catholic bishops make recourse both to the legitimacy of scientific data and an explicit cultural engagement to advance Catholic moral teaching. The abortion issue serves as a good example of this process.[35] In its many public statements since abortion was legalized in America, the National Conference of Catholic Bishops have invoked what they refer to as "a wealth of scientific literature" to support Church teaching that human life begins at conception, hence making abortion "the kind of violent act that can never be justified." The bishops draw on biological evidence demonstrating the development of fetal life to argue against the legalization of abortion and, sharply criticizing the "illogical reasoning" in the Supreme Court's *Roe v. Wade* decision, have argued that the Court was "more impressed by magic than by scientific evidence." The bishops also invoke social scientific data to argue that abortion adversely affects women and families, stating, for example, that abortion violates mother-child bonds and that the "abortion mentality" may be a factor accounting for the mounting evidence of increased child abuse and neglect. In short, the American bishops fused empirical evidence from the social and biological sciences to argue that their position on abortion is "perfectly consistent with modern scientific knowledge."

Because of historical differences in the Catholic Church's cultural status in the United States, being a public church in America presents greater

---

34. These issues are discussed in detail by Cuneo, *Catholics against the Church*.

35. The discussion in this section draws on Michele Dillon, "Religion and Culture in Tension: The Abortion Discourses of the U.S. Catholic Bishops and the Southern Baptist Convention," *Religion and American Culture: A Journal of Interpretation* 5 (1995): 159–80, and Michele Dillon, "Cultural Differences in the Abortion Discourse of the Catholic Church: Evidence from Four Countries," *Sociology of Religion* 57 (1996): 25–36.

challenges than in Ireland or Quebec. The U.S. bishops have to show that the Catholic Church is not only modern but American. And this is indeed something that the bishops have succeeded, rhetorically, in demonstrating. The American bishops' abortion discourse explicitly appeals to and celebrates American political culture. The bishops have framed Catholic opposition to abortion as being consistent with the values enshrined in the U.S. Constitution and Declaration of Independence and have consequently transposed the Church's moral stance into one that is thoroughly American. Through various public statements the bishops typically address their "fellow Americans," and invoke "200 years of *our* history" (emphasis mine) in arguing that abortion is contrary to the principles of "this nation" and its "constitutional guarantee of the right to life." The bishops maintain that the imperative to protect the rights of the unborn is a core "self-evident truth" formalized by the Declaration of Independence and, as they note, grounded in the biblical command: "I set before you life or death. . . . Choose life, then, that you and your descendants may live." Significantly, this is the same Deuteronomic command that John Winthrop and the early Pilgrims used in sanctifying America as the "Promised Land."[36]

The bishops also invoke the American political tradition to affirm the validity of their participation in public debates. Defending the Church against charges of religious involvement in the political process, the bishops have confidently asserted the appropriateness of their public engagement. Paralleling the arguments of Irish bishops, they state that they are not "seeking to impose Catholic moral teaching" on a religiously pluralistic society but, as "citizens of this democracy" and "participants in the American democratic process," are committed to encouraging appropriate political action on abortion. They argue, moreover, that not to be involved in such public policy debates would amount to an abdication of their civic responsibilities. Thus the bishops articulate an "insider" American discourse that places the Church's antiabortion stance squarely in tune with American political and cultural motifs.

Recourse to pluralistic argumentation, therefore, is the primary way the Catholic Church negotiates the public sphere in efforts to advance its

---

36. Robert Bellah discusses the centrality of the Deuteronomic command to the foundation of American culture and the notion that the United States was a "promised land" for the Puritans. See Robert Bellah, *The Broken Covenant: American Civil Religion in Time of Trial* (New York: Seabury Press, 1975), 13–16.

moral teaching as public policy. Paradoxically, moral debates whose outcomes typically attest to the declining authority of the Church in Ireland, Quebec, and the United States at the same time provide the Church with an opportunity to demonstrate that it is an adaptive modern institution adept at couching its moral agenda in a public rather than a purely doctrinal discourse.

Lived Catholicism

The cumulative empirical data available underscores a clear pattern of decline in Catholics' participation in the Church's sacramental practices and acceptance of Catholic moral teaching. This does not, however, in my judgment, necessarily signify the "fall of the Church." When we consider the multiple presences of the Church in everyday life, in terms of both its public institutional activities and its place in ordinary Catholics' lives, we see a more complicated picture, one that suggests a significantly more vibrant church than that indicated by reliance on the criteria of church attendance and moral assent alone.

Civic Catholicism

The preceding section has already highlighted the significant change that has occurred in the Church's status as a public church; it has moved from being a monopoly church (Ireland, Quebec) or a ghettoized immigrant church (United States) to being a fully fledged actor in the public sphere. In this new role, the Church uses the sort of rational arguments expected in civil society rather than the authoritarian or dogmatic claims that were characteristic of its earlier interventions into public policy. Now the Catholic Church is one of a number of publicly engaged collective actors, interacting and at times competing with other churches, the mass media and Internet forums, political lobbies, and diverse social movements as each seeks to project an effective voice in the public realm. The relative success of the Church in carving out a legitimate public institutional/civic role for itself is an important counterpoint to the decline in its confessional power.

Some might argue that the Church's embrace of a pluralistic discourse, including its use of empirically grounded and culturally engaged arguments rather than explicitly doctrinal assertions, is in fact further evidence of the Church's decline. Further, it cannot escape notice that the Church has not won any major policy successes, whether on abortion or on economic redistribution, in the three societies under review, or indeed in any Western nation. Yet, I would argue that if the Church were to retreat to primarily using a confessional or evangelizing discourse, the public accessibility of the Church's stance to Catholics and non-Catholics alike would be severely limited. In contemporary times, people in general, even if they are religiously involved themselves, tend to be uncomfortable with and to misunderstand the public use of sectarian language. This does not mean that doctrinal language cannot be used in the public sphere; it is just less effective in reaching a pluralistic audience.

It is important to keep in mind, moreover, that the Church's use of an empirically grounded rational discourse is always in the service of preserving Catholic values. As such, it eschews confessional discourse to defend a confessional or doctrinal vision. Thus in arguing against divorce or abortion or economic inequality, the Church is fundamentally articulating and defending the value of relational communality, the core of the Catholic ethic. Accordingly, the Church is being very *Catholic* in its role as a public church. But precisely because the Catholic ethic of community contravenes Western, and especially American, individualism, it is very difficult for the Church to be a "winner" in policy debates. The dominant thrust of Western consumer capitalism is to celebrate (and isolate) the individual, and therefore the Catholic Church's efforts to refocus the public's attention on the importance of relational and communal solutions is clearly an uphill struggle. The Church's ideological vision is countercultural. One promising indicator of the emerging recognition that Catholic thought may provide a better way of approaching some of our contemporary social ills is the recent observation by the sociologist Robert Bellah, himself a Protestant and a long-term critic of American individualism, that America could benefit from a greater dose of the Catholic imagination.[37]

Finally, it should be pointed out that openness to reason is a necessary prerequisite to participation in the public sphere. This is a prerequisite for the Church as a public rational actor and for all other participants in civil society. In practice, however, in the deliberations of everyday life, the use

37. Robert Bellah, "Religion and the Shaping of National Culture," *America* 181 (July 31–August 7, 1999): 9–14.

of reason is invariably limited, strategic, and partial. Despite the Church's explicit appeal to the legitimacy of scientific evidence, it is most unlikely that if, for example, the scientific literature were to provide evidence illustrating the unambiguous positive sociological implications of divorce, the Church would abandon its moral opposition to divorce. The overarching moral and doctrinal commitments of the Church do not necessarily detract from its rationality; but they do highlight that reason does not exist in isolation from faith, tradition, power, and the many other nonrational resources that characterize everyday life.

Economic Catholicism

Quite apart from its civic role, the Catholic Church's substantial economic role should be duly recognized. Although the Church's status as an employer of religious personnel (working as pastors, teachers, social workers) has diminished in all three societies as a result of the post-1960s decline in the numbers of priests and nuns, the Church contributes in other direct and indirect ways to the domestic and global economy. In the United States, for example, Catholic Charities continues to be a major provider of social services, with close to fifteen hundred community branches and affiliates, and the implementation of the faith-based service initiatives of the Bush administration is likely to enhance the formal role of local Catholic parishes in the social service arena. Similarly in Ireland, despite the increased secularization of education, health, and social service providers, the Catholic Church continues to be a significant institutional player with a substantial stock of symbolic capital in the welfare field.[38] In Quebec, the establishment and expansion of the Mouvement Desjardins, the largest banking institution in Quebec and the sixth largest in Canada, presents as an enduring symbolic and material testament to the power of the Church to impact the economic sphere.[39]

Communal Catholicism

In addition to the civic and economic presence of the Church there are other strands in lived Catholicism that give pause to the readiness

---

38. See Michel Peillon, *Welfare in Ireland: Actors, Resources, and Strategies* (Westport, Conn.: Praeger, 2001).

39. See Kevin Christiano's chapter, this volume.

with which we might be inclined to accept the "decline and fall" thesis (the title of the conference for which this chapter was invited). In our late-modern, globalized, and pluralistic society, an era in which people are increasingly free to choose "new" identities, it is noteworthy that so many Americans, Irish, and Quebecers choose to still identify as Catholic. Given the decline in the regularity of church attendance and the range of moral and sociosexual issues on which Catholics disagree with the Vatican, one could well imagine a far greater number choosing to eschew a Catholic identity altogether.

Yet, affiliation to the Catholic tradition continues to be meaningful for large numbers: even in Quebec, which has the lowest level of church attendance, over 80 percent still identify as Catholic.[40] This, I suggest, is not solely a nominal identity. It reflects the fact that despite the range of religious and nonreligious identity choices available, many individuals continue to see Catholicism as a meaningful component of what is invariably a multilayered personal and social identity.[41] It also suggests that many non-churchgoing Catholics continue to implicitly view Catholicism as the frame for their basic faith beliefs about God and the afterlife.[42] The enduring cultural appeal of religious and specifically Catholic identity also represents individuals' tacit recognition that "communities of memory," such as provided by a Catholic heritage, are critical anchors in linking the present, past, and future for both individuals and whole regions or societies; recall Kevin Christiano's account of the tourist guide's explanation concerning the crucifix hanging in Quebec's legislature—people cannot afford to forget their past.[43]

40. Ibid.

41. See Michele Dillon, *Catholic Identity: Balancing Reason, Faith, and Power* (New York: Cambridge University Press, 1999), on the significance of Catholicism to feminist and gay Catholics.

42. The vast majority of nominal Catholics in the United States, Ireland, and Quebec believe in God (96 percent, 94 percent, and 80 percent, respectively) and in Heaven (86 percent and 87 percent for U.S. and Ireland, respectively; data not available for Quebec). See Andrew Greeley and Conor K. Ward, "How Secularised Is the Ireland We Live In?" *Doctrine and Life* 50 (2000): 581–617.

43. On communities of memory, see Robert Bellah et al., *Habits of the Heart: Individualism and Commitment in American Life* (Berkeley: University of California Press, 1985).

Sacramental Catholicism

The hold of Catholicism as a religious and as a cultural tradition also underlies the desire of many Catholics to have major calendar events and rites of passage sanctified in church. In all three societies, many noninvolved Catholics attend Easter and Christmas services and value the symbolic importance of church weddings and funerals and of having their children baptized. Even with regard to Quebec, which presents as the most "secularized" of the three case studies, Kevin Christiano comments in this volume that "Catholicism is firmly fixed in the minds and hearts of contemporary Montrealers." Indeed it would seem that Catholics' valuing of the Church's liturgy and sacraments, especially the Mass, is what is core to keeping Catholics attached to the Church, however thinly in some cases. Moreover, the fact that so many divorced Catholics in all three societies increasingly seek Church annulments, though further indicative of the decline of the Church's power to regulate marriage, is also indicative of the desire of many divorced Catholics to preserve their Catholic identity and as such to fully participate in the Mass.[44]

The symbolic importance of the Mass is also a common resource that unites liberal and conservative Catholics and thus provides a significant bridge over the doctrinal polarization that has occurred, especially in the American Church.[45] Of course, unless Catholics continue to go to Mass

44. On Catholic annulments, see Melissa Wilde, "From Excommunication to Nullification: Testing and Extending Supply-Side Theories of Religious Marketing with the Case of Catholic Marital Annulments," *Journal for the Scientific Study of Religion* 40 (2001): 235–49.

45. In previous research, I found, for example, that substantial proportions of "liberal" Catholics (e.g., 56 percent of members of the Women's Ordination Conference, and 46 percent of Dignity/Boston participants) identify the Church's sacramental and liturgical symbol system as core to their personal/Catholic identity (see Dillon, *Catholic Identity*, 203–11). Moreover, while a large proportion of members of the Catholic League for Religious and Civil Rights do not favor women's ordination, at the same time, many are willing to endorse the idea of women priests because with the shortage of male priests, ordaining women would allow for the celebration of the Mass, which they highly value. It would seem, therefore, that for some "conservative" Catholics sacramental celebration is more important than gender ideology/iconic significance. See Michele Dillon, "The Catholic Church and Possible 'Organizational Selves': The Implications for Institutional Change," *Journal for the Scientific Study of Religion* 38 (1999): 386–97. The shared symbolic significance of the Eucharist and other core symbols in Catholicism to liberals and conservatives alike is what makes me feel optimistic about the future prospects for rapprochement between liberal and conservative Catholics.

(even occasionally) and socialize their children into the Church's liturgy and the broader Catholic tradition, the long-term attachment of future generations of Catholics to Catholicism will be seriously attenuated. That current cohorts of Catholic parents continue to recognize the importance of religious socialization is suggested by survey data. Kevin Christiano notes that young married Canadians in Quebec have higher rates of religious involvement than their single peers (44 percent compared to 26 percent, respectively).[46] A similar cultural logic informed by the fact that parents want to ensure the religious socialization of their young children characterizes American and Irish parents.

Apart from church attendance, we also currently see the reemergence of other important devotional symbols and practices in Catholicism. There was a resurgence in Irish devotional life in 2000 when the bones of the Carmelite Saint Thérèse ("The Little Flower"), were displayed in churches in cities and towns around the country, and pilgrimages to the Marian shrine in Knock and to Croagh Patrick continue unabated. Indeed, younger Irish Catholics (those born in the 1970s) are significantly more likely than older cohorts to say that they value the Blessed Virgin Mary (70 percent and 50 percent, respectively).[47] Some of the personal religious practices of young adult Catholics in the U.S. are also remarkably "traditional." Two-thirds (70 percent) of Latinos and a majority (51 percent) of non-Latinos report wearing medals, crucifixes, or scapulars, and substantial proportions also say the rosary (46 percent and 64 percent, respectively).[48]

Local Catholicism

Related to the symbolic importance of the Mass and of other devotional strands in Catholicism is the localism of Catholic life. Despite Catholics' dissent from Vatican teaching, many Catholics maintain a strong loyalty to their local parish and to their local priests.[49] Even at the height of the sex abuse crisis in the United States, for example, whereas 65 percent of Boston Catholics had an unfavorable view of Cardinal Law, only 24

---

46. See Kevin Christiano's chapter, this volume.

47. Greeley and Ward, "How Secularised Is the Ireland We Live In?" 593.

48. Hoge et al., *Young Adult Catholics,* 158.

49. D'Antonio et al., *American Catholics;* Andrew Greeley, *The Catholic Imagination,* 130; Hoge et al., *Young Adult Catholics,* 50–53.

percent had an unfavorable view of their parish priest.[50] Similarly in Ireland, although sex scandals at the highest levels of Church leadership have dampened the confidence of the Irish in their priests, priests nonetheless retain higher credibility than the institutional Church as a whole: 42 percent of Irish Catholics express confidence in their local priests, whereas only 28 percent have confidence in the Church as an institution.[51] The strong activist role assumed by Catholic lay elites in Quebec (Catholic Action) and their denigration of both the Church hierarchy and popular Catholicism may in part account for Quebecers' significantly lower levels of church participation, and presumably also parish loyalty, relative to their Irish and American co-religionists. The comparatively greater disaffection of ordinary Quebecers may rest on the intertwining of their dissent from official Church teaching and their religious disempowerment by lay elites.

In sum, there is plenty of empirical evidence to support the thesis of a decline since 1950 in specific Church practices and in the official authority of the Church hierarchy. Yet, these trends must necessarily be seen in the context of much broader social, economic, political, and cultural shifts in the societies under review during approximately the same time period. As societies change, we should expect religion, too, to change; we should expect change in the religious institutions and traditions themselves and in individuals' attitudes toward religion. In contemporary times, religious identity and church participation is a voluntary activity. Therefore, we should expect it to vary from other times and from other societal contexts when outward displays of religiousness were more "coerced"—either when church attendance was required by law as was common in Reformation Europe[52] or when it was coerced by nationalist (Ireland, Quebec) and ethnic subcultural factors (United States). Moreover, as Philip Gorski argues, patterns of decline are not necessarily permanent or irreversible; as

50. These figures are based on a Boston Globe / WBZ-TV poll of 800 Catholics living in the Boston Archdiocese, conducted April 12–15, 2002.

51. As a sign of decline, however, and as a caution that Catholics' respect for local priests should not be taken for granted, it is noteworthy that the Irish currently have more confidence in their local teachers (60 percent) and police (54 percent). See Greeley, *Religion in Europe*.

52. See Philip Gorski, "Historicizing the Secularization Debate: An Agenda for Research," in Dillon, *Handbook of the Sociology of Religion*, 110–22.

he points out, taking a longer historical and a broader geographical perspective shows that religiousness tends to ebb and flow rather than follow the linear trajectory assumed by secularization theories.[53]

Were we to consider Catholicism since 1850 rather than since 1950, the post-1950 pattern of decline would seem more nuanced. For example, a smaller proportion of American Catholics went to weekly Mass in 1939 (64 percent) than in 1959 (72 percent),[54] and more went to confession in the mid-1980s than in the mid-1970s.[55] Similarly, before the Devotional Revolution (1850–1875) in Ireland, a substantial majority of Catholics did not attend church. Yet, few observers would suggest that America in the 1930s or Ireland in the early 1850s were "secularized" societies. Moreover, the authority of the Church hierarchy prior to the 1950s was not as monolithic as it may retrospectively seem to us in the current moment. Despite the strong political and cultural alliance between Irish Catholic and nationalist leaders, many late-nineteenth- and early-twentieth-century Irish political fighters gave little heed to the Church's condemnation of murder. Similarly, in Quebec, many lay persons' nationalist views were at odds with the pronouncements of the pre–World War II Church hierarchy, which sought to separate religion and nationalism, at least organizationally.[56]

It is precisely because the 1950s was the high point of twentieth-century public religiousness that the post-1950s decline in church attendance and in doctrinal assent seems so sharp. But it is also worth keeping in mind that the Catholicism of the 1950s and 1960s was the object of much criticism. In all three societies, the Catholicism practiced was variously seen by cultural observers as narrow, authoritarian, legalistic, moralistic, conformist, and devoid of spiritual and theological content.[57]

The Church is a living church, and as Vatican II as well as a more long-term historical view of the Church shows, Catholicism is a living tra-

---

53. Ibid.
54. See Hout and Greeley, "The Center Doesn't Hold," 325–45.
55. Gallup and Lindsay, *Surveying the Religious Landscape*, 55.
56. See Gauvreau, "From Rechristianization to Contestation."
57. For criticisms of the nature of pre–Vatican II Catholicism: in Ireland, see, for example, Tom Inglis, *Moral Monopoly: The Catholic Church in Modern Irish Society* (Dublin: Gill and Macmillan, 1987); in Quebec, see Gauvreau, "From Rechristianization to Contestation"; and in America, see Joseph Fichter, *Southern Parish: Dynamics of a City Church* (Chicago: University of Chicago Press, 1951).

dition.[58] We thus expect the lived practices of Catholicism, both in terms of the Church's institutional self-presentation and discourse and in terms of everyday Catholic behavior, to change. Changes in the Church and in how Catholicism is practiced are thus not necessarily indicative of its fall. What may now seem like a "fall" may over time turn out, in fact, to be a transitional fracture or yet another discontinuity in the Church's long history of continuities and discontinuities.[59]

Future Challenges

The contemporary Church nonetheless is confronted with some significant challenges on issues that transcend the Church's presence in any one society. In closing, I point to what I see as three critical and interrelated issues to which the Church needs to be attentive. Most immediately is the crisis of authority that the continuing symbolic and financial fallout from the sex abuse crises presents, especially in America and Ireland but also elsewhere. As discussed earlier in this chapter, the moral authority of the Church hierarchy has been in decline since at least *Humanae vitae.* The sex abuse scandals have recast the question of authority away from moral and doctrinal teaching per se to one that is more squarely concerned with the pastoral credibility of bishops and other Church leaders. As a recent *Boston Globe* poll indicates, in the Boston archdiocese, the epicenter of the sex abuse crisis, increasing numbers of Catholics are giving less money to the Church and are less likely to attend Mass as frequently as they did even in spring 2002, when the crisis was unfolding.[60] It seems urgent, therefore, that bishops reach out and more actively engage in dialogue with ordinary parishioners and also with groups within the Church who, whatever subtexts may be contributing to their activism, appear nonetheless to be sincerely committed to maintaining the relevance

58. See O'Malley, *Tradition and Transition.*

59. The Catholic theologian David Tracy reminds us that there is "no such thing as an unambiguous tradition." See David Tracy, *Plurality and Ambiguity* (San Francisco: Harper and Row, 1987), 36–37.

60. In April 2002, 31 percent of Boston Catholics said that the sex abuse crisis was causing them to donate less money to the church, whereas in May 2003, this figure was 44 percent. In addition, 27 percent said that the crisis has caused them to attend Mass less frequently, and nearly one in five said that they had considered joining a non-Catholic church in the past year. See the *Boston Globe,* May 11, 2003, A1.

of the Church and of Catholicism. In short, notwithstanding the strong loyalty of Catholics to Catholicism and to their parish, the Church hierarchy currently confronts the challenge of earning and rebuilding the trust of Catholics in the local, national, and global church.

A second challenge is posed by the increasing popularity of spiritual vocabularies and practices that are relatively autonomous of institutionalized religion. As opinion poll data and empirical studies show, substantial numbers of individuals are actively committed to a spirituality that takes them beyond the walls of churches and other traditional sites of worship. The prevalence of institutionally autonomous or "personal" religions should not be exaggerated, and their increased presence is a challenge not solely to the Catholic Church but to all organized churches. However, precisely because many spiritual individuals engage in journeys of personal growth that include participation in various aspects of established religious traditions, the appeal of "new" forms of spirituality should alert local Church leaders to rethinking how Catholicism's rich spiritual and mystical tradition might proactively be used to contribute to satisfying the spiritual hunger that is apparent across Western societies.[61]

A third challenge is that presented by the two other global religions, Pentecostalism and Fundamentalism in its varying forms (both Eastern and Western). Both Pentecostalism and Fundamentalism are experiencing an increase in membership worldwide, whereas Catholicism is losing its established share of birth adherents.[62] Beyond the pastoral challenges posed by the increased prominence of both Pentecostalism and Fundamentalism(s)

61. The Vatican recently commented on what it refers to as the New Age Movement in a 90-page booklet, "Jesus Christ the Bearer of the Water of Life: A Christian Reflection on the New Age" (Pontifical Council for Culture, February 2003). The statement recognizes the movement as reflecting the "spiritual hunger of contemporary men and women," and states: "If the Church is not to be accused of being deaf to people's longings, her members need to do two things: to root themselves ever more firmly in the fundamentals of their faith, and to understand the often silent cry in people's hearts, which leads them elsewhere if they are not satisfied by the Church."

62. On the challenges of Pentecostalism and Fundamentalism more generally, see Grace Davie, "The Evolution of the Sociology of Religion," in Dillon, *Handbook of the Sociology of Religion,* 61–75. Using a demographic analysis, Michael Hout observes that given American Catholics' higher fertility from 1920 to 1975 and greater Catholic immigration at both the beginning and end of the twentieth century, we should expect Catholics' share of the U.S. population to have increased rather than remained constant. It should, he argues, be between 32 and 35 percent, and not its current 25 percent. See Hout's "Demographic Methods for the Sociology of Religion," in Dillon, *Handbook of the Sociology of Religion,* 79–84.

is the additional dilemma of how the Catholic Church can continue to craft an effective geopolitical presence in world politics. The Vatican, specifically during the papacy of John Paul II, enjoyed and exercised considerable symbolic capital across diverse geopolitical tensions and controversies, both diplomatic and military. It is yet unknown, however, whether the charismatic authority of Pope John Paul II will be routinized in his successor, Pope Benedict XVI, and, in any event, whether the Vatican can maintain a significant role in attenuating geopolitical conflicts.

In conclusion, since the 1950s the Catholic Church had indeed declined in importance in the everyday lives of its adherents in the United States, Quebec, and Ireland, and it confronts serious pastoral and institutional challenges in these societies and beyond. Yet, before calling its fall, I argue that the comparative data should also be evaluated for evidence of the Church's persistence and of its continuing—though shifting—significance in individual lives and in public culture.

GREGORY BAUM

8. Comparing Post–World War II Catholicism in Quebec, Ireland, and the United States

The title of the conference for which these papers were originally prepared, "Decline and Fall?" suggests a general disappointment with the Catholic Church and an intellectual climate of doom. Paradoxically, at this very time, I am grateful to the Catholic Church (and the other churches in the United States and Canada) for having adopted a critical stance toward the military policies of President George W. Bush. After September 11, 2001, the U.S. churches recommended caution: they demanded that the terrorists be caught and brought to trial, but warned against the use of military violence.[1] They also recommended that the government examine the underlying causes of the attacks on the World Trade Center and the Pentagon and asked whether these attacks were related to American foreign policy in the Middle East and other parts of the world. The churches expressed their doubts about the moral legitimacy of the bombing of Afghanistan.[2] Later, the Catholic bishops and the leaders of the mainline churches argued that a preemptive strike against Iraq had no moral legitimacy.[3] The

1. Gregory Baum, "After September 11: The Dialogue of Religions," *Ecumenist* 39 (Summer 2002): 8–11.

2. The Pastoral Message of the U.S. bishops of November 14, 2001, expressing hesitation regarding military action, was followed on Dec. 17, 2001, by an outright denunciation of the war, signed by thousands of Catholics. See *Ecumenist* 39 (Spring 2002): 4–6.

3. In November 2002 the U.S. Catholic bishops addressed a letter to President Bush in which they argue that according to Catholic teaching on just war, a preemptive strike against Iraq has no moral legitimacy. For the similar evaluations of the other mainline U.S. churches, see Joe Feuerherd, "Opinions Clash on Just War," *National Catholic Reporter*, February 7, 2003, 3.

pope fully shared this opposition to the war.[4] He asked Catholics to make Ash Wednesday, the 5th of March, a day of prayer and fasting in support of peace. Further on in this essay, I shall discuss the spiritual forces behind this political involvement of the Catholic Church.

The essay has three parts. The first compares the secularizing trends in Quebec and Ireland and contrasts them with the experience of American Catholicism, which, despite internal conflicts, continues to thrive. The second deals with a common element: the creativity of Catholicism in Quebec, Ireland, and the United States in the wake of the Vatican Council. I shall argue that the Church has defined its relation to the world and the world religions in accordance with a new paradigm. The third briefly reflects on the refusal of Irish, Quebec, and U.S. Catholics to accept the Church's official teaching on women and sexuality and, related to this, the emergence of a new Catholic culture.

Secularization in Quebec and Ireland Contrasted with the American Experience

There is an obvious similarity between Ireland and Quebec, two small Catholic societies, at one time colonized by a Protestant empire, that struggled to protect their survival and identity. They were both peoples with strong Catholic faith, willingly accepting the clergy as their spiritual leaders. When, in the 1840s, the papacy mobilized the Catholic Church against the emerging liberal society—the ultramontane turn[5]—the Catholic hierarchy in Ireland and Quebec became fiercely antiliberal, a political stance they sustained right up to WW II and, in some cases, even beyond. Yet beginning in 1960, a cultural transformation occurred in Quebec that initiated the secularization of society at a surprisingly rapid pace. Twenty years later, a changing cultural climate in the Irish Republic also led to the loss of Catholic power. Let me begin, therefore, to examine the similarities and differences between these two processes of secularization.

---

4. John Paul II, "The Ten Commandments of Peace," January 24, 2002.

5. Joseph Komonchak, "Modernity and the Construction of Roman Catholicism," *Cristianismo nella Storia* 18 (1997): 353–85.

Secularization in Quebec

World War II had a different impact on the two societies. Since Ireland decided to remain neutral, it did not share the profoundly unsettling experience of the war that shook Europe's traditional institutions and opened the door to both the creative and the nihilistic power of cultural pluralism. Ireland remained undisturbed in its Catholicism.

By contrast, Canada offered immediate support for Britain's war. While there was significant opposition to the war in Quebec, the Quebec bishops stood firmly behind the Canadian government. The war had a modernizing impact on Quebec society: it led to the expansion of many industries, the creation of new jobs in factories and offices, and a rise in the standard of living. The soldiers who went overseas were lifted out of their cultural milieu and experienced religious pluralism in the Canadian army. Quebec was slowly becoming a middle-class society.

Still, after the end of the war and in the 1950s, Quebec society remained faithful to its Catholic inheritance. Almost everyone went to church. Catholicism continued to define Quebec's identity. As Professor Christiano has shown in his essay, under Quebec's conservative premier Maurice Duplessis the province had no ministry of education, no ministry of public health, and no ministry of social assistance. These services were supplied by the Catholic Church through the province-wide network of schools, hospitals, and community centers, producing a unique instance of ecclesiastical power. At the same time, influenced by progressive Catholic thought coming from France—Jacques Maritain and Emmanuel Mounier were read in Quebec—Catholic Action fostered a minor social movement critical of clericalism and political conservatism.

Then, on June 22, 1960, the election of a Liberal government in Quebec released a cultural revolution that affected all classes in Quebec's urban centers. Quebecers wanted to be masters in their own house. Up to that time, because of the economic power exercised by the Anglo elite, the language of work in industry and finance had been English, even though French Canadians made up over 80 percent of the population. Now, the majority wanted to live and work in their own language. People objected to the power exercised by the Anglo minority on the one hand and the Catholic clergy on the other. They wanted to catch up with liberal modernity, yet remain faithful to their tradition of cooperation and solidarity.

What emerged was a social democratic consciousness carried by all classes of society. This cultural transformation, the Quiet Revolution as it was called, allowed Quebecers to transcend the inferiority feelings experienced by colonized peoples and discover their own creativity. A springtime began in literature, music, painting, and architecture.

Professor Gauvreau's account of the Quiet Revolution paid no attention to the political dimension, and even Professor Christiano's excellent essay did not fully acknowledge the change in Quebec's political self-understanding brought about by the Quiet Revolution. Prior to 1960, French Canadians spread over the whole country regarded themselves as a nation, one of Canada's two founding nations. In the Quiet Revolution, the French Canadians living in Quebec defined their province as a nation: they no longer called themselves *les canadiens,* but *les québécois,* thus moving from an ethnic to a territorial nationalism. This had painful consequences for French Canadian minorities living in the rest of Canada: for they were now outsiders to Quebec. At the same time, all citizens of Quebec, whatever their ethnic origin, now came to be looked upon as *québécois.*

Because these events happened during the Vatican Council, which redefined the Church's relation to the modern world, Quebec Catholics were able to join the cultural revolution. In continuity with the Catholic Action movement, they supported social democracy and the curtailment of clerical power. A number of Catholic organizations did oppose the new orientation. Yet before the end of the sixties, all Catholic communities and groups, including the bishops, were fully reconciled to the new Quebec.[6]

The Liberal government, elected in 1960, created public ministries of education, health, and social assistance, thus dismantling the vast ecclesiastical network that had previously served Quebec society. The Church's loss of bureaucratic power was accompanied by another loss. The new Quebec no longer wanted to define its identity in Catholic terms. Quebecers defined themselves as a French-speaking nation, joining the family of nations that made up the modern world. What no one expected in the 1960s was that the Church was about to lose two-thirds of its active mem-

---

6. David Seljak, "The Catholic Church's Reaction to the Secularization of Nationalism in Quebec: 1960–1980" (Ph.D. thesis, McGill University, 1995).

bers. Beginning in the '70s, Catholics drifted out of the Church in ever growing numbers. Quebec became the most secular Canadian province.

The Causes of Secularization

How can we explain this rapid secularization? A process that took a century in European countries occurred in Quebec in a single decade. To explain this we will have to look at the convergence of several historical factors. Some of these factors, as we shall see further on, have also been present in the secularizing trend in Ireland.

The startling changes in Quebec and, later, in Ireland are part of a European drama often referred to as the end of Christendom. The creative fusion between faith and culture and between ecclesiastical and secular institutions that had created Europe's Christian civilization had been challenged by the Enlightenment, defended by Europe's conservative political parties, yet eventually dismantled by the liberal state, though at different speeds in various countries. Emmanuel Mounier wrote *Feu la chrétienté* in 1950.[7] After WWII, Catholic theologians recognized that Christendom had broken down. In the future, they argued, people will be Christians because of their personal decision, not because of their integration into a Christian culture. Vatican Council II recognized this change: in the future, Christian faith will be the result of personal religious experience.[8] Since Quebec and Ireland were societies of resistance in which the Church had unusual cultural power, these two societies were, to a large extent, protected from the impact of modernity. Yet once they opened themselves to these forces, they succumbed to the weight secularity had acquired in European societies. (Since the United States never belonged to European Christendom, U.S. Catholicism, as we shall see further on, has had an entirely different history.)

What does openness to modernity mean? The Enlightenment produced a complex and ambiguous culture. It valued personal autonomy and self-determination and, at the same time, promoted individualism and utilitarianism. In the Quiet Revolution Quebecers opened themselves to this complex set of values. They now insisted on personal autonomy and collective self-determination. Since the Catholic Church had exercised exces-

7. Emmanuel Mounier, *Feu la chrétienté* (Paris: Le Seuil, 1950).
8. *Gaudium et spes*, no. 7.

sive cultural power in Quebec, Catholics now became resentful of clerical rule. They objected to "the unanimity" forced upon them by the Church: no freedom of thought, no dialogue with outsiders, no encouragement of creativity, no space for new experiments. In recent years, Quebec literature, theater, and films have recorded these complaints ad infinitum, often producing an exaggerated picture of the past. A special anger was and still is directed at the Catholic Church for the multiplication of sexual taboos.

To create room for personal autonomy, the Dumont Report (1971–1972), mandated by the Quebec bishops to study the crisis of the Church, recommended the institutionalization of dialogue between hierarchy and people and the recognition of the right to dissent.[9] This turn to new openness, the Dumont Report believed, would allow Quebec's Church to continue to thrive. While the bishops did not implement the report's bold recommendations, they did engage in consultation and dialogue with priests and the laity and did recognize a pluralism of theology, piety, and practice. Yet their welcoming gestures did not halt the process of secularization. While there exists no public, European-style anticlericalism in Quebec—no politician would dream of making an anticlerical remark to be elected—there does exist a widespread resentment against the Church, especially among intellectuals and artists.

Another factor in Quebec's secularization is undoubtedly the individualism and utilitarianism mediated by modern capitalist culture. The commitment of middle-class societies tends to be to upward mobility rather than the life of the spirit. An excessive trust in science and technology also generates a lack of confidence in the invisible order. For a long time, sociologists embraced "the theory of secularization," according to which modern industrial society would bring about the end of religion.[10] The Larochelle Report (1991), commissioned by the Quebec bishops to study the ongoing decline of church membership, still trusted the sociological theory of secularization.[11] The report proposed an argument taken from Emile

---

9. *L'Église du Québec: un héritage, un projet* (Montréal: Fides, 1971); Gregory Baum, "The Dumont Report: Democratizing the Catholic Church," in *The Church in Quebec* (Montreal: Novalis, 1991), 49–65.

10. Gregory Baum, *Religion and Alienation* (New York: Paulist Press, 1975), 140–61.

11. *Risquer l'avenir* (Montréal: Fides, 1992); Gregory Baum, "Catholicism and Secularization in Quebec," in David Lyon, ed., *Rethinking Church, State and Modernity* (Toronto: University of Toronto Press, 2000), 149–65.

Durkheim, according to which a society produces a symbolic culture that creates the citizens in its own image. Thus modern capitalist society creates people that share its values. If the Church wants to survive, the report recommends, it must be willing to imitate the sects and socialize its members in opposition to society. The report recommends that the Church sell the large parish churches, now almost empty on Sundays, and create in their stead small communities of believers. The report even wants to Church to reject the surviving cultural Catholicism, that is, refuse to baptize babies unless their parents are active members of a Christian community. After a lively debate involving clergy and laity, the Church rejected these bold recommendations.

The theoretical weakness of the Larochelle Report was its belief in the theory of secularization, which had never been demonstrated. The great counterexample that has always been cited is the United States, the quintessential modern, capitalist society, in which churches and other religious communities thrive.

Another factor related to the secularization of Quebec society is the growth of the middle class produced by an expanding capitalist economy. The successful capitalist expansion after WWII in the United States had an impact on all of Canada, including the province of Quebec, raising the standard of living and creating new social expectations. Quebec's new middle class, possessed by a new self-confidence, became unwilling to be ruled and spoken to by the clergy as if they were children. In premodern societies priests belonged to the small educated elite accustomed to speak down to the ordinary people. Priests knew what was good for the people, and they expected to be followed. Yet people newly enjoying middle-class self-assurance no longer accepted being spoken to as children. Relying on their faith, Christians wanted to make up their own minds. As we shall see further on, Ireland's remarkable economic success beginning in the 1980s also made Catholics there increasingly impatient with the patronizing discourse of priests and bishops.

Professors Gauvreau and Christiano have suggested that the secularization of Quebec is the unintended consequence of the this-worldly spirituality fostered by the Catholic Action movement in Quebec. Professor Christiano called this "a sociological irony." This raises an important issue to which we will have to return. It is true that with its slogan "see, judge and act," the Catholic Action movement in Europe and Quebec insisted on the social responsibility of laypeople: it offered polite criticism of clerical domination and promoted within society values of personal freedom and social solidarity. Using the vocabulary of Maritain and Mounier, these were personalist values, at odds with liberal individualism on the one hand and communist collectivism on the other. In Quebec, as Professor Christiano has shown, engaged Christians became actively involved in the Quiet Revolution. It is worth remembering that, at this very time, the Vatican Council adopted the personalist orientation of Catholic Action as the new model for the Church's relation to the world. Is the new openness and active engagement of Catholics inevitably the first step toward secularization? We shall have to return to this topic.

Finally, Quebec's Quiet Revolution was an expression of national self-determination. Some Quebecers sought national status for Quebec within the Canadian confederation, while others hoped to attain independent national sovereignty. Quebecers were greatly encouraged by the 1966 Covenants of the United Nations, which recognized people's right to political, cultural, and economic self-determination.[12] I already mentioned the extraordinary cultural creativity that accompanied Quebec's political evolution. In the 1960s and '70s, the people of Quebec were gripped by a collective excitement reminiscent of Emile Durkheim's "effervescence," an outburst of energies capable of transforming the self-understanding of a tribe or people.[13] This effervescence enabled Quebecers in a few years to redefine their collective identity, bracket their Catholic identification, and experience themselves as a French-speaking, North American people, ready to join the family of nations.

None of the above-mentioned factors is able to explain by itself Quebec's rapid secularization. They acted together in a manner that is difficult to reconstruct. In my opinion, the heightened consciousness produced by the struggle for national self-determination accounts for the rapidity of the secularizing process in Quebec.[14]

12. See Walter Laqueur, ed., *The Human Rights Reader* (New York: New American Library, 1990), 215–33.

13. Emile Durkheim, *The Elementary Forms of Religious Life* (New York: Free Press, 1995), 216–25; W. S. F. Pickering, *Durkheim's Sociology of Religion* (London: Routledge and Kegan Paul, 1984), 380–94.

14. This essay is not the place for reporting the imaginative manner in which the Quebec bishops have reacted to the secularization of their society.

Secularization in Ireland

Comparing the wave of secularization that started in Ireland at a later date with that of Quebec reveals similarities and differences. Both societies were remnants of Christendom, pried open by the ambiguous forces of modernity.

The Irish, like the Quebecers, became critical of the Church's cultural power. Impatience with papal sexual teaching started in Ireland in 1968 when Paul VI, against the advice of his study commission, published *Humanae vitae,* ruling out the famous pill that had made life easier and happier for many Catholic couples.[15] While many Catholics disagreed with the Church's teaching on sexual ethics, they remained believing and practicing members of their parishes. According to the historian J. H. Whyte, there exists in the Irish Church a tradition of independence from clerical directives on some issues.[16] As examples he mentions the sympathy for the Fenian movement of the 1860s, the loyalty to Charles Parnell after his fall, and the support for the armed resistance against the Irish Free State in 1922, all of which were repudiated by the Catholic hierarchy. Similarly the disagreement of Catholics with the Church's teaching on women and sexuality did not, at first, weaken their Catholic practice. Yet after 1985, the relative independence from the Church's teaching permitted the creation of a new culture, following the European pattern, that approved unmarried couples living together and tolerated a good deal of sexual nonconformity.[17] Young people were becoming increasingly indifferent to the Catholic Church. Many left the Church in protest over its cultural power. Irish women challenged the Church's teaching on the inequality between the sexes.[18] While the 1993 referendum on abortion still confirmed the Catholic position, Irish culture became increasingly nonconformist.

A second similarity with the Quebec story is the cultural impact of capitalist expansion, the rise in the standard living, the creation of a wid-

15. Séan Fagan, "Humanae vitae: Thirty Years Later," *Doctrine and Life* 49 (1999): 51–54.

16. J. H. Whyte, *Church and State in Modern Ireland, 1923–1979* (Dublin: Gill and Macmillan, 1971), 8–12.

17. Garret FitzGerald, "Marriage in Ireland Today," in Dermot Lane, ed., *New Century, New Society: Christian Perspectives* (Dublin: Columba Press, 1999), 73–92.

18. Linda Hogan, "Women in Culture and Church in Ireland," in Lane, *New Century, New Society,* 140–48.

er middle class, and the discovery of a new self-confidence. Ireland's entry into the European Economic Union made available capital resources that allowed the Irish to reveal their talent in production, commerce, and technology. In the 1990s, people referred to Ireland as the Celtic Tiger. Newly successful Irish men and women no longer accepted being addressed as children by their priests and bishops. More harmful to Catholic faith was that the sudden economic boom made many Irish pursue upward mobility, become indifferent to matters spiritual, and surrender themselves to utilitarian values.[19]

An important difference from Quebec was the historical fact that the Irish had solved their national problem long ago: they had become a sovereign republic. In Quebec the cultural transformation was carried by a passionate effort at national self-determination producing an effervescence that brought about a new collective self-understanding, including a social democratic ethos. The Irish experience was different. Their confident integration into the European Community did not produce the same passion. Nor did it create the social solidarity that characterized Quebec's Quiet Revolution. What I conclude from this analysis is that the wave of secularization in Ireland is not carried by an effervescence and hence will not be as drastic as it has been in Quebec.

In her book *Goodbye to Catholic Ireland,* Mary Kenny offers another reason for the secularization of Ireland. She argued that the Catholic Church's commitment to social justice in the 1970s and early '80s—which I will treat at some length further on—produced a this-worldly orientation of faith that led to the neglect of the spirit. She writes, "Gone are the times when 'Ireland's Spiritual Empire' emphasized the saving of souls and the need to bring Christ to the pagan world."[20] Now, she continues, Catholics want to struggle against apartheid and world hunger. Kenny offers a quotation of J. H. Whyte: "From about 1973 onward, the Catholic Church moved away from its traditional position of power toward the concept—a rather 'Protestant' concept—of being the conscience of society."[21] Kenny writes, "The Irish bishops from 1978 on emphasized 'jus-

---

19. Tony Fahey, "The Culture of Egalitarian Individualism in Modern Ireland," *Doctrine and Life* 49 (1999): 258–66.

20. Mary Kenny, *Goodbye to Catholic Ireland* (London: Sinclair-Stevenson, 1997), 350.

21. Ibid., 349.

tice'—a favorite word of the Christian Left, though it is seldom mentioned in the New Testament."[22] Worldly concern in the name of Christ, Kenny believes, initiates secularization. This is her version of Professor Christiano's "sociological irony."

Finally, an important factor prompting many Irish people to turn their backs on the Church was the sexual scandals among the clergy, beginning in 1992 with the revelation of Bishop Eamon Casey's love affair and child, followed from 1993 on by a series of public scandals related to priests who had sexually abused minors. These misdeeds, carefully recorded in the press, created anger and outrage. As a result many Catholics turned away from the Church. By contrast, the sexual misconduct of the clergy played no role in the secularization of Quebec society. Sexual abuse by the clergy became a public issue there only in the 1990s. The Quebec Church may still be challenged by many more accusations in the future.

How strong is the secularization movement in Ireland? This is hard to measure. On this issue Irish observers are not in agreement. I detected a difference between Professor Keogh's reassurance that attendance at Mass was still high in Ireland and Professor Dillon's declaration that the Church has lost its credibility in Ireland. It may well be that the Irish remain a religious people and at the same time claim independence from Church teaching.[23]

We have looked at the similarities and differences between the movement toward secularization in Quebec and that in Ireland. Because I regard Quebec's Quiet Revolution as a consciousness-transforming event—I used Durkheim's concept of "effervescence"—I have argued that the wave of secularization in Ireland will not move as far as it did in Quebec.

America, a Society in Which Religions Thrive

Europeans and Canadians looking at the United States marvel at the vitality of religion in this enormous country. Visiting America in the 1830s, Alexis de Tocqueville was amazed by the diversity of Christian confessions and the constancy of Americans in their religious practice.[24] America has

---

22. Ibid., 359.

23. See the Report of Andrew Greeley and Conor Ward, *Doctrine and Life* 50 (2000): 581–618.

24. Alexis de Tocqueville, *Democracy in America*, vol. 2 (New York: Vintage Books, n.d.), 21–33.

never been part of Christendom. It was, almost from the beginning, a new civilizational experiment in personal freedom and religious pluralism. Here the separation of church and state was accompanied by a public appreciation of religion and not, as in European countries, by opposition to religion. Tocqueville argued that while Europeans defined their identity in the community where their ancestors had lived for centuries, the highly mobile population of America developed a sense of belonging in the countrywide network of their religious denomination. Max Weber confirmed this observation at the turn of the twentieth century.[25] In more recent times, Andrew Greeley has continued to be impressed by the religious practice of Americans. He argued that in a commercial civilization marked by social mobility and nervous preoccupation with material things, the religious denominations offer Americans a sense of belonging and a source of meaning.[26]

The Catholic minority in the United States believed from the beginning that the innovative creation of the secular state allowed them to develop and thrive, even if the theory behind this political arrangement was at odds with Catholic teaching. In an encyclical of 1897, Leo XIII grudgingly allowed Catholics in America to praise the separation of church and state and the consequent freedom of religion, yet insisted that this was not a political program to be adopted in Europe.[27]

The American Catholic Church grew steadily. It embraced the population of the Mexican territory annexed by the United States in 1848. Following the onset of industrialization in the 1860s, it welcomed waves of immigrants arriving from Catholic parts of Europe. In the last few decades it has received immigrants from the Philippines and immigrants and refugees from the Hispanic parts of the Americas. The Catholic Church embraced communities of many different cultures, speaking different languages and practicing different pieties. American Catholicism was a major experiment in pluralism. Since the Catholic Church embraced the mul-

25. After his return from the United States in 1904, Max Weber wrote "The Protestant Sects and the Spirit of Capitalism," in which he analyzed the amazing vitality of religion in that country. H. H. Gerth and C. Wright Mills, eds., *From Max Weber* (Cambridge: Kegan Paul, Trench and Trubner, 1947), 302–22.

26. Andrew Greeley, *The Denominational Society* (Glenview, Ill.: Scott and Foresman, 1972), 86–107.

27. Gerald P. Fogarty, "Americanism," in Richard McBrian, ed., *Encyclopedia of Catholicism* (San Francisco: Harper, 1989), 40–42.

titude of immigrants, its members tended, for a long time, to belong to the working classes. To preserve its identity and resist public prejudice, Catholicism was at one time willing to constitute itself as a subculture in America, creating its own parallel educational and social institutions so as to remain apart from the mainstream of American life.

I have recalled these well-known facts about American Catholicism to emphasize its difference from Catholicism in Ireland and Quebec. Ireland and Quebec were Catholic societies, belated pockets of European Christendom. What they shared with the American Catholic Church is resistance to Protestant hegemony.

After WWII, American Catholics moved increasingly into the middle class. The Catholic schools and colleges produced competent and ambitious graduates, and the G.I. Bill provided financial support to war veterans who wanted to go to colleges and universities. This educational advance was accompanied by the expansion of American capitalism and the availability of new economic opportunities. Andrew Greeley has argued that the entry of Catholics into the middle class would have provoked turmoil in the Catholic Church, even if there had been no Vatican Council.[28] Educated Catholics would no longer have accepted the authoritarian pastoral style deemed appropriate for the immigrant Church; they would have seen to it that the American values of freedom and participation become respected in the Church. It is not surprising that when the Vatican Council was convoked, the American bishops, wrestling against conservative opposition, offered strong support for the conciliar Declaration of Religious Liberty. In their 1986 pastoral "Economic Justice for All" the bishops wrote: "As we have proposed a new experiment in collaboration and participation in decision making by all those affected at all levels of U.S. society, so we also commit ourselves to become models of collaboration and participation."[29] No other hierarchy has ever written such words.

Freedom and participation are not the only American values. The counter-values of conformity and top-down decision making are also as

28. A theme frequently mentioned by Andrew Greeley. See, for instance, Andrew Greeley, "American Exceptionalism: The Religious Phenomenon," in *The Sociology of Andrew Greeley* (Atlanta: Scholars Press, 1994), 566–87.

29. "Economic Justice for All," in David J. O'Brien and Thomas Shannon, eds., *Catholic Social Thought: The Documentary Heritage* (Maryknoll, N.Y.: Orbis Books, 1992), 572–680, 662.

American as cherry pie. When Pope John Paul II began to appoint conservative yes-men as bishops in the American Church and at the same time restore the monarchical regime of the papacy, American Catholics became increasingly divided between two different visions of the Church, one opting for freedom and participation and the other for conformity and top-down authority. Still, despite these conflicts, American Catholics continue to reveal an extraordinary vitality. While many Catholics have left the Church because of its idea of womanhood, its teaching on sexuality, and its authoritarian practice and while a great number of priests and religious men and women have chosen to drop out, there are no signs that the Catholic Church is suffering anything like the shrinkage experienced in Quebec and Ireland.[30] Even the present crisis, produced by clerics' sexual abuse of minors and the bishops' reluctance to remove them from office, is not causing a major wave of secularization comparable to what has happened in Quebec and Ireland. American Catholics tend to cling to their Church, even when they are angry with it. The creation of the Voice of the Faithful, an association of Catholics angry over the sex scandals, is a symbol of Catholic fidelity, not a sign that Catholics are ready to walk away.

European Christendom has not survived. Its collapse in Quebec and Ireland was a late occurrence. Yet in the United States, Catholicism and organized religions in general were able to thrive. The reasons for this deserve attention, for they may give direction for the future of Christianity in general and Catholicism in particular. One observation that is often made is that religion in America is voluntaristic: people practice their faith because they choose to do so, not because of social or cultural pressures. In America people support their religious community financially and do not rely on assistance from the state. Secondly, American pluralism has allowed no single church to assume a cultural monopoly. In America, the European churches have become "denominations." Like sects, denominations do not aspire to represent the whole, but unlike sects, denominations welcome pluralism and willingly cooperate with other groups in the service of the common good. While the Catholic Church claims to be

---

30. Gerald P. Fogarty, "Die Vereinigten Staaten von Amerika," in Erwin Gatz, ed., *Kirche und Katholizismus seit 1945*, vol. 4 (Paderborn: Ferdinand Schöningh, 2002), 90–143, 143.

the one true church, in the United States it acts like a denomination. The denominational system also allows Jews and other non-Christian religious communities in the U.S. to achieve institutional normalization and fit themselves into the religious landscape. Thirdly, immigrants and their immediate descendants tend to be faithful to their inherited religion; they find in it community and cultural roots. The vibrancy of religion in the U.S. may also be connected to the people's collective faith that God blesses America, that America is "God's own country," in contrast to European countries, and more recently Quebec and Ireland, which have rejected such a religious self-understanding.

The Creativity of Postwar Catholicism

While the lament over the Church's decline after WWII is prominent in these chapters, I wish to move against the stream by describing the extraordinary creativity of post–World War II Catholicism. Let me begin with the opening sentence of *Gaudium et spes,* the conciliar constitution of the Church and in the Modern World.

> The joys and the hopes, the griefs and anxieties of the people of this age, especially those who are poor or in any way afflicted, these too are the joys and hopes, the griefs and anxieties of the disciples of Jesus Christ.

This is a new and startling declaration. No Church Father, no medieval theologian, no witness of the Catholic tradition in the past has ever made an equivalent statement. The heartfelt solidarity with people everywhere, beginning with the poor and afflicted, and the will to accompany them and cooperate with them to lighten their burden is a form of Christian discipleship born after WWII.

A glance at the spiritual books used by priests, religious men and women, and pious laypeople in the past reveals the leap that has been taken. The spiritual life, according to these books, had to do with the quest for holiness and the search for God in the secrecy of one's heart. This literature fostered the supernatural life of faith, hope, and charity, yet never mentioned the world; it made no reference to war, depression, unemployment, or colonization. Since Catholic social teaching prior to John XXIII was exclusively based on natural law theory and did not invoke the supernatural order, this teaching had no impact on the spiritual life. Of course, many Catholics were active in politics and worked for social justice in other ways, yet they regarded these activities as part of the natural order, not the higher order of the spiritual life.

This essay is not the place to render an account of the historical events, the spiritual experiences, and the theological developments that have produced the extraordinary leap in the Church's self-understanding. But let me at least mention three historical experiences that affected dramatic changes in the Church's relation to the world. There was, first, the sorrow of the Church over its relative silence during the persecution of the Jews and their intended extermination. The inherited spirituality failed to prompt the Church to manifest solidarity with a persecuted people. Then, after the overseas colonies achieved their independence, the Church had to apologize to its people for its former loyalty to the colonizer whose protection it had enjoyed. The inherited spirituality had not questioned the Church's relationship to power. Thirdly, Christian voices from the Third World protested against the unjust distribution of wealth and power that produced hunger, despair, and early death in their countries. A *coetus* of Third World bishops at the Vatican Council tried to introduce amendments in the conciliar documents expressing concern for the poor and oppressed.[31] These are three historical experiences that prompted the Church to realize that it cannot be faithful to itself unless it extends solidarity, in the name of the Redeemer, to all human beings, beginning with the poor and afflicted. According to the new teaching, God's self-revelation in Jesus Christ is a world-transforming event, and by working for love, justice, and peace people implicate themselves in God's merciful design.

The Faith-and-Justice Movement

After the Vatican Council, the Church's official teaching continued to clarify the intrinsic connection between faith and justice. While the documents of the council reflected the optimistic reading of the modern world made in the 1960s by the European and North American middle classes, the Latin American Bishops Conference held at Medellin in 1968 looked upon the same modern world from the perspective of a continent on the margin. Influenced by the emerging liberation theology, the Latin Amer-

---

31. Giuseppe Alberigo and Joseph Komonchak, eds., *History of Vatican II*, vol. 2 (Maryknoll, N.Y.: Orbis Books, 1997), 200–203.

ican bishops adopted "the preferential option for the poor," that is, the commitment to look upon society from the perspective of the poor and support their struggle for greater justice.[32] The Medellin Conference influenced the Church's official teaching at Rome and in many countries, including Ireland, Quebec, and the United States. In 1971, Pope Paul VI published his encyclical *Octogesima adveniens* and the World Synod of Bishops held in Rome published their statement *Justia in mundo*. According to the latter document, the salvation brought by Jesus Christ rescues people from sin and sinful conditions, including oppression, and therefore action on behalf of justice is an integral dimension of proclaiming the Good News.[33] According to John Paul II, the proclamation of the Gospel is essentially incomplete if it is not accompanied by the demand for social justice and human rights.[34] The pope has argued that the Enlightenment values of liberty, equality, and solidarity are grounded in biblical revelation and today receive the full support of the Catholic Church.[35]

This dramatic evolution of the Church's social teaching is a reflection of what has been happening among Catholics, their new political engagement, and new theological currents. This essay is not the place for reporting these historical events. What I wish to show is that the Church's new teaching on faith and justice had an impact on Catholicism in Ireland, Quebec, and the United States. In these three societies, as in many other countries, we observe a lively faith-and-justice movement, carried by groups of Catholic laypeople, supported by religious orders, and blessed

32. Gregory Baum, *Theology and Society* (New York: Paulist Press 1987), 3–31.

33. *Justitia in mundo,* nn. 5, 6: "The hopes and forces which are moving the world in its very foundations are not foreign to the dynamism of the Gospel, which though the Power of the Holy Spirit frees humans from personal sin and from its consequences in social life. . . . Action on behalf of justice and participation in the transformation of the world fully appear to us as a constitutive dimension of the preaching of the Gospel." Joseph Gremillion, ed., *The Gospel of Peace and Justice* (Maryknoll, N.Y.: Orbis Books, 1975), 514.

34. "The Church has learnt that an indispensable part of its evangelizing mission is made up of works on behalf of justice and human liberation," from Pope John Paul II's Opening Address at the Latin American Bishops Conference at Puebla (1979) III, 2.; see John Eagleson and Philip Sharper, eds., *Puebla and Beyond* (Maryknoll, N.Y.: Orbis Books, 1979), 66. John Paul II: "The teaching and spreading of the social doctrine are part of the Church's evangelizing mission. . . . To condemn notions of evils and injustices is also part of the ministry of evangelization." *Sollicitudo rei socialis* (1987) n. 41; see O'Brien and Shannon, *Catholic Social Thought,* 425.

35. See, for instance, John Paul II's Address to the United Nations Organization on Oct. 5, 1995.

by the bishops' bold social teaching. Many dioceses opened offices with the task of promoting social justice. The bishops decided to found large organizations to support Third World development and educate the Catholic community at home in regard to the injustices built into the existing order. In Canada, including Quebec, Development and Peace was set up in 1967; in Ireland Trocaire was created in 1973; and in the U.S. the already existing Catholic Relief Services adopted in the 1970s the critical social perspective of the Church's new teaching. A dramatic event was the 32nd General Congregation of the Society of Jesus in 1974, which committed the entire religious community to the preferential option for the poor. The same spirituality led other religious orders to promote the faith-and-justice movement. A glance at the websites of the conference of religious communities in Ireland, Quebec, and the U.S. shows that these communities have not wavered in their commitment.[36]

This how the Canadian bishops in 1976 looked upon the faith-and-justice movement in Canada and Quebec:

> Across Canada today, there are encouraging signs among Christian people who are raising questions [about the relation of the Gospel to the social order.] Much of this activity for social justice and responsible stewardship is occurring on an ecumenical basis. A variety of Christian groups have been working with the poor and oppressed in their communities, organizing educational events on issues of injustice, and pressing leaders of government and industry to change the policies that cause human suffering. Unfortunately, those who are committed to this Christian way of life are presently a minority in the life of the Catholic community. Yet this minority is significant because it is challenging the entire Church to live the Gospel message of serving the needs of the poor. . . . The Gospel calls us to become new men and women in the service of others. It also calls us to a conversion of attitudes leading to a change of the structures that cause human suffering.[37]

To illustrate the leap in the Church's social teaching, I wish to recall the notorious sermon preached by Father John Charles McQuaid, the future archbishop of Dublin, at Blackmore College on March 13, 1932, in which he accused the Declaration of the Rights of Man of 1789 of having

---

36. See the Conference of Religious in Ireland (www.cori.ie), la Conférence religieuse canadienne (www.web.net/crcn), and the Leadership Conference of Women Religious in the United States (www.lcwr.org).

37. "From Words to Action" paragraph 7, Canadian Catholic Conference, September 1976, in E. F. Sheridan, ed., Do Justice: The Social Teaching of the Canadian Bishops (Montréal: Éditions Paulines, 1987), 316.

done the work of Satan.[38] "Human rights set the world against the Church of Christ, they have produced societies that do not recognize God's law, and they allow Jews and Masons to engage in their war against Christian truth and the good of humanity." Compare this with the speech given by Cardinal Cahal Daly in 1998 at the fiftieth anniversary of the UN Declaration of Human Rights on the topic of world poverty, justice, and peace. He mentioned that Pope John Paul II had quoted with approval the statement from the declaration's preamble on "the inherent dignity and equality "of human beings. While the articles of the declaration include people's right to food, shelter and adequate living conditions, Daly continued, what is presently taking place is the spread of poverty in many parts of the world, the widening gap between rich and poor, and in some countries misery caused by obligations imposed by the national debt. Ireland, having joined the well-to-do nations, he went on, must now act responsibly on the international scene. It also must engage in soul-searching over its own treatment of itinerants, refugees, and asylum seekers. Europe's great economic and technical might, Cardinal Daly added, was in need of what Bergson had called "a supplement of soul."[39]

The history of this remarkable evolution has not yet been written. None of the chapters of this volume has recorded the history of the faith-and-justice movement in Ireland, Quebec, and the United States, nor mentioned the pastoral statements of the bishops in support of this movement. Since I have been deeply involved in this movement in Quebec and Canada, I am acquainted with the institutions that promote it, the social projects supported by it, and the bold episcopal teaching that legitimated it in the Church. The story of the Catholic Left in Ireland, Quebec, and the U.S. deserves to be told. All I can do here is to mention a few of the major pastoral letters.

Most important in Ireland was the pastoral letter "The Work of Justice," published by the Irish Bishops Conference in 1976.[40] The Canadian

---

38. John Cooney, *John Charles McQuaid: Ruler of Catholic Ireland* (Dublin: O'Brien Press, 1999), 69–71.

39. See *Furrow* 49 (1998): 131–36.

40. See also the statements of the Irish Bishops Conference in 1999, "Prosperity with a Purpose" and "On Accepting the Stranger into Our Community," arguing that Catholics are summoned by their faith to extend their solidarity to itinerants, refugees, and immigrants.

bishops, including those of Quebec, made a series of public statements in the 1970s and the early part of the '80s that offered a critique of liberal capitalism and supported the search for alternative models of economic development.[41] Since then the bishops of Quebec have continued to promote critical social reflection in their Labor Day statements made every year on the first of May.[42] In producing these statements, the bishops rely on an appointed team that consults Catholics involved in the faith-and-justice movement in various parts of the country. In the United States two pastoral letters, "The Challenge of Peace" (1983) and "Economic Justice for All" (1986) raised to a higher level the socioethical reflection of the Catholic community as well as the public debate in the entire country.[43] Special about these pastoral letters was the method used in their preparation. The first draft made by an appointed committee was sent out to the parishes, Catholics as individuals or in groups were invited to submit their critical remarks, and, eventually, taking account of these proposals, the appointed committee produced the version that received the final approval of the bishops' conference. This was a new style of exercising the Magisterium.

Today, the teaching of the Holy See and the episcopal statements in Ireland, Quebec, and the United States oppose the globalization of the unregulated market system, or "neoliberalism," sustained by the World Bank and the International Monetary Fund. These are the words of John Paul II:

> A system known as "neo-liberalism" increasingly prevails, based on a purely economic conception of the human being. This system considers profit and the law of the market as its only parameter, to the detriment of the dignity and the respect due to individuals and peoples. At times this system has become the ideological justification for certain attitudes and behaviour in the social and political spheres, leading to the neglect of the weaker members of society. Indeed, the poor are becoming ever more numerous, victims of specific policies and structures.[44]

41. Gregory Baum and Duncan Cameron, eds., *Ethics and Economics: The Social Teaching of Canada's Bishops* (Toronto: James Lorimer, 1984); Sheridan, *Do Justice*.

42. Yvonne Bergeron, "Paroles d'évêques à contre-courant: les Messages du 1er mai," in Michel Beaudin et al., eds., *Intervenir à contre-courant* (Montréal: Fides, 1998), 63–92.

43. See O'Brien and Shannon, *Catholic Social Thought*, 492–571, 572–680.

44. *Ecclesia in America*, no. 56, January 22, 1999.

The Canadian bishops addressed this message to the Summit of the Americas held in Quebec City in 2001 about support of the Free Trade Area of the Americas (FTAA).[45]

Welcoming Religious Pluralism

The Church's commitment to peace, justice, and human rights, following Vatican Council II, was accompanied by a bold commitment to religious pluralism, at odds with the Church's antecedent teaching. Despite the repeated repudiation of religious liberty by the popes in the nineteenth century and their insistence that error has no rights, the council affirmed the freedom of religion as a basic human right. For the first time in its history, the Church decided to relate itself to Judaism and the other world religions in a positive way, emphasizing the values held in common and recognizing in the religion of the others ideas and practices that mediate God's saving grace.[46] In several declarations made after the council, the Vatican adopted an entirely new approach to religious pluralism.[47] Instead of looking upon religious pluralism as a historical defect eventually to be corrected by religious unity in Jesus Christ, the Church now recognized religious pluralism as part of God's creation, encouraged interreligious dialogue and cooperation, and invited the world religions to a common witness to the invisible order in a world increasingly committed to secularism.

The Church in Ireland, Quebec, and the United States has followed the lead of the Vatican Council and the example of Pope John Paul II in pursuing a positive approach to religious pluralism. In Ireland the new openness refers mainly to the healing of Catholic-Protestant relations. But in the U.S. and Quebec, where past and present immigration has created a lively religious pluralism, the bishops have initiated and supported interreligious dialogue and solidarity. Again, I can give only a few examples of the changes taking place at this time. In August 2002, a study commission created by the American bishops published a long document, the re-

---

45. Gregory Baum, "The Summit of the Americas," *Ecumenist* 38 (Summer 2001): 14–16.

46. See *Nostra aetate,* the Declaration of the Church's Attitude toward Non-Christian Religions.

47. In 1984 the Vatican Secretariat for Non-Christian Religions published the statement "Dialogue and Mission," and in 1991 the Pontifical Council for Interreligious Dialogue and the Congregation for the Evangelization of Peoples published the joint statement "Dialogue and Proclamation."

sult of a ten-year dialogue with Jewish religious representatives, which argues that, in line with the conciliar statement *Nostra aetate,* God's ancient covenant with the Jewish people retains its validity and that consequently there is no theological legitimacy for an ecclesiastical effort to convert Jews to Christianity.[48] Inspired by the special attention paid to Islam by John Paul II, the American bishops have initiated Catholic-Muslim dialogue on the Atlantic coast, in the Midwest, and in California. On the Web site of the American Catholic Bishops Conference one can find a series of articles promoting Catholic-Muslim friendship, including the collection of the papal statements on Islam. The Quebec bishops also promote interreligious dialogue and cooperation. Quite startling is the changed attitude of the Canadian Church, fully shared by the Quebec bishops, regarding the spiritual inheritance of the Native Peoples. Their rituals and prayers, formerly repudiated as pagan superstitions, are presently honored and granted a place within the Church's liturgy. Let me add that I have been a member of a small committee established by the Quebec bishops that has produced a paper on the Church's response to religious pluralism reviewed by the bishops and subsequently published by them.[49]

The theology behind this new openness offered by the Vatican Council is the revival of the ancient Logos-Christology, formulated by the third-century Egyptian Church Fathers, according to which God's eternal Word, incarnate in Jesus Christ, has addressed human beings throughout their history and initiated them into saving wisdom.[50] Thus world religions and sapiential traditions are bearers of ideas and practices that mediate divine salvation. A lively theological debate on this topic is taking place in the Church at this time. On August 6, 2000, Cardinal Ratzinger, then the president of the Roman Congregation *de doctrina fidei* and now pope, published the instruction *Dominus Iesus,* which defended the Church's traditional teaching and complained that interreligious dialogue had become an ideology. Six weeks later, on September 26, 2000, John Paul II sent a message to an interreligious conference held in Lisbon, presided over by Cardinal Cassidy, then the president of the Pontifical Coun-

---

48. See *Ecumenist* (Spring 2003), 3–6.

49. Assemblée des évêques du Québec, "Le dialogue interreligieux dans un Québec pluraliste" (2007).

50. For the relevant texts, see Jacques Dupuis, *Toward a Christian Theology of Religious Pluralism* (Maryknoll, N.Y.: Orbis Books, 1997), 53–83.

cil for Ecumenism, that praised interreligious dialogue and called for its multiplication in the new millennium.

At the beginning of this article I mentioned the reaction of the Catholic Church to the terrorist attacks on September 11, 2001, its concern for peace, and its expression of solidarity with residents of Arab origin or Muslim religion exposed to prejudice and discrimination. Against the thesis of Samuel Huntington on "the clash of civilizations,"[51] the "clash" produced by the contrasting values of the respective religions, John Paul II, seconded by the American and Quebec bishops, has insisted on "the dialogue of civilizations." Here is a recent text. On February 20, 2003, the pope addressed an interreligious delegation from Indonesia in these words:

> At this time of great tension for the world, you have come to Rome, and I am grateful to have this occasion to speak to you. With the real possibility of war looming on the horizon, we must not permit politics to become a source of further division among the world's religions. In fact, neither the threat of war nor war itself should be allowed to alienate Christians, Muslims, Buddhists, Hindus and members of other religions. As religious leaders committed to peace, we should work together with our own people, with those of other religious beliefs and with all men and women of good will to ensure understanding, cooperation and solidarity.[52]

A New Paradigm

I am prepared to argue that the creativity of post–World War II Catholicism, responding to the challenges of history, has produced a new understanding of the Church's mission in the world. Its commitment to peace, humans rights, social justice, and religious pluralism has led the Church to see itself as sent by the triune God to be the protector of human beings in a murderous world ruled by wealth and power. In fact, a similar evolution is taking place in other religions. While fundamentalism or the return to the boundary is spreading in all religious traditions, including Christianity and Catholicism, a counter-movement is also spread-

---

51. Samuel Huntington, *The Clash of Civilizations* (New York: Simon and Schuster, 1996); Gregory Baum, "The Clash of Civilizations or Their Reconciliation?" *Ecumenist* 39 (Spring 2002): 12–17.

52. "Address of John Paul II to the Members of the Inter-Religious Delegation from Indonesia," Thursday, February 20, 2003. Available on the official Vatican Web site: http://www.vatican.va/phome_en.htm.

ing, reaching out for dialogue and cooperation in support of love, justice, and peace.[53] I wish to argue that if we are to believe the ecclesiastical statements, a paradigm shift has taken place in the self-understanding of the Catholic Church. What has emerged is a this-worldly spirituality, a faith-induced commitment to peace and universal solidarity, beginning with the poor and oppressed. If the ecclesiastical statements are reliable, the Church believes that revealed in Jesus Christ is the eternal God as the transcendent mystery of compassion operative in history, summoning the human family toward peace, justice, and reconciliation.

Should we now return to the question raised above whether a this-worldly spirituality inevitably fosters worldliness and eventually promotes the secularization of society? This is an issue deserving a careful treatment, for which there is no space here. I would want to argue that the faith-and-justice movement in the Catholic Church is sustained by a mystical élan, a fidelity to the Gospel, an energy experienced as grace, an awakening in response to a divine call, and a sense of nonconformity to the wicked world. I am inclined to think that solidarity with the dominant classes is a secularizing force, while solidarity with the victims of history generates spirituality.

Women and Human Sexuality: The Emergence of a New Catholic Culture?

No new thinking has emerged at the Vatican in regard to matters dealing with women and human sexuality. According to the essays in this volume, the majority of Catholics in Ireland, Quebec, and the United States disagree with the Church's official teaching on the role of women in society and the ordination of women to the priesthood. They also disagree with the official teaching that sexual embrace is ethical only in married life and then only if open to conception, and that as a consequence all other sexual practices, including self-pleasuring, are mortal sins deserving eternal punishment. Yet Western culture, confirmed by new social legislation, has rejected the traditional forms of the subjugation of women.

53. The World Conference of Religions for Peace, the Parliament of Religions, and many other interreligious organizations are presently engaged in dialogue and cooperation in the service of peace and justice.

Western culture has also moved beyond the strict sexual norms inherited from the past: it now acknowledges greater freedom in the search for sexual happiness, unfortunately opening the door to the commodification of sexuality in a profitable industry of pleasure. Most Protestant churches, in critical dialogue with the changing culture, have recognized the relationship between men and women as nonhierarchical and hence have decided to ordain women to all ecclesiastical offices. Most of these churches have also moved beyond the inherited norms of sexual ethics, demanding instead that the sexual life of Christians be ruled by consciences formed by the Gospel values of respect, nonexploitation, mutuality, and love.

Research has shown that the Catholic Church's official teaching on women and sexuality, especially after the encyclical *Humanae vitae* (1968), has not been received by the majority of Catholics in the West. The strict orders to obey uttered by Rome have not been able to change this situation. In the theological tradition, the nonreception of an official teaching has its own authority.[54] Today Catholics ask themselves why the Church that has dramatically rethought its relation to the world and the world religions is unable to rethink its understanding of women and humanity's sexual giftedness. In this area the Catholic Church lacks wisdom and suffers confusion. That a group of celibate males wants to define the nature of women and the ethics of sexual love for the whole world is a problematic venture. The committees that make equivalent decisions in the Protestant churches include men and women, married and single, people with nonguilty experiences of sexual love.

It seems to me impossible not to relate the recent scandals—the sexual abuse of minors by members of the clergy—to the confusion about sexuality in the Catholic Church. Rome still thinks that sexuality can be integrated into a fully human life by willpower, by acts of obedience, while contemporary wisdom, universally received in the West, holds that the integration of sexuality takes place in a process of maturing, which demands openness and self-knowledge and includes the cultivation of interpersonal relations. In today's culture, repression does not work; people who run away from self-knowledge will be humiliated by outbursts of unexpected desires.

It is impossible to interpret the sexual abuse of minors by Catholic

---

54. Herman Pottmeyer, "Reception of Doctrine," in McBrien, *Encyclopedia of Catholicism*, 1081–82.

priests without attending to the education they have received in the seminary. Most of these priests are not pedophiles, which is to say they are not sick men; they are ephebophiles, that is, molesters of adolescents, which means that they are immature men, men who have not fully grown up. There are, of course, true vocations to the celibate life. Yet seminary training is oriented toward celibacy whether or not candidates have an inner vocation for it. Such training encourages repression and allows candidates to run away from self-knowledge. When people do not know what stirs within them, they are vulnerable to compulsive behavior that may have destructive consequences and cause great harm.

The anger of Catholics over the sexual abuse scandals in the three countries under study is nourished by several wounds they have received. Their trust in the clergy has been abused: the very men who imposed the strict sexual taboos that have caused Catholics so much guilt now reveal themselves as sexually driven into crime. They are also angry at the clerical culture of secrecy that encourages bishops to hide facts they regard as inconvenient, such as the sexual misdemeanors of their priests and the amount of money paid in compensation and for alimonies.

The sexual abuse scandals are tragic at this very time because, in addition to the harm inflicted on the victims of abuse, they have damaged the Church's credibility when its bold witness for peace, justice, and human rights and its commitment to the dialogue of civilizations could have world-historical significance.

It has been suggested, in a spirit of hope, that the present crisis could become a watershed in the Church's history as it passes from one Catholic culture to another. In the past the spiritual culture promoted in the Church put the main emphasis on obedience. We were to obey the laws and rules formulated by the ecclesiastical authorities. We were not encouraged to develop a critical sense and follow the lead of our own conscience. The hierarchy treated us as immature; they were not interested in what we had to say; they talked down to us and made decisions affecting our lives, like good parents acting on behalf of their children. But the regime of obedience has revealed itself as a failure. In the cultural and ethical pluralism of modern society, Catholic faith will survive only if it is firmly grounded in personal consciousness. Obedience to rules does not produce self-motivated adult Catholics capable of discerning the creative and destructive potential of their cultural world.

An alternative spiritual culture, not based on obedience, was already promoted by a number of twentieth-century Catholic leaders, most influential among them the Belgian priest, later a cardinal, Joseph Cardijn, a founder of the Catholic Action movement. His motto was "see, judge, and act." Here people of faith were asked to look at the reality before them, evaluate it in the light of the Gospel, and intervene responsibly to bring society into greater conformity with God's will. Since this motto did not assign a high priority to ecclesiastical obedience, participants in Catholic Action often found themselves at odds with their bishop. "See, judge, and act" meant that Catholics, guided by faith in the Gospel, were to develop a critical conscience and assume responsibility for their action in society.

After Vatican Council II a growing number of Catholics adopted the spiritual culture of see, judge, and act. Their lives were defined by faith, discernment, and responsibility. *Gaudium et spes* acknowledged "the emergence of a new humanism, one in which human beings are defined first of all by their responsibility toward their brothers (and sisters) and towards history."[55] At certain moments, obedience to authorities is indeed necessary; this is true in all organizations. But obedience is not the guide of life. What guides these Catholics is faith, hope, and love, the critical evaluation of society and culture, and the taking of personal responsibility for their actions. These Catholics do not want their bishops to speak to them like children. They are unhappy with clericalism. Still, they are eager to hear the teaching of popes and the bishops; they want to learn how the Church's authoritative leaders see the meaning and power of the Gospel in today's culture. But they feel free to reflect on these messages, compare them with their own understanding of faith, and then make up their own mind and assume personal responsibility for their actions. That this new freedom has taken place in regard to Catholic sexual ethics has been demonstrated empirically.

The present crisis in the Church, it has been argued, is an occasion for the rapid spread of the new Catholic culture. Even bishops recognize that the present troubles cannot be repaired by a renewed emphasis on obedience. Demanding that the angry Catholic laity shut up and that seminaries enforce ever stricter rules will not solve the Church's present problem.

---

55. *Gaudium et spes,* no. 55.

What is needed in the present culture are Catholics with profound convictions generated by their faith, ready to see, judge, and act in the world in which they find themselves.

Pope John Paul II created his own vocabulary to describe this new self-understanding, new at least in the Catholic Church. Humans, we are told, are meant to be "subjects" or historical agents, bearing responsibility for their lives and the institutions to which they belong. John Paul II speaks here of people's "subjectivity" and demands that institutions respect the "subjectivity" of their members. Even if a government introduces legislation that serves the common good, it sins against the people's "subjectivity" if it has not consulted them and taken their judgment seriously.[55] The word "subjectivity" is the pope's vocabulary for the watchword of Catholic Action, "see, judge, and act." It is puzzling that John Paul II does not apply his theory to the Church itself: the Church, it would appear, need not respect the subjectivity of its members. Still, Catholics increasingly demand that their consciences be respected. The present crisis and the loss of the Church's credibility in matters dealing with women and human sexuality may well become an important milestone in the passage from a Catholic culture of obedience to a new Catholic culture of faith-based responsibility.

The new paradigm defining the Church's relation to the world and the world religions is likely to be accompanied by a new paradigm for the self-understanding of Catholic men and women.

55. See John Paul II's encyclical *Sollicitudo rei socialis* (1987), no. 15.

Contributors

R. SCOTT APPLEBY is the John M. Regan Jr. Director of the Joan B. Kroc Institute for International Peace Studies and professor of history at the University of Notre Dame. He is the author of numerous books and articles on U.S. religious history and the challenges to religion in the modern world.

GREGORY BAUM is a widely published theologian who attended Vatican II as an expert on ecumenism, and also a prolific sociologist. He is professor emeritus of religious studies at McGill University in Montreal.

KEVIN J. CHRISTIANO is associate professor in the Department of Sociology at the University of Notre Dame. He has published widely on the sociology of religion and is past president of the American Council for Québec Studies (2003–2005).

JAMES D. DAVIDSON is professor of sociology at Purdue University, where he specializes in the sociology of religion and especially research on American Catholics. He is a recent past president of the Association for the Sociology of Religion.

MICHELE DILLON is professor of sociology at the University of New Hampshire and past chair of the section for the sociology of religion of the American Sociological Association. She has written extensively about both U.S. and Irish Catholicism.

MICHAEL GAUVREAU is professor of history at McMaster University in Ontario, Canada. He has written extensively on the history of religion in Canada, including a recent book on religious transformation in Quebec.

DERMOT KEOGH is professor of history at University College, Cork, and a former journalist. He has written and reported widely on religion in Ireland, including church-state relations, and on Irish foreign policy. He is a member of the Royal Irish Academy.

LAWRENCE TAYLOR is professor of anthropology at the National University of Ireland, Maynooth. He has done fieldwork in rural Ireland and along the U.S./Mexican border, and has published extensively on Irish popular religion and on contemporary border issues.

LESLIE WOODCOCK TENTLER is professor of history at the Catholic University of America. She writes mainly on American religious history, particularly U.S. Catholicism.

Index